KT-441-098

Good Housekeeping

STEP-BY-STEP
Baking

Good Housekeeping

STEP-BY-STEP
Baking

TED SMART

A TED SMART Publication 1999

1 3 5 7 9 10 8 6 4 2

First published in the United Kingdom in 1999 by Ebury Press,
Random House, 20 Vauxhall Bridge Road, London SW1V 2SA

Random House Australia (Pty) Limited
20 Alfred Street, Milsons Point, Sydney,
New South Wales 2061, Australia

Random House New Zealand Limited
18 Poland Road, Glenfield,
Auckland 10, New Zealand

Random House South Africa (Pty) Limited
Endulini, 5A Jubilee Road
Parktown 2193, South Africa

Random House UK Limited Reg. No. 954009

A CIP catalogue record for this book is available from the British Library.

MANAGING EDITOR: Janet Illsley
DESIGN: Christine Wood
SPECIAL PHOTOGRAPHY: Gus Filgate
SPECIAL TECHNIQUES PHOTOGRAPHY: Craig Robertson
STYLIST: Penny Markham
FOOD STYLISTS: Joanna Farrow, Louise Pickford and Julie Beresford
OTHER PHOTOGRAPHS: Jean Cazals, Laurie Evans, David Gill, Graham Kirk, Sandra Lousada,
James Murphy, Philip Webb, Harry Cory-Wright, Elizabeth Zeschin

MAIN CONTRIBUTING AUTHORS: Joanna Farrow, Louise Pickford and Charlotte Coleman-Smith
OTHER RECIPES: The Good Housekeeping Institute, Maxine Clark, Lyn Rutherford, Janet Smith,
Linda Fraser
RECIPE TESTING: Pascale Harzic and Julia Alger
ADDITIONAL EDITORIAL ASSISTANCE: Hilary Bird, Fiona Hunter, Kim Griffiths

Printed and bound in Singapore by Tien Wah Press

CONTENTS

COOKERY NOTES

◆ Both metric and imperial measures are given for the recipes. Follow either set of measures, not a mixture of both, as they are not interchangeable.

◆ All spoon measures are level unless otherwise stated. Use measuring spoons, available in metric and imperial, for accurate quantities.

◆ Ovens must be preheated to the specified temperature. Grills should also be preheated. Cooking times in the recipes are based on this assumption.

◆ Large eggs should be used except where otherwise specified. Free-range eggs are recommended.

◆ Use freshly ground black pepper and sea salt unless otherwise specified.

◆ Use fresh rather than dried herbs unless dried herbs are stipulated.

THE FOLLOWING SYMBOLS APPLY IN THE COLOUR INDEX:

❅ indicates that the recipe is suitable for freezing

🕐 identifies recipes which can be prepared and baked in 30 minutes

❏ denotes baked items which have good keeping qualities

THE RECIPES INCLUDE THE FOLLOWING INFORMATION:

◆ Preparation and cooking times, plus additional time for proving etc.

◆ Suitability for freezing. Where the dish should be frozen at the end of a certain stage of the method (rather than at the end), this stage is indicated.

◆ Calorie counts are given per serving or appropriate portion of the dish. Where the calorie count ranges from a higher to a lower figure, this reflects that the number the recipe serves is variable. The lower count will apply if you are serving the larger number, as the portion size will be smaller.

colour index

LAMB AND CHESTNUTS EN CROÛTE
Lamb fillets are wrapped in spinach leaves
and ham, then baked in a crisp pastry crust.
Serves 8   page 80   ❋

BEEF AND GUINNESS PIE
A richly flavoured stew of meltingly tender beef under a blanket of crisp,
light homemade flaky pastry.
Serves 6-8   page 80   ❋

TURKEY AND HAM PIE WITH
CHESTNUTS
Topped with a crumbly potato pastry crust,
this festive pie includes piquant cranberries.
Serves 8-10   page 82   ❋

SMOKED HADDOCK, SALMON AND
PRAWN PIE
This wonderfully rich, creamy fish pie is
delicately flavoured with tarragon.
Serves 6   page 78

SALMON EN CROÛTE WITH SPINACH
Chunks of fresh salmon and peeled prawns,
layered with spinach in a puff pastry crust.
Serves 6   page 77

CHICKEN AND ARTICHOKE PIE
Chicken breasts and artichoke hearts in a
cream cheese and wine sauce, topped with
crunchy filo speckled with sesame seeds.
Serves 4   page 82

FESTIVE NUT AND CRANBERRY
TERRINE
A vegetarian hot water crust pie, encasing a
tasty cheese, walnut and herb filling.
Serves 8   page 83

MOROCCAN FILO PIE
This delicious spinach, lentil and feta cheese
pie is scented with garlic, spices and herbs.
Serves 6-8   page 83   ❊

LEEK AND MASCARPONE TART
A wonderfully creamy flan, filled with sweet, melting leeks and scattered
with Parmesan.
Serves 8   page 86   ❊

GAME AND HERB PIE
A wintry medley of game, mushrooms,
bacon and shallots cooked in a creamy
wine sauce, then baked in puff pastry shells.
Serves 8   page 84

QUICHE LORRAINE
Classic creamy quiche, with a smoky bacon,
onion and gruyère filling.
Serves 6-8   page 86   ❊

SPINACH AND SWEET ONION TART
Caramelised, whole baby onions, fresh
spinach and crème fraîche in a melting crust.
Serves 6-8   page 87

GRILLED PEPPER AND CHICK PEA TART
A vibrant tart of spicy chick peas and sweet peppers baked in a creamy custard. Serve with a radicchio and tomato salad.
Serves 6-8   page 89 ✳

SWEET POTATO AND SMOKED CHEESE FLAN
Wafer-thin sweet potato slices, layered with spicy chorizo and smoked Cheddar.
Serves 6-8   page 88

ONION AND POTATO TART
A tasty cheese topped flan, flavoured with capers, olive paste and fresh herbs.
Serves 4   page 88

ROQUEFORT TART
A superb creamy blue cheese tart with a tasty garlic and walnut topping.
Serves 6-8   page 88

MEDITERRANEAN TART
A colourful tart with a deep, satisfying flavour and a subtle fragrance of mint.
Serves 6-8   page 87 ✳

TOMATO TARTE TATIN
Filled with roasted plum tomatoes, this attractive tart is served topped with garlic and basil flavoured ciabatta crumbs.
Serves 6   page 92

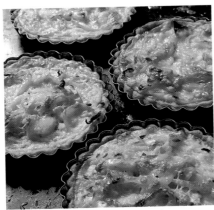

FENNEL, ONION AND GRUYÈRE
TARTLETS
Delicious cheese pastry tartlets with an
aromatic, creamy fennel and onion filling.
Serves 4   page 94 ✳

PARMESAN TARTLETS WITH BROAD
BEAN PESTO
Parmesan pastry cases filled with a broad
bean pesto, olives and tomatoes.
Serves 4   page 95 ✳

CHICORY FLAN
Chicory bulbs are braised until meltingly tender, then baked in a savoury cheese
custard topped with Parma ham.
Serves 6-8   page 90

AVOCADO AND PARMA HAM PUFFS
Puff pastry rounds topped with avocado
slices, Parma ham and piquant gremolata.
Serves 6   page 95

CRAB FILO TART
A crisp filo shell filled with flaked crab meat,
flavoured with spring onions, fresh ginger
and chopped coriander.
Serves 8   page 92

PARSNIP TATIN
Baby parsnips, moistened with cider, are
encased in a walnut pastry in this delicious
upside down tart.
Serves 6   page 92

SALMON AND HERB PASTIES
Crammed with salmon, prawns and fragrant summer herbs, these luxurious pasties make
perfect outdoor eating.
Serves 6   page 96   ✳

BAKED GARLIC AND GOAT CHEESE PARCELS
Small savoury parcels stuffed with caramelised garlic purée, goat's cheese and fresh herbs.
Serves 6   page 98

WILD MUSHROOM PITHIVIERS
Elegant, individual pies – ideal as a
vegetarian alternative Christmas dinner.
Serves 6   page 98   ✳

FILO MUSHROOM TARTLETS
Individual tarts filled with tasty mushrooms,
topped with a whole egg, then baked
to perfection.
Serves 6   page 98

ONION, FETA AND PINE NUT TARTS
Sweet caramelised onions, pine nuts and
crumbled feta in puff pastry cases.
Serves 4   page 95   ✳

EASY-BAKE PIZZA
Children will enjoy making their own pizzas
with this easy-to-follow recipe.
Serves 2-4   page 102

**TOMATO PIZZA WITH PARMA HAM
AND ROCKET**
Thin pizza with a stylish topping of Parma
ham, rocket leaves and Parmesan shavings.
Serves 2-4   page 102

**OLIVE CRUST PIZZA WITH
LEEK CONFIT**
Pizza crust flavoured with black olives, and
topped with melting cheese and leeks.
Serves 2-4   page 103

PIZZA FIORENTINA
Authentic Italian pizzas topped with Parma ham and fresh spinach, scattered
with grated Parmesan and baked with a whole egg in the centre.
Serves 2   page 104

GARLIC AND CAMEMBERT PIZZETTE
Sweet roast garlic gives these small pizzas a
superb flavour. A tasty starter or snack.
Serves 4   page 106

**FOUR CHEESE PIZZA WITH
SUN-DRIED TOMATOES**
Thin pizzas topped with melting dolcelatte,
mozzarella, mascarpone and Parmesan.
Serves 4   page 106

TALEGGIO PIZZETTE WITH PANCETTA AND RED ONION
Liberally flavoured with garlic, fresh basil and thyme, these pizzas are very tasty.
Serves 4   page 107

FENNEL AND BRESAOLA PIZZA
Elegant pizzas with a delicious topping of grilled fennel slices, bresaola, pecorino shavings and extra-virgin olive oil.
Serves 2-4   page 107

MUSHROOM AND CRÈME FRAÎCHE PIZZA
Assorted full flavoured fresh mushrooms give this pizza topping a sublime quality.
Serves 2   page 108

PISSALADIÈRE PARCEL
In this Provençal style pizza, meltingly soft onions, goat's cheese and anchovies are baked in a crisp dough crust.
Serves 6-8   page 108

PIZZA WITH SPINACH, FETA AND PINE NUTS
Spinach, onion and garlic pizzas dotted with feta, mascarpone and pine nuts.
Serves 2-4   page 110

ARTICHOKE AND DOLCELATTE PIZZA
Rich pizza, topped with sun-dried tomato paste, artichoke hearts and dolcelatte.
Serves 2-4   page 110

PIZZA CALAMARI
Thin tomato pizzas, topped with crisp fried squid and served with a lemon dressing.
Serves 2   page 110

PROSCIUTTO AND FONTINA CALZONE
'Double crust' pizza filled with Parma ham, sun-dried tomatoes, basil and fontina.
Serves 2-4   page 112

PRAWN AND SWEET CHILLI PIZZA
This recipe is inspired by the flavours of Pacific rim cooking, with tiger prawns, kaffir lime leaves, ginger and sweet hot chilli jam.
Serves 2   page 109

BEETROOT AND TALEGGIO PIZZA
Deep-base pizza with an original topping, equally good hot or cold – as picnic food.
Serves 6-8   page 114

ROASTED ONION AND OLIVE CALZONE
A double crust pizza, enclosing a creamy cheese and roasted red onion filling.
Serves 4   page 114 ✳

FOCCACIA PIZZA
Half pizza, half bread, topped with fresh plum tomatoes, mozzarella and anchovies.
Serves 6-8   page 115

FARMHOUSE LOAF
Traditional country-style loaf, with a wholemeal variation.
Makes 1; 16 slices   page 118 ✳

HOMESTYLE CIABATTA
This polenta enriched dough closely resembles home-baked Italian ciabatta. Delicious plain or toasted – drizzled with extra-virgin olive oil.
Makes 2; each 10 slices   page 118 ✳

GRANARY BREAD
A delicious full-flavoured loaf, made with malted granary flour and rolled oats.
Makes 1; 16 slices   page 118 ✳

SOURDOUGH
Made with a starter dough, this bread has a characteristic, slightly sour flavour.
Makes 1; 16 slices   page 120 ✳

SEEDED BARLEY BREAD
A 'healthy' nutty, seeded loaf with a delicious flavour – great toasted or dunked into soups.
Makes 1; 18 slices   page 122 ✳

MULTIGRAIN LOAF
Enriched with sunflower, poppy and sesame seeds, this moist granary bread has a wonderful nutty taste.
Makes 2; each 12 slices   page 122 ✳

SODA BREAD
Classic Irish bread which relies on bicarbonate of soda to both raise and flavour the dough.
Makes 1; 14-16 slices   page 123   ✳

APRICOT AND HAZELNUT BREAD
This flavoured granary bread has a superb moist texture and an excellent flavour.
Makes 2; each 12 slices   page 123   ✳

CORNBREAD
A golden close-textured American-style loaf with a distinctive flavour.
Makes 1; 16 slices   page 123   ✳

BEER BREAD
A wonderfully robust bread with a moist texture and slightly sour, yeasty flavour. Best eaten simply spread with butter.
Makes 1; 20 slices   page 124   ✳

DARK RYE BREAD
A dense, moist loaf with the distinctive flavour of molasses. Best thinly sliced, plain or toasted, with butter and jam.
Makes 2; each 10 slices   page 124   ✳

HERBED CHEESE STICK
Savoury batons with an enticing aroma of fresh rosemary and herbes de Provence.
Makes 2; each serves 4   page 123   ✳

CHEESE AND ONION BREAD
This Greek-style bread is first pan-fried, then baked with a cheesy red onion and thyme topping.
Makes 2; each serves 4   page 125

CHILLI CORNBREAD
Wheat-free savoury bread, flavoured with sweetcorn, spring onions, red chilli and grated Parmesan.
Makes 1; 10 slices   page 125   ✳

SPICED NAAN
This superb variation of Indian stuffed naan is surprisingly easy to make.
Makes 4   page 125

TURKISH FLAT BREAD
Reminiscent of traditional Turkish flat breads, this one has an authentic soft, fluffy texture and milky flavour.
Makes 1; 15 slices   page 128

PUMPKIN BREAD
This savoury loaf with its light, cake-like texture makes the perfect soup or salad accompaniment.
Makes 2; each 8-10 slices   page 128   ❊

WALNUT AND CRANBERRY BREAD
A nutty, savoury bread with a hint of sweetness from the cranberries.
Makes 2; each 10 slices   page 126   ❊

OLIVE BREAD ROLLS
Speckled with chopped black olives, these delicious rolls are brushed with olive oil and sprinkled with coarse sea salt after baking.
Makes 6 rolls   page 132   ❊

SCIACCIATA
An Italian pizza-style flat bread with a tasty garlic, sage and olive oil topping.
Makes 2; each serves 4   page 129   ❊

SUN-DRIED TOMATO AND FENNEL ROLLS
Fragrant rolls with a dense, slightly moist texture – perfect for sandwich fillings.
Makes 10 rolls   page 129   ❊

SPINACH AND CHEESE BREAD
A light bread dough rolled around a tasty spinach and feta cheese filling. Serve as a picnic snack, or with salad.
Makes 1; 16 slices   page 130

PARMESAN AND CHIVE ROLLS
These tasty cheese and herb rolls are particularly good served with soups.
Makes 8 rolls   page 132 ❊

SESAME RINGS
Served as street snacks in many eastern Mediterranean countries, these tasty sesame rings are ideal for a brunch or mid-morning snack.
Makes 12   page 132

FOCACCIA
Popular Italian flat bread, served as an accompaniment to salads, soups and stews.
Makes 2; each serves 6   page 134 ❊

HERB YOGURT BREAD
Like soda bread, this quick non-yeast bread doesn't need to rise before baking. It is particularly good with soups.
Makes 1; 16 slices   page 134 ❊

CHEESE MUFFINS
Light, savoury muffins with a peppery 'kick'. Best eaten on the day they are made, while still warm if possible.
Makes 12   page 134 ❊

KUGELHOPF
A light, raisin and almond studded yeast bread – traditionally eaten at Christmas in Germany and Austria.
Serves 12   page 138   ❈

STICKY FRUIT BRIOCHE
A rich, buttery brioche style bread, lightly scented with rosewater and packed with dried fruit and nuts.
Serves 8-10   page 138   ❈

PRUNE AND SAFFRON BUNS
Saffron lends a warm colour and mild, spicy aroma to these fruity yeast buns.
Makes 8 large buns   page 140   ❈

SPICED FIG AND RICOTTA BREAD
Sweet, light cinnamon-scented bread with layers of fresh figs and creamy ricotta.
Serves 8   page 139

BLUEBERRY FOUGASSE
This flat, dimpled sweet vanilla bread is piled up with colourful blueberries.
Serves 8   page 142

KRINGLE
Cardamom is the predominant flavour in this fragrant, festive Danish bread.
Serves 12   page 145 ✻

APPLE STROMBOLI
Tart dessert apples, mild spices and butter are rolled in a simple dough to make a fresh, light tasting bread that's particularly good warmed through for breakfast.
Serves 8   page 143

PANNETONE
Light, yet buttery and rich, this Italian classic favourite is studded with dried fruit and candied peel.
Makes 10-12 slices   page 144 ✻

CHRISTMAS STOLLEN
Richly fruited, lightly spiced festive yeast bread with an almond paste centre.
Makes 10 slices   page 142 ✻

SWEET MOCHA BREAD
This brioche-style bread sandwiches a delicious chocolate and coffee flavoured filling.
Serves 10   page 144 ✻

GOOSEBERRY CUSTARD CRUMBLE
For a new twist on this classic pudding, a creamy custard is poured over the fruit layer before topping with the crumble.
Serves 6   page 150

RED FRUIT CHARLOTTE WITH ORANGE SABAYON
Assorted berry fruits baked in a brioche crust and served with a superb sabayon.
Serves 4   page 150

BRAMBLE OAT CRUNCH
A wonderful combination of hedgerow fruits and toasted oats enriched with nuts.
Serves 8   page 151   ❋

FRANGIPANE BAKED PEARS
Poached fresh pears are stuffed with macerated raisins and almonds, then baked in a frangipane mixture.
Serves 6   page 156   ❋

PEACH BROWN BETTY
Fresh peach slices layered with a mildly spiced, buttery crumb mixture and baked in ramekins.
Serves 4   page 151

SPICED RAISIN PUDDINGS
Light, airy sponges speckled with raisins and ginger. A demerara lemon butter is the perfect accompaniment.
Serves 8   page 152   ❋

CHOCOLATE, WALNUT AND MAPLE PUDDINGS
Exceptionally light 'steamed puddings' made from a whisked egg mixture.
Serves 8   page 152   ❋

APRICOT AND CARDAMOM CRUMBLE
Fresh apricots baked under a hazelnut and oat crumble, flavoured with cardamom.
Serves 6   page 151

DOUBLE LEMON PUDDING
On baking this tangy pudding separates to form a light, golden sponge over a layer of zesty, thick lemon custard.
Serves 6-8   page 156

CLAFOUTIS
Sweet cherries are baked in a custard-like batter and served warm with a dusting of vanilla sugar.
Serves 6   page 157

PINEAPPLE, APPLE AND ALMOND PUDDINGS
Attractive individual puddings, topped with caramelised apple slices and served with cardamom-scented custard.
Serves 6   page 152 ✳

COCONUT AND SAFFRON RICE PUDDING
This fragrant pudding is enriched with coconut milk, dates and toasted pistachios.
Serves 4   page 157

APRICOT EGG CUSTARD
Fresh, juicy apricots are baked in an egg-rich batter for this light adaptation of a clafoutis.
Serves 8   page 157

CHOCOLATE MOUSSE PUDDINGS
Rich, gooey fudge-like puddings, served topped with vanilla-flavoured Greek yogurt or lightly whipped cream.
Serves 4-6   page 154

COCONUT AND LIME SYRUP CAKE
A sensational, light coconut cake soaked in a tangy lime syrup flavoured with lime leaves. Serve with Greek yogurt or crème fraîche as a refreshing dessert.
Serves 6   page 160

GOLDEN CROISSANT PUDDING
For this gourmet bread and butter pudding, flaky croissants and sultanas are baked in a creamy egg custard.
Serves 6   page 160   ✻

CHOCOLATE BREAD AND BUTTER PUDDING
Fruited bread baked in a vanilla custard with pockets of gooey chocolate sauce.
Serves 6   page 160

CARAMELISED APPLE CREAMS
Crème caramels coated with a delicious, slightly sharp, apple juice and honey glaze.
Serves 8   page 158

TROPICAL FRUIT CAKE
This striking pudding has a sticky base, topped with tropical fruits and caramel.
Serves 8   page 162

DOUBLE CHOCOLATE BAKED ALASKAS
Guaranteed to be popular, this spectacular pudding is surprisingly easy-to-prepare.
Serves 6   page 164   ✻

HOT ORANGE SOUFFLÉ
An impressive baked soufflé flavoured with
Grand Marnier and fresh orange.
Serves 6   page 164

GINGER RICOTTA CAKE
An enticing cheesecake flavoured with stem
ginger – served warm with a ginger and
whisky cream sauce.
Serves 6-8   page 168 ❋

BAKED CHEESECAKE WITH EXOTIC FRUITS
A traditional deep American style cheesecake, baked until just set – served topped with a
medley of tropical fruits.
Serves 8-10   page 169

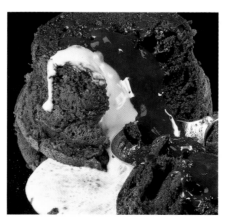

PECAN STREUSEL CHEESECAKE
A rich, smooth cheesecake, topped with a
crunchy caramelised pecan mixture and
served with a warm maple sauce.
Serves 6   page 168

CHOCOLATE SOUFFLÉS
These divine soufflés conceal a hidden
centre of melting chocolate. A frothy vanilla
cream is the perfect complement.
Serves 8   page 164

TIRAMISU TORTE
An outrageously rich cheesecake with an
irresistible soft gooey texture, based on the
delectable ingredients of tiramisu.
Serves 8-10   page 166 ❋

COCONUT AND MANGO TART
A luxurious tart of poached mangoes under a blanket of velvet smooth coconut custard, topped with toasted coconut.
Serves 10   page 172

FRENCH APPLE TART
Ever-tempting popular flan of fresh apple purée flavoured with Calvados, topped with a glazed arrangement of apple slices.
Serves 10   page 176

TARTE TATIN
This classic French dessert is cooked upside down, then inverted to serve, so the apples sit atop the rich pastry base.
Serves 8   page 176 ❊

RASPBERRY TART
A creamy, vanilla scented custard tart topped with flavourful fresh raspberries and a liberal dusting of vanilla sugar.
Serves 6   page 176

CHOCOLATE AND CHERRY AMARETTI TART
Tart morello cherries give this classic flavour combination a wonderful quality.
Serves 8   page 177 ❊

GOLDEN PASSION FRUIT TART
This exotic fruit tart is complemented by a tangy mango and citrus sauce. For a special touch, decorate with caramel bark.
Serves 8   page 179 ❊

GLAZED PRUNE TART
Plump prunes are steeped overnight in brandy, then baked in a sweet flan case – enveloped in a rich, creamy custard.
Serves 8   page 178 ❊

SUMMER FRUIT AND PRALINE TART
An elegant tart of fresh berries on a delicious praline flavoured custard.
Serves 10   page 178

PEAR TART RENVERSÉE
Halved pears are poached in a red wine syrup, then topped with pastry and baked. To serve, the tart is inverted.
Serves 6   page 179

TREACLE TART
Breadcrumbs are mixed with golden syrup and lemon to cut the sweetness, then baked in a deep pastry case.
Serves 8-10   page 182   ❊

RATAFIA BAKEWELL TART
A deep almondy sponge set on a layer of apricot conserve in a crisp pastry case.
Serves 8   page 184   ❊

DARK CHOCOLATE TART WITH HAZELNUT AND ORANGE SYRUP
A sensational smooth, slightly bitter, dark chocolate tart contrasted by a sweet, tangy hazelnut syrup.
Serves 10   page 182

VANILLA TART WITH BLUEBERRY COMPOTE
A delicately flavoured vanilla custard baked in a shallow pastry shell and served cold with a contrasting blueberry compote.
Serves 8   page 174

LEMON TART WITH FROSTED BERRIES
The addition of frosted seasonal berries to a classic lemon tart makes this version extra special.
Serves 8   page 180   ❊

PECAN, MAPLE AND WHISKY PIE
A decadent tart of toasted pecan nuts in a whisky flavoured filling, served drizzled with maple syrup.
Serves 6-8   page 182   ❋

PLUM AND ALMOND TART
Plums' natural affinity with almonds is used to excellent effect in this easy sourdough pastry tart.
Serves 6-8   page 184   ❋

ITALIAN EASTER TART
An irresistible ricotta cheese and arborio rice tart, delicately flavoured with orange, cinnamon and raisins.
Serves 6-8   page 188

LEMON AND LIME PAVLOVA PIE
A sumptuous special occasion dessert featuring a tangy lemon and lime filling piled high with soft mallowy meringue.
Serves 6   page 185

BERRY MILLE FEUILLES
Summer fruits add mouth-watering appeal to this crisp pastry and creamy custard pâtisserie classic.
Serves 8-10   page 190

FREE-FORM FIG TART
Glazed fresh figs baked on a sweet flan pastry base, served with scoops of honey ice cream.
Serves 6-8   page 186

PLUM AND MARZIPAN KUCHEN
Fresh plums set on a layer of almond paste in a delicious crumbly, almond pastry case.
Serves 6-8   page 188   ❋

PITHIVIERS
Attractive sugar-glazed French puff pie with a dried fruit and ground almond filling, spiked with orange liqueur.
Serves 10   page 188   ❋

MAPLE AND WALNUT MILLE FEUILLES
Filo pastry layered with custard, walnuts,
pistachios, dates and maple syrup.
Serves 8   page 192

APPLE STRUDEL WITH MAPLE
FUDGE SAUCE
A creamy fudge sauce is the perfect foil for
this filo roll, filled with tangy apples.
Serves 6-8   page 194

PISTACHIO BAKLAVA
Pistachios, pine nuts and spices are sandwiched between crisp layers of filo,
then soaked in a honey syrup – fragrant with cardamom and rosewater.
Serves 6-8   page 192

SPICED NUT STRUDEL
Assorted nuts, glacé cherries and raisins
flavoured with spices and enveloped in
buttery layers of filo pastry.
Serves 8-10   page 195   ✳

FESTIVE MINCE PIES
Rich shortcrust pies, filled with luxury
mincemeat and topped with festive
pastry shapes.
Makes 12   page 195   ✳

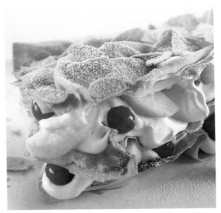

APPLE AND ALMOND MILLE FEUILLES
Crisp filo sheets interleaved with sweet
almond paste and tangy poached fruits.
Serves 6   page 192

WHITE CHOCOLATE TARTLETS
These spectacular, satin-textured white chocolate tarts are the ultimate indulgence.
Serves 8   page 196 ✼

CRANBERRY AND GINGER SLICE
Tart cranberries and silky smooth mascarpone complement each other perfectly in this smart, wintry dessert. Serve warm or chilled with the accompanying ginger syrup.
Serves 6-8   page 194

BAKEWELL TARTLETS WITH PLUM SAUCE
Crumble-topped, almond sponge tartlets, served with a tangy fresh plum sauce.
Serves 6   page 198 ✼

RHUBARB CRUMBLE TARTS
These attractive filo tarts are an excellent way to serve fresh rhubarb. An orange syrup sauce is the perfect complement.
Serves 6   page 199

PEACH CINNAMON TARTLETS
Fresh, ripe peach halves baked on puff pastry rounds spread with a delicious cinnamon butter.
Serves 4   page 198 🕐

PEAR GALETTES WITH CHOCOLATE SAUCE
These attractive pastries are easy to make with ready-to-bake dough.
Serves 6   page 199 🕐

SHORTBREAD
Melt-in-the mouth Scottish shortbread with
a sublime, rich buttery taste.
Makes 18-20   page 202

NOVELTY BISCUITS
Fun biscuits for children to make and
decorate, with easy to follow instructions.
Makes 18-20   page 202 ❋

MACADAMIA NUT COOKIES
Ground macadamia nuts give these smooth-textured crescent-shaped cookies
a wonderful buttery flavour.
Makes 24-26   page 202 ❋ ❑

ORANGE FLOWER BISCUITS
Delicate, thin biscuits scented with orange
flower water, plus variations.
Makes 20-24   page 204 🕐

DOUBLE CHOCOLATE COOKIES
American style, crumbly cookies – laden
with dark and white chocolate chunks.
Makes 18   page 204 ❋ 🕐 ❑

GINGER CHOCOLATE CHIP COOKIES
Crisp, light cookies flavoured with
crystallised ginger and dark chocolate.
Makes 32-34   page 204 ❋ 🕐

ALMOND FUDGE CRUMBLES
Easy cookies enriched with crushed almond flakes and niblets of chewy fudge.
Makes 24   page 205 ❄ ⏱ ❏

LEMON ZESTIES
Quick, easy biscuits with a melting texture and a refreshing lemon tang.
Makes 16-18   page 205 ❄ ⏱ ❏

ORANGE CINNAMON SABLÉS
These subtly flavoured biscuits have a crisp, yet melting texture.
Makes 20   page 205 ❄ ⏱ ❏

CHOCOLATE SOFT CENTRES
These crackled, crumbly biscuits conceal a velvet smooth chocolate centre.
Makes 18   page 208 ❄ ⏱

PANFORTE DE SIENA
This scented spicy, thin 'cake' packed with candied peel, honey and nuts is a traditional Italian Christmas treat.
Makes 12 slices   page 208 ❏

PAMPERATO
A variation of panforte, richly flavoured with nuts, brandy-soaked raisins, chocolate and candied peel.
Makes 3; each 4 slices   page 209 ❏

BISCOTTI
Light, crunchy biscuits studded with toasted almonds and flavoured with a hint of orange.
Makes about 50   page 209   ❑

BRANDY SNAPS
Lacy, rolled dessert biscuits with a slightly chewy texture, plus variations for baskets to hold ices and sorbets.
Makes 12-16   page 210   ❊

FLORENTINES
Elegant chewy biscuits, rich with nuts, fruit and sunflower seeds. After baking the edges are rolled in melted chocolate for a decorative effect.
Makes 12   page 206

GINGER GLASS BISCUITS
These crisp, light semi-transluscent biscuits are the perfect foil for creamy desserts.
Makes 18   page 210   ❊ ⏱

PISTACHIO THINS
Variation of crunchy biscotti, flavoured with pistachio nuts and anise.
Makes about 30   page 210   ❑

ROSEMARY TUILES
Pretty dessert biscuits, with a subtle fragrance of rosemary and lemon.
Makes 28-30   page 212

TRADITIONAL SCONES
Oven fresh scones served with jam and whipped cream are as popular as ever.
Makes 8   page 216   ❄ ⏱

BLUEBERRY SCONES
Bursting as they bake, blueberries give these simple scones a lovely, juicy flavour.
Makes 10-12   page 216   ❄ ⏱

CARROT AND RAISIN SCONES
Serve these mildly spiced scones topped with spoonfuls of cream cheese or mascarpone.
Makes 9   page 216   ⏱

POPPY SEED, ORANGE AND ALMOND SCONE RING
An unusual scone round, flavoured with orange marmalade and poppy seeds.
Makes 8 large scones   page 218   ❄

PLUM AND HAZELNUT SLICE
Puréed plums give this traybake a moist texture. Served warm with yogurt or cream, it doubles up as a simple dessert.
Makes 10 slices   page 220   ❄

ORANGE FLAPJACKS
Nutty sunflower seeds and tangy orange zest add a twist to this chewy traybake.
Makes 18   page 220   ❄ ❑

GINGER FLAPJACKS
Baked in a deep tin, these flapjacks have a delicious crumbly, moist texture and a subtle ginger flavour.
Makes 18   page 220   ✳❑

COCONUT SQUARES
Made with ground rice, hazelnuts and coconut, these tasty cakes are gluten-free.
Makes 12   page 222   ✳❑

WHITE CHOCOLATE HAZELNUT BROWNIES
Sugar-crusted and laden with white chocolate ... once tasted, never forgotten!
Makes 12   page 221   ✳❑

RICH CHOCOLATE BROWNIES
Deliciously rich, with a characteristic soft, gooey texture, these dark chocolate brownies are simply the best!
Makes 24   page 221   ✳❑

APPLE AND GINGER TEABREAD
Fresh apples and preserved stem ginger are a perfect partnership here.
Makes 8-10 slices   page 222   ✳❑

RIPPLED DATE AND BANANA LOAF
A lovely, moist teabread with a distinctive banana flavour and a layer of date purée.
Makes 8-10 slices   page 224   ✳❑

CHOCOLATE AND SWEET POTATO LOAF
Moist sweet potato based cake enriched with chocolate and toasted almonds.
Makes 8-10 slices   page 224   ✳❑

FRUIT AND SPICE PARKIN
Full of flavours, this cake is best left to
mature for 1-2 weeks before it is eaten.
Makes 12 slices   page 224   ✳ ❑

APRICOT TEABREAD WITH MARMALADE
Flavoured with a tangy orange marmalade and plenty of dried apricots, this teabread is also
glazed with marmalade.
Makes 10 slices   page 222   ✳ ❑

FRUITED TEABREAD
Richly flavoured with tea-soaked dried
apricots, prunes and raisins, this moist
teabread is topped with a honey glaze.
Makes 10 slices   page 225   ✳ ❑

BANANA TEABREAD
A nutty banana teabread topped with dried
banana chips and toasted walnuts.
Makes 8-10 slices   page 225   ❑

**MOLASSES, PRUNE AND
WALNUT TEABREAD**
A chunky, wholesome loaf that's good for
breakfast – on its own or lightly buttered.
Makes 10 slices   page 225   ✳ ❑

PEAR AND CARDAMOM TEABREAD
Flavoured with fresh pear slices and
cardamom, this iced teabread is excellent.
Makes 10 slices   page 226   ✳ ❑

MADELEINES
Delicate, attractive sponges baked in
traditional shell shaped tins.
Makes 24   page 230   ✳

PEAR AND CINNAMON BUNS
Dotted with dried pears and sultanas, these
buns are topped with a sugary glaze.
Makes 14   page 230   ✳ ⏱

GREEK EASTER CAKES
Lemony sponge cakes steeped in a spiced
orange syrup – fragrant with cinnamon,
cardamom and cloves.
Makes 8   page 230

FIG AND OATMEAL MUFFINS
Flavoured with dried figs and sultanas, these
muffins are best eaten warm on the day
they are made.
Makes 12   page 232   ✳ ⏱

CRANBERRY MUFFINS
These moist muffins bursting with tangy
cranberries are perfect for a winter brunch.
Makes 12   page 232   ✳ ⏱

WHOLEMEAL BANANA MUFFINS
High fibre muffins topped with dried banana
chips and walnuts in a tangy orange glaze.
Makes 6   page 232   ✳

DOUBLE CHOCOLATE MUFFINS
These rich muffins contain chunks of dark
and white chocolate to give morsels of
pure delight!
Makes 14   page 233   ✳

PECAN AND ORANGE PUFFS
Melt-in-the-mouth rough puff pastries with a delicious caramelised pecan and orange filling.
Makes 9   page 234

MARZIPAN AND RAISIN WHIRLS
Resembling Danish pastries, these spirals enclose a spiced raisin and almond filling.
Makes 12   page 236   ❋

MOROCCAN ALMOND CRESCENTS
Crisp pastries delicately scented with orange flower water and filled with a moist almond paste.
Makes 18   page 236

APRICOT PATTIES
These quick and easy patty cakes are irresistibly moist. They are delicious served warm at teatime, or with crème fraîche as a dessert.
Makes 12   page 233   ❋ ◷

CITRUS ECCLES CAKES
These flaky, light lattice-topped pastries are filled with citrus peel, currants and muscovado sugar.
Makes 20   page 237   ❋

RASPBERRY PALMIERS
Ready-made puff pastry rolled around fresh raspberries and baked with a sugar glaze to delicious effect.
Makes 16   page 237   ◷

CARAMELISED STRAWBERRY TARTLETS
Pretty filo cases filled with lemony mascarpone and pan-fried strawberries.
Makes 12   page 238

PEACH FILOS
Filo rings filled with a spiced mixture of ground almonds and dried peaches, steeped in a citrus syrup after baking.
Makes 8   page 240

LEMON SHORTBREAD TARTLETS
A wonderfully tangy lemon posset set in melting shortbread cases.
Makes 10   page 240

CHERRY TARTLETS
Elegant tartlets filled with pitted canned cherries in a soft set cheesecake mixture.
Makes 8   page 237

FLORENTINE TARTLETS
Delicate, little tartlets filled with frangipane and topped with glacé cherries, flaked almonds and pumpkin seeds.
Makes 12   page 240

REDCURRANT AND RASPBERRY MERINGUE SHORTBREADS
Red fruits set in almond shortbread cases and topped with swirls of meringue.
Makes 12   page 241

PASSION FRUIT ÉCLAIRS
Light, fresh-tasting éclairs flavoured with passion fruit juice and kirsch.
Makes 12-15   page 242   ❈

COFFEE AND PECAN LAYER CAKE
A moist coffee cake enriched with chopped pecans, and coated with a coffee frosting.
Makes 10 slices   page 246 ❋

WALNUT TORTE
A light, airy sponge flavoured with toasted walnuts, ricotta and a hint of orange. Served topped with chocolate shavings.
Makes 8-10 slices   page 246

FROSTED LIME SPONGE
An interesting variation on a classic Victoria Sandwich, filled and topped with a tangy lime and cream cheese frosting.
Makes 10 slices   page 246 ❋

LAVENDER MADEIRA CAKE
Fresh lavender gives a subtle, summery flavour to this buttery Madeira cake. Dried lavender can be used as an alternative.
Makes 10 slices   page 248 ❋ ❑

DANISH APPLE CAKE
This cake is so moist and delicious, it is difficult to resist. Serve warm with pouring cream for optimum appreciation.
Makes 8 slices   page 250

ICED ROSEMARY CAKE
A sweet orange glaze contrasts perfectly with this unusual, subtly fragrant cake.
Makes 12 slices   page 250 ❋ ❑

LEMON AND HAZELNUT CAKE
Light whisked sponge flavoured with poached whole lemon and ground nuts.
Makes 8 slices   page 254 ❋

CARROT CAKE WITH MASCARPONE
A wonderfully moist cake with a creamy mascarpone frosting and an unusual decoration of crisp-fried carrot shavings.
Makes 8-10 slices   page 251 ❋

AMARETTI PLUM CAKE
Crushed amaretti biscuits provide pockets of flavour in this almond cake, and add a tasty crunch to the fresh plum topping.
Makes 12-16 slices   page 251 ✻

CRUMBLE TOPPED FRUIT CAKE
An easy cake, dotted with dried fruit and scattered with a sugary crumbly crust.
Makes 12 slices   page 252 ✻ ❑

BRAZIL NUT AND POLENTA CAKE
Polenta gives this moist cake an interesting grainy texture and accentuates the flavour of the brazil nuts.
Makes 10 slices   page 253 ✻ ❑

GREEK YOGURT CAKE
A simple cake soaked in lemon syrup after baking to delicious effect. Served with fresh oranges, it makes a good dessert.
Makes 10 slices   page 252

SUMMER BERRY CRUNCH CAKE
Crushed sugar cubes tossed with lemon juice make a zesty topping for this juicy fresh fruit cake.
Makes 8 slices   page 253

CHERRY AND APPLE STREUSEL
Encased in a buttery, almond crumble is a mouth-watering filling of vanilla-scented cherries and sautéed apples.
Makes 10 slices   page 254 ✻

CAERPHILLY AND APPLE CAKE
A light, crumbly apple and sultana cake with a hidden layer of tart Caerphilly cheese.
Makes 10 slices   page 254 ❋

DARK, MOIST CHOCOLATE CAKE
This scrumptious chocolate cake, enriched with ground almonds, keeps well.
Makes 12 slices   page 258 ❋ ❑

FRUITED BUTTERMILK CAKE
A flavoursome, easy fruit cake, made with ready-mixed luxury dried fruit and dark muscovado sugar.
Makes 12 slices   page 255 ❋ ❑

FRUITED GINGERCAKE
A deliciously moist gingerbread, packed with plenty of dried and glacé fruit, nuts and ginger pieces.
Makes 16 slices   page 256 ❋ ❑

PISTACHIO ANGEL CAKE
Light, airy sponge speckled with pistachios and coated with a smooth coconut frosting.
Makes 12 slices   page 258

CHERRY AND ALMOND CAKE
A deliciously rich almond cake dotted with natural glacé cherries and slivered almonds.
Makes 18 slices   page 258 ❋ ❑

ITALIAN MERINGUES
Soft-centred meringues sandwiched with whipped cream and served with strawberries or other seasonal fruits.
Serves 6   page 262 ✺

PAVLOVA
A colourful medley of fruits nestling in whipped cream on a luscious deep, mallowy meringue.
Serves 8   page 263

CHOCOLATE AND RASPBERRY TORTE
An elegant gâteau, comprising a chocolate sponge case filled with cream – spiked with liqueur and dotted with fresh raspberries, ginger and grated chocolate.
Makes 12 slices   page 266

CHOCOLATE AND HAZELNUT MERINGUES
Flavoured meringues served topped with berry fruits and chocolate shavings.
Serves 6   page 263 ✺

CHOCOLATE AND CHESTNUT MACAROON
Layers of hazelnut meringue sandwiched together with a creamy chestnut filling.
Serves 6   page 263 ✺

COCONUT ROULADE WITH CHERRIES
Deliciously moist sponge enriched with creamed coconut and filled with cherries flavoured with kirsch.
Serves 8   page 264

CHOCOLATE ROULADE
Melt-in-the-mouth baked chocolate mousse mixture rolled around vanilla-scented whipped cream.
Serves 10   page 264   ❉

CHOCOLATE AND CHERRY GÂTEAU
A magical chocolate cake topped with fresh or canned cherries and a wickedly rich chocolate ganache.
Makes 10-12 slices   page 265   ❉

CITRUS MOUSSE CAKE WITH PLUMS
Whisked egg whites give this sponge a wonderfully moist texture. Poached plums are the perfect complement.
Makes 12 slices   page 265

RICH CHOCOLATE LACE GÂTEAU
An impressive, yet easy-to-make lacy chocolate collar embraces a rich liqueur-drizzled chocolate sponge – hidden under a creamy ganache.
Makes 12 slices   page 270

CHOCOLATE GÂTEAU WITH BRANDIED PRUNES
Prunes in a brandy syrup are layered with cream between chocolate sponge rounds.
Makes 16 slices   page 268   ❉

BUTTERSCOTCH AND BRAZIL NUT GÂTEAU
Thin sponge rounds enriched with nuts and layered with a butterscotch mixture.
Makes 12 slices   page 268

EXOTIC FRUIT GÂTEAU
A delicious tropical fruit gâteau, mildly spiced with star anise and cinnamon.
Makes 12 slices   page 269

PEAR AND GINGER WINE GÂTEAU
Fresh pear slices set in ginger wine jelly make an attractive integral decoration for this fresh-tasting gâteau.
Makes 12 slices   page 272

CHOCOLATE ORANGE TRUFFLE TORTE
A chocolate sponge base is drizzled with
orange liqueur, then topped with a divine
chocolate and orange truffle mixture.
Makes 12 slices   page 273 ✳

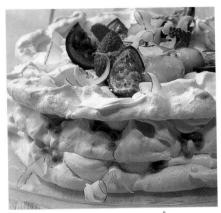

PASSION FRUIT MERINGUE GÂTEAU
Crisp, light coconut meringue layered with a
fragrant passion fruit cream.
Serves 10   page 273

CHOUX RING WITH PEACHES AND CARAMEL
This variation of Paris Brest is topped with caramel and filled with fresh peach slices in a
liqueur flavoured mascarpone cream.
Serves 10-12   page 276

DOUBLE CHOCOLATE RIBBON CAKE
This deliciously rich cake makes an
irresistible treat. The chocolate ribbons
add a stylish finishing touch.
Makes 10 slices   page 274 ✳

BLUEBERRY AND VANILLA MALLOW
Soft vanilla-scented meringue sandwiched
together with a creamy filling, toasted
almonds and fresh blueberries.
Serves 8   page 276

ICED BERRY MERINGUE
An iced meringue gâteau filled with a
homemade soft fruit ice cream.
Serves 10   page 276 ✳

IVORY CELEBRATION CAKE
Elegant iced rich fruit cake which can be adapted to suit any occasion, from birthdays to weddings.
Makes 36-40 slices page 281 ❏

THE ULTIMATE CHRISTMAS CAKE
This moist cake is full of enticing Christmas flavours and decorated simply with ready-to-roll icing.
Makes 16-20 slices page 284 ❇ ❏

TIERED CELEBRATION CAKE
This sophisticated two-tier cake is casually coated with royal icing and decorated with muslin drapes, frosted flowers and sugared strawberries.
Makes 80-100 slices page 282 ❏

CHOCOLATE CROWN
For adults and older children, this extravagant chocolate novelty cake is wrapped in a decorative collar and piled high with luxury chocolates.
Makes 12 slices page 286 ❇

CANDLELIT CHRISTMAS CAKE
Frosted bay leaves and nightlights make a simple, effective decoration for this light alternative to a traditional dark fruit cake.
Makes 24-30 slices   page 285 ❇ ❏

WHITE AND DARK CHOCOLATE GÂTEAU
This impressive rich, chocolate cake hidden beneath a white chocolate drape is surprisingly easy to make.
Makes 12-14 slices page 286 ❇

SPICED ALMOND EASTER CAKE
This variation of a simnel cake has a layer of sticky almond paste through the middle and a wonderful spicy flavour.
Makes 10 slices page 288 ❄ ❑

BIRTHDAY BEAR CAKE
Ready-to-roll icing, plus a selection of bright food colourings and ribbons are all you need to decorate this delightful cake.
Makes 24 slices page 292 ❄ ❑

SNOW COTTAGE
This charming variation of a gingerbread house is made with non-spicy biscuits to appeal to young children. For extra excitement, sweets can be piled inside the cottage.
Makes 10 slices page 290

TRAIN CAKE
The simplicity of this novelty cake design is wonderfully effective, making it a perfect choice for young children.
Makes 16-20 slices page 292 ❄ ❑

CARAMEL GARLAND CAKE
Elegant, yet simple iced sponge surrounded by a garland of fresh fruit and caramel shapes. Suitable for any special occasion, from birthdays to special wedding anniversaries.
Makes 12 slices page 288 ❄ ❑

INTRODUCTION

A detailed guide to essential ingredients,
baking equipment, basic preparation techniques
and storage, including freezing

Butter

Butter is one of the most important flavours in baking – how often do we hear baked things praised just because they taste 'buttery'? Butter provides cakes, biscuits and pastry with a rich, yet restrained flavour and a warm, subtle colour. Although in the past butter was salted in order to preserve it, in this country we've retained the habit and most of the butter sold here is still salted or slightly salted. However, in baking, unsalted butter really does makes the best-flavoured cakes and biscuits.

Butter is made by vigorously churning pasteurised cream until it forms a solid mass, that can be gathered, washed and shaped into blocks. The remaining liquid – buttermilk – is drained off and used separately.

Unsalted butter is pale in colour with a smooth, firm texture and a delicious nutty, slightly sweet taste. It carries other flavours beautifully and can also stand on its own in simple recipes where it makes up a large proportion of the ingredients. If you do use salted butter in baking, always taste before adding any more salt to the mixture – saltiness varies from brand to brand and too much can spoil the finished product. Unsalted butter is the best choice for pastry because it stays firm and can be rubbed into flour more successfully.

Storing butter

Butter sops up flavours like a sponge, so any strong-tasting foods that are in the fridge at the same time are likely to affect its taste. To avoid this, wrap tightly in greaseproof paper or foil and store the butter in a separate fridge compartment. Normally, chilled salted butter keeps well for up to 1 month, unsalted butter for up to 2 weeks. If necessary, you can freeze butter for up to 6 months.

Cooking with butter

Using butter at the correct temperature is an important factor. If you are making pastry or following any recipe with a rubbing-in method of incorporating butter, then it should be cold and firm. This ensures that the butter can be evenly mixed in, but still retains some form. However, when baking biscuits, cakes and breads, the butter should be soft all the way through but not actually melting, so that it can be creamed with sugar successfully. If you forget to take the butter out of the fridge well in advance, soften it in the microwave on low for 10-20 seconds if necessary.

◆ To melt butter, first cut into small pieces so that it will melt quickly and evenly, then place in a small, heavy-based pan over a low heat until melted; don't allow to boil or it may become bitter. Take the pan off the heat as soon as the butter has melted.

Alternatives to butter

Most margarines are a blend of vegetable oils, milk and animal fats, though pure vegetable margarines – essential for strict vegetarians – are now widely available. Although margarine

Butter is derived from very fresh cream, by slow churning. Unsalted butter, sometimes described as 'sweet butter' is preferred for most baking purposes.

does not give the same creamy taste as butter, it can be used in much the same way. In general, block margarine is the best type to use in baking; it should be removed from the fridge half an hour before you're ready to use it. Soft-tub margarine is too soft for rubbing into flour, and although it is very easy to cream with sugar, it doesn't always give good results in cake-making. Low-fat margarines and spreads have a high water content and are not suitable for baking.

◆ White cooking fats are whipped from blended vegetable oils or a mix of vegetable and animal fats or fish oils. They are totally flavourless, but give light results in baking and make crumbly, 'short' textured pastry and biscuits – hence their alternative name 'shortenings'. These white cooking fats are often used in conjunction with butter. Lard is a clear, hard fat with a bland taste. It is made from rendered pork belly fat and was once used regularly for pastry-making. Nowadays, however, white vegetable fat is generally used in preference to lard, except in traditional recipes.

Sugar

Most sugar is derived from two sources: sugar cane which grows in the tropics and sub-tropics, and sugar beet which is produced in temperate climates, including this country. There are many types of sugar for the cook to choose from for baking. At one end of the spectrum there is unrefined molasses sugar – a fine-grained, dark substance with a texture like damp sand and a raw, treacly taste. At the other end, there is icing sugar, its pale, refined cousin – a powdery sugar with an uncomplicated, one-dimensional sweetness. It's hard to believe that the two are related, but both types have distinct uses in baking.

White sugars

White sugar has been refined from sugar cane or sugar beet by a lengthy process and contains less then 1% vitamins or minerals.

◆ Granulated sugar is perhaps the most familiar white sugar, as it gazes up at us from sugar bowls across the country. In baking, it is good for crunchy biscuits or in certain recipes which have a rubbing-in method, but in cakes its coarse grains can create a speckled appearance.

◆ Caster sugar has a much finer grain and dissolves much more quickly. It is the sugar most often used in baking as it creams well with butter and is perfect for light sponge cakes, biscuits and for sprinkling over shortbread. Golden caster and granulated sugars are also available; these are tossed with a little molasses to add colour and impart a little flavour.

◆ Vanilla sugar lends a subtle sophistication wherever it is used. It is simply caster sugar enhanced with pure vanilla. Rather than buy vanilla sugar, which is flavoured with vanilla extract, make your own by burying a vanilla pod in a jar of caster sugar and leaving it for about 2 weeks. You can also infuse sugar with whole spices, such as cinnamon sticks.

◆ Icing sugar is very sweet, with a powdery texture and dissolves almost instantly. Use it to make smooth icings for cakes, and for sifting over pies, sponge cakes and desserts as decoration. Icing sugar isn't generally used in cake mixtures as it does not create enough volume when creamed.

◆ Rock sugar is made of crystallised raw cane sugar. It is familiar as pale brown crystals served with coffee, but makes an attractive decoration for cakes and biscuits, too. Multi-coloured rainbow rock sugar is also available.

Brown sugars

Unrefined or raw brown sugar is cane juice that has been separated and crystallised, and contains varying amounts of molasses. It ranges in colour from pale gold to volcanic black. Brown sugar has more depth and character than white sugar and adds a richer flavour to cakes and biscuits. Once opened, brown sugar may go hard in the bag or jar – cover it with a damp cloth for a few hours until it softens up again, or add a crust of bread, seal the container tightly and leave it for a day or overnight.

To make your own vanilla sugar, keep a vanilla pod buried in a jar of caster sugar to impart a subtle flavour.

◆ Molasses sugar is dark, soft, fine-grained and damp with a strong flavour. It is used for rich, moist fruit cakes and puddings. One notch down, dark muscovado is an unrefined, slightly less intense sugar with a treacly flavour which is perfect for rich, dark, mature cakes containing fruit and alcohol, as well as treacle cakes and gingerbread. Light muscovado is lighter still, and is used widely in cakes, muffins, teabread and parkin. If you want to add brown-sugar richness without overpowering other flavours, this is the sugar to use. (Muscovado is Portuguese for unrefined.)

◆ Demerara sugar has large, coarse, golden crystals with a slight flavour of molasses and is sold refined and unrefined. It is often used for sprinkling over cakes and teabreads before baking, but is not generally used in cakes that require creaming because it gives a gritty texture.

◆ Light and dark soft brown sugars are usually refined white sugars that have been tossed in syrup or molasses. They are drier than other unrefined brown sugars and don't have as much flavour, but they can be used in the same way as muscovado sugars to colour biscuits and cakes.

Flour

Wheat flours are made up of three types of wheat grain – hard, soft and durum. Hard grains are used in 'strong' bread flours because they produce the most gluten, while soft grains are low in gluten and are used in 'soft' plain flours for cakes and biscuits. All wheat flours are made from various combinations of these three types of wheat.

Plain flours

Plain white flour, like white sugar, is the most refined type of flour you can buy – during processing, the bran and germ are removed from every grain. The flour is then fortified with vitamins and treated with chlorine to whiten it. Unbleached flour has been left to whiten naturally without the use of chlorine – this process takes longer and as a result the flour tends to be more expensive.
◆ Soft plain flour is made from 100% soft wheat. It is fine-textured and ideal for making pastry, cakes and biscuits.
◆ Strong plain white flour, by contrast, is milled from hard wheat with a high gluten content. It is used for making bread and produces loaves with a good, open texture.
◆ Italian type '00' flour is milled to a finer texture than ordinary plain flour and tends to cook faster, so the floury taste cooks out more quickly. It is the flour used for pasta, but also makes good pastry.

Self-raising flour

Self-raising flour is used in cake-making because, as the name suggests, it helps the cake to rise. It is made from plain white flour to which baking soda and salt have been added. Do not keep a bag of self-raising flour for longer than 3 months as the potency of the baking soda will have diminished. If you want to substitute plain flour for self-raising in a recipe, add 10ml (2 tsp) baking powder to each 225g (8oz) flour.

Wholemeal flours

Wholemeal flour or wholewheat flour is milled from the entire wheat kernel (the bran and germ) and contains all the natural nutrients and flavours of the grain. It is coarser and heavier than white flour and does not rise as much. There are stone-ground wholewheat flours as well as roller-milled flours; stone-ground flour tends to have a better flavour, but won't keep as well. It can be combined with strong plain flour in equal quantities for a milder taste. Brown flour contains 80-90% of the bran and wheat germ. It is lighter than wholemeal flour and will produce smoother results. It can be used for bread, biscuits and pastry. Granary flour is brown flour with malted wheat flakes added and lends a delicious nutty taste.

Other flours

The following flours are used to a limited extent in baking.
◆ Polenta flour or fine cornmeal flour is ground from white, yellow or blue corn. Yellow or white cornmeal is used to make Italian polenta; in the USA cornmeal flour is widely used

to make cornbread. Fine or coarse cornmeal flour is good for making muffins, and any bread where a corn flavour and a slightly gritty texture are desired.
◆ Buckwheat flour is made from ground grains of buckwheat, a plant which grows prolifically in north-eastern Europe. It is a fruit, rather than a type of wheat. Buckwheat is usually added to other, lighter flours when used in bread-making.
◆ Rye flour is very low in gluten and produces a heavy loaf, with a distinctive flavour. It is usually combined with a high-gluten flour for a lighter result. Pumpernickel bread is made from coarse ground rye flour, while fine ground rye flour is used for black breads.
◆ Cornflour is a fine, white powder made from the heart of the maize kernel. It is low in gluten and is often added to cakes, shortbread and biscuits to give a fine texture.
◆ Rice flour is produced from very finely ground polished white rice. It can be used to make 'wheat-free' cakes for those with a gluten intolerance.
◆ Potato flour is a very fine, soft gluten-free powder made from pure potato starch. It gives a light, dry texture in baking and can be used by itself or mixed with wheat flour. Potato flour is tasteless and therefore good for delicately flavoured puddings and sauces.
◆ Chestnut flour is a light brown nutty flour ground from chestnuts, and is perfect for cakes, breads, biscuits and soufflés – especially for those with an intolerance to gluten. It is obtainable from specialist Italian food shops.

Eggs

Dark brown, speckled, white or beige – it makes no odds which you choose as the flavour of an egg isn't affected by the colour of its shell. However, this is one time when size really does matter. In this book all recipes use large eggs (unless otherwise indicated), so make sure you have the right size. The egg itself should bear the Lion Quality mark of freshness. Lion eggs are monitored by the British Egg Information Bureau and are stamped with a sell-by date so you can tell how old your egg is even when you've thrown away the box. Only buy eggs from a farm that you know have been laid in the last 7 days. Eggs from 'caged bird' or battery hens should reach supermarket shelves within 24 hours of laying, while free-range eggs get there within 3 days. Don't use eggs that have been around for too long – the British Egg Information Bureau recommends that eggs should not be older than 21 days.

Storing and checking for freshness

Like butter, eggs like to absorb flavours from foods that share the same breathing space. Keep them in the fridge in their box or in a separate container and sit them pointed end downwards. This will stop moisture from the egg evaporating and air filling the sac inside the egg between the shell and membrane. If you hold an egg up to a strong light you can check the size of the sac (before the advent of electricity, this test used to be known as candling).

◆ A fresh egg cracked on to a plate will have two layers of white, one thick and one thin, with a 'proud' yolk, which keeps its shape. As time passes, the proteins will break down, the white will thin out and become watery and the yolk will look flat. If a fresh egg is immersed horizontally in cold water it should sink to the bottom without tilting – if it tilts, it may be up to a week old, if it floats vertically, then it's getting on and is probably better discarded. Don't take a chance if you think an egg may be past its best, and always discard eggs which are cracked or dirty.

Egg safety

Eggs are susceptible to salmonella, one of the bacteria responsible for food poisoning. This is because their shells are porous and can absorb the bacteria if they come into contact with it. Thorough cooking will destroy salmonella, but raw or lightly cooked eggs are used in many classic recipes – including meringues, lemon curd, some sauces and ice creams. Although the risk is small, those who are particularly vulnerable – including the young, the elderly, pregnant women and those with an immune-deficiency disease – should not eat raw or lightly cooked eggs.

Baking with eggs

Eggs are indispensable in cooking. Nutritionally, they are a marvellous complete food, but they also have unique culinary properties. They can be used whole or as separate yolks or whites to bind a mixture, to add richness and create volume. To get the best out of them, make sure eggs are at room temperature before baking; if they are too cold they won't blend well with other ingredients, and the whites won't trap air properly and whisk up to a good volume.

◆ Always use a clean, completely grease-free bowl when whisking egg whites – glass, stainless steel or copper are preferable, as plastic tends to hold grease. Be careful not to overbeat or the air bubbles will burst and your cake or soufflé may fall flat. Whipped egg whites lose volume very quickly, so only whip them immediately before using.

◆ Egg yolks are liable to curdle if they are too cold, or if they are added to a mixture too quickly. Add beaten egg or egg yolks to a cake mixture, a little at a time, sprinkling in a tablespoon of flour if it starts to curdle. Curdling won't affect the taste, but the texture of the cake may be a little coarse and dense.

Separating eggs

To separate eggs, take two bowls and crack the egg sharply but firmly in the centre on the side of one bowl. Holding it upright over the bowl, ease the top half of the shell away leaving the yolk resting in the bottom half. Allow any escaping egg white to drop into the first bowl, then transfer the egg yolk from shell to shell, all the while collecting the white in the first bowl. When there is no more white left in the shell, drop the egg yolk carefully into the second bowl. If the yolk breaks into the white, you will have to start again as egg white won't whisk if there is any trace of yolk. If this sounds daunting, you can buy a special egg separator – simply crack the whole egg into the cup which has a slit at the side through which the white can escape.

Chocolate

In many baking recipes chocolate is a key ingredient and the quality of the chocolate you use is an important factor. Generally, sweet milk chocolate with a low content of cocoa solids should be avoided, as should synthetic-tasting 'cooking chocolate' or 'cake covering' which is sold in the baking section of most supermarkets. Instead, choose a bittersweet, plain, or semi-sweet chocolate that has at least 70% cocoa solids – very often, these are stocked in the confectionery section along with the sweets and eating chocolates and are labelled as continental or luxury chocolate. If you're making a pudding or cake where chocolate is the main ingredient and the dominant taste, it's important to use a fine quality brand. You could ruin the taste if you use inexpensive chocolate.

◆ Couverture is a fine quality plain chocolate often used by professional cooks for decoration and in sweet-making. It contains a high level of cocoa butter which makes it very runny when melted and produces a thin, even, glossy coating. Couverture chocolate is invariably tempered before use (see below). It can be bought as bittersweet, semi-sweet and milk chocolate, but is usually only sold by specialist food stores and some delicatessens.

◆ White chocolate contains cocoa butter, but no cocoa solids – hence its opaque, creamy colour. It sets less firmly than dark chocolate and is not as easy to work with because it overheats very easily. Some supermarkets have started to sell a 'luxury' brand – favour this over ordinary white chocolate, which is often overpoweringly sweet when melted.

Storing chocolate

To store chocolate, wrap it well in foil and keep it in a cool, dry place. If it becomes too warm, a whitish 'bloom' will appear – this is the cocoa butter rising to the surface. This does not affect the taste, but may alter the texture of your recipe. In hot weather chocolate can be kept in the fridge for a short while if necessary, but it will develop a 'bloom' if refrigerated for any length of time. Bring to room temperature before you use it.

Melting chocolate

The most important thing to remember when melting chocolate is to treat it gently. Break it up into small pieces and place it in the top half of a double boiler or in a heatproof bowl over a pan of gently simmering water – the water should not be boiling. Make sure the bowl doesn't touch the water. Heat slowly without stirring until the chocolate is soft, then stir until smooth. Remove the chocolate from the heat once all of it has melted.

◆ Don't try to hurry up the melting process, and never allow the chocolate to overheat. Avoid letting any moisture or steam come into contact with it, or the chocolate may seize and harden. While it is still of pouring consistency, melted chocolate can be combined with other ingredients – but make sure any liquids you add are of similar temperature. Melted

chocolate can be allowed to set and melted again, but each time it is reused it will get thicker. If you do want to re-melt it, mix it with the same amount of fresh chocolate.

◆ 'Tempering' chocolate make it easier to work with and ensures a glossy appearance. To temper chocolate, melt it in the usual way, then pour two thirds on to a marble slab or clean surface and move it back and forth with a plastic scraper or palette knife until it is thick and on the point of setting. Quickly return to the rest of the chocolate and re-melt, stirring constantly. The chocolate is now ready to use.

Chocolate curls (caraque)

These make an attractive decoration for desserts and cakes. To make them, spread a thin layer of fine quality melted dark or white chocolate (or tempered chocolate) over a marble slab or other clean, smooth surface. When it has just set, push a large knife across the chocolate at an angle of about 25° to scrape off curls. Store in an airtight container between sheets of greaseproof paper in a cool place for up to 1 week.

Yeast

Yeast is a living, single-celled organism used in baking as a raising agent. It starts working as soon as it comes into contact with warmth, moisture and food and converts the natural sugars present in flour into little bubbles of carbon dioxide. These become trapped and, during baking, expand and cause the dough to rise. The flour must be strong, or high in gluten, in order for it to contain these bubbles.

Dried yeast

◆ Fast-action dried yeast, also called easy-blend yeast, has revolutionised bread-making. It is a powdered yeast that is very simple to use and does not need dissolving in liquid – you simply mix it straight into the flour and other dry ingredients. It allows the flavour of the bread to come through without being too yeasty. Fast-action dried yeast is widely available and comes in 7g (¼oz) sachets.

◆ Ordinary dried yeast is grainier than fast-action dried yeast. It needs to be blended with tepid liquid and a pinch of sugar before mixing with flour, then put in a warm place until frothy. Make sure the liquid you use is not too hot, or it may kill the yeast. If the mixture does not froth up, the yeast is not fresh and should not be used.

Ordinary dried yeast has largely been replaced by fast-action dried because the latter works so well. However, it can be used for any of the breads in this book: 15ml (1 tbsp) ordinary dried yeast is equivalent to 15g (½oz) fresh yeast or 7g (¼oz) fast-action dried. Ordinary dried yeast should be stored in a cool, dark place and will keep up to 6 months – throw it away after this time.

Fresh yeast

Fresh yeast is a creamy, beige soft solid, which, as easy-blend yeast becomes more popular, is not always easy to find – although you may track it down at a specialist baker's shop or a larger supermarket with a fresh bakery. Fresh yeast should have a clean, sweet smell and break apart cleanly without crumbling. You can keep it in the fridge loosely wrapped for up to 5 days, or freeze it for up to 3 months – thaw it thoroughly and return to room temperature before using.

Fresh yeast is easy to use. Simply blend it with a little tepid liquid and a little flour (from the recipe) and leave it in a warm place for 20 minutes before you mix it with the other ingredients. If you're using fresh yeast in place of fast-action dried yeast, 15g (½oz) fresh yeast is equivalent to 7g (¼oz) fast-action dried. Fresh yeast gives the most authentic, yeasty taste to bread, and for this reason it is still favoured by purists and keen bread makers.

Other raising agents

The following commercially prepared raising agents are used in scones, some cakes and non-yeast breads. They must be measured carefully, as too much or too little will adversely affect the end result. They must be kept in a dry place and used within their use-by date.

◆ Baking powder is a mixture of cream of tartar and bicarbonate of soda. When it comes into contact with liquid it releases carbon dioxide bubbles which expand during baking.

◆ Bicarbonate of soda is an alkaline substance which gives off carbon dioxide when mixed with an acid, such as lemon juice, cream of tartar or buttermilk, in a cake or soda bread recipe. Bicarbonate of soda has a fairly strong taste and is therefore only suitable for certain recipes.

Equipment

The beauty of baking is that it requires very little in the way of sophisticated equipment. Despite the fact that the food processor and electric mixer are well-established members of a modern cook's armoury, there's still room for originals such as the wooden spoon and the rolling pin. In fact, it's now possible to make a chic, back-to-basics style statement with simple implements such as these. They are the comforters of the kitchen drawer, and together with a few sturdy mixing bowls, tins, and baking sheets may be all you need to get started. However, if time is short and your pace of life demands that you emerge from the lazy haze of nostalgia that surrounds the traditional image of baking, then electronic equipment also has an important role to play.

Measuring

Almost all of us have some residual knowledge of baking, even if our memories are only of licking out the bowl or decorating a cake with hundreds and thousands. One thing that may have been far from our minds as we enjoyed these childhood pleasures is the importance of accuracy, probably the key word for successful baking. Before you even begin, make sure that you have the equipment to measure your ingredients properly. Kitchen scales and a set of measuring spoons are essential for baking. Kitchen scales can be electronic, spring-operated or balance-based.

◆ Most electronic scales of today come with an add-and-weigh function, which allows you to reset the display or dial to zero once you have weighed an item – you can then weigh other ingredients on top. Digital displays can usually be switched from metric to imperial instantly. Some electronic scales don't come with a bowl or jug – you simply use your own and set to zero. The best electronic scales have a memory that displays the weight even when the bowl has been removed.

◆ Spring-operated scales use the tension stored in the spring to balance against the ingredients. Sometimes these can only weigh small loads, depending on the strength of the spring – check before buying.

◆ Balance scales are the simplest, most basic form of weighing. The weights are set on one tray and the ingredients to be weighed on the other. Working on a seesaw principle the weight is attained when the two sides exactly match.

◆ Most people have wildly varying sizes of spoons rattling around in their kitchen drawers, so a set of measuring spoons is really necessary where exact measures are crucial. The spoons usually come joined together in 1.25ml (¼ tsp), 2.5ml (½ tsp), 5ml (1 tsp) and 15ml (1 tbsp) sizes. If you ever use American or Australian recipes, you will need a set of measuring cups too.

◆ A sugar thermometer is the most reliable way to check the temperature of boiling sugar syrup for crème au beurre, Italian meringue, caramel etc. If the thermometer is made of glass, warm it in hot water before use to prevent cracking.

Beating and blending

Beating and blending by hand is still sometimes the most effective way of mixing ingredients. By all means cream butter and sugar together with an electric mixer, but when it comes to folding in the flour for a cake mixture, for example, it's best to use a large metal spoon slowly and carefully so that you don't knock the air out. Electronic equipment won't give you the control you need for folding in.

◆ An electric whisk is almost an essential item. For creaming and whisking hand-held electric beaters are often more convenient to use than free-standing ones because they allow you to control the movement around a bowl. However, for long sessions of beating or for arduous kneading of bread dough, a free-standing electric mixer which can be fitted with a dough hook as well as a whisk or beater is most useful – some models move around the bowl independently.

◆ Balloon whisks are excellent for beating air into egg whites by hand as they produce a good, airy froth (an electric food mixer can make the texture a little dense). Make sure the handle of the whisk has a good grip. A flat coil whisk is good for quickly whisking up small amounts of egg white and for scooping up stubborn liquid that may be hiding at the sides of a bowl or pan.

◆ Blenders can be used for whisking up small quantities of egg yolks, as well as puréeing vegetables and fruit, and pulverising nuts. Small, hand-held blenders that look like wands are good for using directly over a bowl or pan and are excellent for whipping cream.

◆ A set of wooden spoons, a large oval metal spoon and a large plastic spatula with a flexible blade are basic essentials for mixing and folding ingredients together.

Food processors

Hands are, of course, the original and best tool for making pastry, but unless you have a naturally cool touch you may want to use a food processor – ideally one fitted with a pulse button and a stainless steel bowl which can be chilled first. Food processors can be called on for a wide range of baking tasks, including kneading bread dough, all-in-one cake making, blending and creaming, although they may not incorporate quite as much air as whisking by hand allows you to. Choose one that's quiet to use and that has a large-capacity bowl.

Bread-making machines

These are marvellous inventions for those who don't mind handing over all the fun of kneading and knocking back to a machine, and are an affordable revelation for many people. You simply put all of your ingredients in the non-stick bread pan (usually wet ingredients first), then set the timer, which may have a delay of up to 13 hours so you can bake overnight, if you wish. A viewing window allows you, like an expectant father, to see how everything's getting along and the whole task can be completed in 2½ hours.

Most machines have a maximum capacity of 900g (2lb), a drawback if you want to make large batches of bread (and you may damage the motor if you try and overload it). You should always start a new machine off with a small (450g/1lb) simple white loaf as a control experiment. All machines are different, and you need to get to know how yours performs before you can use it to its full potential. The dough produced by the machine should be smooth and only slightly sticky to the touch. You can add water or flour if it looks too wet or too dry – lift the lid to check at intervals, but leave the machine well alone while the dough is proving and baking. There should be an option for selecting the darkness of your crust, but be careful not to choose a setting that is too light or too dark, or you may find that the machine over- or underbakes your loaf. Most bread-making machines allow you to remove the dough and bake it in the oven if you prefer – punch it down, knead it and leave it to rise before transferring it to the oven.

Once you have got to know your machine, you're free to experiment with as many different flavours and types of bread as you can dream up – dried fruit, different flours, bread with caraway seeds, sunflower seeds, garlic, herbs or cheese – all of these are possible. Seeds, nuts and raisins can be added during a special mix cycle which the machine announces with a beep.

Baking tins, trays and other containers

Good quality cake tins, loaf pans and baking sheets are essential. To avoid baking in several batches, buy baking sheets that are large (but make sure they fit comfortably on your oven shelves). If you think about the extreme heat that baking equipment has to put up with, it makes sense to buy the sturdiest stuff you can find. Look for tins and pans made of heavy-gauge metal – the gauge or thickness of a pan determines its efficiency in reflecting heat: the thicker the gauge the less likely it is to warp or develop hot spots.

◆ Aluminium is one of the most common metals used in cookware. It is lightweight, inexpensive and easy to clean, as well as responding quickly to changes in heat. However, aluminium is soft and if you drop an aluminium cake tin on the floor, it will dent very easily. For this reason, it is often anodised to toughen it. Heavy-gauge anodised aluminium is particularly good for baking tins – they can be used on direct heat, under the grill or in the oven.

◆ Tin is a popular metal for baking containers as it heats up very quickly. However, taking care of it can be labour-intensive as it rusts easily – after washing a tin pan it should be put in a warm oven to dry off completely.

◆ Stainless steel looks good, but conducts heat slowly and is therefore not the best choice for bakeware.

◆ Non-stick pans and baking sheets are useful, but may become scratched if you use metal implements. If you use pans with a dark non-stick lining, you may need to reduce the oven temperature slightly – dark colours absorb heat, while shiny ones reflect it from the contents of the pan.

◆ When you've baked your loaf –or cake, biscuits or pastries – you'll need a wire rack for cooling so that the air can move freely round the cooling object. Sogginess may set in if hot things are left to sit in their own steam.

CAKES AND BISCUITS Choosing the right tin when baking cakes is the last, best compliment you can pay your mixture before it goes into the oven. Using the correct-sized tin is as important to the end result as measuring the ingredients precisely. Build up a basic stock of different sized tins from those described here. You will almost certainly require

20cm (8 inch) and 23cm (9 inch) round tins, although it's possible to buy a multi-size cake tin with an inner ring that can be inserted for smaller cakes.

◆ To check the size of a tin, measure it straight across the top from one inside edge to the other, then the depth from top to bottom. To work out the volume, fill it with water to the top and transfer it to a measuring jug.

◆ Deep round or square cake tins are suitable for large cakes and fruit cakes. A good depth encourages a cake to rise, so if in doubt, err on the deeper side. Loose-bottomed tins make it easier to turn the cake out. Spring-release cake tins with loose bottoms and sides which open out are used for soft cakes and gâteaux which would not normally be inverted after cooking, and for cheesecakes. Round, shallow sponge or sandwich tins (around 4cm/1½in depth) are used for making layer cakes. Gingerbread is usually baked in a shallow, square or rectangular tin. For storage convenience, adjustable square tins are now available, in which the sides can be reduced or enlarged as required.

◆ For Swiss rolls and roulades, you'll need a shallow, rectangular Swiss roll tin; these come in several different sizes. For chocolate brownies, flapjacks and other traybakes, you'll need a smaller, slightly deeper rectangular tin: 27x19cm (10½x7½ inches) is a good size.

◆ 12-hole bun tins are used to make fairy cakes; for muffins you'll need a larger 12-hole muffin tray; there are also mini-bun and mini-muffin trays available. If you want to make more than 12, it's best to do this in batches so that you don't overcrowd the oven. Line the tin with paper or foil cases, or if it's non-stick, grease the holes lightly. If you use foil cases, you can lay them out on an ordinary baking sheet, spaced well apart, and they will retain their shape as long as you don't overfill the cases. For baking classic French madeleines, there are madeleine trays with 12 indents shaped like shells; these should be greased and dusted with flour before using.

◆ Ring tins and tube tins are available for special cakes, such as Kugelhopf and Angel cake.

BREAD AND PIZZAS For these, you will need a good selection of baking sheets in different sizes, including at least two large ones. Make sure that they are made of robust, thick-gauge metal so that they won't buckle under high temperatures. Breads and pizzas need maximum exposure to heat in order to crisp and brown properly.

◆ If you are a keen pizza-maker, you may want to invest in a special pizza stone – a clay slab which reproduces the intense dry heat of a professional pizza oven. Like a baking sheet, the stone should be preheated before baking. Breads such as ciabatta, focaccia and flatbreads can also be baked on a pizza stone.

◆ If you're making traditional shaped loaves, you'll need loaf tins. These are available in two sizes: 450g (1lb) and 900g (2lb). If you intend to batch-bake bread, it's worth investing in two of the smaller 450g (1lb) tins. Loaf tins can also be used for teabreads, those wonderfully compact and sensible-looking cakes whose innocent appearance conceals a multitude of calories.

PASTRY The best flan tins for pastry have a dull interior or non-stick lining which allow the pastry to brown and crisp properly. Although ceramic dishes are aesthetic if you are serving from the oven to the table, they are not good at conducting heat and can make pastry go soggy. It is best to buy a loose-bottomed metal tin so the flan can be removed easily without breaking the pastry. To unmould, place the flan tin on a can of beans and gently pull down the ring, leaving the finished tart on the base suspended on the can.

For deep, open fruit tarts use a deep-rimmed pie dish with straight or sloping sides. Enamelled pie plates are good for pies and tarts, as the metal conducts the heat quickly and evenly. For individual tarts and sweet dessert pastries, buy individual flan tins or tartlet moulds with loose bases. If you are cooking large batches, you may want to use a 12-hole tartlet tray.

BAKED PUDDINGS AND SOUFFLÉS Deep pudding and pie dishes are used for sweet baked milk puddings, crumbles, gratins and savoury pasta bakes. They are usually oval, with a large surface area so that a good proportion of the pudding is exposed and will brown successfully. Soufflé dishes should be straight-sided so the mixture can rise easily. For individual puddings, porcelain ramekins and dariole moulds are ideal. The size of these individual dishes varies; make sure that you have the correct capacity for the recipe – especially if you are making individual soufflés.

Puddings and soufflés are usually served straight from the oven from their original container, so make sure that the dish you use is presentable. Wipe around the edges before putting it in the oven so you don't end up with baked-on spots of mixture which will spoil the look of the finished dish. Ovenproof clear glass (pyrex) is good for a simple look and allows you to inspect the sides of the pudding while it is baking. As long as you don't drop it on a hard or stone floor, a pyrex dish should last a long while, although may become scratched over time. Dishes made from enamelled cast iron are heavy but durable and will withstand more than a few hard knocks; earthenware or porcelain dishes look good but need careful handling.

Lining papers

Cake tins and pans usually need to be lined with a non-stick paper to prevent sticking and to make it easier to unmould. Sometimes you will need to grease a tin as well as line it – always follow the instructions in the recipe.

◆ Greaseproof paper has a waterproof coating and can be used for lining tins and trays as well as for wrapping cakes and biscuits for storage.

◆ Silicone paper is a slightly thicker paper coated with silicone and can cope with higher temperatures than greaseproof paper.

◆ Non-stick baking parchment is a very strong, stiff paper which is also heat- and grease-resistant.

◆ Edible rice paper is useful for lining the bottom of cake tins when you are baking a very sticky mixture, such as panforte, as it needn't be removed once the cake is cooked.

Bread-making

Basic bread-making techniques are straightforward and once you have mastered them you will be able to create your own versions of commercial speciality breads at a fraction of the cost. Look to the recipes here for inspiration but don't be afraid to experiment: flavour savoury doughs with different cheeses, fresh herbs, olives, or sun-dried tomatoes; sweet doughs with vanilla sugar or scented spices like cardamom and cinnamon, as well as dried fruits and nuts.

Bread ingredients

Various different flours are used for bread-making. Strong flours give the best results because they are high in gluten – the substance which stretches the dough and traps in air as it cooks, to give an open texture. Bread made with wholemeal flour has a distinctive flavour and texture; it is also an excellent source of fibre. For a lighter loaf, use brown (wheatmeal) flour, or half wholemeal and half white flour. Granary flour, with its added malted wheat flakes, gives bread a characteristic nutty flavour. Rye and buckwheat flours also make interesting breads, but as these are both low in gluten, they should be mixed with a strong flour. The quantity of liquid specified in a recipe should always be regarded as an approximate guide because flour absorbency varies according to the type of flour, and from brand to brand.

It is, of course, yeast with its unique properties that enables bread to rise. Although not difficult to use, yeast must be handled in the right way in order to work effectively (see page 55). Salt improves the flavour of bread, but it also slows down the action of yeast, so don't add too much. Be guided by the amount specified in the recipe.

Some recipes call for a little fat to be rubbed into the flour before the yeast is added. This helps the keeping quality of the bread and imparts extra flavour, but too much fat will slow down the action of the yeast.

Mixing the dough

Some recipes recommend warming the flour and mixing bowl in advance. If using fresh or 'ordinary' dried yeast, or if you are working in a cold room, this helps speed things up a little, but otherwise it isn't necessary.

Kneading

After mixing, the dough must be kneaded vigorously to strengthen the gluten in the flour, make the dough elastic and ultimately to achieve a good rise. If you omit this stage, the dough will not rise. There's nothing difficult about kneading and, contrary to popular belief, it doesn't take long to do by hand – 5-10 minutes should be long enough.

Turn the dough onto a floured surface, fold it firmly towards you, then quickly and firmly push it down and away from you with the heel of your hand. Give it a quarter turn and continue kneading until the dough feels elastic and smooth: it shouldn't be sticky.

As an alternative to kneading by hand, you can use a large mixer with a dough hook attachment, or a food processor. In either case, it is essential to avoid overloading the machine; follow the manufacturer's guidelines on maximum quantities.

Rising

Shape the kneaded dough into a ball and place in a clean bowl. Cover with a clean tea-towel, an oiled polythene bag or oiled cling film to prevent a skin forming. Leave in a warm place until the dough has doubled in size and springs back when pressed. The time it takes to rise will depend on the ambient temperature. If you put the bowl near a warm oven or in an airing cupboard, rising can take as little as 30 minutes, while at cooler temperatures it may take over an hour. Don't be tempted to put it somewhere hot to speed things up; you will end up with an uneven-textured loaf, or you could kill the yeast. For a slower rise, leave the dough in the refrigerator overnight; bring it to room temperature before shaping.

Knocking back

After the initial rising, the dough is 'knocked back' to smooth out any large pockets of air and ensure the end result has an even texture. A brief kneading is sufficient, just 2-3 minutes, before shaping the dough.

Shaping

The simplest way to shape bread dough is to form it into a round or oval, flatten slightly and bake it directly on a baking sheet. For a decorative effect, slash the top of the dough or score in a diamond pattern.

◆ To shape a baton, form the dough into a long roll with tapering ends.
◆ For a traditional tin loaf, flatten the dough to an oblong, the length of the tin, but three times as wide. Fold in three, then place in the tin, to two-thirds fill it.

◆ For a cottage loaf, cut off one third of the dough. Shape both pieces into rounds and place the smaller one on top of the larger round. Push the handle of a wooden spoon down through the middle.
◆ For a plait, divide the dough into three. Shape each piece into a long roll, pinch the ends together and plait loosely. Rolls can be formed into any of the above shapes.

Proving the dough

Leave the shaped dough once again in a warm place until it has doubled in size and springs back when pressed. This proving stage is quicker than the first rising.

Glazing

Applying a glaze before baking gives bread an attractive finish.
◆ For a golden, shiny glaze, brush the proved dough with beaten egg or egg beaten with a little water or milk.
◆ For a crusty finish, brush with salted water, made by dissolving 10ml (2 tsp) salt in 30ml (2 tbsp) water.
◆ For a soft golden crust, brush with milk.
◆ Any topping, such as sesame seeds, poppy seeds, nuts, grated cheese or coarse sea salt is applied after glazing the bread.
◆ Some breads and yeast buns are glazed after baking, with warmed honey or syrup.

Baking

Bread is baked in a hot oven to kill the yeast and halt its action. If the bread shows signs of browning too quickly during baking, cover loosely with foil. When cooked, the bread should be well risen, firm to the touch and golden brown; if you turn it over and tap it on the bottom with your knuckles, the loaf should sound hollow.
◆ To crisp large loaves all over, place them upside down on the hot baking sheet for about 10 minutes. Always remove bread from loaf tins before cooling on wire racks. Serve while still slightly warm, if possible.

Pastry-making

The art of successful pastry making lies in accurate measuring, using the correct proportion of fat to flour, and light, careful handling. With the exceptions of choux pastry and hot water crust pastry, everything needs to be kept cool when making pastry – the work surface, equipment, ingredients and your hands. It is important to 'rest' pastry before baking, otherwise it will shrink during baking. Most pastries are best rested in the refrigerator well wrapped in cling film. Pastries which are handled a great deal, such as puff, must be rested before and after shaping.

The main types of pastry are short pastries, of which shortcrust is the most familiar, and flaked pastries, such as puff. Other pastries include hot water crust, choux pastry and filo pastry.

Ready-made pastries

If you haven't the time or inclination to make your own pastry, choose from the wide range of ready-made chilled fresh and frozen pastries which are now available. Ready-made puff pastry is so successful and quick to use that most people opt to buy rather than make it.

◆ Filo pastry is particularly time-consuming and difficult to make, but packets of ready-made filo sheets are widely available and give excellent results. (For this reason a recipe for filo pastry is not included in this book.) Note that the size of filo sheets varies considerably between brands. Check the size of filo sheets specified in the recipe before buying. It is essential to keep filo sheets covered as you work to prevent them from drying out and becoming brittle.

Pastry ingredients

For most pastries, plain white flour works best, as it gives a light, crisp result. Self-raising flour produces a soft spongy pastry. Wholemeal flour gives a heavier dough which is more difficult to roll. For wholemeal pastry, it is therefore preferable to use half wholemeal and half white flour. Puff pastry is usually made with strong plain (bread) flour as this contains extra gluten to strengthen the dough, enabling it to withstand intensive rolling and folding. A little lemon juice is usually added to puff pastry to soften the gluten and make the dough more elastic.

Traditionally shortcrust pastry is made with a mixture of lard (for shortness) and either butter or margarine (for flavour). However it is now more often made with a mixture of white vegetable fat and butter or margarine, or all butter for a rich flavour. White vegetable fat – like lard – gives a short texture. If margarine is preferred, it should be hard, block margarine rather than the soft-tub alternative.

Care must be taken when adding the liquid to a dough: too much will result in a tough end result; too little will produce a crumbly pastry which is difficult to handle. Use chilled water and add just enough to bind the dough. Egg yolks are often used to enrich pastry.

Mixing pastry by hand

Most pastry-making involves rubbing the fat into the flour. To do this, cut the fat into the small pieces, then add to the flour and salt and mix briefly with a round-bladed knife, to coat the pieces with flour. Then, using your fingertips, pick up a small amount of the mixture at a time and rub the fat and flour together to break the fat down into tiny pieces. Do this as lightly and quickly as possible until the mixture resembles fine crumbs; avoid using the palms of your hands.

When adding the liquid, sprinkle this evenly over the surface of the rubbed-in mixture; uneven addition may cause blistering once the pastry is cooked. Use a round-bladed knife to mix in the liquid. You may need a little more or less than the quantity stated in the recipe because the absorbency of flours varies. For this reason, don't add it all at once. Once the dough begins to hold together, collect it into a ball and knead lightly for a few seconds.

Mixing pastry in a food processor

Using a machine rather than your hands to mix pastry is one way of keeping the dough cool. Short pastries, including enriched flan pastries, can be made very successfully and quickly in a food processor. To ensure that the dough is not over-worked, use the pulse button in short bursts, checking the consistency all the time.

◆ Blend the dry ingredients first for 5-10 seconds, then add the fat and blend for another 10-15 seconds. Add the water 1 tbsp at a time and pulse until the dough is just beginning to hold together in a clump. Avoid making too large a quantity at one time or the result will be disappointing.

Pastry quantities

Where a recipe specifies a weight of pastry, this generally refers to the weight of flour in the recipe rather than the combined weight of the ingredients. For example, if a recipe calls for 225g (8oz) shortcrust pastry, you will need this amount of flour and 110g (4oz) fat, as the correct proportion of fat is 2:1.

◆ Recipes for basic pastries appear on page 76; sweet pastries on page 172. If your pie or flan(s) needs more (or less) than the basic recipe quantity, simply increase (or decrease) the pastry ingredients in proportion.

◆ When buying ready-made pastry, the weight specified on the packet is the combined weight of the ingredients, not the flour weight. As a guide, a 375g (13oz) packet of shortcrust pastry is roughly equivalent to homemade pastry made with 225g (8oz) flour. Approximately 750g (1lb 10oz) ready-made puff pastry is equivalent to homemade puff pastry made with 450g (1lb) flour.

Quantity guide for flans

Flan tins, including individual ones, vary in depth, which affects the quantity of pastry required to line them. Therefore the following is an approximate guide only.

Flan tin size	Pastry (flour weight)
18cm (7 inch)	125g (4oz)
20cm (8 inch)	175g (6oz)
23cm (9 inch)	200g (7oz)
25cm (10 inch)	225g (8oz)
Four 10cm (4 inch) individual	150g (5oz)
Six 7.5cm (3 inch) individual	150g (5oz)

Rolling out pastry

A cool surface, such as marble or granite, is ideal for rolling out pastry. Alternatively use a large plastic (rather than wooden) board, or roll pastry directly on a formica work surface. Dust the work surface and rolling pin – never the pastry – very lightly with flour. Roll the dough lightly and evenly in one direction only – until thin. Always roll away from you, using light, firm strokes and rotate the pastry frequently to keep an even shape and thickness. Avoid over-rolling, pulling or stretching the pastry as you roll it or it will shrink badly during cooking. The usual thickness for rolling out

pastries is 3mm ($\frac{1}{8}$ inch), though puff pastry is sometimes rolled out to a 5mm ($\frac{1}{4}$ inch) thickness, depending on the use.

Shaping pastry

Pastry is most often used to line flan tins and cover pies (see pages 65-7). Pastry can also be folded around fillings to form pasties, or wrapped around whole boned fish or meat, as in salmon or beef en croûte.

Glazing pastry

Glazing pastry seals the surface and gives pies an attractive sheen. Using a pastry brush, lightly brush the pastry with egg yolk beaten with a little water, or with beaten whole egg. Alternatively, for a less shiny finish, brush with milk. Part-baked pastry cases are sometimes glazed, then baked for a little longer to seal before filling. Glaze the surface of pies before positioning pastry leaves or cut-out decorations, then brush the decorations with more glaze.

Lining a flan case

1 Roll out the pastry on a lightly floured surface until it is 5-7.5cm (2-3 inches) larger all round than the flan tin, depending on depth of tin. Using the rolling pin, lift the pastry over the tin.

2 Lift the edges of the pastry so that it falls down into the tin, then gently press the pastry against the side of the tin so there are no gaps between pastry and tin.

3 Turn any surplus pastry outwards over the rim, then trim away using a sharp knife to leave a neat edge. Chill in the refrigerator for 20-30 minutes to rest the pastry; this helps to minimise shrinkage during baking.

4 If a recipe tells you to 'bake blind' you need to bake, or part-bake the pastry case without its filling. It is either partially cooked before filling, or completely cooked if the filling doesn't need baking. Prick the base with a fork, then line with a large piece of greaseproof paper. Fill with ceramic baking beans or dried pulses. Bake at the suggested temperature for 10-15 minutes or until the case looks set, then remove paper and beans and bake for a further 5 minutes until the base is firm and lightly coloured; or a further 15 minutes until crisp and golden brown if the pastry requires complete baking.

Covering a pie dish

1 Using the inverted pie dish as a guide, roll out the pastry on a lightly floured surface until it is 5cm (2 inches) larger all round than the dish. Cut off a 2.5cm (1 inch) strip from around the edge. Moisten the rim of the pie dish and position the strip on the rim; brush with water.

2 Fill the pie dish generously so that the surface of the filling is slightly rounded; use a pie funnel if there isn't quite enough filling to do this. Use the rolling pin to help lift the pastry lid into position. Press the edges together to seal.

3 Using a sharp knife, held at an angle away from the dish, trim off excess pastry. Make a hole in the top of the pie.

4 Knock up the pastry edge by holding the blunt edge of a knife horizontally against the rim and tapping sharply; this seals the edge and stops the filling leaking out.

Pastry finishes

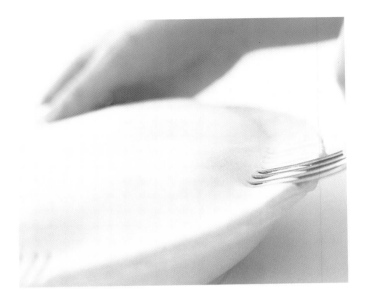

FORKED EDGE Simply press all around the edge of the pie with the back of a floured fork.

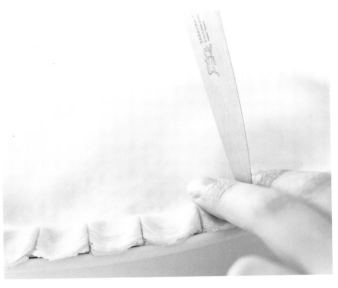

FLUTED OR SCALLOPED EDGE Press your forefinger and middle finger on the rim of the pastry. At the same time gently draw back the floured blade of a round-bladed knife in between your fingers, about 1cm (½ inch) towards the centre. Repeat at 2.5cm (1 inch) intervals around the edge to create a decorative finish.

CRIMPED EDGE Push your thumb into the rim of the pastry and, using the thumb and forefinger of the other hand, gently pinch the pastry so that it is pushed up by this action. Continue around the edge of the pie.

PASTRY LEAVES Cut strips from the pastry trimmings, then cut these diagonally into diamonds. Use the back of the knife to mark veins and pinch one end to form a stem. Roll small balls to resemble berries. Glaze the surface of the pie before positioning the decorations to ensure they adhere.

Cake-making

Successful cake-baking is at least partly dependent on the use of good basic techniques, including lining cake tins, creaming, whisking and careful folding in. It is most important to use good quality ingredients and to measure them accurately – using scales and measuring spoons. Most cake recipes require the fat to be used at room temperature. Eggs should also be used at room temperature; if taken straight from the refrigerator they are more likely to curdle a mixture.

Once the cake is in the oven resist the temptation to open the door – a sudden gush of cold air will make it sink in the middle. Instead wait until the cooking time is almost up before testing. If your cake appears to be browning too quickly, cover with greaseproof paper towards the end of cooking.

◆ To test a baked sponge, carefully remove from the oven and touch the centre with one hand – it should feel spongy and give very slightly. A whisked sponge cake should just be shrinking from the sides of the tin. If necessary return the cake to the oven for a few minutes, closing the door very gently so that vibration does not cause the cake to sink in the centre.

◆ To test a fruit cake, take it out of the oven, insert a skewer into the centre and remove: it should come away cleanly. If any mixture is sticking to the skewer, bake for a little longer.

Apart from very light sponges, all cakes are best left to stand in their tin for several minutes after baking to firm up slightly before turning out.

CREAMING Using an electric whisk or wooden spoon, beat the softened butter and sugar together in a large bowl until pale and fluffy, and very light in consistency. If creaming by hand with a wooden spoon, you will need to beat very vigorously. Beat the eggs into the creamed mixture, a little at a time, beating well after each addition. To prevent curdling, a little of the measured flour can be added with the eggs. Traditional Victoria sandwiches and similar cakes are made using this method.

WHISKING Put the eggs and sugar in a large heatproof bowl over a pan of hot water and whisk until the mixture is thick enough to leave a trail when the whisk is lifted from the bowl. Remove the bowl from the heat and continue whisking for about 5 minutes or until the mixture is cool. Classic, fatless sponges made by the whisking method are very light in texture. A Genoese sponge uses the same technique but, after whisking, melted butter is very carefully folded in with the flour to make a richer cake.

FOLDING IN Sift the flour over the creamed or whisked cake mixture, sifting high so that plenty of air is incorporated. Use a large metal spoon to gently fold in the flour, cutting and carefully folding it into the mixture using a figure-of-eight movement.

NOTE When mixing an 'all-in-one' cake, the ingredients are beaten to a similarly creamy consistency in one go. If the mixture seems too firm, beat in a dash of milk.

LINING A ROUND CAKE TIN Place the cake tin on a piece of greaseproof paper and draw around it. Cut out, just inside the line. Cut strip(s) of paper, about 2cm (¾ inch) wider than the depth of the tin. Fold up the bottom edge by 1cm (½ inch), then make cuts, 2.5cm (1 inch) apart, from the edge to the fold. Grease the cake tin lightly. Position the paper strip(s) around the side of the tin so the snipped edge sits on the base. Lay the paper circle in the base. Lightly grease all of the paper. (A square cake tin is lined in a similar way, but you will need to cut the side strip(s) to fit at the corners.)

LINING A SWISS ROLL TIN OR SHALLOW BAKING TIN Grease the base and sides of the tin. Cut a rectangle of greaseproof paper or non-stick baking parchment, 7.5cm (3 inches) wider and longer than the size of the tin. Press the paper into the tin, cutting the paper at the corners and folding to fit neatly. Grease the paper.

LINING A LOAF TIN Grease the loaf tin. Cut a strip of greaseproof paper, the length of the tin base and wide enough to cover the base and long sides. Press into position. Cut another greaseproof strip, the width of the tin base and long enough to cover the base and ends of the tin; position. Grease all of the paper.

NOTE If only the base and long sides of a loaf tin need lining, use a double paper thickness so the cake can easily be lifted.

PREPARING A TIN FOR A RICH FRUIT CAKE Extra protection is needed to prevent the edges of a fruit cake overcooking. First line the inside of the cake tin (see above left), then cut a double thick strip of brown paper, the circumference of the tin and 2.5cm (1 inch) deeper. Wrap the brown paper around the outside of the tin and secure with string.

Covering a cake with almond paste

Almond paste or marzipan is applied to rich fruit cakes to keep in the moisture and flavour, and to create a smooth foundation for the icing. It is therefore important to apply it neatly. You can either make your own almond paste (see page 280), or buy it. Choose white, rather than yellow ready-made almond paste, as it is less likely to discolour the icing. The flavour of homemade almond paste is, of course, far superior.

Care must be taken when applying almond paste to avoid over-handling as this encourages the oils to flow from the ground almonds. These oils may seep through the iced surface of the cake, causing staining.

Once you have applied the almond paste, you will need to allow time for it to dry before covering with icing. Homemade almond paste takes a little longer to dry out than the ready-made variety. Leave the cake in a cool, dry place to dry out thoroughly for at least 24 hours before covering with ready-to-roll icing. Allow to dry for at least 2 days before applying smooth Royal icing.

1 Trim the top of the cake level if necessary, then place on a cake board, which should be at least 5cm (2 inches) larger than the cake. Brush the top of the cake with apricot glaze.

2 Roll out half of the almond paste on a surface dusted with icing sugar to fit top of cake. Lift the almond paste round (or square) on top of the cake and smooth over, neatening the edges.

3 Cut a piece of string the same height as the cake with its almond paste top, and another to fit around side of cake. Roll out the remaining almond paste and, using the string as a guide, trim the paste to size. Brush the sides of the cake and the almond paste rim with apricot glaze. Roll up the almond paste strip loosely. Place one end against the side of the cake and unroll to cover it. Use a palette knife to smooth over the sides and joins of the paste.

Applying ready-to-roll icing (sugar paste)

1 Dust the work surface and rolling pin with cornflour. Knead the icing until pliable, then roll out into a round or square 5-7.5cm (2-3 inches) larger than the cake all round. With the help of a rolling pin, lift the icing on top of the cake and allow it to drape over the edges.

2 Dust your hands with cornflour and press the icing onto the sides of the cake, easing it down to the board.

3 Using a sharp knife, trim off the excess icing at the base to neaten. Reserve the trimmings to make decorations if required.

4 Using your fingers dusted with a little cornflour, gently rub the surface in a circular movement to buff the icing and make it smooth.

Storage

Bread

Bread is best stored in a dry, well ventilated bread bin, not the refrigerator, and eaten on the day it is made. Enriched bread with a high fat or sugar content should keep well for 2-3 days, but other homemade bread tends to stale quite quickly. Quick yeastless breads, leavened with baking powder or bicarbonate of soda rather than yeast – like scones – quickly stale. They are invariably at their best eaten fresh and warm from the oven.

Bread freezes well for a short time – up to 1 month – after which time the crust begins to deteriorate and lift off. In general, it is best to avoid freezing bread and pizza doughs, as the freezing process affects the way the yeast works. To freeze loaves or rolls, allow to cool completely, then pack in polythene bags to freeze. Defrost at room temperature when required. Once defrosted, the bread can be freshened by popping briefly into a warm oven.

Pastry

With the exception of choux pastry, uncooked pastry doughs will keep, well wrapped in cling film, in the refrigerator for 2-3 days. Raw pastry dough can be frozen, but it must be allowed to defrost fully before attempting to roll out, or it may crack. In most cases, pastry can be shaped and frozen before baking, then baked straight from the freezer quite successfully. Mince pies are particularly convenient to freeze in this way, as you can prepare them well ahead of the festivities and bake as, and when required. Uncooked flan cases freeze well too, though you will need to pack these in rigid containers once frozen, to ensure they do not get broken in the freezer.

Cakes and biscuits

Everyday cakes, such as Madeira and Victoria sandwich-type cakes keep well for 4-5 days in a cake tin or large plastic container. Rich fruit cakes and gingerbread actually improve with keeping. However, most cakes and biscuits are best enjoyed freshly baked.

If storing is necessary, make sure that the cake is completely cold before you put it into the container. If you haven't a large enough container, wrap the cake in a double layer of greaseproof paper and overwrap with foil. In any event, this is the best way to store rich fruit cakes; once wrapped, place in a cardboard cake box if you have one. Avoid putting rich fruit cakes in direct contact with foil, because the fruit may react with it. Never seal a fruit cake in an airtight plastic container for long periods of time as this may encourage mould growth. Always store cakes in a cool, dry place.

Biscuits should never be stored in the same tin as a cake, and preferably not with other types of biscuits, as they quickly soften and absorb other flavours.

Most cakes, particularly sponges, freeze beautifully, but they are generally best frozen before filling and decorating. If freezing a finished gâteau, open freeze on a board or tray, then transfer to a rigid container to protect the decoration. Allow to defrost at room temperature.

the recipes

PIES AND SAVOURY FLANS

Comforting deep-filled pies, individual pasties crammed with tasty ingredients, and irresistible creamy flans with all manner of flavourful fillings to choose from

SHORTCRUST PASTRY

This is the most widely used of all pastries. The proportion of flour to fat is 2:1. The choice of fat is largely a matter of taste – butter gives a rich flavour, while using half white vegetable fat improves the texture.

MAKES a 225g (8oz) quantity ◆ PREPARATION 10 minutes, plus resting
◆ FREEZING Suitable

225g (8oz) plain white flour	110g (4oz) butter, or other fat, cut into pieces
pinch of salt	45-60ml (3-4 tbsp) cold water

1 Sift the flour and salt into a bowl. Add the fat and mix lightly, then using your fingertips, rub into the flour until the mixture resembles fine breadcrumbs.
2 Sprinkle the water evenly over the surface and stir with a round-bladed knife until the mixture begins to stick together in large lumps. If it seems dry, add a little extra water. With one hand, collect the dough together into a ball.
3 Knead gently on a lightly floured surface for a few seconds to form a smooth, firm dough. Wrap in cling film and rest in the refrigerator for 30 minutes before rolling out.

NOTES
◆ To make the pastry in a food processor, put the flour and salt in the processor bowl with the butter. Process until the mixture resembles fine crumbs, then add the water. Pulse until the dough comes together in a ball. Continue as above.
◆ Shortcrust pastry can be stored in the refrigerator for up to 3 days, or frozen.

VARIATIONS
◆ WHOLEMEAL PASTRY Replace half of the white flour with wholemeal flour. A little extra water may be needed.
◆ NUT PASTRY Mix in 25g (1oz) finely chopped or ground walnuts, hazelnuts or almonds before adding the water.
◆ CHEESE PASTRY Stir in 45-60ml (3-4 tbsp) freshly grated Parmesan or 75g (3oz) Cheddar cheese and a pinch of mustard powder before adding the water.

RICH FLAN PASTRY

Also known as pâte brisée, this is an enriched smooth, pliable dough which is rolled out thinly and used for savoury tarts. A sweetened version is used for sweet flans (see page 172).

MAKES a 125g (4oz) quantity ◆ PREPARATION 15 minutes, plus resting
◆ FREEZING Suitable

110g (4oz) plain white flour	1 egg yolk
50g (2oz) unsalted butter, at room temperature, cut into cubes	pinch of salt
	25ml (1½ tbsp) cold water

1 Sift the flour into a mound on a clean work surface and make a large well in the centre. Place the butter in the well with the egg yolk, salt and water.
2 Using the fingertips and a 'pecking' motion, 'peck' the butter, egg yolk, salt and water together until the mixture resembles scrambled eggs.
3 Gradually work in the flour, using the fingertips until the mixture forms large crumbs. Add a little extra cold water if the dough looks too dry.
4 Turn out on to a lightly floured work surface. Lightly push the dough away from you, using the heel of your hand to push it across the surface. Scrape the dough together with a dough scraper or palette knife. Repeat until the dough is smooth and pliable, like putty.
5 Gather into a ball. Wrap in cling film and chill for at least 30 minutes to relax the pastry and reduce shrinkage during baking. Return to room temperature before rolling out.

PUFF PASTRY

The richest of all pastries, puff pastry requires patience, practice and very light handling. It is not practical to make less than a 450g (1lb) flour weight quantity.

MAKES a 450g (1lb) quantity ◆ PREPARATION 40 minutes, plus resting
◆ FREEZING Suitable

450g (1lb) strong plain white flour	300ml (½ pint) chilled water (approximately)
pinch of salt	15ml (1 tbsp) lemon juice
450g (1lb) butter, chilled	

1 Sift the flour and salt together into a bowl. Cut off 50g (2oz) of the butter and flatten the remaining large block with a rolling pin to a slab, about 2cm (¾ inch) thick; set aside.
2 Cut the 50g (2oz) butter into small pieces and rub into the flour, using the fingertips.
3 Using a round-bladed knife, stir in enough water and the lemon juice to make a soft, elastic dough.
4 Turn out on to a lightly floured work surface and quickly knead the dough until smooth. Cut a cross through half of the depth, then open out to form a star. Roll out, keeping the centre four times as thick as the flaps. Place the slab of butter in the centre. Fold the flaps over the dough, envelope-style.
5 Press gently with a rolling pin and roll out to a rectangle, measuring 40x20cm (16x8 inches). Fold the bottom third up and the top third down, keeping the edges straight. Wrap in cling film and leave to rest in the refrigerator for 30 minutes.
6 Put the pastry on a lightly floured work surface with the folded edges to the sides. Repeat the rolling, folding and resting sequence 5 times.
7 Shape the puff pastry as required, then rest in the refrigerator for at least 30 minutes before baking.

NOTE 750g (1lb 10oz) ready-made puff pastry is roughly equivalent to this quantity.

SALMON EN CROÛTE WITH SPINACH

Chunks of fresh salmon and peeled prawns in a creamy sauce, layered with spinach and encased in a puff pastry crust.

SERVES 6 ◆ PREPARATION 40 minutes, plus cooling
◆ COOKING TIME 30-35 minutes ◆ FREEZING Not suitable
◆ 660 CALS PER SERVING

500g (1lb 2oz) packet ready-made puff pastry

FILLING
25g (1oz) butter
2 shallots, peeled and finely chopped
5ml (1 tsp) chopped fresh thyme
60ml (4 tbsp) plain white flour
5ml (1 tsp) mustard powder
300ml (½ pint) single cream

freshly grated nutmeg
salt and pepper
450g (1lb) salmon fillet, skinned and cut into cubes
225g (8oz) peeled raw prawns
15ml (1 tbsp) lemon juice
30ml (2 tbsp) chopped fresh dill
225g (8oz) frozen leaf spinach, thawed

TO FINISH
1 egg, beaten, to glaze

1 Divide the pastry in half and roll out each piece thinly on a lightly floured surface to a large rectangle, about 33x20cm (13x8 inches). Cover with a clean tea-towel and leave to rest.
2 To make the filling, melt the butter in a saucepan, add the shallots and thyme, and fry gently for 3 minutes. Stir in the flour and mustard and cook for 30 seconds. Off the heat, stir in the cream, then stir over a medium heat until thickened. Cook, stirring, for a further 2 minutes.
3 Remove from the heat and season with the nutmeg, salt and pepper. Cover the surface closely with dampened greaseproof paper and set aside to cool. When cold, stir in the salmon, prawns, lemon juice and dill.
4 Preheat a baking sheet on the middle shelf of the oven at 220°C/fan oven 210°C (425°F) Mark 7. Drain the spinach, squeezing out as much liquid as possible; season with a little salt and pepper. Lift one pastry rectangle on to a large cold baking sheet and spread the spinach on top, to about 4cm (1½ inches) from the edges.
5 Spoon the fish mixture on top of the spinach and brush the pastry edges with beaten egg. Lay the other pastry rectangle on top and press the edges together to seal in the filling.
6 Trim the pastry, leaving a 1cm (½ inch) border all round the pie, then knock up and flute the edges. Brush with egg and pierce the top to allow steam to escape. Bake on the preheated baking sheet for 20 minutes, then reduce setting to 190°C/fan oven 180°C (375°F) Mark 5 and bake for a further 10-15 minutes until the pastry is risen and golden.

SMOKED HADDOCK, SALMON AND PRAWN PIE

This wonderfully rich, creamy fish pie is perfect for a dinner party. Serve with a green vegetable or mixed leafy salad.

SERVES 6 ◆ PREPARATION 40 minutes, plus chilling ◆ COOKING TIME 30 minutes ◆ FREEZING Not suitable ◆ 745 CALS PER SERVING

500g (1lb 2oz) packet ready-made puff pastry

FILLING
25g (1oz) butter
2 shallots, finely chopped
finely grated rind of 1 lemon
40g (1½oz) plain white flour
300ml (½ pint) double cream
15ml (1 tbsp) chopped fresh tarragon

pinch of freshly grated nutmeg
salt and pepper
300g (10oz) smoked haddock fillet, skinned
300g (10oz) salmon fillet (preferably undyed), skinned
225g (8oz) peeled raw prawns

TO FINISH
1 egg, beaten with a little water, to glaze

1 To make the filling, melt the butter in a small pan, add the shallots with the lemon rind and fry gently for 5 minutes until softened. Add the flour, stir for 30 seconds then remove from the heat and whisk in the cream. Return to a low heat and stir until thickened. Stir in the tarragon and season with nutmeg and pepper to taste. Cover the surface closely with dampened greaseproof paper and set aside to cool.

2 Remove any small residual bones from the smoked haddock and salmon with tweezers, then cut the fish into large cubes. Fold into the cooled cream sauce, together with the prawns. Cover the surface once again.

3 Preheat a large baking sheet in the oven at 230°C/fan oven 220°C (450°F) Mark 8. Divide the pastry in half. Roll out one piece on a lightly floured surface to a 25cm (10 inch) square and place on a second lightly greased large baking sheet.

4 Spoon the fish mixture over the pastry, to approximately 2.5 cm (1 inch) from the edges. Brush the pastry edges sparingly with water.

5 Roll out the second piece of pastry to a slightly larger square. Lay over the filling and press the pastry edges together to seal. Trim to neaten, then knock up and flute the edges.

6 Make 2 small holes in the centre of the pie and brush the pastry with egg glaze. Slide the baking sheet on top of the preheated one. Bake in the hot oven for 15 minutes, then reduce setting to 190°C/fan oven 180°C (375°F) Mark 5 and bake for a further 15 minutes or until crisp and golden.

LAMB AND CHESTNUTS EN CROÛTE

Lamb fillets are wrapped in spinach leaves and ham to seal in the juices, keeping the meat deliciously moist and tender, and ensuring that the pastry crust stays crisp.

SERVES 8 ◆ PREPARATION 40 minutes, plus chilling
◆ COOKING TIME 35-50 minutes ◆ FREEZING Suitable (stage 5)
◆ 645 CALS PER SERVING ◆ COLOUR INDEX Page 8

2 racks of lamb, trimmed, each 350g (12oz)
100g (3½oz) trimmed spinach leaves
50g (2oz) butter
75g (3oz) shallots, peeled and chopped
225g (8oz) mixed mushrooms, chopped
3 garlic cloves, peeled and crushed
45ml (3 tbsp) balsamic vinegar
100g (3½oz) cooked, vacuum-packed chestnuts, chopped

5ml (1 tsp) chopped fresh thyme
150ml (¼ pint) double cream
salt and pepper
4 thin slices cooked ham
500g (1lb 2oz) packet ready-made puff pastry
1 egg, beaten

PORT GRAVY
750ml (1¼ pints) well flavoured lamb stock
150ml (¼ pint) port
5ml (1 tsp) redcurrant jelly

1 Bone the lamb racks, removing each fillet in one piece; reserve bones for stock. Immerse the spinach in boiling water for 1-2 seconds. Drain, refresh with cold water and pat dry.
2 Melt the butter in a pan, add the shallots and cook, stirring, for 2-3 minutes. Add the mushrooms and cook for 3-4 minutes. Stir in the garlic and vinegar; cook for 1 minute. Add the chestnuts, thyme and cream. Bring to the boil and let bubble for 10 minutes or until reduced to a sticky glaze. Season to taste; set aside to cool slightly.
3 Lay 2 ham slices on a piece of cling film, overlapping to form a 20x15cm (8x6 inch) rectangle. Cover with half of the spinach. Season one lamb fillet; place in the middle. Spread with half of the mushroom mixture. Wrap the meat tightly in the spinach and ham, sealing with the cling film. Repeat with the other lamb fillet. Refrigerate.
4 Roll out 125g (4oz) of the pastry to a 30x20cm (12x8 inch) rectangle. Place on a baking sheet and prick well; chill for 30 minutes. Cook at 220°C/fan oven 210°C (425°F) Mark 7 for 15 minutes. Cool, then cut into two 20x15cm (8x6 inch) rectangles. Place one lamb fillet on each piece of baked pastry. Trim pastry to the same dimensions.
5 Thinly roll out remaining pastry to 56x23cm (22x9 inches). Cut into two 28x23cm (11x9 inch) pieces. Brush with beaten egg, then wrap around the lamb (glazed-side down). Trim, leaving 2.5 cm (1 inch) to tuck under the cooked pastry base. Brush with egg; decorate with leaves cut from the pastry trimmings. Cover lightly with cling film; chill for 1 hour.
6 Brush the pastry again with egg. Bake at 230°C/fan oven 220°C (450°F) Mark 8 allowing 20-30 minutes for medium-rare lamb; 30-35 minutes for well done meat. Cover pastry towards end of cooking if it appears to be overbrowning.

7 Meanwhile make the gravy. Add the port and jelly to the stock and boil briskly for 20-30 minutes until syrupy and reduced to about 450ml (¾ pint). Check seasoning.
8 Allow the meat to stand for 5 minutes before slicing. Serve with the port gravy, mashed sweet potatoes and broccoli.

BEEF AND GUINNESS PIE

A richly flavoured stew of meltingly tender beef is baked under a blanket of crisp, light homemade flaky pastry. If preferred, you could use a 350g (12oz) packet ready-made puff pastry as an alternative.

SERVES 6-8 ◆ PREPARATION 30 minutes, plus pastry and chilling
◆ COOKING TIME 2 hours for filling; 35 minutes baking ◆ FREEZING Suitable
◆ 685-515 CALS PER SERVING

PIE FILLING
700g (1½lb) stewing steak, cut into 3cm (1¼ inch) cubes
salt and pepper
flour, for coating
175g (6oz) pancetta or bacon lardons, diced
50g (2oz) butter
2 onions, peeled and diced
2 garlic cloves, peeled and crushed
15ml (1 tbsp) chopped fresh thyme
grated rind of ½ orange
2.5ml (½ tsp) ground allspice

300ml (½ pint) Guinness
150ml (¼ pint) beef stock
30ml (2 tbsp) tomato paste
2 bay leaves
225g (8oz) button mushrooms

PASTRY
300g (10oz) plain white flour
5ml (1 tsp) salt
175g (6oz) butter
180-200ml (6-7fl oz) iced water
beaten egg, mixed with a little water, to glaze

1 Toss the beef in seasoned flour to coat, shaking off excess.
2 Heat a flameproof casserole or heavy-based pan, add the bacon and dry-fry until the fat is released and the bacon is browned; remove with a slotted spoon. Add half of the butter to the pan, then fry the beef in batches for about 5 minutes until golden on all sides. Return all beef to the pan and stir in the onions, garlic, thyme, orange rind and spice. Fry gently for 10 minutes, and then return the bacon to the pan.
3 Pour in the Guinness and bring to a simmer. Add the stock, tomato paste and bay leaves, then cover and simmer very gently for 2 hours or until the beef is tender. Melt remaining butter in another pan and fry the mushrooms until lightly browned. Add to the beef, then transfer to a 1.5 litre (2½ pint) pie dish. Set aside until cold. Discard the bay leaves.
4 Meanwhile, make the pastry. Sift the flour and salt into a bowl and rub in 50g (2oz) of the butter. Gradually work in sufficient water to form a soft dough. Knead on a lightly floured surface until smooth. Wrap in cling film and chill for 15 minutes.
5 Roll out the dough on a lightly floured surface to a 30x15cm (12x6 inch) rectangle, 5mm (¼ inch) thick. Dot 25g (1oz) of the remaining butter over the top two thirds of the

dough, fold the uncovered third back over half the buttered dough, then fold once more to enclose all the butter. Press the edges together, wrap and chill for 15 minutes.

6 Unwrap the dough, turning so a narrow side is towards you, then re-roll flat to a similar sized rectangle. Repeat the process with the butter, folding and chilling three more times, turning the dough once each time before rolling. Wrap and chill until required.

7 Roll out the pastry on a lightly floured surface until a little larger than the pie dish. Cut 4 long strips about 2.5 cm (1 inch) wide from the edges of the pastry, and press on to the rim of the pie dish, dampening the rim as you do so. Place a pie funnel in the centre (if you have one).

8 Brush the pastry rim with a little water. Cut a cross in the centre of the pastry, then carefully position over the pie so that the cross in the centre fits over the pie funnel. Trim off excess pastry, then knock up and scallop the edges. Roll out the trimmings and cut out leaves; use to decorate the pie.

9 Brush with egg glaze and bake at 220°C/fan oven 210°C (425°F) Mark 7 for 20 minutes. Reduce setting to 200°C/fan oven 190°C (400°F) Mark 6 and bake for a further 15 minutes until the pastry is golden.

1 Toss the turkey meat in seasoned flour to coat. Melt the butter in a large frying pan. Add half of the turkey and fry quickly on all sides until golden. Remove with a slotted spoon and set aside; fry the rest of the turkey; remove.

2 Add the onions to the pan and cook gently for 10 minutes until soft. Stir in the stock, plenty of nutmeg and seasoning; cook, stirring, until thickened. Combine the turkey, ham, chestnuts and thyme in a flameproof casserole and pour on the stock mixture. Cover and cook very gently for 30 minutes. Stir in the cranberries and cream.

3 Using a slotted spoon, transfer the mixture to a 2 litre (3½ pint) shallow pie dish. Place a pie funnel in the centre and add enough of the cooking juices to half fill the dish; reserve any remaining liquid. Allow the filling to cool.

4 Meanwhile, make the pastry. Cook the potato in boiling salted water until tender; drain well and mash. Sift the flour into a bowl and rub in the fats, using fingertips. Add the potato and stir with a round-bladed knife, adding a little cold water to mix to a smooth, firm dough. Wrap in cling film and chill for 30 minutes.

5 Roll out the pastry and use to cover the pie. Make a hole in the centre and decorate with a pastry rose and leaves shaped from the trimmings if liked. Brush with beaten egg to glaze and scatter with a little coarse salt. Bake at 200°C/fan oven 190°C (400°F) Mark 6 for 40 minutes until the pastry is crisp and golden. Serve hot, with seasonal vegetables and any reserved cooking juices in a sauceboat.

TURKEY AND HAM PIE WITH CHESTNUTS

This festive pie works well with ready diced packs of raw turkey from the supermarket; it is also an excellent way of using up Christmas leftovers. The flavourful juices are laced with cream, and cranberries provide a piquant contrast. All are encased under a delicious crumbly potato pastry crust.

SERVES 8-10 ◆ PREPARATION 50 minutes, plus cooling
◆ COOKING TIME 40 minutes for filling; 40 minutes baking ◆ FREEZING Suitable
◆ 945-755 CALS PER SERVING

PIE FILLING
900g (2lb) boneless turkey (preferably a mixture of breast and thigh meat), chopped
45ml (3 tbsp) plain white flour
salt and pepper
50g (2oz) butter
2 large onions, peeled and chopped
750ml (1¼ pints) chicken stock
freshly grated nutmeg
350g (12oz) cooked ham, chopped
350g (12oz) vacuum-packed chestnuts

15ml (1 tbsp) chopped fresh thyme
150g (5oz) fresh or frozen cranberries
150ml (¼ pint) double cream

PASTRY
1 large potato, peeled and diced
450g (1lb) plain white flour
125g (4oz) butter, in pieces
150g (5oz) white vegetable fat, in pieces

TO FINISH
beaten egg, to glaze
coarse salt, for sprinkling

CHICKEN AND ARTICHOKE PIE

SERVES 4 ◆ PREPARATION 20 minutes ◆ COOKING TIME 30-35 minutes
◆ FREEZING Not suitable ◆ 350 CALS PER SERVING ◆ COLOUR INDEX Page 8

3 skinless chicken breasts, about 350g (12oz)
150ml (¼ pint) dry white wine
225g (8oz) soft cheese with garlic and herbs
salt and pepper

400g can artichoke hearts in water, drained and quartered
4 sheets filo pastry, about 40g (1½oz)
olive oil, for brushing
5ml (1 tsp) sesame seeds

1 Put the chicken in a wide, shallow pan. Add the wine, cover tightly and poach for 10 minutes. Remove the chicken with a slotted spoon and set aside. Add the soft cheese to the wine and mix until smooth. Bring to a simmer and let bubble until thickened. Season with salt and pepper to taste.

2 Cut the chicken into bite-sized pieces. Stir into the sauce with the artichokes; check the seasoning. Place in a shallow ovenproof dish.

3 Brush the filo pastry lightly with oil, scrunch slightly and place on top of the chicken. Sprinkle with sesame seeds.

4 Cook at 200°C/fan oven 190°C (400°F) Mark 6 for 30-35 minutes or until the pastry topping is crisp.

FESTIVE NUT AND CRANBERRY TERRINE

SERVES 8 ◆ PREPARATION 45 minutes, plus cooling
◆ COOKING TIME 45-50 minutes ◆ FREEZING Not suitable
◆ 490 CALS PER SERVING ◆ COLOUR INDEX Page 9

FILLING
125g (4oz) long-grain rice
60ml (4 tbsp) olive oil
1 onion, peeled and finely chopped
1 leek, thinly sliced
4 celery sticks, thinly sliced
60ml (4 tbsp) chopped mixed fresh herbs, such as sage, parsley and thyme
40g (1½oz) fresh white breadcrumbs
40g (1½oz) walnuts, toasted and roughly ground
125g (4oz) dolcelatte cheese, crumbled
1 egg, lightly beaten
125ml (4fl oz) crème fraîche

salt and pepper

HOT WATER CRUST PASTRY
225g (8oz) plain white flour
pinch of salt
100ml (3½fl oz) water
40g (1½oz) white vegetable fat
15g (½oz) butter

TOPPING
125g (4oz) redcurrant jelly
5ml (1 tsp) lemon juice
15ml (1 tbsp) water
125g (4oz) cranberries or redcurrants

TO GARNISH
bay leaves

1 Cook the rice in boiling salted water according to the packet instructions until just tender; refresh under cold water, drain thoroughly and set aside.
2 Heat the oil in a frying pan, add the onion, leek, celery and herbs and fry gently for 10 minutes until softened; transfer to a bowl. Add the rice and remaining filling ingredients; stir until evenly combined and season well; set aside to cool.
3 For the pastry, sift the flour and salt into a bowl and make a well in the middle. Heat the water, fat and butter in a pan until the liquid comes to the boil. Pour into the flour and work together, using a wooden spoon, until evenly mixed.
4 When cool enough to handle, bring the dough together with your hands and knead lightly until smooth. Roll out on a lightly floured surface to a 25×20cm (10×8 inch) rectangle and use to line a 900g (2lb) loaf tin, pressing the dough into the corners; trim the overhanging pastry and reserve.
5 Spoon the filling into the pastry case and smooth the surface. Divide the pastry trimmings in half and roll each piece into a long thin rope. Plait the two lengths together.
6 Dampen the edges of the pastry in the tin and top with the pastry plait, pressing down gently. Bake at 220°C/fan oven 210°C (425°F) Mark 7 for 45-50 minutes until golden and a skewer inserted into the centre comes out hot. Leave to cool.
7 For the topping, heat the redcurrant jelly in a small pan with the lemon juice and water until melted, then simmer for 3 minutes. Remove from the heat and stir in the fruit.
8 To unmould the pie, upturn and tap gently, then set on an oblong plate or board. Spoon the cranberry or redcurrant topping on top of the pie and leave to set. When cold, garnish with bay leaves and cut into slices to serve.

MOROCCAN FILO PIE

SERVES 6-8 ◆ PREPARATION 20 minutes ◆ COOKING TIME 40-45 minutes
◆ FREEZING Suitable (stage 5) ◆ 540-410 CALS PER SERVING

12 sheets filo pastry
75g (3oz) unsalted butter, melted

FILLING
60ml (4 tbsp) olive oil
1 onion, peeled and finely chopped
2-3 garlic cloves, peeled and crushed
10ml (2 tsp) ground coriander
5ml (1 tsp) ground cumin

450g (1lb) spinach leaves, shredded
two 400g (14oz) cans green lentils, drained
2 eggs, beaten
175g (6oz) feta cheese
25g (1oz) Parmesan cheese, freshly grated
60ml (4 tbsp) chopped fresh herbs, such as coriander, mint and parsley
salt and pepper

1 To prepare the filling, heat the oil in a saucepan, add the onion, garlic and spices and fry gently for 10 minutes.
2 Add the spinach and cook until wilted. Stir in the lentils, cover and heat through for 5 minutes. Mash the lentils slightly with a fork, then transfer to a bowl; let cool slightly.
3 Stir in the eggs, then crumble in the feta, and add the Parmesan, herbs and seasoning. Toss to mix, then set aside.
4 Lay one sheet of filo pastry in the base of a lightly oiled 25×20cm (10×8 inch) baking tin, trimming to fit as necessary, and brush with butter. Layer five more filo sheets in the tin, brushing each with butter.
5 Spoon in the filling and level the surface. Layer the remaining filo sheets on top, again brushing each with butter.
6 Score the top of the pie in a diamond pattern, using a sharp knife. Bake at 180°C/fan oven 170°C (350°F) Mark 4 for 40-45 minutes until golden brown. Leave to stand for 5 minutes, then cut into squares and serve with a salad.

GAME AND HERB PIE

SERVES 8 ◆ PREPARATION 40 minutes, plus chilling
◆ COOKING TIME 35-40 minutes ◆ FREEZING Not suitable
◆ 995 CALS PER SERVING

900g (2lb) ready-made puff pastry
beaten egg, for brushing

FILLING
700g (1½lb) boneless mixed game, such as rabbit and pheasant
15ml (1 tbsp) crushed, dried green peppercorns
flour, for coating
30ml (2 tbsp) oil
75g (3oz) butter
175g (6oz) rindless smoked streaky bacon (preferably in one piece), roughly chopped
225g (8oz) shallots or button onions, peeled
4 garlic cloves, peeled and crushed
600ml (1 pint) dry white wine

salt and pepper
450ml (¾ pint) double cream
15ml (1 tbsp) chopped fresh thyme
225g (8oz) brown-cap mushrooms, halved
700g (1½lb) trimmed spinach
30ml (2 tbsp) each chopped fresh basil, parsley, mint and tarragon

TO GARNISH
fresh or deep-fried herb sprigs
fried garlic slices (optional)
cracked green peppercorns (optional)

1 Roll out the pastry on a lightly floured surface to a 3mm (⅛ inch) thickness and use to line eight 7.5cm (3 inch) base-measurement brioche moulds (see note). Prick the bases well. Chill for 10 minutes, then line with greaseproof paper and fill with baking beans. Cook at 200°C/fan oven 190°C (400°F) Mark 6 for 20 minutes, then remove the paper and beans, brush lightly with beaten egg to seal and return to the oven for a further 5 minutes or until light golden.

2 Meanwhile, make the filling. Cut the game into bite-sized pieces, season with crushed peppercorns and coat with flour. In a large flameproof casserole, heat the oil with 50g (2oz) of the butter. Fry the game and bacon in batches for 1-2 minutes until golden. Remove from the pan and set aside.

3 Halve any large onions, then add to the pan with the garlic and fry for 3-4 minutes or until golden brown. Pour in the wine. Bring to the boil and let bubble for about 10 minutes until reduced to a syrupy consistency.

4 Return the game and bacon to the pan. Season and bring to the boil, then add the cream and thyme. Simmer for a further 8-10 minutes or until the liquid is reduced by half. Cover and simmer gently for 20 minutes or until the game is very tender.

5 Heat the remaining 25g (1oz) butter in a wide-based pan and fry the mushrooms over a high heat until golden; remove and set aside. In the same pan, cook the spinach for 2-3 minutes, with just the water clinging to the leaves after washing, until just wilted. Drain and squeeze out all liquid. Roughly chop and season well.

6 Divide the spinach between the baked pastry cases. Add the chopped herbs and fried mushrooms to the game mixture, then spoon into the cases. Cover loosely with foil and cook at 180°C/fan oven 170°C (350°F) Mark 4 for 10-15 minutes until piping hot to the centre. Serve garnished with herb sprigs, fried garlic slices and peppercorns if wished.

VARIATION To make one large pie, use a 5 cm (2 inch) deep, 23cm (9 inch) flan tin. Bake at stage 1 for 40 minutes.

3 Line the pastry case with greaseproof paper and baking beans. Place on a baking sheet and bake for 15 minutes. Remove paper and beans and bake for a further 10-12 minutes until the pastry is crisp and golden.

4 Using a slotted spoon, transfer the cooked leeks to the pastry case. Whisk the eggs, mascarpone and cream together with half of the Parmesan; season well.

5 Spoon the mixture over the vegetables, top with the olives and bake for 35-40 minutes until the filling is set and golden. Scatter over the remaining cheese. Serve warm.

QUICHE LORRAINE

SERVES 6-8 ◆ PREPARATION 35 minutes, plus chilling ◆ COOKING TIME 55 minutes
◆ FREEZING Suitable ◆ 865-650 CALS PER SERVING ◆ COLOUR INDEX Page 9

PASTRY	**40g (1½oz) butter**
200g (7oz) plain white flour	**125g (4oz) shallots or onions, peeled and finely chopped**
pinch of salt	**400ml (14fl oz) crème fraîche**
100g (3½oz) butter, diced	
1 egg	**100g (3½oz) gruyère cheese, grated**
15ml (1 tbsp) cold water	**salt and pepper**
FILLING	
5 eggs, lightly whisked	
225g (8oz) streaky bacon (preferably in one piece), derinded and cut into strips	

1 To make the pastry, put the flour and salt into a food processor with the butter. Process until the mixture resembles fine crumbs, then add the egg and water. Process until the mixture just comes together in a ball. Turn out on to a lightly floured surface and knead lightly until smooth. Wrap in cling film and chill for at least 30 minutes.

2 Roll out the pastry on a lightly floured surface and use to line a 3cm (1¼ inch) deep, 23cm (9 inch) loose-based flan tin. Chill for 20 minutes.

3 Prick the base, then line with greaseproof paper and baking beans. Place the flan tin on a baking sheet. Bake blind at 200°C/fan oven 190°C (400°F) Mark 6 for 10 minutes. Remove paper and beans and bake for a further 10 minutes until the pastry is golden. Brush with a little of the beaten egg and return to the oven for 5 minutes, to seal. Lower the setting to 190°C/fan oven 180°C (375°F) Mark 5.

4 Put the bacon in a pan with cold water to cover, bring to the boil, then drain and pat dry. Melt the butter in a frying pan, add the shallots and cook for 1 minute. Add the bacon and cook, stirring, until browned. Drain, then place in the pastry case.

5 In a bowl, beat the eggs with the crème fraîche and cheese; season. Pour the mixture over the bacon in the pastry case. Bake for 30 minutes, or until golden and set. Allow to stand for 10 minutes before serving, with a salad.

LEEK AND MASCARPONE TART

A deliciously creamy flan filled with sweet roasted leeks, and scattered with olives and grated Parmesan.

SERVES 8 ◆ PREPARATION 35 minutes, plus chilling
◆ COOKING TIME 25 minutes for filling; 1 hour baking ◆ FREEZING Suitable
◆ 480 CALS PER SERVING

Shortcrust Pastry, made with 225g (8oz) flour (see page 76)	**salt and pepper**
	3 medium eggs, lightly beaten
FILLING	**225g (8oz) mascarpone**
6-8 trimmed leeks, about 700g (1½lb)	**90ml (3fl oz) single cream**
30ml (2 tbsp) olive oil	**75g (3oz) Parmesan cheese, freshly grated**
15-30ml (1-2 tbsp) chopped fresh sage	**40g (1½oz) pitted black olives, halved**

1 Roll out the pastry on a lightly floured surface and use to line a 2.5 cm (1 inch) deep, 25 cm (10 inch) fluted flan tin. Prick the base with a fork and chill for 30 minutes.

2 Cut the leeks into 2.5 cm (1 inch) slices. Toss with the olive oil, sage, salt and pepper and roast at 230°C/fan oven 220°C (450°F) Mark 8 for 25 minutes, stirring occasionally until golden and tender. Allow to cool. Reduce oven setting to 200°C/fan oven 190°C (400°F) Mark 6.

SPINACH AND SWEET ONION TART

SERVES 6-8 ◆ PREPARATION 45 minutes, plus chilling
◆ COOKING TIME 40 minutes ◆ FREEZING Not suitable
◆ 480-360 CALS PER SERVING ◆ COLOUR INDEX Page 9

PASTRY
200g (7oz) plain white flour
pinch of salt
75g (3oz) butter, diced
15g (½oz) walnuts, toasted and ground
1 egg yolk
30-45ml (2-3 tbsp) cold water

FILLING
225g (8oz) baby onions, peeled
50g (2oz) butter
6 garlic cloves, peeled

2 fresh thyme sprigs, bruised
2 fresh bay leaves, bruised
salt and pepper
30ml (2 tbsp) balsamic vinegar
450g (1lb) spinach leaves, stalks removed
pinch of freshly grated nutmeg
200ml (7fl oz) crème fraîche
25g (1oz) Parmesan cheese, freshly grated

1 To make the pastry, sift the flour and salt into a bowl and rub in the butter until the mixture resembles fine breadcrumbs. Stir in the walnuts, then gradually work in the egg yolk and water to form a soft dough. Wrap in cling film and chill for 30 minutes.

2 Preheat a baking sheet in the oven at 200°C/fan oven 190°C (400°F) Mark 6. Roll out the dough on a lightly floured surface and use to line a 3cm (1¼ inch) deep, 23cm (9 inch) loose-based flan tin. Prick the base and chill for 15 minutes.

3 Line the pastry case with greaseproof paper and baking beans and bake on the hot baking sheet for 10-12 minutes. Remove paper and beans and bake for a further 10 minutes; set aside to cool. Increase oven setting to 230°C/fan oven 220°C (450°F) Mark 8.

4 Meanwhile, for the filling, blanch the whole onions in boiling water for 2 minutes; drain and dry on kitchen paper. Melt half of the butter in a frying pan. Add the whole onions and garlic cloves with the herbs and fry over a medium heat for 20 minutes until golden and caramelised. Stir in 2.5ml (½ tsp) salt and the balsamic vinegar; cook for a further 5 minutes. Discard the herbs; allow to cool.

5 Cook the spinach in a large saucepan over a low heat, with just the water clinging to the leaves after washing, for 3-4 minutes until wilted. Refresh under cold water and squeeze out excess liquid. Chop finely and return to the pan. Heat gently to dry thoroughly, stir in the remaining butter and season with the nutmeg, salt and pepper.

6 Arrange the onion mixture and spinach in the pastry case and spoon over the crème fraîche, spreading to the edges. Sprinkle with the grated Parmesan and bake in the oven for about 20 minutes until the filling is golden and bubbling. Leave to stand for 10 minutes. Serve warm.

NOTE The filling should still be soft when the tart is served.

MEDITERRANEAN TART

SERVES 6-8 ◆ PREPARATION 45 minutes, plus chilling
◆ COOKING TIME 45 minutes ◆ FREEZING Suitable ◆ 535-400 CALS PER SERVING

150g (5oz) plain white flour
pinch of salt
50g (2oz) butter, diced
15g (½oz) Parmesan cheese, freshly grated
1 egg yolk

FILLING
350g (12oz) aubergine
30ml (2 tbsp) olive oil
10ml (2 tsp) balsamic vinegar

1 small garlic clove, peeled and crushed
salt and pepper
125g (4oz) cherry tomatoes, halved
125g (4oz) feta cheese, diced
3 eggs, lightly beaten
300ml (½ pint) double cream
30ml (2 tbsp) chopped fresh mint

1 Sift the flour and salt into a bowl and rub in the butter until the mixture resembles fine breadcrumbs. Stir in the cheese, then work in the egg yolk and 30ml (2 tbsp) cold water to form a soft dough. Knead lightly, wrap and chill for 30 minutes.

2 Roll out the dough on a lightly floured surface and use to line a greased 22 cm (8½ inches) square pastry tin. Prick the base with a fork and chill for a further 30 minutes.

3 Line the pastry case with greaseproof paper and baking beans and bake blind at 200°C/fan oven 190°C (400°F) Mark 6 for 12 minutes. Remove paper and beans and bake for a further 8-10 minutes. Preheat a baking sheet in the oven.

4 Meanwhile, prepare the filling. Cut the aubergine into 5mm (¼ inch) slices. Mix the olive oil with the vinegar, garlic and seasoning. Brush over the aubergine slices and grill for 3-4 minutes each side until charred and tender. Leave to cool.

5 Arrange the aubergine slices, tomatoes and feta in the pastry case. Beat the remaining ingredients together in a bowl, season lightly and pour into the pastry case. Transfer to the hot baking sheet and bake for 25 minutes or until golden and set. Leave to stand for 5-10 minutes. Serve warm.

ONION AND POTATO TART

SERVES 4 ◆ PREPARATION 30 minutes, plus chilling ◆ COOKING TIME 40 minutes
◆ FREEZING Not suitable ◆ 605 CALS PER SERVING ◆ COLOUR INDEX Page 10

Shortcrust Pastry, made with 175g (6oz) flour (see page 76)

FILLING
3 small potatoes, about 225g (8oz)
60ml (4 tbsp) olive oil
2 onions, peeled and sliced
2 garlic cloves, peeled and crushed

10ml (2 tsp) chopped fresh thyme
10ml (2 tsp) chopped fresh sage
30ml (2 tbsp) olive paste
30ml (2 tbsp) capers in brine, drained
125g (4oz) gruyère or Cheddar cheese, grated
salt and pepper

1 Preheat a baking sheet in the oven at 220°C/fan oven 210°C (425°F) Mark 7. Roll out the pastry on a lightly floured surface to a 30cm (12 inch) round, then lift on to a cold baking sheet. Using fingers and thumbs, form a slight rim around the edge. Prick the base and line with greaseproof paper and baking beans.

2 Slide the baking sheet on to the hot baking sheet and bake blind for 10 minutes. Remove the paper and beans and bake for a further 5-8 minutes or until the pastry is crisp.

3 Meanwhile, cook the potatoes in lightly salted boiling water for 10-15 minutes until just tender. Drain and immediately refresh under cold water. Pat dry and cut into thin slices.

4 Heat the oil in a frying pan, add the onions, garlic and herbs and fry gently for 10 minutes until soft and golden.

5 Spread the olive paste over the pastry base, then top with the potatoes, onion mixture and capers. Scatter over the cheese and season well. Bake for 20-25 minutes until the filling is golden. Serve at once, with a tomato salad.

NOTE For convenience, you can buy a 225g (8oz) packet ready-made shortcrust pastry, rather than make your own.

SWEET POTATO AND SMOKED CHEESE FLAN

SERVES 6-8 ◆ PREPARATION 15 minutes, plus chilling
◆ COOKING TIME 15-20 minutes ◆ FREEZING Not suitable
◆ 475-355 CALS PER SERVING ◆ COLOUR INDEX Page 10

350g (12oz) packet ready-made puff pastry
350g (12oz) sweet potatoes, scrubbed
15ml (1 tbsp) olive oil

125g (4oz) smoked Cheddar cheese, grated
125g (4oz) spicy chorizo sausage, thinly sliced
salt and pepper

1 Roll out the pastry thinly on a lightly floured surface to a 23x33cm (9x13 inch) rectangle and press into a Swiss roll tin (of the same dimensions). Prick base and chill for 30 minutes.

2 Preheat a baking sheet on the middle shelf of the oven at 220°C/fan oven 210°C (425°F) Mark 7. Cut the sweet potatoes into thin slices, no more than 3 mm (1/8 inch) thick. Brush with oil and place on the grill rack. Grill for 3-5 minutes each side until golden and just tender. Allow to cool.

3 Arrange the sweet potato slices and chorizo slices over the pastry base and scatter with the grated cheese. Bake on the preheated baking sheet for 15-20 minutes until risen and golden. Serve with a green salad.

ROQUEFORT TART

SERVES 6-8 ◆ PREPARATION 30 minutes, plus chilling
◆ COOKING TIME 45-50 minutes ◆ FREEZING Not suitable
◆ 905-680 CALS PER SERVING ◆ COLOUR INDEX Page 10

PÂTE BRISÉE
250g (9oz) plain white flour
5ml (1 tsp) salt
125g (4½oz) butter, softened
1 egg yolk

FILLING
225g (8oz) cream cheese
150ml (¼ pint) crème fraîche or double cream
3 eggs, beaten
175g (6oz) Roquefort cheese

pepper
freshly grated nutmeg
45ml (3 tbsp) chopped fresh chives

TOPPING
30ml (2 tbsp) olive oil
3 garlic cloves, peeled and sliced
125g (4oz) walnut halves
15ml (1 tbsp) walnut oil
45ml (3 tbsp) chopped fresh parsley

1 To make the pastry, sift the flour and salt on to a sheet of greaseproof paper. Put the butter and egg yolk in a food processor and blend until smooth. Shoot in the flour and work until just combined. Turn out on to a lightly floured surface and knead gently until smooth. Wrap in cling film and chill for at least 30 minutes. Bring to room temperature before rolling out.

2 Beat the cream cheese in a bowl until softened, then beat in the cream and eggs. Crumble in the Roquefort and mix gently. Season liberally with pepper and a little nutmeg. Stir in the chives; set aside.

3 Roll out the pastry on a lightly floured surface. Use to line a 25cm (10 inch) loose-based flan tin. Chill for 20 minutes.

4 Prick the pastry base. Line with greaseproof paper and baking beans and place the flan tin on a baking sheet. Bake blind at 200°C/fan oven 190°C (400°F) Mark 6 for 10 minutes. Remove paper and beans and bake for a further 5 minutes. Let cool slightly. Lower the oven setting to 190°C/fan oven 180°C (375°F) Mark 5.

5 Pour the filling into the pastry case and bake for 30-35 minutes or until puffed and lightly browned.

6 Meanwhile, prepare topping. Heat the oil in a frying pan and fry the garlic and walnuts, stirring, until the garlic is golden. Stir in the walnut oil and parsley. Scatter the topping over the tart and serve warm or cold, with a salad.

GRILLED PEPPER AND CHICK PEA TART

A vibrant tart of spicy chick peas and sweet peppers baked in a creamy custard. Serve with a radicchio and tomato salad.

SERVES 6-8 ◆ PREPARATION 40 minutes, plus chilling ◆ COOKING TIME 50 minutes ◆ FREEZING Suitable ◆ 515-385 CALS PER SERVING

Shortcrust Pastry, made with 225g (8oz) flour (see page 76)

FILLING
2 red peppers, cored, deseeded and quartered
45ml (3 tbsp) olive oil
1 onion, peeled and finely chopped
1 garlic clove, peeled and crushed

5ml (1 tsp) turmeric
2.5ml (½ tsp) paprika
400g (14oz) can chick peas, drained
30ml (2 tbsp) chopped fresh coriander
15ml (1 tbsp) lemon juice
3 eggs, beaten
300ml (½ pint) soured cream
salt and pepper

1 Roll out the pastry on a lightly floured surface and use to line a 25cm (10 inch) flan tin. Prick the base and chill for 30 minutes.

2 Line the pastry case with greaseproof paper and baking beans and place on a baking sheet. Bake blind at 200°C/fan oven 190°C (400°F) Mark 6 for 15 minutes. Remove the paper and beans and bake for a further 10-12 minutes until golden and crisp.

3 Brush the pepper quarters with 15ml (1 tbsp) of the olive oil and grill for 3-4 minutes each side until charred and tender. Cover and leave to cool, then peel the peppers and cut the flesh into thin strips.

4 Heat the remaining oil in a frying pan and gently fry the onion, garlic and spices for 5 minutes until softened. Add the chick peas and mash lightly, then add the peppers, coriander and lemon juice. Spoon into the pastry case.

5 Beat the eggs, cream and a little seasoning together in a bowl, then pour into the pastry case. Bake for 25 minutes or until the filling is golden and set. Allow to stand for about 10 minutes. Serve warm.

CHICORY FLAN

Chicory bulbs are braised until meltingly tender, then baked in a savoury cheese custard topped with Parma ham.

SERVES 6-8 ◆ PREPARATION 45 minutes, plus chilling
◆ COOKING TIME About 1 hour ◆ FREEZING Not suitable
◆ 600-450 CALS PER SERVING

Shortcrust Pastry, made with 225g (8oz) flour (see page 76)

FILLING
50g (2oz) butter
6 heads white chicory, about 600g (1¼lb) in total, halved lengthwise
5ml (1 tsp) caster sugar
50ml (2fl oz) vegetable or chicken stock

2 eggs
2 egg yolks
200ml (7fl oz) double cream
15ml (1 tbsp) wholegrain mustard
50g (2oz) gruyère cheese, grated
salt and pepper
5-6 slices Parma ham, cut into pieces

1 Roll out the pastry on a lightly floured surface and use to line a 25cm (10 inch) fluted flan tin. Prick the base with a fork and chill for 30 minutes.

2 Line the pastry case with greaseproof paper and baking beans, place on a baking sheet and bake at 200°C/fan oven 190°C (400°F) Mark 6 for 15 minutes. Remove beans and paper and bake for a further 10-12 minutes until the pastry is crisp and golden. Allow to cool. Reduce oven setting to 190°C/fan oven 180°C (375°F) Mark 5.

3 Meanwhile, prepare the filling. Melt the butter in a frying pan. Add the chicory, cut-side down, and fry gently for 5 minutes, then turn and fry for a further 5 minutes; you may need to do this in batches. Add the sugar and stock, cover and braise for 30 minutes or until the chicory is tender. Remove with a slotted spoon and leave to cool.

4 Beat the eggs, egg yolks, cream, mustard and cheese together in a bowl until evenly blended. Season with pepper and a little salt.

5 Arrange the chicory, cut-side up, in the pastry case, with the tips radiating from the centre (like the spokes of a wheel); trim to fit as necessary.

6 Pour the egg mixture over the chicory and top with the Parma ham. Bake for 35-40 minutes until the filling is firm. Allow to cool slightly. Serve warm.

NOTE If the chicory heads are plump, quarter lengthways or cut into chunks to ensure they cook through.

CRAB FILO TART

SERVES 8 ◆ PREPARATION 20 minutes, plus cooling ◆ COOKING TIME 55 minutes
◆ FREEZING Not suitable ◆ 260 CALS PER SERVING ◆ COLOUR INDEX Page 11

175g (6oz) filo pastry
30ml (2 tbsp) olive oil

FILLING
25g (1oz) butter
1 bunch spring onions, finely chopped
10-15ml (2-3 tsp) grated fresh root ginger
450g (1lb) fresh or vacuum-packed white crab meat

200ml (7fl oz) single cream
3 egg yolks
30ml (2 tbsp) chopped fresh coriander
salt and pepper

TO GARNISH
coriander leaves

1 Preheat a baking sheet on the middle shelf of the oven at 200°C/fan oven 190°C (400°F) Mark 6. Keep the filo pastry covered with a damp tea-towel. Taking one sheet at a time, brush with oil and place in a deep 23cm (9 inch) flan tin, allowing the edges to overhang slightly. Continue to add oiled filo sheets to fill the tin and form a shell. Prick the base.

2 Bake on the preheated baking sheet for 10 minutes, then set aside to cool. Reduce oven setting to 190°C/fan oven 180°C (375°F) Mark 5.

3 To make the filling, melt the butter in a frying pan and gently fry the spring onions and ginger for 2-3 minutes until softened. Allow to cool.

4 Flake the crab meat into a bowl. Add the cooled onion mixture, with all of the remaining filling ingredients. Stir well, seasoning generously. Spoon into the filo case.

5 Carefully cover the overhanging filo edges with foil to prevent overbrowning and bake for 45 minutes until golden and just set. Leave to stand for 10 minutes. Serve warm, garnished with coriander.

TOMATO TARTE TATIN

SERVES 6 ◆ PREPARATION 50 minutes, plus chilling
◆ COOKING TIME 30-40 minutes ◆ FREEZING Not suitable
◆ 310 CALS PER SERVING ◆ COLOUR INDEX Page 10

90ml (6 tbsp) olive oil
30ml (2 tbsp) tomato paste
400g (14oz) can chopped tomatoes
1 fresh thyme sprig
salt and pepper
20ml (4 tsp) caster sugar
1.1kg (2½lb) plum tomatoes
50g (2oz) ciabatta
2 garlic cloves, crushed
45ml (3 tbsp) chopped fresh basil or thyme

PASTRY
75g (3oz) chilled butter, cut into cubes
125g (4oz) plain white flour
60-75ml (4-5 tbsp) soured cream

TO SERVE
garlic-infused olive oil (see note)
chervil or parsley sprigs
crushed black peppercorns

1 Heat 30ml (2 tbsp) olive oil in a pan, add the tomato paste and cook, stirring, for 1 minute. Add the canned tomatoes, thyme, seasoning and 5ml (1 tsp) caster sugar. Bring to the boil, lower the heat and simmer gently, uncovered, for 45 minutes or until the sauce is reduced and very thick. Discard the thyme; allow to cool.

2 Meanwhile, halve the plum tomatoes lengthwise and place on a baking sheet, cut-side up. Season, sprinkle with remaining sugar and drizzle with 15ml (1 tbsp) olive oil. Cook under a preheated grill for about 15 minutes until charred. Cool.

3 To make the pastry, place the butter and flour in a food processor. Pulse until the mixture resembles coarse crumbs, add the cream and pulse again until the dough comes together. Wrap in cling film and chill for at least 30 minutes.

4 Process the ciabatta with the garlic and 45ml (3 tbsp) olive oil to rough crumbs; season well and place on a baking sheet. Bake at 200°C/fan oven 190°C (400°F) Mark 6 for 5-10 minutes or until golden. Mix with the chopped basil or thyme.

5 Arrange the tomatoes, cut-side down, over the base of a 25cm (10 inch) ovenproof frying pan or non-stick cake tin. Spoon over any juices and season. Spread the tomato sauce over the tomatoes. Roll the pastry out on a lightly floured surface to a 25cm (10 inch) round, place on top of the tomatoes and trim the edges. Cut steam holes in the pastry and bake in the oven for 30-40 minutes or until golden.

6 Invert the tart on to a serving plate and scatter over the garlic and herb crumb mixture. Drizzle with garlic-infused oil, garnish with herbs and season with crushed peppercorns.

NOTE For garlic-infused oil, put 2 thinly sliced garlic cloves in a pan with 90ml (6 tbsp) olive oil and warm gently until the garlic is golden; remove from the heat.

PARSNIP TATIN

Serve this delicious savoury upside down tart with a dollop of crème fraîche or soured cream.

SERVES 6 ◆ PREPARATION 30 minutes, plus chilling
◆ COOKING TIME 20-25 minutes ◆ FREEZING Not suitable
◆ 390 CALS PER SERVING

PASTRY
200g (7oz) plain white flour
2.5ml (½ tsp) salt
100g (3½oz) chilled butter, diced
15g (½oz) walnuts, toasted and ground
1 egg yolk
15ml (1 tbsp) cold water

FILLING
40g (1½oz) butter
8 baby parsnips, about 7.5 cm (3 inches) long, halved lengthwise
15ml (1 tbsp) brown sugar
salt and pepper
90ml (3fl oz) dry cider

1 To make the pastry, sift the flour and salt into a bowl. Rub in the butter until the mixture resembles fine breadcrumbs, then stir in the walnuts. Gradually work in the egg yolk and

water to form a soft dough. Knead briefly, then wrap in cling film and chill in the refrigerator for 30 minutes.

2 For the filling, melt the butter in a 20-23cm (8-9 inch) heavy-based ovenproof frying pan (see note). Add the parsnips, cut-side down, arranging them like the spokes of a wheel, with the narrow ends at the centre. Sprinkle with the sugar and season with salt and pepper. Fry over a medium heat for 15 minutes, turning halfway through cooking until evenly golden. Add the cider, bring to the boil, then remove from the heat.

3 Meanwhile, roll out the pastry on a lightly floured surface to a round, slightly larger than the frying pan. Carefully position the pastry over the parsnips, pressing lightly and well down the side of the pan to enclose the parsnips. Bake in the oven at 200°C/fan oven 190°C (400°F) Mark 6 for 20-25 minutes until golden.

4 Invert a warm serving plate over the pan, then carefully flip over to unmould the tart on to the plate. Spoon over the pan juices and serve at once, with crème fraîche.

NOTE Ideally you need a non-stick frying pan with an integral metal handle, which can be put into the oven. If your pan isn't ovenproof, transfer the cooked parsnips to a well greased cake tin before covering with the pastry.

oil. Divide the onion mixture between them, leaving a 1cm (½ inch) margin round the edges. Season with salt and pepper.

5 Place the tarts on the hot baking sheets and bake in the oven for 15 minutes or until the pastry is crisp, golden and risen around the edges. Garnish with oregano sprigs to serve.

NOTE These tarts can be reheated from frozen at 220°C/ fan oven 210°C (425°F) Mark 7 for 10 minutes.

VARIATION Flavour the caramelised onion filling with anchovies instead of raisins. Season with pepper only.

FENNEL, ONION AND GRUYÈRE TARTLETS

SERVES 4 ◆ PREPARATION 25 minutes, plus chilling ◆ COOKING TIME 35 minutes ◆ FREEZING Suitable ◆ 670 CALS PER SERVING ◆ COLOUR INDEX Page 11

CHEESE PASTRY
175g (6oz) plain white flour
75g (3oz) lightly salted butter, in pieces
50g (2oz) gruyère cheese, grated
1 egg yolk
30ml (2 tbsp) cold water

FILLING
225g (8oz) onion, peeled
225g (8oz) fennel bulb
45ml (3 tbsp) olive oil
5ml (1 tsp) fennel seeds
1 egg
150ml (¼ pint) double cream
salt and pepper
25g (1oz) gruyère cheese, grated

1 To make the pastry, sift the flour into a bowl. Rub in the butter, using your fingertips, then stir in the cheese. Add the egg yolk and cold water and mix to a firm dough. Knead lightly until smooth, then wrap in cling film and chill in the refrigerator for 30 minutes.

2 Roll out the pastry thinly on a lightly floured surface and use to line four 2cm (¾ inch) deep, 10cm (4 inch) individual flan tins.

3 Line with greaseproof paper and baking beans and bake blind at 200°C/fan oven 190°C (400°F) Mark 6 for 10 minutes until beginning to colour around the edges. Remove the paper and beans and bake for a further 5 minutes.

4 Meanwhile, prepare the filling. Slice the onion and fennel as thinly as possible. Heat the oil in a large frying pan and add the onion and fennel, with the fennel seeds. Fry very gently for 10 minutes or until softened. Allow to cool slightly.

5 In a bowl, beat together the egg, cream and a little seasoning. Divide the fennel mixture between the pastry cases and pack down lightly. Pour on the egg mixture and sprinkle with the cheese. Bake for about 20 minutes until the custard is just set. Serve warm.

VARIATION For classic onion tarts, omit the fennel and fennel seeds, and double the quantity of onion.

ONION, FETA AND PINE NUT TARTS

Sweet caramelised onions, olives, pine nuts, sun-dried tomatoes and crumbled feta cheese in puff pastry cases.

SERVES 4 ◆ PREPARATION 30 minutes, plus chilling ◆ COOKING TIME 15 minutes ◆ FREEZING Suitable (see note) ◆ 710 CALS PER SERVING

450g (1lb) ready-made puff pastry
60ml (4 tbsp) olive oil, plus extra for brushing
700g (1½lb) onions, peeled and sliced
25g (1oz) pine nuts
25g (1oz) raisins (optional)
50g (2oz) feta cheese, crumbled

25g (1oz) pitted black olives
25g (1oz) sun-dried tomatoes, roughly chopped
25g (1oz) capers
salt and pepper
oregano sprigs, to garnish

1 Roll out the puff pastry on a lightly floured surface and cut out four 15cm (6 inch) rounds, using an inverted saucer as a guide. Chill for 30 minutes.

2 Preheat two baking sheets in the oven at 220°C/fan oven 210°C (425°F) Mark 7.

3 Meanwhile, heat the oil in a large heavy-based frying pan. Add the onions and cook over a low heat for 10-15 minutes, stirring occasionally, until golden and caramelised. Allow to cool, then stir in the pine nuts, raisins if using, feta cheese, olives, sun-dried tomatoes and capers.

4 Prick the pastry rounds with a fork and brush with a little

PARMESAN TARTLETS WITH BROAD BEAN PESTO

SERVES 4 ◆ PREPARATION 20 minutes, plus chilling
◆ COOKING TIME 20-25 minutes ◆ FREEZING Suitable (stage 3)
◆ 535-565 CALS PER SERVING ◆ COLOUR INDEX Page 11

PASTRY
150g (5oz) plain white flour
pinch of salt
50g (2oz) butter, diced
15g (½oz) Parmesan cheese, freshly grated
1 egg yolk
30ml (2 tbsp) cold water

BROAD BEAN PESTO
225g (8oz) broad beans, thawed if frozen
1 garlic clove, peeled and crushed
50g (2oz) pecorino or Parmesan cheese, grated
15-30ml (1-2 tbsp) lemon juice, to taste

10ml (2 tsp) creamed horseradish
15ml (1 tbsp) chopped fresh mint
90-100ml (3-3½fl oz) extra-virgin olive oil
salt and pepper

TOPPING
50g (2oz) pitted black olives
2 ripe tomatoes, peeled, deseeded and diced
15ml (1 tbsp) chopped fresh parsley
15ml (1 tbsp) lemon juice
30ml (2 tbsp) extra-virgin olive oil

1 To make the pastry, sift the flour and salt into a bowl and rub in the butter until the mixture resembles fine breadcrumbs. Stir in the Parmesan, then gradually work in the egg yolk and water to form a soft dough. Knead lightly, wrap in cling film and chill for 30 minutes.

2 Meanwhile preheat a baking sheet on the middle shelf of the oven at 200°C/fan oven 190°C (400°F) Mark 6. Divide the pastry into 4 pieces. Roll each out thinly on a lightly floured surface to a round and use to line four individual 10cm (4 inch) fluted flan tins. Chill for 30 minutes.

3 Line the pastry cases with greaseproof paper and baking beans and bake blind on the hot baking sheet for 15 minutes. Remove paper and beans; bake for a further 5-10 minutes to crisp the base. Leave until cold.

4 Meanwhile, prepare the pesto. Cook the beans in lightly salted boiling water for 3 minutes. Drain, refresh under cold water and pat dry. Place in a food processor with the garlic, cheese, 15ml (1 tbsp) lemon juice, horseradish, mint, 90ml (3fl oz) oil and seasoning; purée until smooth. Add the extra oil and/or lemon juice if required.

5 For the topping, mix the olives, tomatoes, parsley, lemon juice and oil together in a bowl and season with salt and pepper to taste. Divide the bread bean pesto between the pastry cases and spoon the olive mixture on the top. Serve at once, with a mixed green salad.

AVOCADO AND PARMA HAM PUFFS

SERVES 6 ◆ PREPARATION 15 minutes, plus chilling
◆ COOKING TIME 12-15 minutes ◆ FREEZING Not suitable
◆ 320 CALS PER SERVING

350g (12oz) ready-made puff pastry
60ml (4 tbsp) sun-dried tomato paste
30ml (2 tbsp) mascarpone
1 small avocado
15ml (1 tbsp) lemon juice
6 slices Parma ham

GREMOLATA
2 garlic cloves, peeled and crushed
30ml (2 tbsp) chopped fresh basil
grated rind of 1 lemon
pepper

1 Roll out the pastry on a lightly floured surface and cut out six 12cm (5 inch) rounds, using an inverted fluted flan tin or saucer as a guide. Prick the bases and chill for 30 minutes.

2 Preheat a baking sheet on the middle shelf of the oven at 220°C/fan oven 210°C (425°F) Mark 7. Mix the tomato paste and mascarpone together and spread over the pastry bases.

3 Peel, halve and stone the avocado, then cut the flesh into wafer-thin slices and brush with the lemon juice. Arrange on the pastry bases. Transfer to the preheated baking sheet and cook for 12-15 minutes until risen and golden.

4 Meanwhile, mix the gremolata ingredients together in a bowl. Arrange the Parma ham slices on the puffs; warm through in the oven for 1 minute if required. Scatter over the gremolata and serve immediately.

SALMON AND HERB PASTIES

Crammed with salmon, prawns and summer herbs, these luxurious pasties make perfect outdoor eating.

SERVES 6 ◆ PREPARATION 40 minutes, plus chilling ◆ COOKING TIME 25 minutes
◆ FREEZING Suitable (stage 5) ◆ 880 CALS PER PASTY

PASTRY

350g (12oz) plain white flour

salt and pepper

250g (9oz) butter, frozen for 1 hour

150ml (¼ pint) cold water (approximately)

FILLING

450g (1lb) salmon fillet, skinned and cubed

1 large garlic clove, peeled and crushed

25g (1oz) flat-leafed parsley, finely chopped

15g (½oz) fresh mint leaves, finely chopped

100g (3½oz) cooked peeled prawns (optional)

2 lemons

25g (1oz) butter

125g (4oz) leeks, finely sliced

30ml (2 tbsp) mascarpone

TO FINISH

1 egg, lightly beaten

dried crushed chillies or coarse sea salt flakes

1 To make the pastry, sift the flour into a bowl, add 2.5ml (½ tsp) salt and a little pepper. Coarsely grate the frozen butter into the flour and mix lightly. Using a fork, stir in enough cold water to form a dough. Gather together into a ball, wrap in cling film and chill for 30 minutes.

2 For the filling, put the salmon, garlic, herbs, and prawns if using in a bowl. Using a zester, pare the rind from the lemons in strips and add to the salmon mixture. Melt the butter in a frying pan, add the leeks and cook briskly, stirring, for about 10 minutes until just golden. Allow to cool.

3 Add the cooked leeks to the salmon mixture and toss to mix. Season with salt and pepper to taste, then set aside. Divide the chilled pastry into 12 equal pieces.

4 On a floured surface, roll out 6 pieces of pastry and cut out 12cm (5 inch) circles; roll out the remaining pieces and cut six 15cm (6 inch) circles, using saucers as guides.

5 Brush the edges of the smaller circles with beaten egg and place two heaped tablespoonfuls of filling in the centre of each one. Postion the larger circles on top, press the pastry edges together to seal, then flute decoratively. Cut a cross in the middle of each pasty and fold back the tips of each cross. Transfer the pasties to a non-stick baking sheet.

6 Spoon 5ml (1 tsp) mascarpone into each pasty, then chill for 30 minutes. Preheat a baking sheet in oven at 200°C/fan oven 190°C (400°F) Mark 6. Brush pasties with egg and sprinkle with crushed chillies or sea salt. Place on the hot baking sheet, loosely cover with foil and bake for 20 minutes. Remove foil and cook for a further 5 minutes or until golden.

NOTE The pasties can be baked from frozen; allow an extra 10-15 minutes after removing the foil.

WILD MUSHROOM PITHIVIERS

SERVES 6 ◆ PREPARATION 1 hour, plus chilling ◆ COOKING TIME 20-25 minutes
◆ FREEZING Suitable (stage 5) ◆ 1040 CALS PER SERVING
◆ COLOUR INDEX Page 12

two 500g packets ready-made puff pastry
1 egg, beaten

FILLING
450g (1lb) assorted wild mushrooms
450g (1lb) floury potatoes
300ml (½ pint) milk
200ml (7fl oz) double cream
2 garlic cloves, peeled and crushed
salt and pepper
freshly grated nutmeg

50g (2oz) butter
10ml (2 tsp) chopped fresh thyme

PORT SAUCE
40g (1½oz) butter
4 shallots, peeled and finely chopped
150ml (¼ pint) port or Madeira
600ml (1 pint) vegetable stock

TO GARNISH
thyme sprigs

1 To make the filling, rinse the wild mushrooms to remove any grit, then pat dry with kitchen paper and slice thickly.
2 Peel and thinly slice the potatoes. Pour the milk and cream into a large, heavy-based saucepan, add the garlic and bring to the boil. Add the potatoes, return to the boil and simmer gently, stirring occasionally, for 15-20 minutes or until tender. Season generously with salt, pepper and nutmeg. Cool.
3 Melt the butter in a large frying pan. As it starts sizzling, add the mushrooms and fry, stirring, over a high heat, for 5-7 minutes or until they are cooked and the juices have completely evaporated. Season with salt and pepper, stir in the chopped thyme, then set aside to cool.
4 Roll out the pastry thinly on a lightly floured surface. Cut out six 15cm (6 inches) rounds for the lids and six 14cm (5½ inches) rounds for the bases. Place the smaller pastry bases on a large baking sheet and brush the edges with beaten egg.
5 Spoon the cooled potato mixture on to the pastry bases, leaving a 1cm (½ inch) margin. Top with the mushroom mixture. Position the pastry lids and press the pastry edges together to seal. Chill for 30 minutes-1 hour.
6 Preheat a large baking sheet in the oven at 220°C/fan oven 210°C (425°F) Mark 7. Knock up and scallop the pastry edges, then brush the tops with beaten egg. Use the back of a knife to lightly score the tops of the pithiviers decoratively. Slide the tray of pithiviers on to the hot baking sheet and bake for 20-25 minutes or until deep golden brown.
7 Meanwhile, make the port sauce. Melt the butter in a frying pan, add the shallots and cook for 2-3 minutes. Pour in the port and bubble to reduce by half. Add the stock, bring to the boil and bubble for 10-15 minutes or until syrupy; season.
8 Transfer the pithiviers to warmed plates, garnish with thyme and serve with the port sauce and steamed baby leeks.

NOTE The pithiviers can be baked from frozen; allow an extra 10-15 minutes.

FILO MUSHROOM TARTLETS

SERVES 6 ◆ PREPARATION 30 minutes ◆ COOKING TIME 25-30 minutes
◆ FREEZING Not suitable ◆ 375 CALS PER SERVING ◆ COLOUR INDEX Page 12

8-10 sheets filo pastry
sunflower oil, for brushing

FILLING
15ml (1 tbsp) sunflower oil
2 small red onions, peeled and finely chopped
2 garlic cloves, peeled and crushed
225g (8oz) mixed flat and chestnut mushrooms, finely chopped

5 sun-dried tomatoes in oil, drained and finely chopped
10ml (2 tsp) lemon juice
15ml (1 tbsp) chopped fresh parsley
salt and pepper
6 medium eggs
15g (½oz) Parmesan cheese, freshly grated

1 Lightly oil six 2.5cm (1 inch) deep, 9cm (3½ inch) individual flan tins. Cut eighteen 11cm (4½ inch) squares from the filo pastry. Brush each square with a little sunflower oil. Layer 3 filo squares in each tin, arranging them at an angle to each other so the points form a star. Press the pastry into the edges of the tins. Bake at 190°C/fan oven 180°C (375°F) Mark 5 for 10-15 minutes until just golden.
2 Meanwhile, heat the oil in a pan, add the onions and fry gently until softened. Add the garlic and mushrooms to the pan and cook until the juices start to run. Add the sun-dried tomatoes, lemon juice, parsley and seasoning.
3 Divide the filling between the filo pastry cases. Press a hollow in the centre of one with the back of a spoon. Break an egg into a small saucer or small cup, then slide into one of the hollows; repeat with the other eggs.
4 Sprinkle with the Parmesan and bake for 14-16 minutes until the eggs are softly set and creamy. Serve with a mixed leaf salad drizzled with balsamic vinegar.

BAKED GARLIC AND GOAT CHEESE PARCELS

These small savoury parcels – stuffed with caramelised garlic purée, goat's cheese and fresh herbs – make a perfect starter or light lunch. Serve with a tomato relish and a leafy salad.

SERVES 6 ◆ PREPARATION 15 minutes
◆ COOKING TIME 45 minutes for filling; 20-25 minutes baking
◆ FREEZING Not suitable ◆ 310 CALS PER SERVING

1-2 heads garlic (see note)
1 fresh thyme sprig
15ml (1 tbsp) olive oil
salt and pepper
375g (12oz) packet ready-made puff pastry

175g (6oz) log goat's cheese, cut into slices
30ml (2 tbsp) chopped fresh herbs, to include basil, mint and thyme
beaten egg, mixed with a little water, to glaze

1 Cut a thin slice from the top of the garlic bulb(s) and place on a large sheet of foil. Put the thyme sprig on top, drizzle with the olive oil and season with salt and pepper. Bring the edges of the foil over the top and fold together to seal.

2 Place the parcels on a baking sheet and bake at 220°C/fan oven 210°C (425°F) Mark 7 for 45 minutes. Unwrap the garlic and leave to cool, then carefully squeeze the soft flesh into a bowl. Season with a little salt and pepper to taste.

3 Roll out the pastry to a 38x25cm (15x10 inch) rectangle, then cut into six 12cm (5 inch) squares. Spread a circle of garlic paste in the middle and top with slices of cheese and a sprinkling of herbs.

4 Brush the pastry edges sparingly with water, then bring the corners up over the filling and press together to seal. Brush with a little egg glaze, transfer to a baking sheet and bake in the oven for 20-25 minutes until golden. Leave to stand for 5 minutes before serving.

NOTES
◆ For speed, you could buy ready rolled puff pastry, cutting slightly smaller squares if necessary.
◆ Use 2 heads of garlic for a more pronounced flavour.
◆ For extra flavour, sprinkle cracked pepper or sea salt over the pastries before baking.

PIZZAS

Easy to make pizza crusts, with sensational savoury toppings to suit all tastes. Choose from authentic Italian pizzas and original combinations, such as prawn and sweet chilli, or beetroot and taleggio cheese

PIZZA BASE DOUGH

It is surprisingly quick and easy to make your own pizza dough, using fast-action dried yeast. If you are very short of time, use a pizza base mix instead: a 140g (5oz) packet is roughly equivalent to this basic recipe quantity.

MAKES 1 LARGE OR 2 SMALL PIZZA BASES ◆ PREPARATION 15 minutes, plus rising

225g (8oz) strong plain white flour
2.5ml (½ tsp) salt
2.5ml (½ tsp) fast-action dried yeast

150ml (¼ pint) warm water
15ml (1 tbsp) extra-virgin olive oil

1 Sift the flour and salt into a bowl and stir in the yeast. Make a well in the centre and gradually work in the water and oil to form a soft dough.
2 Knead the dough on a lightly floured surface for 8-10 minutes (or using a large food mixer with a dough hook) until smooth and elastic.
3 Place in an oiled bowl, turn the dough once to coat the surface with oil and cover the bowl with cling film. Leave to rise in a warm place for approximately 1 hour until doubled in size.
4 Knock back the pizza dough and shape as required.

NOTE If preferred, use 15g (½oz) fresh yeast instead of fast-action dried yeast. Mix with 30ml (2 tbsp) of the flour, a pinch of sugar and the warm water. Leave in a warm place for 10 minutes until frothy, then add to the rest of the flour and salt. Mix to a dough and continue as above.

EASY-BAKE PIZZA

Children will enjoy making their own pizzas with this easy-to-follow recipe. Choose 3 or 4 topping ingredients from those listed below.

SERVES 2-4 ◆ PREPARATION 20 minutes, plus rising
◆ COOKING TIME 15-20 minutes ◆ FREEZING Not suitable
◆ 650-320 CALS PER SERVING ◆ COLOUR INDEX Page 13

140g (5oz) packet pizza base mix
½ jar pizza topping

TOPPINGS
½ small onion, peeled and thinly sliced
50g (2oz) button mushrooms, sliced
50g (2oz) frozen peas, thawed
50g (2oz) canned sweetcorn, drained

75g (3oz) tuna fish, drained
125g (4oz) cooked chicken breast, sliced
75g (3oz) cherry tomatoes, halved

TO FINISH
75g (3oz) Cheddar cheese, grated, or 125g (4oz) mozzarella, sliced

1 Preheat a baking sheet in the oven at 220°C/fan oven 210°C (425°F) Mark 7. Place the pizza mix in a bowl and add

water according to the packet instructions. Combine with a fork, then continue to mix with your hands until it forms a soft dough, adding a little more flour if it's too sticky.
2 Once the dough has come together in a ball, sprinkle flour over the work surface and turn out the dough. Knead it for 5 minutes until smooth, shiny and elastic.
3 Sprinkle more flour over the work surface and rolling pin. Roll out the dough to a 20cm (8 inch) circle then, using the rolling pin, transfer it to a baking sheet.
4 Spread the pizza topping over the dough, then add your favourite toppings. Sprinkle with the grated Cheddar or arrange the sliced mozzarella on top.
5 Leave in a warm place for 10 minutes to rise, then carefully slide the pizza on to the hot baking sheet and cook for 15-20 minutes until golden. Leave to stand for a few minutes before serving.

TOMATO PIZZA WITH PARMA HAM AND ROCKET

SERVES 2-4 ◆ PREPARATION 30 minutes, plus rising
◆ COOKING TIME 10-15 minutes ◆ FREEZING Not suitable
◆ 750-375 CALS PER SERVING ◆ COLOUR INDEX Page 13

1 quantity Pizza Base Dough (see left)
400g (14oz) can chopped tomatoes
2 garlic cloves, peeled and crushed
grated rind of ½ lemon
45ml (3 tbsp) extra-virgin olive oil

30ml (2 tbsp) chopped fresh basil
pinch of caster sugar
salt and pepper
50g (2oz) rocket leaves
6 slices Parma ham
25g (1oz) Parmesan cheese shavings

1 Make the pizza dough and leave to rise for 1 hour or until doubled in size.
2 Meanwhile, place the tomatoes, garlic, lemon rind, 30ml (2 tbsp) oil, the basil, sugar, salt and pepper in a saucepan and bring to the boil. Cover and simmer gently for 15 minutes, then cook uncovered for a further 10 minutes until reduced and thickened. Leave to cool.
3 Preheat a baking sheet on the top shelf of the oven at 230°C/fan oven 220°C (450°F) Mark 8. Knock back the pizza dough and roll out thinly on a floured board to a 30-35cm (12-14 inch) round, according to preferred thickness of pizza. Transfer to a second baking sheet.
4 Spread the tomato sauce over the dough, almost to the edges. Transfer the pizza to the hot baking sheet and bake for 10-15 minutes until the dough is crisp and golden.
5 Meanwhile, toss the rocket in the remaining 15ml (1 tbsp) olive oil. On removing the pizza from the oven, immediately top with the slices of Parma ham, rocket, salt and pepper, and finally the Parmesan shavings. Serve at once.

OLIVE CRUST PIZZA WITH LEEK CONFIT

The pizza crust is flavoured with chopped black olives, adding a savoury flavour that balances the sweetness of the topping.

SERVES 2-4 ◆ PREPARATION 25 minutes, plus rising
◆ COOKING TIME About 15 minutes ◆ FREEZING Not suitable
◆ 1215-610 CALS PER SERVING

PIZZA DOUGH

225g (8oz) strong plain white flour, plus extra for sprinkling

5ml (1 tsp) sea salt

2.5ml (½ tsp) fast-action dried yeast

pinch of sugar

150ml (¼ pint) warm water

50g (2oz) pitted black olives, finely chopped

TOPPING

45ml (3 tbsp) olive oil

450g (1lb) leeks, thinly sliced

1 garlic clove, crushed

30ml (2 tbsp) chopped fresh sage

salt and pepper

100g (3½oz) mascarpone

225g (8oz) dolcelatte cheese, cubed

pinch of crushed dried red chillies (optional)

sage sprigs, to garnish

1 Sift the flour and salt into a bowl and stir in the yeast and sugar. Make a well in the centre and work in the water to form a soft dough.

2 Knead on a lightly floured surface for 8-10 minutes (or using a large food mixer with a dough hook). Add the olives and sprinkle with some extra flour to prevent the dough becoming wet. Knead gently for a further 2 minutes.

3 Shape the dough into a ball, place in an oiled bowl, cover and leave to rise in a warm place for at least 1 hour.

4 Meanwhile, prepare the topping. Heat the oil in a frying pan, then add the leeks, garlic, sage and seasoning. Fry gently for about 20 minutes until the leeks are softened and golden. Allow to cool, then stir in the mascarpone.

5 Preheat 2 baking sheets in the oven at 230°C/fan oven 220°C (450°F) Mark 8. Knock back the dough on a lightly floured board. Divide in half and roll each piece out thinly to a 23-25cm (9-10 inch) round, according to preferred thickness of pizza. Transfer to oiled baking sheets and top with the leek confit. Scatter over the dolcelatte and crushed chillies, if using.

6 Slide the pizzas on to the hot baking sheets and bake for 15 minutes or until the base is crisp and the topping is bubbling. Serve at once, garnished with sage.

PIZZA FIORENTINA

Thin, crisp pizzas topped with fresh spinach, Parma ham, Parmesan and a whole egg.

SERVES 2 ◆ PREPARATION 30 minutes, plus rising
◆ COOKING TIME About 15 minutes ◆ FREEZING Not suitable
◆ 850 CALS PER SERVING

1 quantity Pizza Base Dough (see page 102)

450g (1lb) spinach leaves, stalks removed

40g (1½oz) butter

salt and pepper

freshly grated nutmeg (optional)

1 egg yolk, beaten, for brushing

4 slices Parma ham, cut into pieces

2 eggs

25g (1oz) Parmesan cheese, freshly grated

TO SERVE

extra-virgin olive oil or truffle oil, for drizzling

1 Make the pizza dough and leave to rise for 1 hour or until doubled in size. Preheat 2 baking sheets in the oven at 230°C/fan oven 220°C (450°F) Mark 8. Drain the spinach leaves well after washing and pat dry on kitchen paper, then shred roughly.

2 Melt the butter in a large pan, add the spinach and cook gently until just wilted. Drain thoroughly, squeezing out excess liquid. Season with salt, pepper, and nutmeg if using. Set aside to cool.

3 Knock back the dough on a floured board. Divide in half and roll each piece out thinly to a 23-25cm (9-10 inch) round, according to preferred thickness of pizza. Brush with egg yolk.

4 Top each pizza base with the Parma ham, then the spinach. Transfer to the hot baking sheets and make a small indentation in the centre of the spinach. Bake for 8 minutes.

5 Remove from the oven and crack an egg into the indentation on each pizza.

6 Sprinkle over the cheese and bake for a further 6-8 minutes until the base and egg are cooked. Serve drizzled with extra-virgin olive oil or truffle oil.

NOTES
◆ If you prefer hard-cooked eggs, add them to the pizzas at the start of baking.
◆ You can use 300-350g (10-12oz) frozen leaf spinach in place of fresh. Defrost, drain and squeeze out excess liquid.

3 Increase the setting to 220°C/fan oven 210°C (425°F) Mark 7 and preheat 2 baking sheets in the oven. Squeeze out the flesh from the garlic cloves and reserve.
4 Knock back the dough and divide into 4 pieces. Roll each piece out thinly on a lightly floured board to a 15cm (6 inch) round.
5 Transfer the pizza bases to the hot baking sheets. Drizzle each with a little olive oil and spread with the garlic paste. Scatter over the chilli, top with slices of camembert and bake for 12-15 minutes. Sprinkle with sea salt, pepper and thyme leaves to serve.

VARIATION Instead of roasting the garlic, divide the garlic bulb into individual cloves and blanch these in their skins in boiling water for 20 minutes until soft. Drain, cool slightly, then squeeze out the garlic and chop finely. Spread over the pizza bases as above.

GARLIC AND CAMEMBERT PIZZETTE

Sweet roast garlic gives these small pizzas a wonderful depth of flavour. Alternatively, blanched garlic cloves works well, too (see variation). Serve these pizzette as a starter or snack.

SERVES 4 ◆ PREPARATION 20 minutes, plus rising
◆ COOKING TIME 12-15 minutes ◆ FREEZING Not suitable
◆ 230 CALS PER PIZZETTE

1 quantity Pizza Base Dough (see page 102)
1-2 heads of garlic
2 fresh thyme sprigs
3 tbsp extra-virgin olive oil
1 red chilli, deseeded and cut into thin strips

225g (8oz) camembert cheese, thinly sliced
sea salt and pepper
thyme leaves, to garnish

1 Make the pizza dough and leave to rise for 1 hour or until doubled in size.
2 Meanwhile, cut a thin slice from the top of each garlic bulb and place on a sheet of foil. Top with the thyme sprigs and drizzle with half of the oil. Fold the foil over to enclose and seal the edges to make a parcel. Bake at 200°C/fan oven 190°C (400°F) Mark 6 for 1 hour. Remove from the oven and allow to cool slightly.

FOUR CHEESE PIZZA WITH SUN-DRIED TOMATOES

A tasty pizza with a rich topping of sun-dried tomatoes, mozzarella, dolcelatte, ricotta and Parmesan. Serve accompanied by a crisp, mixed leaf salad.

SERVES 4 ◆ PREPARATION 30 minutes, plus rising ◆ COOKING TIME 10-15 minutes
◆ FREEZING Not suitable ◆ 690 CALS PER SERVING ◆ COLOUR INDEX Page 13

1 quantity Pizza Base Dough (see page 102)
50g (2oz) drained sun-dried tomatoes in oil, sliced
125g (4oz) mozzarella cheese, grated
125g (4oz) dolcelatte cheese, diced
125g (4oz) mascarpone
50g (2oz) Parmesan cheese, freshly grated
5ml (1 tsp) dried oregano
salt and pepper

1 Make the pizza dough and leave to rise for 1 hour or until doubled in size.
2 Preheat a baking sheet on the top shelf of the oven at 230°C/fan oven 220°C (450°F) Mark 8. Knock back the risen dough and divide into 4 equal pieces.
3 On a well floured board, roll out each piece of dough to a thin 18cm (7 inch) round. Top with the sun-dried tomatoes and cheeses, then sprinkle with the oregano and season with salt and pepper to taste.
4 Carefully transfer the pizzas to the hot baking sheet and bake in the oven for 10-15 minutes until bubbling and golden. Serve at once.

NOTE You will need a large baking sheet to take all 4 pizzas; alternatively you may prefer to cook them in 2 batches.

FENNEL AND BRESAOLA PIZZA

SERVES 2-4 ◆ PREPARATION 30 minutes, plus rising
◆ COOKING TIME 18-25 minutes ◆ FREEZING Not suitable
◆ 650-325 CALS PER SERVING

1 quantity Pizza Base Dough (see page 102)
30ml (2 tbsp) extra-virgin olive oil
1 garlic clove, peeled and crushed
400g (14oz) can chopped tomatoes
15ml (1 tbsp) chopped fresh basil
pinch of sugar

salt and pepper
2 fennel bulbs, thinly sliced
25g (1oz) pecorino cheese, freshly grated

TO FINISH
8 slices bresaola or Parma ham
pecorino cheese shavings
extra-virgin olive oil, for drizzling

1 Make the pizza dough and leave to rise for 1 hour or until doubled in size.
2 Meanwhile, put 15ml (1 tbsp) of the oil in a small pan with the garlic, tomatoes, basil, sugar, salt and pepper, and bring to the boil. Lower the heat and simmer, uncovered, for about 20 minutes until thickened. Set aside to cool.
3 Brush the fennel slices with the remaining oil, season lightly and grill for 5-6 minutes on each side until tender and golden.
4 Preheat a baking sheet on the top shelf of the oven at 220°C/fan oven 210°C (425°F) Mark 7. Knock back the dough and roll out thinly on a floured board to a 30-35cm (12-14 inch) round, according to preferred thickness of pizza.
5 Transfer the dough to the hot baking sheet and spread with the tomato sauce. Arrange the fennel over the top, dust with the grated cheese and bake for 18-25 minutes until the base is crisp.
6 On removing the pizza from the oven, immediately top with the slices of bresola and pecorino shavings. Serve at once, drizzled with a little extra-virgin olive oil.

TALEGGIO PIZZETTE WITH PANCETTA AND RED ONION

SERVES 4 ◆ PREPARATION 30 minutes, plus rising ◆ COOKING TIME 30-35 minutes
◆ FREEZING Not suitable ◆ 630 CALS PER SERVING ◆ COLOUR INDEX Page 14

two 140g (5oz) packets pizza-base mix
60ml (4 tbsp) Dijon mustard
50g (2oz) fresh basil leaves
1 red onion, peeled and cut into wedges
4 garlic cloves, peeled and finely sliced

200g (7oz) pancetta or streaky bacon rashers
300g (10oz) taleggio cheese, sliced (see note)
16 fresh thyme sprigs, or 15ml (1 tbsp) dried
pepper
extra-virgin olive oil, for drizzling

1 In a large mixing bowl, make up the pizza-base mix according to the packet instructions. Divide the dough into 4 equal portions. On a lightly floured board, roll each portion out thinly to a 22cm (8½ inch) round.
2 Preheat 2 baking sheets in the oven at 200°C/fan oven 190°C (400°F) Mark 6 for 5-10 minutes.
3 Meanwhile, spread each pizza base with 15ml (1 tbsp) mustard, then scatter over the basil leaves, red onion, garlic and pancetta. Place the taleggio cheese in the middle with the thyme sprigs or a pinch of dried thyme. Season with pepper. Transfer to 2 large greased baking sheets and drizzle lightly with oil.
4 Lift the pizzas on to the hot baking sheets and bake for 30-35 minutes or until golden.

NOTE If taleggio cheese isn't available, use brie or camembert instead.

PISSALADIÈRE PARCEL

In this variation of the famous Provençal onion pizza, meltingly soft onions, goat's cheese and anchovies are baked in a crisp dough crust.

SERVES 6-8 ◆ PREPARATION I hour, plus rising
◆ COOKING TIME 45 minutes- I hour ◆ FREEZING Not suitable
◆ 470-355 CALS PER SERVING ◆ COLOUR INDEX Page 14

YEAST DOUGH
375g (13oz) strong plain white flour
5ml (I tsp) salt
2.5ml (½ tsp) fast-action dried yeast
30ml (2 tbsp) olive oil

FILLING
60ml (4 tbsp) olive oil
900g (2 lb) onions, peeled and finely sliced
3 garlic cloves, peeled and finely sliced

10ml (2 tsp) finely chopped fresh rosemary, or 5ml (I tsp) dried
200g (7oz) goat's cheese, crumbled
8 anchovy fillets, chopped

TO FINISH
beaten egg, for brushing
rosemary sprigs
sea salt, for sprinkling

I For the filling, heat the oil in a pan, then add the onions, garlic and rosemary. Lay a disc of greaseproof paper on top and cover the pan with a tight-fitting lid. Simmer over a low heat for 45 minutes, stirring occasionally, and adding a little water if the onions look dry. Drain the onions, reserving the liquid.

2 Meanwhile make the dough. Sift the flour and salt into a bowl and stir in the yeast. Make a well in the centre. Make the reserved onion liquid up to 300ml (½ pint) with warm water, then add to the well with the oil and mix to a soft dough. Knead for 10 minutes until smooth. Shape into a ball and place in an oiled bowl. Cover the bowl with cling film and leave to rise for 45 minutes or until doubled in size.

3 Mix the goat's cheese and anchovies into the cooked onion mixture.

4 Roll the dough out to a 30cm (12 inch) round. Lift on to a lightly floured baking sheet. Spread the filling over the dough, leaving a 6cm (2½ inch) border all round. Lightly brush the border with water. Bring up the edges of the dough over the filling to make a parcel and press together to seal well.

5 Place another non-stick baking sheet on top of the parcel, then invert both baking sheets to turn the parcel over, so the seal is underneath. Press down lightly, then remove the top baking sheet.

6 Make deep, diagonal slashes across the top of the dough, I cm (½ inch) apart. Leave to prove for 30 minutes or until spongy.

7 Brush the dough lightly with beaten egg, then sprinkle with rosemary and sea salt. Bake at 220°C/fan oven 210°C (425°F) Mark 7 for 45 minutes- I hour until the pastry is crisp, covering with greaseproof paper if it appears to be overbrowning. Leave to stand for 5 minutes before serving.

VARIATION Flavour the filling with finely chopped fresh thyme, rather than rosemary.

MUSHROOM AND CRÈME FRAÎCHE PIZZA

SERVES 2 ◆ PREPARATION 20 minutes, plus rising
◆ COOKING TIME About 15 minutes ◆ FREEZING Not suitable
◆ 1015 CALS PER SERVING

I quantity Pizza Base Dough (see page 102)
15g (½oz) dried porcini mushrooms
60ml (4 tbsp) olive oil
350g (12oz) assorted fresh mushrooms, sliced
I garlic clove, peeled and crushed

15ml (I tbsp) chopped fresh sage
200g (7oz) tub crème fraîche
25g (Ioz) Parmesan cheese, freshly grated
salt and pepper

I Make the pizza dough and leave to rise for I hour or until doubled in size.

2 Meanwhile, for the topping, soak the dried porcini in boiling water to cover for 20 minutes. Drain and pat dry.

3 Heat the oil in a frying pan. Add the sliced mushrooms, porcini, garlic and sage and sauté for 3-4 minutes until just softened and lightly golden. Set aside. Preheat 2 baking sheets in the oven at 230°C/fan oven 220°C (450°F) Mark 8.

4 Knock back the dough, then divide in half. Roll out each half thinly on a lightly floured board to a 23-25cm (9-10 inch) round, according to preferred thickness of pizza.

5 Carefully slide the pizzas on to the hot baking sheets and top with the mushrooms, crème fraîche and Parmesan. Season with salt and pepper to taste. Bake for about 15 minutes until bubbling and golden. Serve at once.

PRAWN AND SWEET CHILLI PIZZA

This recipe is inspired by the flavours of Pacific rim cooking, with lime leaves, ginger and sweet hot chilli jam.

SERVES 2 ◆ PREPARATION 50 minutes, plus rising ◆ COOKING TIME 15-20 minutes
◆ FREEZING Not suitable ◆ 710 CALS PER SERVING

1 quantity Pizza Base Dough (see page 102)

10ml (2 tsp) sesame oil

1 garlic clove, peeled and crushed

5ml (1 tsp) grated fresh root ginger

225g (8oz) cherry tomatoes, halved

4 kaffir lime leaves, finely shredded

12 large raw tiger prawns, peeled and deveined

salt and pepper

few fresh basil, mint and coriander leaves

SWEET CHILLI JAM

1 beef tomato, quartered

1 red onion, peeled and roughly chopped

1 red chilli, seeded and roughly chopped

60ml (4 tbsp) caster sugar

15ml (1 tbsp) dark soy sauce

15ml (1 tbsp) red wine vinegar

1 Start by making the sweet chilli jam. Put the tomato, onion and chilli in a food processor and process briefly until finely chopped. Transfer to a pan, then add the remaining ingredients, seasoning with a little salt. Bring to the boil. Simmer, uncovered, stirring occasionally, for 30 minutes until thickened to a jam-like consistency. Leave until cold.

2 Next, make the pizza dough and leave to rise in a warm place for 1 hour until doubled in size. For the topping, combine the sesame oil, garlic and ginger in a bowl.

3 Preheat 2 baking sheets in the oven at 230°C/fan oven 220°C (450°F) Mark 8. Knock back the dough, then divide in half. Roll out each half thinly on a lightly floured board to a 23-25cm (9-10 inch) round, according to preferred thickness of pizza.

4 Carefully transfer the bases to the hot baking sheets and spread with the sesame oil mixture. Top with the tomatoes, lime leaves and prawns. Season with a little salt and pepper. Bake for 15-20 minutes until the bases are crisp and the prawns are cooked.

5 Scatter over the fresh herbs and top with a little chilli jam. Hand the remaining chilli jam separately.

PIZZA WITH SPINACH, FETA AND PINE NUTS

SERVES 2-4 ◆ PREPARATION 30 minutes, plus rising
◆ COOKING TIME About 15 minutes ◆ FREEZING Not suitable
◆ 1200-600 CALS PER SERVING ◆ COLOUR INDEX Page 14

1 quantity Pizza Base Dough (see page 102)	salt and pepper
45ml (3 tbsp) olive oil, plus extra for drizzling	25g (1oz) raisins (optional)
1 large onion, peeled and thinly sliced	30ml (2 tbsp) sun-dried tomato paste
2 garlic cloves, peeled and crushed	125g (4oz) feta cheese
	150g (5oz) mascarpone cheese
450g (1lb) frozen leaf spinach, thawed and drained	15g (½oz) pine nuts

1 Make the pizza dough and leave to rise for 1 hour or until doubled in size.

2 Preheat 2 baking sheets on the top shelf of the oven at 230°C/fan oven 220°C (450°F) Mark 8. Heat 30ml (2 tbsp) olive oil in a frying pan, add the onion and garlic and fry gently for 10 minutes until softened.

3 Squeeze out excess water from the spinach and chop finely, then mix with the onion, remaining olive oil, seasoning, and raisins if using.

4 Knock back the risen dough and divide in half. Roll out each piece on a lightly floured board to a 23cm (9 inch) round and place on cool baking sheets. Spread each one with tomato paste and top with the spinach mixture.

5 Cream the feta and mascarpone together in a bowl, then dot over the pizza. Sprinkle with the pine nuts.

6 Slide the pizzas on to the hot baking sheets and bake for 15 minutes or until melted and bubbling. Serve at once.

ARTICHOKE AND DOLCELATTE PIZZA

A wonderfully rich pizza, topped with artichoke hearts, olives and dolcelatte cheese.

SERVES 2-4 ◆ PREPARATION 25 minutes, plus rising
◆ COOKING TIME 15-20 minutes ◆ FREEZING Not suitable
◆ 995-495 CALS PER SERVING ◆ COLOUR INDEX Page 14

1 quantity Pizza Base Dough (see page 102)	175g (6oz) dolcelatte cheese, derinded and diced
TOPPING	10ml (2 tsp) dried oregano
45ml (3 tbsp) sun-dried tomato paste	25g (1oz) Parmesan cheese, freshly grated
400g (14oz) can artichoke hearts, drained, rinsed and halved	pepper
25g (1oz) pitted black olives	extra-virgin olive oil, for drizzling

1 Make the pizza dough and leave to rise for 1 hour or until doubled in size.

2 Preheat a baking sheet on the top shelf of the oven at 230°C/fan oven 220°C (450°F) Mark 8. Knock back the risen dough and roll out on a lightly floured board to a 30cm (12 inch) round.

3 Using fingertips and thumbs, form a shallow rim around the edge of the dough. Prick with a fork.

4 Transfer the dough to a lightly greased baking sheet and spread with the tomato paste. Scatter over the artichokes, olives, dolcelatte, oregano, Parmesan and pepper to taste.

5 Slide the pizza on to the hot baking sheet and bake for 15-20 minutes until the base is crisp and the topping is golden. Drizzle with olive oil and serve with a tomato salad.

PIZZA CALAMARI

Thin pizza bases, spread with a fresh-tasting tomato salsa and baked until crisp, then served topped with a tangle of crisp fried squid – drizzled with a lemon dressing.

SERVES 2 ◆ PREPARATION 35 minutes, plus rising ◆ COOKING TIME 12-15 minutes
◆ FREEZING Not suitable ◆ 810 CALS PER SERVING

1 quantity Pizza Base Dough (see page 102)	**TOMATO SALSA**
	15ml (1 tbsp) extra-virgin olive oil
TOPPING	4 ripe plum tomatoes, diced
15ml (1 tbsp) extra-virgin olive oil	2 garlic cloves, peeled and finely chopped
350g (12oz) large squid, cleaned and sliced into strips, tentacles reserved whole (if wished)	4 spring onions, finely sliced
	1 red chilli, deseeded and finely chopped
DRESSING	15ml (1 tbsp) chopped fresh coriander leaves
30ml (2 tbsp) extra-virgin olive oil	salt and pepper
10ml (2 tsp) lemon juice	

1 Make the pizza dough and leave to rise for 1 hour or until doubled in size. Preheat 2 baking sheets in the oven at 230°C/fan oven 220°C (450°F) Mark 8.

2 To make the tomato salsa, combine all of the ingredients in a bowl, seasoning with salt and pepper to taste.

3 Knock back the dough, then divide in half. Roll out each half thinly on a lightly floured board to a 23-25cm (9-10 inch) round, according to preferred thickness of pizza. Carefully transfer to the hot baking sheets and spread with the tomato salsa. Bake for 12-15 minutes until crisp.

4 Meanwhile, for the topping, heat the oil in a large, non-stick frying pan. Fry the squid strips and tentacles, if using, in batches over a high heat for 2-4 minutes until crisp, adding extra oil as necessary; drain on kitchen paper. For the dressing, whisk the oil and lemon juice together in a bowl to combine; season with salt and pepper.

5 Arrange the squid on top of the pizzas and drizzle with the lemon dressing. Serve immediately.

PROSCIUTTO AND FONTINA CALZONE

Calzone is simply a regular pizza folded in half before baking to form a 'double crust' pizza.

SERVES 2-4 ◆ PREPARATION 25 minutes, plus rising
◆ COOKING TIME About 20 minutes ◆ FREEZING Not suitable
◆ 1480-740 CALS PER SERVING

2 x quantity Pizza Base Dough (see page 102)
15-30ml (1-2 tbsp) olive oil
8 slices Parma ham
75g (3oz) drained sun-dried tomatoes in oil, roughly chopped

8-10 fresh basil leaves
225g (8oz) fontina cheese, diced

1 Make the pizza dough and leave to rise in a warm place for 1 hour until doubled in size.

2 Preheat a large baking sheet on the middle shelf of the oven at 220°C/fan oven 210°C (425°F) Mark 7. Knock back the risen dough on a floured board and divide in half. Wrap one half in cling film.

3 Roll out the other half of the dough thinly to a 30cm (12 inch) round.

4 Brush the dough with half the olive oil, then arrange half of the Parma ham, sun-dried tomatoes, basil leaves and cheese over one half of the round.

5 Brush the edges with water and fold the dough over the filling, pressing the edges together to seal. Repeat to make 2 calzone. Place a roasting tin half filled with hot water in the bottom of the oven.

6 Carefully transfer the calzone to the hot baking sheet and bake in the oven for 18-22 minutes until risen and golden. Allow to cool slightly for a few minutes before serving.

NOTE Steam from the roasting tin of water in the bottom of the oven helps to keep the calzone crust moist.

4 Knock back the dough on a floured surface, roll out and use to line a 35x23cm (13x9 inch) Swiss roll tin. Scatter over the cooked beetroot and juices, chopped sage and cheese.

5 Place the tin on the hot baking sheet and bake the pizza for 20-25 minutes until risen and golden. Leave in the tin for 10 minutes, then carefully transfer to a wire rack and leave until cold. Serve cut into squares.

NOTE If taleggio cheese is unobtainable, use brie instead.

VARIATION To serve hot, use 1 quantity of Pizza Base Dough. Shape into 2 thin pizzas, apply the topping as above and bake for 10-12 minutes.

ROASTED ONION AND OLIVE CALZONE

This folded pizza encloses a delicious filling of roasted red onions, olive paste and melting cheese.

SERVES 4 ◆ PREPARATION 40 minutes, plus rising ◆ COOKING TIME 15 minutes
◆ FREEZING Suitable ◆ 475 CALS PER SERVING ◆ COLOUR INDEX Page 15

1 quantity Pizza Base Dough (see page 102)	**5ml (1 tsp) grated lemon rind**
FILLING	**60ml (4 tbsp) olive oil**
4 red onions, peeled and cut into wedges	**125g (4oz) ricotta cheese**
1 garlic clove, peeled and crushed	**125g (4oz) fontina or mozzarella cheese, diced**
5ml (1 tsp) chopped fresh rosemary	**30ml (2 tbsp) olive paste**
	salt and pepper

1 Make up the pizza base dough and leave to rise for 1 hour or until doubled in size.

2 Meanwhile, make the filling. Place the onions in a roasting tin with the garlic, rosemary and lemon rind, add the oil and toss well. Roast at 230°C/fan oven 220°C (450°F) Mark 8 for 30 minutes, stirring occasionally until the onions are softened and browned. Turn into a bowl; allow to cool.

3 Add the ricotta, fontina or mozzarella, and olive paste to the cooled onion mixture. Season with salt and pepper to taste. Preheat a baking sheet on the top shelf of the oven.

4 Knock back the risen dough and divide into 4 equal pieces. Keeping the other 3 pieces covered with cling film, roll out one piece thinly on a floured board to a 20cm (8 inch) round.

5 Spoon a quarter of the onion mixture on to one half of the dough and dampen the edges with a little water. Fold over the other half of the dough and press the edges together well to seal. Repeat to make 4 calzone in total.

6 Transfer the calzone to the hot baking sheet and bake on the top shelf of the oven for 15 minutes until puffed up slightly and golden. Leave to stand for 5 minutes, then serve with a tomato salad.

BEETROOT AND TALEGGIO PIZZA

This deep-base pizza is great served cold as a picnic food. It is also delicious eaten hot (see variation).

SERVES 6-8 ◆ PREPARATION 1½ hours ◆ COOKING TIME 20-25 minutes
◆ FREEZING Not suitable ◆ 445-335 CALS PER SERVING

1½ x quantity Pizza Base Dough (see page 102)	**salt and pepper**
450g (1lb) baby or small beetroot, trimmed	**15ml (1 tbsp) balsamic vinegar**
2 garlic cloves, peeled and crushed	**15ml (1 tbsp) chopped fresh sage**
2 fresh sage sprigs	**350g (12oz) taleggio cheese, derinded and cut into 1cm (½ inch) cubes**
30ml (2 tbsp) olive oil	

1 Make the pizza dough and leave to rise for 1 hour or until doubled in size.

2 Meanwhile, cut the beetroot into small wedges and place in a small roasting pan. Sprinkle with the garlic, sage sprigs, 15ml (1 tbsp) oil and 30ml (2 tbsp) water. Season with salt and pepper.

3 Roast in the oven at 200°C/fan oven 190°C (400°F) Mark 6 for 30 minutes, then add the balsamic vinegar and bake for a further 15 minutes. Allow to cool. Place a baking sheet on the top shelf of the oven to heat.

FOCCACIA PIZZA

Topped with fresh plum tomatoes, melting mozzarella and anchovies, this half pizza, half bread makes a sustaining snack.

SERVES 6-8 ◆ PREPARATION 30 minutes, plus rising
◆ COOKING TIME 30 minutes ◆ FREEZING Not suitable
◆ 465-350 CALS PER SERVING

450g (1lb) strong plain white flour

10ml (2 tsp) fast-action dried yeast

10ml (2 tsp) sea salt

15ml (1 tbsp) fresh thyme leaves

15ml (1 tbsp) chopped fresh rosemary

60ml (4 tbsp) olive oil

280-300ml (9-10 floz) warm water

TOPPING

6 ripe plum tomatoes, sliced

200g (7oz) buffalo mozzarella cheese, thinly sliced

50g (2oz) canned anchovy fillets, drained and sliced

25g (1oz) Parmesan cheese, freshly grated

extra-virgin olive oil, for drizzling

1 Sift the flour into a bowl, then stir in the yeast, salt and herbs. Make a well in the centre and gradually work in the olive oil and enough warm water to form a soft dough. Knead for 10 minutes.

2 Transfer the dough to an oiled bowl, cover and leave to rise in a warm place for 1 hour until doubled in size.

3 Knock back the dough on a floured board and roll out to a 5mm (¼ inch) thick round. Transfer to an oiled baking sheet, cover loosely with oiled cling film and leave to rise for a further 30 minutes.

4 Carefully arrange the sliced plum tomatoes and mozzarella cheese evenly over the dough, in neat rows, starting and ending with a row of tomatoes. Scatter over the anchovies and grated Parmesan.

5 Drizzle with olive oil and bake at 200°C/fan oven 190°C (400°F) Mark 6 for 30 minutes or until risen and golden. Transfer to a wire rack to cool. Serve warm.

BREADS

Traditional farmhouse loaves and nutty wholegrain
breads, plus a tempting collection of savoury breads
which are as satisfying to make as they are to eat

FARMHOUSE LOAF

MAKES I LOAF; 16 SLICES ◆ PREPARATION 20 minutes, plus rising
◆ COOKING TIME 30-35 minutes ◆ FREEZING Suitable ◆ 160 CALS PER SLICE
◆ COLOUR INDEX Page 16

575g (1¼lb) strong plain white flour	7g sachet fast-action dried yeast (see note)
125g (4oz) strong plain wholemeal flour	25g (1oz) butter, diced
15ml (1 tbsp) salt	450ml (¾ pint) warm water (approximately)
5ml (1 tsp) caster sugar	extra flour, for sprinkling

I Sift the white flour into a bowl and stir in the wholemeal flour, salt, sugar and yeast. Rub in the butter. Make a well in the centre and add the warm water. Work to a smooth, soft dough, adding a little extra water if necessary.

2 Knead for 10 minutes until smooth, then shape into a ball and place in an oiled bowl. Cover with a tea-towel and leave to rise in a warm place for 1-2 hours, until doubled in bulk.

3 Knock back the dough on a lightly floured surface. Shape into a large oval loaf and place on a floured baking sheet, or press into an oiled 900g (2lb) loaf tin. Cover loosely and leave to rise for a further 30 minutes.

4 Slash the top of the loaf with a knife, sprinkle with a little flour and bake at 230°C/fan oven 220°C (450°F) Mark 8 for 15 minutes. Reduce oven setting to 200°C/fan oven 190°C (400°F) Mark 6 and bake for a further 15-20 minutes or until the bread is risen and sounds hollow when tapped underneath. Cool on a wire rack.

NOTE If available, use 15g (½oz) fresh yeast instead of dried. Crumble into a bowl, add the sugar, 150ml (¼ pint) of the warm water and 60ml (4 tbsp) of the plain flour. Stir well to dissolve the yeast, then leave in a warm place for 20 minutes until very frothy. Continue as above, adding the frothy yeast to the dry ingredients with the rest of the water.

VARIATION

WHOLEMEAL BREAD Use 225g (8oz) white flour and 450g (1lb) wholemeal flour. Increase the fast-action dried yeast to 1½ sachets (or use 20g/¾oz fresh yeast).

GRANARY BREAD

MAKES I LOAF; 16 SLICES ◆ PREPARATION 20 minutes, plus rising
◆ COOKING TIME 30-35 minutes ◆ FREEZING Suitable ◆ 155 CALS PER SLICE
◆ COLOUR INDEX Page 16

125g (4oz) strong plain wholemeal flour	7g sachet fast-action dried yeast (see note)
450g (1lb) malted strong granary flour	150ml (¼ pint) warm milk
10ml (2 tsp) salt	300ml (½ pint) warm water (approximately)
15g (½oz) butter, diced	15ml (1 tbsp) malt extract
125g (4oz) rolled oats	rolled oats, for dusting

I Put the flours into a bowl and stir in the salt. Rub in the butter, then stir in the oats and yeast. Make a well in the centre and add the warm milk, water and malt extract. Work to a soft dough, adding a little extra water if necessary.

2 Knead for 10 minutes until smooth, then shape into a ball and place in an oiled bowl. Cover with a tea-towel and leave to rise in a warm place for 1-2 hours until doubled in bulk.

3 Knock back the dough on a lightly floured surface and shape into a large round. Place on a baking sheet, cover and leave to rise for a further 30 minutes.

4 Cut a cross on top of the loaf and sprinkle with oats. Bake at 230°C/fan oven 220°C (450°F) Mark 8 for 15 minutes. Reduce oven setting to 200°C/fan oven 190°C (400°F) Mark 6 and bake for a further 15-20 minutes or until the bread sounds hollow when tapped underneath. Cool on a wire rack.

NOTE If available, use 20g (¾oz) fresh yeast instead of dried. Proceed as for Farmhouse Loaf (see note, left).

HOMESTYLE CIABATTA

This polenta enriched dough resembles home-baked breads found in Italy, more closely than our familiar supermarket ciabattas. Its lengthy rising time is well worth the wait. Delicious plain or toasted – drizzled with extra-virgin olive oil.

MAKES 2 LOAVES; EACH 10 SLICES ◆ PREPARATION 25 minutes, plus standing
◆ COOKING TIME 30-35 minutes ◆ FREEZING Suitable ◆ 165 CALS PER SLICE

15g (½oz) fresh yeast (or 7g sachet fast-action dried yeast)	5ml (1 tsp) caster sugar
450-500ml (15-16fl oz) warm water	15ml (1 tbsp) olive oil
10ml (2 tsp) salt	675g (1½lb) strong plain white flour
	225g (8oz) polenta or cornmeal

I Blend the yeast with 150ml/¼ pint of the water until smooth. Combine the remaining ingredients in a bowl and work in the yeast mixture and enough of the remaining water to form a soft dough. Shape into a ball and place in an oiled bowl. Cover with oiled cling film and leave to rise for 3 hours.

2 Knock back the dough on a lightly floured surface for 2-3 minutes. Divide in half and place each piece in a large oiled polythene bag; tie to seal. Refrigerate for 24 hours.

3 The following day, remove dough from refrigerator 1 hour before baking. Knead gently on a floured surface and shape each into an oval. Tap to flatten and transfer the doughs to a large, floured baking sheet. Cover with oiled cling film and leave to rise in a warm place for 1 hour until doubled in size.

4 Place a small roasting pan half-filled with warm water in the bottom of the oven at 230°C/fan oven 220°C (450°F) Mark 8 and heat for 1-2 minutes, then put the breads into the oven. Bake for 15 minutes, then lower the setting to 190°C/fan oven 180°C (375°F) Mark 5. Bake for a further 15-20 minutes or until the bread is golden and sounds hollow when tapped underneath. Cool on a wire rack.

SOURDOUGH

A starter dough is made, then left to stand for a few days before being added to the bread dough. This bread has a characteristic slightly sour flavour and keeps well, wrapped in foil, for up to 3 days. The starter dough can be kept on the go for as long as you require. To replenish it, simply add a little of the frothed yeast each time you make a loaf.

MAKES 1 LOAF; 16 SLICES ◆ PREPARATION 20 minutes, plus standing and rising
◆ COOKING TIME 35-40 minutes ◆ FREEZING Suitable ◆ 175 CALS PER SLICE

SOURDOUGH STARTER
15g (½oz) fresh yeast (see note)

600ml (1 pint) warm water

225g (8oz) strong plain white flour

BREAD DOUGH
15g (½oz) fresh yeast (see note)

15ml (1 tbsp) caster sugar

400-450ml (14-15fl oz) warm water

450g (1lb) strong plain white flour

225g (8oz) rye flour

15ml (1 tbsp) salt

125ml (4fl oz) starter dough

1 Make the sourdough starter 3 days in advance. Mix the yeast with a little of the warm water in a bowl. Stir in the remaining water and flour until smooth. Cover with a damp tea-towel and leave in a warm, dark place for 3 days, stirring and spraying with a little water from time to time.

2 To make the bread, in a small bowl, cream the yeast with the sugar, a little of the water and a little of the white flour until smooth. Leave to froth in a warm place for 10 minutes. (Add a tablespoon of this frothed mixture to the starter.)

3 Mix the remaining flours and salt in a bowl and gradually work in 125ml (4fl oz) of the starter dough, the frothed yeast mixture and enough of the remaining water to form a soft dough. Knead for 10 minutes.

4 Shape the dough into a ball and place in an oiled bowl. Cover with a tea-towel and leave to rise in a warm place for 1½ hours or until doubled in size.

5 Knock back the dough on a lightly floured surface and shape into a flattish round. Carefully score the surface in a diamond pattern. Place on a floured baking sheet, cover with oiled cling film and leave to rise for 30 minutes.

6 Bake at 230°C/fan oven 220°C (450°F) Mark 8 for 15 minutes, then lower the setting to 190°C/fan oven 180°C (375°F) Mark 5 and bake for a further 20-25 minutes until the bread sounds hollow when tapped underneath. Transfer to a wire rack to cool.

NOTE Fresh yeast is traditional for a sourdough, but easy blend dried yeast works successfully. Substitute a 7g sachet fast-action dried yeast for each of the fresh yeast quantities.

5 Bake at 230°C/fan oven 220°C (425°F) Mark 8 for 30-35 minutes until the bread is risen and sounds hollow when tapped underneath. Leave in the tin for 10 minutes, then transfer to a wire rack to cool.

NOTE If you prefer to use fresh yeast, blend 20g (¾oz) with the sugar, 150ml (¼ pint) of the water and 60ml (4 tbsp) of the wholemeal flour until smooth; leave to froth in a warm place for 10 minutes. Add at stage 2.

MULTIGRAIN LOAF

Enriched with sunflower, poppy and sesame seeds, this moist granary bread has a superb nutty taste.

MAKES 2 LOAVES; EACH 12 SLICES ◆ PREPARATION 20 minutes, plus rising
◆ COOKING TIME 30-35 minutes ◆ FREEZING Suitable ◆ 115 CALS PER SLICE
◆ COLOUR INDEX Page 16

225g (8oz) strong plain wholemeal flour
350g (12oz) strong granary flour
125g (4oz) rye flour
25g (1oz) butter, diced
10ml (2 tsp) salt
7g sachet fast-action dried yeast (see note)
5ml (1 tsp) caster sugar
40g (1½oz) rolled oats or barley, or millet flakes

30ml (2 tbsp) each sesame seeds, poppy seeds and sunflower seeds
450ml (¾ pint) warm water
30ml (2 tbsp) malt extract

TO FINISH
egg, beaten with a little water, to glaze
few extra sesame, poppy and sunflower seeds

1 Mix the wholemeal, granary and rye flours together in a large bowl. Rub in the butter, then stir in all the remaining dry ingredients.
2 Make a well in the centre and gradually work in the warm water and malt extract to form a soft dough.
3 Knead the dough for 10 minutes, then transfer to an oiled bowl, cover with oiled cling film and leave to rise in a warm place for 2 hours or until doubled in size.
4 Lightly oil two 900g (2lb) loaf tins. Knock back the dough, divide in half and shape each one into an oblong.
5 Press into the prepared tins, cover loosely with oiled cling film and leave to rise for 30 minutes until the dough reaches the top of the tins.
6 Carefully brush each loaf with egg glaze and scatter over some extra seeds. Bake at 220°C/fan oven 210°C (425°F) Mark 7 for 30-35 minutes until the breads are risen and golden brown. To test whether the loaves are cooked, tap them on the base – they should sound hollow. Leave in the tins for 10 minutes, then transfer to a wire rack to cool.

NOTE If available, use 20g (¾oz) fresh yeast instead of dried. Blend with the sugar, 150ml (¼ pint) of the water and 60ml (4 tbsp) of the wholemeal flour until smooth; leave to froth in a warm place for 10 minutes. Add at stage 2.

SEEDED BARLEY BREAD

This 'healthy' nutty, seeded loaf has a delicious flavour. It is great toasted or dunked into soups.

MAKES 1 LARGE LOAF; 18 SLICES ◆ PREPARATION 20 minutes, plus rising
◆ COOKING TIME 30-35 minutes ◆ FREEZING Suitable ◆ 170 CALS PER SLICE

225g (8oz) pearl barley
225g (8oz) strong plain white flour
225g (8oz) strong plain wholemeal flour
15ml (1 tbsp) salt
15ml (1 tbsp) caster sugar

1½ x 7g sachets fast-action dried yeast (see note)
125g (4oz) sunflower seeds
60ml (4 tbsp) poppy seeds
30ml (2 tbsp) linseed
400-450ml (14-15fl oz) warm water

1 Dry-fry the pearl barley in a heavy-based frying pan over a low heat for about 5 minutes until lightly browned. Cool slightly, then grind in batches to a coarse-grained flour, using a spice grinder or blender.
2 Combine the flours, salt, ground barley flour, sugar, yeast, and all of the seeds in a bowl. Gradually work in sufficient warm water to form a soft dough.
3 Knead for 10 minutes until smooth, then shape into a ball and place in an oiled bowl. Cover with a tea-towel and leave to rise in a warm place for 1½-2 hours, until doubled in size.
4 Knock back the dough on a lightly floured surface, shape into an oval and press into a lightly oiled 900g (2lb) loaf tin. Cover loosely with oiled cling film and leave to rise for a further 45 minutes.

APRICOT AND HAZELNUT BREAD

MAKES 2 LOAVES; EACH 12 SLICES ◆ PREPARATION 20 minutes, plus rising
◆ COOKING TIME 30-35 minutes ◆ FREEZING Suitable ◆ 125 CALS PER SLICE
◆ COLOUR INDEX Page 17

450g (1lb) strong granary flour

225g (8oz) strong plain white flour

10ml (2 tsp) salt

25g (1oz) butter, diced

75g (3oz) hazelnuts, toasted and chopped

75g (3oz) ready-to-eat dried apricots, chopped

7g sachet fast-action dried yeast

30ml (2 tbsp) molasses

350ml (12fl oz) warm water

milk, for brushing

1 Put the flours into a large bowl. Add the salt, then rub in the butter. Stir in the hazelnuts, dried apricots and dried yeast.
2 Make a well in the centre and gradually work in the molasses and warm water to form a soft dough.
3 Knead for 8-10 minutes until smooth, then transfer the dough to an oiled bowl. Cover with a tea-towel and leave to rise in a warm place for 1-1½ hours until doubled in size.
4 Preheat a large baking sheet on the top shelf of the oven set at 220°C/fan oven 210°C (425°F) Mark 7. Knock back the dough, then divide in half. Shape each portion into a small flattish round and place on a floured baking sheet. Cover loosely and leave to rise for a further 30 minutes.
5 Using a sharp knife, cut several slashes on each round, brush with a little milk and transfer to the heated baking sheet. Bake for 15 minutes, then reduce the oven setting to 190°C/fan oven 180°C (375°F) Mark 5 and bake for a further 15-20 minutes or until the bread is risen and sounds hollow when tapped underneath. Cool on a wire rack.

SODA BREAD

MAKES 1 LOAF; 14-16 SLICES ◆ PREPARATION 15 minutes
◆ COOKING TIME 30-35 minutes ◆ FREEZING Suitable ◆ 125-110 CALS PER SLICE
◆ COLOUR INDEX Page 17

350g (12oz) plain wholemeal flour

125g (4oz) coarse oatmeal

10ml (2 tsp) bicarbonate of soda

5ml (1 tsp) salt

5ml (1 tsp) thin honey

300ml (½ pint) buttermilk

30-45ml (2-3 tbsp) milk

1 Combine all of the dry ingredients in a large bowl. Make a well in the centre and gradually beat in the honey, buttermilk and enough milk to form a soft dough.
2 Knead for 5 minutes until smooth. Shape the dough into a 20cm (8 inch) round and place on a lightly oiled baking sheet.
3 Using a sharp knife, cut a deep cross on top of the dough. Brush with a little milk and bake at 200°C/fan oven 190°C (400°F) Mark 6 for 30-35 minutes until the bread is slightly risen and sounds hollow when tapped underneath. Cool on a wire rack; eat the same day.

CORNBREAD

MAKES 1 LOAF; 16 SLICES ◆ PREPARATION 15 minutes, plus rising
◆ COOKING TIME 25-30 minutes ◆ FREEZING Suitable ◆ 125 CALS PER SLICE
◆ COLOUR INDEX Page 17

225g (8oz) coarse cornmeal

225g (8oz) strong plain white flour

7g sachet fast-action dried yeast

5ml (1 tsp) salt

2.5ml (½ tsp) caster sugar

400ml (14fl oz) milk

15g (½oz) butter or margarine

1 Combine the dry ingredients in a bowl. Heat the milk and butter in a pan until the butter is melted, cool until tepid, then work into the dry ingredients to form a soft dough.
2 Knead for 8-10 minutes until smooth, then transfer the dough to a greased bowl. Cover with a tea-towel and leave to rise in a warm place for 1-1½ hours until doubled in size.
3 Oil a 20cm (8 inch) square cake tin. Knock back the dough and shape into a square a little smaller than the prepared tin. Press into the tin, cover loosely and leave to rise for a further 30 minutes.
4 Bake at 220°C/fan oven 210°C (425°F) Mark 7 for 25-30 minutes until risen and golden. Leave in tin for 10 minutes, then transfer to a wire rack. Serve cold, cut into fingers.

HERBED CHEESE STICK

MAKES 2 LOAVES; EACH SERVES 4 ◆ PREPARATION 20 minutes, plus rising
◆ COOKING TIME 25 minutes ◆ FREEZING Suitable ◆ 240 CALS PER SERVING
◆ COLOUR INDEX Page 17

450g (1lb) strong plain white flour

5ml (1 tsp) salt

½ x 7g sachet fast-action dried yeast

15ml (1 tbsp) dried herbes de Provence

25g (1oz) gruyère cheese, finely grated

250-300ml (9-10fl oz) warm water

30ml (2 tbsp) olive oil

50g (2oz) sultanas

2 fresh rosemary sprigs

1 Sift the flour and salt into a bowl and stir in the yeast, herbs and cheese. Make a well in the centre and gradually work in sufficient warm water and the oil to make a soft dough. Knead for 10 minutes.
2 Turn the dough on to a lightly floured surface and knead in the sultanas. Shape into a ball and place in an oiled bowl. Cover with a tea-towel and leave to rise in a warm place for 1 hour or until doubled in size.
3 Knock back the dough on a lightly floured surface, divide in half and shape each piece into a baton. Place on a large baking sheet and sprinkle with flour. Slash along the length of each stick and top with the rosemary sprigs. Cover loosely and leave to rise for a further 30 minutes.
4 Bake at 220°C/fan oven 210°C (425°F) Mark 7 for about 25 minutes until risen and golden. Transfer to a wire rack to cool slightly. Serve warm.

BEER BREAD

MAKES I LARGE OVAL LOAF; 20 SLICES ◆ PREPARATION 20 minutes, plus rising ◆ COOKING TIME 35-40 minutes ◆ FREEZING Suitable ◆ 155 CALS PER SLICE

250g (9oz) buckwheat flour
350g (12oz) wholemeal bread flour
225g (8oz) strong plain white flour
10ml (2 tsp) salt
7g sachet fast-action dried yeast

375ml (13fl oz) stout or other strong, dark beer
25g (1oz) butter, melted
125ml (4fl oz) warm water
15ml (1 tbsp) thin honey, warmed
TO GLAZE
30ml (2 tbsp) thin honey, warmed

1 Mix the flours and salt in a large bowl and stir in the yeast. Make a well in the centre. Gradually work in the beer, melted butter, warm water and honey to form a soft dough.
2 Knead for 10 minutes until smooth, then shape the dough into a ball and place in an oiled bowl. Cover with a tea-towel and leave to rise in a warm place for 1-1½ hours or until doubled in size.
3 Heat a clean terracotta tile, pizza stone or baking sheet on the middle oven shelf at 200°C/fan oven 190°C (400°F) Mark 6.
4 Knock back the dough on a lightly floured surface and shape into a large oval. Place on a well floured baking sheet, slash the top in several places with a sharp knife and cover with oiled cling film. Leave to rise for a further 45 minutes.
5 Carefully transfer the risen dough to the hot tile or stone and bake for 35-40 minutes until the bread is risen and sounds hollow when tapped underneath. On removing from the oven, brush with the warm honey. Cool on a wire rack.

DARK RYE BREAD

A dense, moist loaf with the distinctive flavour of molasses which keeps well, wrapped in foil, for up to 3 days. It is best eaten thinly sliced, plain or toasted, with butter and jam.

MAKES 2 LOAVES; EACH 10 SLICES ◆ PREPARATION 20 minutes, plus rising ◆ COOKING TIME 40-45 minutes ◆ FREEZING Suitable ◆ 135 CALS PER SLICE

150ml (¼ pint) warm milk
20ml (1½ tbsp) molasses
225g (8oz) wholemeal bread flour
450g (1lb) rye flour
7g sachet fast-action dried yeast

10ml (2 tsp) salt
15ml (1 tbsp) caraway seeds
25g (1oz) butter, melted
275-300ml (9-10fl oz) buttermilk

1 Mix the warm milk with the molasses.
2 Combine the flours, yeast, salt and caraway seeds in a bowl. Make a well in the centre and add the molasses mixture, butter and enough buttermilk to form a soft, tacky dough.
3 Knead for 10 minutes until the dough is smooth, then transfer to an oiled bowl, cover with a tea-towel and leave to rise in a warm place for 2 hours.
4 Knock back the dough on a lightly floured surface, divide in half and press into two oiled 450g (1lb) loaf tins. Cover with oiled cling film and leave to rise for a further 1 hour.
5 Bake at 190°C/fan oven 180°C (375°F) Mark 5 for 40-45 minutes until the bread sounds hollow when tapped underneath. Leave in the tins for 10 minutes, then transfer to a wire rack to cool.

CHEESE AND ONION BREAD

MAKES 2 LOAVES; EACH SERVES 4 ◆ PREPARATION 20 minutes, plus rising
◆ COOKING TIME 25-30 minutes ◆ FREEZING Not suitable
◆ 115 CALS PER SERVING ◆ COLOUR INDEX Page 17

450g (1lb) strong plain white flour	**TOPPING**
5ml (1 tsp) salt	**1 red onion, peeled and finely sliced**
½ x 7g sachet fast-action dried yeast	**10ml (2 tsp) chopped fresh thyme**
2.5ml (½ tsp) caster sugar	**50g (2oz) Cheddar cheese, grated**
300ml (½ pint) warm water	**pepper**
	oil, for brushing

1 Sift the flour and salt into a bowl, stir in the yeast and sugar, then make a well in the centre. Gradually work in the warm water to form a soft dough.

2 Knead for 8-10 minutes until smooth and elastic, then transfer the dough to an oiled bowl. Cover with a tea-towel and leave to rise in a warm place for 1-1½ hours until doubled in size.

3 Knock back the dough, divide in half and knead briefly. Roll each portion out to a 20cm (8 inch) flat round, transfer to a well floured baking sheet or board, cover loosely and leave to rise for a further 30 minutes.

4 Meanwhile, for the topping, mix the onion with the thyme, cheese and pepper.

5 Brush a cast-iron griddle or ovenproof skillet with oil and heat until starting to smoke. Carefully transfer one dough round to the pan, immediately lower the heat and cook for 10 minutes until the base is golden.

6 Remove from the heat and sprinkle half the onion mixture on top of the bread. Bake at 200°C/fan oven 190°C (400°F) Mark 6 for 15-20 minutes or until the dough is risen and firm to the touch.

7 In the meantime, repeat to make the second loaf. Transfer to a wire rack to cool. Serve warm.

CHILLI CORNBREAD

MAKES 1 LOAF; 10 SLICES ◆ PREPARATION 20 minutes
◆ COOKING TIME 45 minutes ◆ FREEZING Suitable ◆ 150 CALS PER SLICE
◆ COLOUR INDEX Page 17

1 large egg	**pinch of cayenne pepper**
200ml (7fl oz) Greek yogurt	**1 large red chilli, deseeded and finely chopped**
25g (1oz) butter, melted	**75g (3oz) spring onions, finely sliced**
150g (5oz) fine cornmeal	**125g (4oz) canned sweetcorn kernels, drained**
25g (1oz) potato flour	**50g (2oz) Parmesan cheese, freshly grated**
15ml (1 tbsp) baking powder	
5ml (1 tsp) salt	

1 Base-line a 450g (1lb) non-stick loaf tin with non-stick baking parchment. In a large bowl, whisk the egg until frothy, then stir in the yogurt and melted butter.

2 Stir in the cornmeal, potato flour, baking powder, salt and cayenne pepper. Add the remaining ingredients and mix until thoroughly combined.

3 Turn the mixture into the prepared loaf tin and bake at 180°C/fan oven 170°C (350°F) Mark 4 for 45 minutes or until a skewer inserted into the centre comes out clean.

4 Leave in the tin for 10 minutes, then turn out on to a wire rack to cool. When completely cold, cut into slices and serve.

SPICED NAAN

This Indian stuffed naan bread has a wonderful, spicy filling and is surprisingly easy to make.

MAKES 4 ◆ PREPARATION 30 minutes, plus rising ◆ COOKING TIME 10-12 minutes
◆ FREEZING Not suitable ◆ 395 CALS PER NAAN ◆ COLOUR INDEX Page 17

350g (12oz) strong plain white flour	**5ml (1 tsp) grated fresh root ginger**
5ml (1 tsp) salt	**10ml (2 tsp) ground coriander**
½ x 7g sachet fast-action dried yeast	**5ml (1 tsp) ground cumin**
5ml (1 tsp) thin honey	**5ml (1 tsp) ground cinnamon**
175ml (6fl oz) warm water	**pinch of chilli powder**
15g (½oz) butter, melted	**25g (1oz) sultanas, chopped**
FILLING	**25g (1oz) desiccated coconut**
25g (1oz) butter or margarine, melted	**30ml (2 tbsp) water**
1 onion, peeled and diced	
2 garlic cloves, peeled and crushed	

1 Sift the flour and salt into a bowl and stir in the yeast. Make a well in the centre and gradually work in the honey, warm water and melted butter to form a soft dough.

2 Knead for 8-10 minutes until smooth and elastic, then transfer the dough to a greased bowl. Cover and leave to rise in a warm place for 1-1½ hours until doubled in size.

3 Meanwhile, prepare the filling. Melt the butter in a frying pan, add the onion, garlic, ginger and spices and fry gently for 10-15 minutes until softened. Stir in the sultanas, coconut and water. Cover and simmer for 10 minutes. Set aside to cool.

4 Knock back the dough and divide into 4 pieces. Roll each out to a 20cm (8 inch) round. Divide the filling between the rounds, spreading it over one half of each round.

5 Fold the bread over and carefully reshape, pressing the edges together to seal. Roll out again, to form flat ovals, about 20cm (8 inch) long. Transfer the breads to a well floured baking sheet, cover loosely and leave to rise for 15 minutes. Meanwhile, preheat a large baking sheet on the top shelf of the oven at 230°C/fan oven 220°C (450°F) Mark 8.

6 Carefully transfer the breads to the hot baking sheet and bake for 10-12 minutes until puffed up and golden. Serve hot.

WALNUT AND CRANBERRY BREAD

A savoury loaf with a hint of sweetness from dried cranberries makes the perfect breakfast treat, toasted and served warm with butter and jam. This bread will keep for 2 days, wrapped in foil; it is also good toasted.

MAKES 2 LOAVES; EACH 10 SLICES ◆ PREPARATION 20 minutes, plus rising
◆ COOKING TIME 30 minutes ◆ FREEZING Suitable ◆ 185 CALS PER SLICE
◆ FREEZING Suitable

225g (8oz) strong plain wholemeal flour
450g (1lb) malted granary flour
15ml (1 tbsp) salt
125g (4oz) rolled oats
two 7g sachets fast-action dried yeast

125g (4oz) walnuts, chopped
75g (3oz) dried cranberries
450ml (¾ pint) warm water
30ml (2 tbsp) thin honey

1 Mix the wholemeal and granary flours, salt, oats, yeast, walnuts and cranberries in a bowl. Work in the warm water with the honey to form a soft dough.

2 Knead for 10 minutes, then shape into a ball, place in an oiled bowl, cover with a tea-towel and leave to rise in a warm place for 1 hour or until doubled in size.

3 Place a clean terracotta tile or pizza stone on the middle shelf of the oven at 220°C/fan oven 210°C (425°F) Mark 7 to heat up. Knock back the dough on a lightly floured surface and divide in half.

4 Shape each piece of dough into a round and transfer to a well floured baking sheet.

5 Snip the surface with a pair of scissors, cover with oiled cling film and leave to rise for a further 30 minutes.

6 Carefully transfer the risen doughs to the hot tile or stone and bake for 15 minutes, then lower the setting to 170°C/fan oven 160°C (325°F) Mark 3 and bake for a further 15 minutes until the bread sounds hollow when tapped underneath. Cool on a wire rack. Serve warm.

NOTE It is not essential to bake the breads on a tile or pizza stone. You can use a preheated baking sheet instead.

TURKISH FLAT BREAD

Reminiscent of traditional Turkish flat breads, this one has an authentic soft, fluffy texture and milky flavour.

MAKES I LOAF; 15 SLICES ◆ PREPARATION 20 minutes, plus rising
◆ COOKING TIME 25-30 minutes ◆ FREEZING Not suitable ◆ 110 CALS PER SLICE

450g (1lb) strong plain white flour
10ml (2 tsp) salt
7g sachet fast-action dried yeast

10ml (2 tsp) thin honey
150ml (¼ pint) warm milk
150ml (¼ pint) warm water (approximately)
milk, to glaze

1 Sift the flour and salt into a bowl and stir in the yeast. Add the honey and gradually work in the warm liquid, adding sufficient to form a soft dough.
2 Knead for 10 minutes, then shape the dough into a ball. Place in an oiled bowl, cover with a tea-towel and leave to rise in a warm place for 1 hour or until doubled in size.
3 Preheat a clean terracotta tile, pizza stone or baking sheet on the middle oven shelf at 220°C/fan oven 210°C (425°F) Mark 7.
4 Knock back the dough on a lightly floured surface and roll out to form a flat oval, about 1cm (½ inch) thick. Transfer to an oiled baking sheet and carefully score the surface with a sharp knife to form a diamond pattern. Cover with oiled cling film and leave to rise for a further 30 minutes.

5 Carefully brush the bread with milk, then transfer to the hot tile or stone. Bake for 25-30 minutes until risen and golden. Wrap in a clean tea-towel and leave to cool.

PUMPKIN BREAD

This savoury loaf with its light, cake-like texture makes the perfect soup or salad accompaniment. If you have any leftover the following day, toast and spread with butter.

MAKES 2 LOAVES; EACH 8-10 SLICES ◆ PREPARATION 35 minutes, plus rising
◆ COOKING TIME 35 minutes ◆ FREEZING Suitable ◆ 180-145 CALS PER SLICE

450g (1lb) peeled pumpkin, diced
675g (1½lb) strong plain white flour
10ml (2 tsp) salt
1½ x 7g sachets fast-action dried yeast

5ml (1 tsp) caster sugar
30ml (2 tbsp) chopped fresh sage
125g (4oz) red Leicester cheese, grated
180-200ml (6-7fl oz) warm water

1 Steam the pumpkin for 15 minutes until cooked. Drain well, then dry on kitchen paper. Return to the saucepan and mash well. Stir over a medium heat for a few minutes to drive off excess moisture. Set aside to cool.

2 Sift the flour and salt into a bowl and stir in the yeast and sugar. Gradually work in the puréed pumpkin, chopped sage, 90g (3oz) of the cheese, and enough warm water to form a firm dough. Knead for 8-10 minutes until soft.

3 Shape into a ball and place in an oiled bowl. Cover with a tea-towel and leave to rise in a warm place for 1 hour until doubled in size.

4 Knock back the dough on a lightly floured surface. Divide in half and shape each half into an oval. Press into two oiled 450g (1lb) loaf tins, cover loosely with oiled cling film and leave to rise for a further 30 minutes.

5 Bake at 200°C/fan oven 190°C (400°F) Mark 6 for 30 minutes, then carefully sprinkle with the remaining cheese and bake for a further 5 minutes or until the bread is risen and sounds hollow when tapped underneath. Leave in the tins for 10 minutes, then turn out and cool on a wire rack.

SCIACCIATA

An Italian pizza-style flat bread with a tasty garlic, sage and olive oil topping. Other fresh herbs, such as thyme or basil, can be used in place of sage.

MAKES 2; EACH SERVES 4 ◆ PREPARATION 15 minutes, plus rising
◆ COOKING TIME 15-20 minutes ◆ FREEZING Suitable ◆ 265 CALS PER SERVING
◆ COLOUR INDEX Page 18

450g (1lb) strong plain white flour
½ x 7g sachet fast-action dried yeast
5ml (1 tsp) sea salt
2.5ml (½ tsp) caster sugar
30ml (2 tbsp) extra-virgin olive oil
250-300ml (8-10fl oz) warm water

TOPPING
60ml (4 tbsp) extra-virgin olive oil
2 garlic cloves, peeled and crushed
15ml (1 tbsp) chopped fresh sage
sea salt

1 Sift the flour into a large bowl and stir in the yeast, salt and sugar. Make a well in the centre and gradually work in the oil and sufficient warm water to form a soft dough.

2 Knead for 8-10 minutes until smooth and elastic, then transfer the dough to a greased bowl. Cover with a tea-towel and leave to rise in a warm place for 1-1½ hours until doubled in size.

3 Preheat a large baking sheet on the top shelf of the oven set at 220°C/fan oven 210°C (425°F) Mark 7. Knock back the dough, divide in half and roll each piece out to a 25x12cm (10x5 inch) oval. Transfer to a well floured baking sheet, cover loosely and leave to rise for a further 30 minutes.

4 To prepare the topping, in a small bowl, mix the oil with the garlic, sage and a little salt.

5 Make 4 deep slashes along each oval and transfer to the preheated baking sheet. Quickly drizzle over the garlic oil and bake for 15-20 minutes until the bread is risen and golden. Transfer to a wire rack to cool. Serve warm.

SUN-DRIED TOMATO AND FENNEL ROLLS

MAKES 10 ROLLS ◆ PREPARATION 20 minutes, plus rising
◆ COOKING TIME 20-25 minutes ◆ FREEZING Suitable ◆ 295 CALS PER ROLL

675g (1½lb) strong plain white flour
15ml (1 tbsp) salt
7g sachet fast-action dried yeast
5ml (1 tsp) caster sugar
125g (4oz) sun-dried tomatoes (preferably not in oil), finely chopped
60ml (4 tbsp) sun-dried tomato paste
15ml (1 tbsp) fennel seeds, roasted and roughly ground
300-350ml (10-12fl oz) warm water
sea salt, for sprinkling

1 Sift the flour and salt into a bowl, then stir in the yeast, sugar, chopped sun-dried tomatoes, tomato paste, fennel seeds and enough warm water to form a soft dough.

2 Knead for 10 minutes, then shape into a round and place in an oiled bowl. Cover with a tea-towel and leave to rise in a warm place for 1 hour or until doubled in size.

3 Knock back the dough on a lightly floured surface. Divide into 10 pieces. Shape into balls, flatten slightly and place on an oiled baking sheet. Cover loosely with oiled cling film and leave to rise for a further 30 minutes.

4 Sprinkle the rolls with sea salt and bake at 200°C/fan oven 190°C (400°F) Mark 6 for 20-25 minutes until risen and golden. Cool on a wire rack.

SPINACH AND CHEESE BREAD

A light bread dough rolled around a tasty spinach and feta cheese filling. Serve as a picnic snack, or with salad.

MAKES 1; 16 SLICES ◆ PREPARATION 30 minutes
◆ COOKING TIME 25-30 minutes ◆ FREEZING Not suitable ◆ 160 CALS PER SLICE

400g (14oz) wholemeal bread flour
125g (4oz) chick pea (gram) flour
10ml (2 tsp) salt
10ml (2 tsp) sugar
7g sachet fast-action dried yeast
300ml (½ pint) warm milk

FILLING
30ml (2 tbsp) olive oil
4 spring onions, finely chopped
1 garlic clove, peeled and crushed
5ml (1 tsp) ground cumin
450g (1lb) chopped fresh spinach leaves
30ml (2 tbsp) chopped fresh dill
175g (6oz) feta cheese, diced
salt and pepper

1 Mix the flours, salt, sugar and yeast together in a bowl and make a well in the centre. Gradually work in the milk to form a soft dough.

2 Knead for 10 minutes, then shape the dough into a ball and place in an oiled bowl. Cover with a tea-towel and leave to rise in a warm place for 1 hour.

3 Meanwhile, prepare the filling. Heat the oil in a frying pan, add the spring onions, garlic and cumin, and fry gently for 3-4 minutes until softened. Add the spinach and dill and fry until just wilted. Set aside to cool.

4 Stir the feta cheese into the cooled filling and season with salt and pepper to taste. Place in a sieve and press out any excess moisture; the mixture should be quite dry.

5 Knock back the dough on a lightly floured surface and roll out thinly to a 35x25cm (14x10 inch) rectangle. Carefully spread the spinach mixture on top of the dough to within 1cm (½ inch) of the edges.

6 Starting from a narrow edge, roll up as for a roulade, dampening the edges to seal. Place seam-side down on an oiled baking sheet, cover with oiled cling film and leave to rise for a further 30 minutes. Bake at 200°C/fan oven 190°C (400°F) Mark 6 for 25-30 minutes until golden and the bread sounds hollow when tapped underneath. Cool on a wire rack. Cut into slices to serve.

OLIVE BREAD ROLLS

Studded with chopped black olives and glazed with olive oil and sea salt, these large flat rolls taste delicious.

MAKES 6 ROLLS ◆ PREPARATION 15 minutes, plus rising
◆ COOKING TIME 15-20 minutes ◆ FREEZING Suitable ◆ 310 CALS PER ROLL
◆ COLOUR INDEX Page 18

450g (1lb) strong plain white flour, plus an extra 25g (1oz)

10ml (2 tsp) salt

7g sachet fast-action dried yeast

pinch of caster sugar

5ml (1 tsp) dried rosemary (optional)

30ml (2 tbsp) olive oil

300ml (½ pint) warm water

125g (4oz) pitted black olives, finely chopped

TO FINISH
olive oil, for brushing
coarse sea salt, for sprinkling

1 Sift all but 25g (1oz) of the flour with the salt into a bowl and stir in the yeast, sugar, and rosemary if using. Make a well in the centre and add the olive oil and warm water; work to a soft dough. Knead for 10 minutes until smooth.
2 Pat the olives dry and add to the dough with the extra 25g (1oz) flour; knead in gently. Shape into a ball, then transfer the dough to a greased bowl. Cover with a tea-towel and leave to rise in a warm place for 1 hour.
3 Knock back the dough and divide into 6 pieces. Shape into balls, then press lightly to form flat rolls, about 12cm (5 inches) in diameter. Transfer to a baking sheet, cover loosely with oiled cling film and leave to rise for 30 minutes.
4 Make finger indentations over each roll, then brush with olive oil and sprinkle with coarse sea salt. Bake at 220°C/fan oven 210°C (425°F) Mark 7 for 15-20 minutes until risen and golden. Cool on a wire rack.

PARMESAN AND CHIVE ROLLS

MAKES 8 ◆ PREPARATION 20 minutes, plus rising ◆ COOKING TIME 15-20 minutes
◆ FREEZING Suitable ◆ 270 CALS PER ROLL ◆ COLOUR INDEX Page 19

450g (1lb) strong plain white flour

5ml (1 tsp) salt

7g sachet fast-action dried yeast

pinch of sugar

60ml (4 tbsp) chopped fresh chives

65g (2½oz) Parmesan cheese, freshly grated

300ml (½ pint) milk

25g (1oz) butter

1 Sift the flour and salt into a bowl and stir in the yeast, sugar, chives, and all but 15g (½oz) of the cheese.
2 Heat the milk and butter in a small pan until the butter is melted; cool slightly until tepid. Gradually add to the dry ingredients and work together to form a soft dough.

3 Knead the dough for 8-10 minutes until smooth, then transfer to a greased bowl. Cover with a tea-towel and leave to rise in a warm place for 1 hour.
4 Knock back the dough and divide into 8 pieces. Shape into balls, flatten slightly and place on an oiled large baking sheet. Cover loosely with oiled cling film and leave to rise for 30 minutes.
5 Sprinkle the remaining Parmesan over the rolls and bake at 220°C/fan oven 210°C (425°F) Mark 7 for 15-20 minutes until risen and golden. Cool on a wire rack.

SESAME RINGS

These tasty sesame rings are served as street snacks in many eastern Mediterranean countries. They make an excellent brunch or mid-morning snack.

MAKES 12 ◆ PREPARATION 20 minutes, plus rising ◆ COOKING TIME 25 minutes
◆ FREEZING Not suitable ◆ 260 CALS PER RING

450g (1lb) strong plain white flour

10ml (2 tsp) salt

20ml (4 tsp) caster sugar

7g sachet fast-action dried yeast

125g (4oz) fine semolina

300ml (½ pint) warm water

25g (1oz) butter, melted

TO FINISH
2 eggs, beaten
125g (4oz) sesame seeds
coarse sea salt, for sprinkling

1 Sift the flour and salt into a bowl and stir in the sugar, yeast and semolina. Make a well in the centre and gradually work in the warm water and butter to form a soft dough.
2 Knead for 10 minutes, then shape the dough into a ball and place in an oiled bowl. Cover with a tea-towel and leave to rise in a warm place for 1 hour or until doubled in size.
3 Knock back the dough on a lightly floured surface, then divide into 12 pieces. Roll each piece into a 30cm (12 inch) stick and form into a ring, pinching the ends together.
4 Dip the rings into the beaten egg, then into the sesame seeds to coat. Place on 2 large, oiled baking sheets. Cover with oiled cling film and leave to rise for a further 30 minutes.
5 Sprinkle with sea salt and bake at 220°C/fan oven 210°C (425°F) Mark 7 for 10 minutes, then reduce the setting to 170°C/fan oven 160°C (325°F) Mark 3 and bake for a further 15 minutes or until golden. Cool on a wire rack.

FOCACCIA

MAKES 2; EACH SERVES 6 ◆ PREPARATION 30 minutes, plus rising
◆ COOKING TIME 20-25 minutes ◆ FREEZING Suitable ◆ 275 CALS PER SERVING
◆ COLOUR INDEX Page 19

675g (1½ lb) strong plain white flour
pinch of salt
7g sachet fast-action dried yeast
450ml (¾ pint) warm water
45ml (3 tbsp) extra-virgin olive oil

TO FINISH
60ml (4 tbsp) olive oil
coarse sea salt or crystal salt, for sprinkling

1 Sift the flour and salt into a large bowl and stir in the yeast. Make a well in the centre and gradually work in the warm water and olive oil to form a soft dough.
2 Knead for 10 minutes until smooth and elastic, then place in a greased bowl. Cover with a tea-towel and leave to rise in a warm place for 1½-2 hours until doubled in size. If too soft, knead in a little more flour.
3 Lightly oil two shallow 25cm (10 inch) metal pizza tins or pie plates. Knock back the dough and divide in half. Roll out each piece to a 25cm (10 inch) circle. Transfer to the oiled tins. Cover with a damp tea-towel and leave to rise for 30 minutes.
4 Using your fingertips, make deep dimples all over the surface of the dough. Drizzle with the olive oil, sprinkle generously with salt and spray with water. Bake at 200°C/fan oven 190°C (400°F) Mark 6 for 20-25 minutes, spraying with water twice during cooking. Transfer to a wire rack to cool slightly. Serve warm on the same day.

VARIATIONS
◆ OLIVE AND SUN-DRIED TOMATO FOCACCIA Drain 50g (2oz) sun-dried tomatoes in oil, slice and knead into the dough at stage 2. Scatter 225g (8oz) black or green olives over the dough at stage 4.
◆ SAGE AND ONION FOCACCIA Knead 15-20 chopped fresh sage leaves into the dough at stage 2. Sprinkle the focaccia with extra sage leaves and 2 peeled, thinly sliced red onions at stage 4 before baking.

HERB YOGURT BREAD

Like soda bread, this quick non-yeast bread doesn't need to rise before baking. It is particularly good with soups.

MAKES 1; 16 SLICES ◆ PREPARATION 15 minutes
◆ COOKING TIME 40-45 minutes ◆ FREEZING Suitable ◆ 150 CALS PER SLICE
◆ COLOUR INDEX Page 19

350g (12oz) strong plain white or wholemeal flour
125g (4oz) fine cornmeal
10ml (2 tsp) salt
10ml (2 tsp) baking powder
5ml (1 tsp) bicarbonate of soda
30ml (2 tbsp) chopped mixed fresh herbs (parsley, thyme and fennel or dill)

50g (2oz) butter, melted
2 eggs, beaten
300ml (½ pint) yogurt
30ml (2 tbsp) thin honey

TO FINISH
5ml (1 tsp) chopped fresh thyme leaves

1 Grease a 23cm (9 inch) round cake tin. Mix the dry ingredients together in a bowl, stir in the mixed herbs and make a well in the centre.
2 In another bowl, beat together the melted butter, eggs and yogurt; pour into the well. Work together until evenly combined, then transfer the mixture to the prepared tin and level the surface.
3 Scatter the thyme leaves over the surface of the dough and bake at 180°C/fan oven 170°C (350°F) Mark 4 for 40-45 minutes until risen and a skewer inserted into the middle comes out clean. Leave in the tin for 10 minutes, then turn out and cool on a wire rack.

CHEESE MUFFINS

Light, savoury muffins with a peppery 'kick'. They should be eaten on the day they are made, while still warm if possible.

MAKES 12 ◆ PREPARATION 10 minutes ◆ COOKING TIME 15-20 minutes
◆ FREEZING Not suitable ◆ 285 CALS PER MUFFIN

225g (8oz) plain white flour
225g (8oz) fine cornmeal
10ml (2 tsp) sugar
5ml (1 tsp) salt
30ml (2 tbsp) baking powder
15-30ml (1-2 tbsp) coarsely ground black peppercorns

50g (2oz) Parmesan cheese, freshly grated
4 medium eggs, lightly beaten
450ml (¾ pint) milk
60ml (4 tbsp) sunflower oil
50g (2oz) Cheddar cheese, grated

1 Line a 12-hole muffin tin with paper muffin cases. Combine the flour, cornmeal, sugar, salt, baking powder, pepper and Parmesan in a large bowl and make a well in the centre.
2 Beat the eggs, milk and sunflower oil together, then pour into the well. Beat with a wooden spoon until well combined.

3 Spoon the muffin mixture into the prepared tin, dividing it equally. Sprinkle with the grated Cheddar cheese. Bake at 220°C/fan oven 210°C (425°F) Mark 7 for 15-20 minutes until well risen, and a skewer inserted into the centre comes out clean.

4 Leave in the tin for 5 minutes, then transfer the muffins to a wire rack to cool. Serve warm.

VARIATION

SUN-DRIED TOMATO AND CHILLI MUFFINS Replace the coarsely ground peppercorns with 4 sun-dried tomatoes in oil, drained and finely chopped, and 1 small red chilli, deseeded and diced.

SWEET YEAST BREADS

Inspired by recipes from Scandinavia, Austria, Italy, and France, these delicious enriched breads are laden with fruit and fragrant with spices

rectangle and brush with a little melted butter. Sprinkle half of the filling evenly over the dough. Roll up from a long side, pinching the ends together, to make a long sausage.

5 Repeat with the remaining dough and filling. Place the 2 rolls, side by side and twist together into a rope. Transfer to a greased baking sheet, bringing the ends together into a round, leaving a small hole in the middle. Cover loosely with oiled cling film and leave for about 1 hour until doubled in size.

6 Brush the brioche with any remaining butter. Bake at 190°C/fan oven 180°C (375°F) Mark 5 for 40-50 minutes until risen and golden, and the underside feels hollow when tapped, covering loosely with foil after about 20 minutes to prevent overbrowning. Transfer to a wire rack to cool.

7 For the icing, mix the icing sugar with the rosewater. Spoon the icing over the brioche to decorate.

STICKY FRUIT BRIOCHE

A rich, buttery brioche style bread, lightly scented with rosewater and packed with dried fruit and nuts. Allow plenty of time for the dough to rise and prove.

SERVES 8-10 ◆ PREPARATION 25 minutes, plus rising
◆ COOKING TIME 40-50 minutes ◆ FREEZING Suitable (before icing)
◆ 485-355 CALS PER SLICE ◆ ILLUSTRATED WHOLE Page 137

300g (10oz) strong plain white flour

75g (3oz) firm unsalted butter, diced

30ml (2 tbsp) light muscovado sugar

3 egg yolks

7g sachet fast-action dried yeast

90ml (3fl oz) warm milk

45ml (3 tbsp) rosewater

FILLING

100g (3½oz) blanched almonds, roughly chopped

125g (4oz) currants

50g (2oz) chopped candied or mixed peel

75g (3oz) light muscovado sugar

15g (½oz) unsalted butter, melted

ICING

125g (4oz) icing sugar

20-25ml (4-5 tsp) rosewater

1 Sift the flour into a bowl, then rub in the butter, using fingertips. Stir in the sugar, egg yolks and yeast. Add the milk and rosewater and mix to a firm dough, adding a little more warm milk if the mixture feels dry.

2 Turn out on to a floured surface and knead for 5-10 minutes until the dough is smooth and elastic. Transfer to a lightly oiled bowl and cover with cling film. Leave to rise in a warm place for about 2 hours until doubled in size.

3 For the filling, mix together the almonds, currants, candied peel and sugar.

4 Knead the dough lightly on a floured surface, then divide in half. Thinly roll out one half to a 46x18cm (18x7 inch)

KUGELHOPF

MAKES 12 SLICES ◆ PREPARATION 45 minutes, plus overnight chilling and rising
◆ COOKING TIME 50-55 minutes ◆ FREEZING Suitable ◆ 390 CALS PER SERVING
◆ COLOUR INDEX Page 20

200g (7oz) seedless raisins

45ml (3 tbsp) light rum

10ml (2 tsp) fast-action dried yeast

300g (11oz) strong plain white flour

4 eggs

100ml (3½fl oz) milk

225g (8oz) unsalted butter, softened

75g (3oz) caster sugar

pinch of salt

finely grated rind of 1 lemon

100g (3½oz) split blanched almonds, lightly toasted

icing sugar, for dusting

glacé fruits, nuts and dragées (optional), to decorate

1 Soak the raisins in the rum overnight.

2 Place the yeast and flour in a food mixer. Whisk the eggs and milk together lightly in a bowl. With the machine running on a slow speed, pour in the egg mixture and mix for approximately 10 minutes or until the dough is smooth, shiny and elastic. (Or mix by hand.)

3 Meanwhile, beat the butter, sugar, salt and lemon rind together in a bowl. With the machine running, gradually add this mixture to the dough until evenly incorporated. Turn into a large bowl, cover with cling film and refrigerate overnight.

4 Generously butter a 2 litre (3½ pint) kugelhopf ring mould, then press a third of the almonds on the inside; refrigerate.

5 Roughly chop the remaining almonds and knead into the dough by hand, with the raisins and rum. Carefully place in the prepared mould. Cover and leave in a warm place until the dough has risen to within 2cm (¾ inch) of the rim.

6 Bake below the centre of the oven at 200°C/fan oven 190°C (400°F) Mark 6 for 10 minutes. Lower the setting to 190°C/fan oven 180°C (375°F) Mark 5. Cover the kugelhopf with greaseproof paper and bake for a further 40-45 minutes or until the underside sounds hollow when tapped.

7 Leave in the tin for 15 minutes, then turn out on to a wire rack to cool. Serve dusted with icing sugar and decorated with glacé fruits, nuts and dragées if wished. Eat within 2 days.

SPICED FIG AND RICOTTA BREAD

SERVES 8 ◆ PREPARATION 25 minutes, plus rising ◆ COOKING TIME 35 minutes
◆ FREEZING Not suitable ◆ 315 CALS PER SERVING

300g (10oz) strong plain white flour
5ml (1 tsp) ground mixed spice
5ml (1 tsp) ground cinnamon
7g sachet fast-action dried yeast
50g (2oz) caster sugar
1 egg
45ml (3 tbsp) olive oil
100ml (3½fl oz) warm water

TO ASSEMBLE
12 fresh ripe figs
250g (9oz) ricotta cheese
60ml (4 tbsp) double cream
50g (2oz) caster sugar
milk, for brushing
60ml (4 tbsp) icing sugar
thin honey, to serve

1 Sift the flour and spices into a bowl. Stir in the yeast and sugar, then make a well in the centre. Beat the egg with the oil and warm water, then add to the well. Mix to a firm dough, adding a little extra water if the dough is too dry.

2 Turn the dough on to a lightly floured surface and knead for about 5 minutes until smooth and elastic. Transfer to a lightly oiled bowl, cover with foil and leave in a warm place to rise for about 1½ hours until doubled in size.

3 Thinly slice 4 figs; quarter the rest. Beat the ricotta, cream and sugar together in a bowl until evenly blended.

4 Turn the dough on to a lightly floured surface and knead gently, then divide in half. Roll out one half thinly to a 26cm (10½ inch) round and place on a lightly greased baking sheet. Spread to within 2cm (¾ inch) of the edges with half of the ricotta mixture. Arrange the sliced fig evenly on top. Brush the edges of the dough with milk.

5 Roll out the remaining dough to a round of the same size and position over the first, sandwiching the filling. Pinch the edges together to seal, then bend upwards, to form a case. Spread the remaining ricotta mixture over the top and scatter with the fig wedges. Cover loosely with foil and leave for about 45 minutes until risen.

6 Dust with the icing sugar and bake at 190°C/fan oven 180°C (375°F) Mark 5 for 35 minutes, covering with foil after about 20 minutes if the bread appears to be browning too quickly. Leave on the baking sheet for 30 minutes, then drizzle with honey and serve warm.

PRUNE AND SAFFRON BUNS

Saffron lends a warm colour and spicy, aromatic flavour to this sweet yeast dough, which is enriched with plump prunes, raisins and dried apricots to delicious effect. Because the dough is rich, you need to allow plenty of time for it to rise.

MAKES 8 BUNS ◆ PREPARATION 25 minutes, plus rising
◆ COOKING TIME About 30 minutes ◆ FREEZING Suitable ◆ 510 CALS PER BUN

1 sachet saffron strands	125g (4oz) raisins
450g (1lb) strong plain white flour	225ml (7½fl oz) warm milk
good pinch of salt	50g (2oz) ready-to-eat dried apricots, roughly chopped
175g (6oz) firm unsalted butter, diced	
25g (1oz) caster sugar	beaten egg or milk, to glaze
7g sachet fast-action dried yeast	45ml (3 tbsp) golden syrup
200g (7oz) ready-to-eat prunes, roughly chopped	40g (1½oz) sugar cubes, lightly crushed

1 Put the saffron in a small bowl with 30ml (2 tbsp) boiling water and leave to infuse for 5 minutes. Sift the flour and salt into a bowl. Rub in the butter, then stir in the sugar, yeast and two thirds of the prunes and raisins. Add the milk and saffron with its liquid; mix to a soft dough.

2 Turn the dough out on to a floured surface and knead for 5-10 minutes until smooth and elastic. Transfer to a lightly oiled bowl, cover with cling film and leave to rise in a warm place for about 2 hours until doubled in size.

3 Mix the remaining prunes and raisins with the apricots. Turn the dough on to a floured surface and knead lightly to eliminate some of the air. Cut into 8 even sized pieces. Shape each piece into a ball and space well apart on a lightly greased baking sheet.

4 Press a deep hole in the centre of each bun (to resemble ring doughnuts).

5 Pack half the dried fruit mixture into the holes, then press well down. Cover loosely with lightly oiled cling film and leave to rise for about 45-60 minutes until doubled in size. Brush the buns with egg or milk and bake in the oven at 200°C/fan oven 190°C (400°F) Mark 6 for 15 minutes. Pile the remaining fruit into the centres, pressing down gently. Bake for a further 15 minutes, covering with foil if necessary to prevent overbrowning.

6 Transfer to a wire rack to cool. Heat the syrup in a pan until slightly thinned, then brush over the buns while still warm. Scatter with the coarse sugar.

VARIATION Omit the saffron and sift in 10ml (2 tsp) ground mixed spice with the flour.

2 Turn out on to a floured surface and knead for about 5 minutes until smooth and elastic. Transfer to a lightly oiled bowl and cover with cling film. Leave to rise in a warm place for 1-1½ hours until doubled in size.

3 Turn the dough on to a floured surface and knead lightly to eliminate some of the air. Roll out to an oval shape, about 35x20cm (14x8 inches). Transfer to a lightly greased baking sheet, cover loosely with oiled cling film and leave for about 30 minutes until risen.

4 Use your middle finger and forefinger to push deep holes into the dough, about 5cm (2 inches) apart. Push half the blueberries into the holes. Brush with melted butter and bake at 200°C/fan oven 190°C (400°F) Mark 6 for about 12 minutes until golden. Remove from the oven and reduce the setting to 180°C/fan oven 170°C (350°F) Mark 4.

5 Pile the remaining blueberries over the holes. Scatter with sugar and return to the oven for a further 5-10 minutes until the blueberries have softened. Serve warm or cold.

CHRISTMAS STOLLEN

MAKES 10 SLICES ◆ PREPARATION 20 minutes, plus rising
◆ COOKING TIME 40 minutes ◆ FREEZING Not suitable ◆ 320 CALS PER SERVING
◆ COLOUR INDEX Page 21

350g (12oz) strong plain white flour	**25g (1oz) glacé cherries**
2.5ml (½ tsp) salt	**25g (1oz) chopped mixed peel**
2.5ml (½ tsp) ground mixed spice	**50g (2oz) chopped almonds**
50g (2oz) unsalted butter, diced	**1 small egg, beaten**
7g sachet fast-action dried yeast	**120-150ml (4-5fl oz) warmed milk**
25g (1oz) caster sugar	**125g (4oz) ready-made almond paste**
125g (4oz) mixed sultanas, currants and raisins	**icing sugar, for dusting**

1 Sift the flour, salt and spice into a bowl and rub in the butter. Stir in the rest of the ingredients, except the almond paste, adding sufficient warm milk to mix to a soft dough.

2 Turn on to a lightly floured surface and knead for about 10 minutes, then shape into a ball. Place in an oiled bowl, cover with cling film and leave to rise in a warm place for 2 hours or until doubled in size.

3 Knock back the dough, then shape into a long oval, about 1cm (½ inch) deep.

4 Roll the almond paste into a log, a little shorter than the length of the oval. Make a slight indentation along the length of the dough. Lay the almond paste in this groove and fold the dough over to enclose it; press the edges together to seal.

5 Transfer to a lightly oiled large baking sheet, cover and leave to rise for a further 30 minutes.

6 Bake at 180°C/fan oven 170°C (350°F) Mark 4 for 40 minutes until deep golden. Transfer to a wire rack to cool. Serve dusted with icing sugar. Eat within 1-2 days.

BLUEBERRY FOUGASSE

Based on a traditional fougasse, the dimples impressed in this flat bread are filled with colourful blueberries. Once baked, the flavour of the softened blueberries with the sweet vanilla bread is superb – perfect for breakfast, or later in the day. Serve warm for optimum flavour.

SERVES 8 ◆ PREPARATION 20 minutes, plus rising
◆ COOKING TIME About 20 minutes ◆ FREEZING Not suitable
◆ 220 CALS PER SERVING

250g (9oz) strong plain white flour	**100ml (3½fl oz) warm water**
pinch of salt	
50g (2oz) firm unsalted butter, diced	**TO FINISH**
30ml (2 tbsp) caster sugar	**150-175g (5-6oz) fresh blueberries**
7g sachet fast-action dried yeast	**15g (½oz) unsalted butter, melted**
1 egg	**45ml (3 tbsp) granulated or caster sugar**
10ml (2 tsp) vanilla extract	

1 Sift the flour and salt into a bowl. Rub in the butter, using fingertips, then stir in the sugar and yeast and make a well in the centre. Beat together the egg, vanilla extract and water, then add to the well. Mix to a soft dough.

APPLE STROMBOLI

Tart dessert apples, mild spices and butter, rolled in a simple dough make a fresh, light tasting bread that's particularly good warmed through for breakfast. When baked the bread rises, then deflates as it cools, resulting in a very moist texture.

SERVES 8 ◆ PREPARATION 25 minutes, plus rising ◆ COOKING TIME 40 minutes ◆ FREEZING Not suitable ◆ 285 CALS PER SERVING

350g (12oz) strong plain white flour
large pinch of salt
75g (3oz) unsalted butter
25g (1oz) caster sugar
7g sachet fast-action dried yeast
275ml (9fl oz) warm water

FILLING
4 Granny Smith's or other crisp apples

15ml (1 tbsp) lemon juice
75g (3oz) light muscovado sugar
10ml (2 tsp) ground cinnamon
2.5ml (½ tsp) freshly grated nutmeg

TO FINISH
milk, for brushing
icing sugar, for dusting

1 Sift the flour and salt into a bowl. Melt 25g (1oz) of the butter and add to the bowl with the sugar and yeast. Gradually stir in the warm water to make a soft dough, adding a little more if the dough is too dry.

2 Turn out on to a floured surface and knead for 5-10 minutes until smooth and elastic. Transfer to a lightly oiled bowl, cover with cling film and leave in a warm place to rise for about 1½ hours until doubled in size.

3 Meanwhile peel, quarter and core the apples. Cut each apple quarter into 4 slices and put in a bowl of cold water with the lemon juice added to prevent discoloration.

4 Mix together the muscovado sugar, cinnamon and nutmeg. Turn the dough out on to a floured surface and knead gently. Roll out to a 33cm (13 inch) square.

5 Drain the apples thoroughly, dry on kitchen paper, then scatter over the dough to within 2cm (¾ inch) of the edges. Sprinkle over the spiced sugar and dot with the remaining butter. Roll up the dough, Swiss-roll style, to enclose the filling. Pinch the ends together well to seal, then place on a greased baking sheet with the edge face upwards.

6 Cover loosely with oiled cling film and leave to prove for 45-60 minutes until doubled in size.

7 Brush with milk to glaze, then bake at 220°C/fan oven 210°C (425°F) Mark 7 for 15 minutes. Reduce oven setting to 180°C/fan oven 170°C (350°F) Mark 4 and bake for a further 25 minutes until deep golden, covering with foil to prevent overbrowning. Transfer to a wire rack and dust with icing sugar. Serve warm or cold, cut into slices.

PANNETONE

This classic Italian favourite is really a cross between a bread and a cake. Light, yet buttery and rich, it is studded with dried fruit and candied peel. Because of the high butter content, pannetone keeps well. It is normally eaten with coffee, or a glass of dessert wine, Marsala or sherry.

MAKES 10-12 SLICES ◆ PREPARATION 25 minutes, plus rising
◆ COOKING TIME 35 minutes ◆ FREEZING Suitable
◆ 415-320 CALS PER SERVING ◆ COLOUR INDEX Page 21

450g (1lb) strong plain white flour	**1 egg**
10ml (2 tsp) salt	**4 egg yolks**
75g (3oz) caster sugar	**150ml (¼ pint) warm milk**
1½ x 7g sachets fast-action dried yeast	**175g (6oz) unsalted butter, softened**
finely grated rind of 1 lemon	**75g (3oz) chopped mixed candied orange and citron peel**
finely grated rind of 1 orange	**125g (4oz) raisins**

1 Line a 15cm (6 inch) deep cake tin with a double layer of non-stick baking parchment which extends 12cm (5 inches) above the rim.

2 Sift the flour and salt into a bowl and stir in the sugar, yeast and citrus rinds. Make a well in the centre. Beat the egg and egg yolks together and add to the well with the warm milk. Mix to an elastic dough, adding a little more flour if necessary, but keeping the dough quite soft. Work in the softened butter.

3 Cover with cling film and leave to rise for 2-4 hours until doubled in volume.

4 Knock back the dough and knead in the chopped peel and raisins. Place in the prepared tin and cut a deep cross on the top with a very sharp knife. Cover and leave to rise until the dough is 2.5cm (1 inch) above the top of the tin.

5 Bake at 200°C/fan oven 190°C (400°F) Mark 6 for 15 minutes, then lower the heat to 180°C (350°F) Mark 4 and bake for a further 40 minutes until well risen and golden. Leave in the tin for 10 minutes, then transfer to a wire rack to cool.

6 To serve, cut off the top and slice horizontally. To store, replace the top, wrap the whole pannetone in cling film or foil and refrigerate. Bring to room temperature to serve.

NOTE Most sweet egg and butter enriched doughs take a long time to rise, so start them early in the day. Don't put them to rise in a very warm place once the butter is incorporated, or it will melt and make the dough greasy.

SWEET MOCHA BREAD

This brioche-style bread sandwiches a delicious chocolate and coffee flavoured filling. When shaping the bread in the tin, make sure the layers of dough are firmly pinched together so the filling does not seep out. Because of the richness of the dough, allow plenty of rising time.

MAKES 10 SLICES ◆ PREPARATION 25 minutes, plus rising
◆ COOKING TIME 45 minutes ◆ FREEZING Suitable ◆ 475 CALS PER SERVING

	FILLING AND TOPPING
425g (15oz) strong plain white flour	**75g (3oz) caster sugar**
5ml (1 tsp) salt	**60ml (4 tbsp) instant coffee granules**
7g sachet fast-action dried yeast	**200g (7oz) plain chocolate, chopped**
75g (3oz) caster sugar	**50g (2oz) pecan nuts, chopped**
3 eggs	
150ml (¼ pint) double cream	
50g (2oz) butter, melted	

1 Sift the flour and salt into a bowl. Stir in the yeast and sugar, then make a well in the centre. Lightly beat the eggs, cream and butter together in another bowl, then add to the well. Mix to a soft dough.

2 Turn the dough on to a floured surface and knead for 5-10 minutes until smooth and elastic. Transfer to a lightly oiled bowl, cover with cling film and leave in a warm place to rise until doubled in size.

3 For the filling, put 50g (2oz) of the sugar in a small pan with 75ml (5 tbsp) water and heat gently until the sugar is dissolved. Stir in the coffee granules and bring to the boil. Simmer for 1 minute, then set aside to cool.

4 Grease and line a 20cm (8 inch) spring-release cake tin. Turn the dough out on to a floured surface and divide into 4 pieces. Roll out one piece to a 25cm (10inch) round and press into the base of the tin so the edges come slightly up the sides of the tin. Scatter with 50g (2oz) of the chopped chocolate, then spoon over about a third of the coffee syrup.

5 Roll out another piece of dough to a 25cm (10inch) round and lay over the first, letting the excess dough come up the sides of the tin and pinching the edges firmly into the first layer of dough. Repeat the layering, finishing with a round of dough. Brush the top of the dough lightly with water and scatter with the pecan nuts.

6 Cover the tin with lightly oiled cling film and leave to rise in a warm place until the dough nearly reaches the top of the tin.

7 Bake the bread at 220°C/fan oven 210°C (425°F) Mark 7 for 15 minutes, then reduce the setting to 170°C/fan oven 160°C (325°F) Mark 3. Cover the tin with foil and bake for a further 30 minutes.

8 Put the remaining sugar in a small pan with 60ml (4 tbsp) water and heat gently until the sugar dissolves. Bring to the boil and boil for 1 minute. Remove from the heat and stir in the remaining chocolate. Transfer the bread to a wire rack and drizzle with the chocolate sauce. Leave to cool.

KRINGLE

Cardamom is the predominant flavour in this fragrant, festive Danish bread. A spiced butter enclosed in the dough seeps into the bread during baking. It's best eaten within 2 days, but freezes well – defrost at room temperature and warm through before icing.

SERVES 12 ◆ PREPARATION 25 minutes, plus rising
◆ COOKING TIME 25-30 minutes ◆ FREEZING Suitable (before icing)
◆ 265 CALS PER SERVING

12-15 large green cardamom pods
350g (12oz) strong plain white flour
40g (1½oz) caster sugar
finely grated rind of 2 lemons
7g sachet fast-action dried yeast
75g (3oz) unsalted butter, melted
1 egg
1 egg yolk
100ml (3½fl oz) warm milk

SPICED BUTTER
100g (3½oz) unsalted butter, softened
40g (1½oz) caster sugar
10ml (2 tsp) ground cinnamon

TO FINISH
beaten egg, to glaze
25g (1oz) flaked almonds
75g (3oz) icing sugar
15ml (1 tbsp) lemon juice

1 Snip open the cardamom pods with scissors and tip the seeds into a pestle and mortar; crush the seeds. Sift the flour into a bowl. Stir in the sugar, lemon rind, crushed cardamom and yeast. Make a well in the centre.

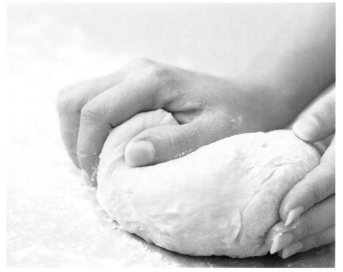

2 Add the melted butter, egg, egg yolk and milk and mix to a soft dough, adding a little more milk if the mixture feels dry. Turn the dough on to a floured surface and knead for 5-10 minutes until soft and elastic. Transfer to a lightly oiled bowl, cover with cling film and leave to rise in a warm place for about 2 hours until doubled in size.

3 Meanwhile, mix together the spiced butter ingredients until evenly combined. Lightly knead the dough to eliminate most of the air, then roll it into a long 'sausage' on a floured surface. Using a rolling pin, flatten to a 60×15cm (24×6 inch) rectangle. Spread to within 2cm (¾ inch) of the edges with the spiced butter.

4 Roll up the dough from a long edge, then press firmly along the join and pinch the ends together to prevent the butter seeping out.

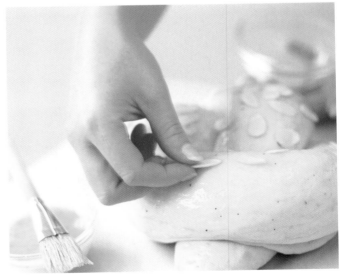

5 Transfer to a greased baking sheet, bringing the ends round and twisting them together to make a large knot; avoid overstretching the dough. Cover loosely with oiled cling film and leave for about 1 hour until doubled in size.

6 Brush with beaten egg and scatter with the almonds. Bake at 200°C/fan oven 190°C (400°F) Mark 6 for 25-30 minutes until deep golden, covering with foil after 15 minutes to prevent overbrowning. Cool on a wire rack. Blend the icing sugar with the lemon juice; drizzle over the cooled bread.

NOTE Like many enriched dough, this takes a while to start rising so allow plenty of time. Don't worry if the bread splits to reveal the spicy layer during baking; this adds to its appeal.

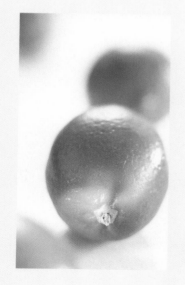  

BAKED
PUDDINGS

Sensational new recipes for all kinds of puddings, from moist
fruity sponges, crunchy charlottes and warming crumbles to creamy
bread-and-butter puddings and irresistible cheesecakes

3 Whisk the egg yolks and sugar together in a bowl, then stir in the infused cream and strain into a clean pan. Heat gently, stirring, until the custard thickens enough to coat the back of the spoon. Cool slightly, then carefully spoon over the gooseberries.

4 To make the crumble, sift the flour into a bowl and rub in the butter until the mixture resemble rough crumbs. Stir in the oats, sugar and 15ml (1 tbsp) water, then scatter over the custard layer. Bake at 200°C/fan oven 190°C (400°F) Mark 6 for 30 minutes until bubbling and golden. Serve hot.

NOTE If fresh gooseberries are unobtainable, use frozen ones, increasing the quantity to 800g (1¾lb).

RED FRUIT CHARLOTTE WITH ORANGE SABAYON

SERVES 4 ◆ PREPARATION 30 minutes ◆ COOKING TIME 25 minutes
◆ FREEZING Not suitable ◆ 560 CALS PER SERVING ◆ COLOUR INDEX Page 22

50g (2oz) unsalted butter
1 small orange
125g (4oz) blackberries
50g (2oz) caster sugar
2.5ml (½ tsp) ground mixed spice
60ml (2fl oz) water
1 large or 6 individual brioches (one-day old)
75g (3oz) raspberries

75g (3oz) strawberries, halved

ORANGE SABAYON
4 egg yolks
60ml (4 tbsp) caster sugar
juice of ½ orange
15ml (1 tbsp) Grand Marnier

1 Base-line 4 timbales or custard cups and grease generously, using most of the butter.

2 Finely grate the rind of the orange. Put the blackberries, sugar, spice, water and half of the orange rind in a pan. Bring to a simmer and cook gently for 5 minutes. Leave to cool.

3 Cut the brioche into thin slices. Cut out 4 small rounds to fit the base of the moulds and 4 larger ones, the diameter of the rims. Cut remaining slices into strips. Press the smaller rounds into the base of the moulds; line the sides with strips.

4 Peel and segment the orange, discarding all white pith, and place in a bowl. Stir in the cooked blackberry mixture, raspberries and strawberries. Spoon into the lined moulds.

5 Press the 4 larger brioche circles on top and brush with the remaining melted butter. Place on a baking sheet and bake at 200°C/fan oven 190°C (400°F) Mark 6 for 25 minutes, covering the tops with foil after about 10 minutes.

6 Meanwhile for the sabayon, whisk the egg yolks, sugar and remaining orange rind in a bowl until pale. Place over a pan of gently simmering water, add the orange juice and liqueur and whisk until frothy and doubled in volume; keep warm.

7 Leave the puddings to stand for 5 minutes, then carefully unmould on to warm plates and serve with the sabayon.

GOOSEBERRY CUSTARD CRUMBLE

For a new twist on this classic pudding, a creamy custard – flavoured with a hint of Sauternes – is poured over the fruit layer before topping with the crumble.

SERVES 6 ◆ PREPARATION 30 minutes ◆ COOKING TIME 30 minutes
◆ FREEZING Not suitable ◆ 540 CALS PER SERVING

700g (1½lb) gooseberries, trimmed
50g (2oz) sultanas
15g (½oz) butter
30ml (2 tbsp) caster sugar
3 cloves

CUSTARD
200ml (7fl oz) double cream
45ml (3 tbsp) Sauternes wine or sweet sherry

1 vanilla pod, split
3 egg yolks
30ml (2 tbsp) caster sugar

CRUMBLE
150g (5oz) plain white flour
75g (3oz) butter, diced
25g (1oz) rolled oats
50g (2oz) caster sugar

1 Put the gooseberries in a pan with the sultanas, butter, sugar, cloves and 30ml (2 tbsp) water. Heat gently for 5-10 minutes until the fruit just starts to soften. Transfer to a 1.5 litre (2½ pint) pie dish, or 6 individual dishes.

2 For the custard, pour the cream and Sauternes into a pan, add the vanilla pod and slowly bring to the boil. Take off the heat and leave to infuse for 20 minutes. Discard the vanilla pod, scraping the seeds into the cream.

BRAMBLE OAT CRUNCH

SERVES 8 ◆ PREPARATION 25 minutes ◆ COOKING TIME 50 minutes
◆ FREEZING Suitable (stage 3) ◆ 400 CALS PER SERVING
◆ COLOUR INDEX Page 22

1.4 kg (3lb) crisp dessert
apples, peeled, cored and
chopped
225g (8oz) blackberries
25g (1oz) caster sugar
100g (3½oz) porridge oats
25g (1oz) plain white flour

200g (7oz) mixed nuts,
such as hazelnuts, almonds
and pecans, roughly
chopped
100g (3½oz) soft brown
sugar
125g (4oz) butter, melted

1 Base-line a 20cm (8 inch) spring-release cake tin. Put the apples in a large pan with the blackberries, caster sugar and 150ml (¼ pint) water. Cook gently for 20 minutes or until tender and most of the liquid has evaporated.
2 Scatter the nuts and oats on a baking sheet and toast under a preheated grill until golden, stirring occasionally.
3 Combine the chopped nuts, oats, flour and brown sugar in a large bowl. Add the melted butter and stir well. Press half of this mixture over the base of the cake tin, then cover with the fruit.
4 Top with the remaining nut mixture and bake at 190°C/fan oven 180°C (375°F) Mark 5 for 20 minutes or until golden and crisp. Leave in the tin to cool, then turn out and serve with ice cream.

PEACH BROWN BETTY

SERVES 4 ◆ PREPARATION 15 minutes ◆ COOKING TIME 30 minutes
◆ FREEZING Not suitable ◆ 295 CALS PER SERVING ◆ COLOUR INDEX Page 22

2 firm peaches
50g (2oz) unsalted butter
50g (2oz) caster sugar
30ml (2 tbsp) double
cream
75g (3oz) fresh wholemeal
breadcrumbs

25g (1oz) soft brown sugar
15g (½oz) plain white flour
5ml (1 tsp) ground mixed
spice
pinch of freshly grated
nutmeg (optional)

1 Halve, stone and thinly slice the peaches.
2 Place the butter, caster sugar and cream in a small pan and heat gently until the butter is melted and the sugar dissolved. Divide half of this buttery mixture between 4 ramekins.
3 Mix the breadcrumbs with the brown sugar, flour and spice.
4 Divide half the peach slices between the ramekins, then cover with half of the breadcrumb mixture. Repeat these layers, then drizzle over the rest of the buttery mixture. Bake at 190°C/fan oven 180°C (375°F) Mark 5 for 30 minutes until bubbling.
5 Let stand for 5 minutes, then turn out the puddings on to plates. Serve topped with whipped cream, sprinkled with a little nutmeg if liked.

APRICOT AND CARDAMOM CRUMBLE

SERVES 6 ◆ PREPARATION 15 minutes ◆ COOKING TIME 25-30 minutes
◆ FREEZING Not suitable ◆ 230 CALS PER SERVING

700g (1½lb) apricots,
stoned and quartered
30-45ml (2-3 tbsp) caster
sugar
3-4 green cardamom pods,
split, seeds extracted and
crushed
50g (2oz) plain white flour

50g (2oz) jumbo rolled
oats
50g (2oz) light brown
soft sugar
50g (2oz) butter, diced
25g (1oz) hazelnuts,
toasted and roughly
chopped

1 Mix the apricots with the caster sugar and place in a 1.3 litre (2¼ pint) pie dish or 6 individual dishes.
2 Place the crushed cardamom seeds, flour, oats and brown sugar in a large bowl, then rub in the butter using fingertips. Stir in the chopped hazelnuts.
3 Spoon the crumble mixture over the fruit. Bake at 190°C/fan oven 180°C (375°F) Mark 5 for 25-30 minutes or until bubbling and golden brown. Serve warm, with Greek yogurt or crème fraîche.

SPICED RAISIN PUDDINGS

Light, spicy sponge speckled with raisins and stem ginger and 'steamed' in the oven. A syrupy lemon butter is the perfect accompaniment.

SERVES 8 ◆ PREPARATION 25 minutes ◆ COOKING TIME 40-45 minutes
◆ FREEZING Suitable (stage 4) ◆ 560 CALS PER SERVING
◆ COLOUR INDEX Page 22

175g (6oz) unsalted butter, softened
175g (6oz) caster sugar
3 eggs, lightly beaten
225g (8oz) self-raising white flour
7.5ml (1½ tsp) baking powder
5ml (1 tsp) ground mixed spice
2.5ml (½ tsp) ground cinnamon

75g (3oz) raisins
1 piece preserved stem ginger in syrup, about 15g (½oz), finely chopped
30-45ml (2-3 tbsp) milk

LEMON SAUCE
75g (3oz) unsalted butter
175g (6oz) demerara sugar
grated rind and juice of 2 small lemons

1 Grease 8 individual 175ml (6fl oz) pudding basins.
2 Cream the butter and sugar together in a bowl until pale and fluffy. Add the eggs, a little at a time, beating well after each addition, and adding a little of the flour to prevent curdling.
3 Sift the remaining flour, baking powder and spices over the bowl. Add the raisins and chopped ginger and gradually fold in, using a large metal spoon. Stir in sufficient milk to give a soft, dropping consistency.
4 Divide the mixture between the pudding basins and level the surface.
5 Stand in a roasting tin and pour in sufficient boiling water to give a 1cm (½ inch) depth. Cover the roasting tin with foil. Bake at 180°C/fan oven 170°C (350°F) Mark 4 for 40-45 minutes until risen and firm to the touch.
6 Meanwhile, make the sauce. Melt the butter in a small pan. Add the sugar and heat gently for 2-3 minutes until bubbling. Add the lemon rind and juice and cook gently to make a buttery syrup.
7 Loosen the edges of the puddings with a knife, then invert on to warmed serving plates. Pour a little sauce over each one and serve with cream or crème fraîche.

NOTE Both the Spiced Raisin and Chocolate Walnut and Maple Puddings (right) can be baked from frozen, allowing an extra 5-10 minutes in the oven.

VARIATIONS
◆ Use chopped dates, dried figs or prunes instead of raisins.
◆ Replace the lemon in the sauce with orange rind and juice.

CHOCOLATE, WALNUT AND MAPLE PUDDINGS

SERVES 8 ◆ PREPARATION 25 minutes ◆ COOKING TIME 30 minutes
◆ FREEZING Suitable (stage 4) ◆ 525 CALS PER SERVING
◆ COLOUR INDEX Page 22

150g (5oz) unsalted butter, softened
175g (6oz) light muscovado sugar
1.25ml (¼ tsp) ground nutmeg
25g (1oz) plain white flour
60ml (4 tbsp) cocoa powder

5 eggs, separated
125g (4oz) ground almonds
50g (2oz) fresh white breadcrumbs
50g (2oz) walnuts, chopped

TO SERVE
maple syrup, for drizzling
few chopped walnuts

1 Grease 8 individual 175ml (6fl oz) pudding basins and line the bases with greaseproof paper.
2 In a bowl, cream the butter with 50g (2oz) of the sugar and the nutmeg until fluffy. Sift the flour and cocoa powder over the mixture. Beat in the egg yolks, then add the ground almonds, breadcrumbs and walnuts; fold in until combined.
3 Whisk the egg whites in a clean bowl until stiff. Gradually whisk in the remaining sugar. Fold a quarter into the chocolate mixture to lighten it, using a metal spoon. Carefully fold in the remaining mixture.
4 Spoon the mixture into the prepared basins, filling them no more than two-thirds full.
5 Stand the pudding basins in a roasting tin and pour in sufficient boiling water to give a 1cm (½ inch) depth. Cover the roasting tin with foil and bake at 180°C/fan oven 170°C (350°F) Mark 4 for 30 minutes or until the puddings feel firm.
6 Loosen the edges of the puddings with a knife and turn out on to warmed serving plates. Drizzle with maple syrup and sprinkle with chopped walnuts. Serve hot, with crème fraîche.

PINEAPPLE, APPLE AND ALMOND PUDDINGS

SERVES 6 ◆ PREPARATION 20 minutes ◆ COOKING TIME 35-40 minutes
◆ FREEZING Suitable ◆ 230 CALS PER SERVING

1 Granny Smith's apple, cut into 6 slices
75g (3oz) caster sugar, plus extra for dusting
50g (2oz) plain white flour
5ml (1 tsp) baking powder
pinch of salt
50g (2oz) butter, diced
50g (2oz) ground almonds
100g (3½oz) cooking apple, peeled, cored and diced

100g (3½oz) pineapple, peeled, cored and diced
1 large egg, lightly beaten
1.25ml (¼ tsp) almond extract

TO DECORATE
mint sprigs
crystalised violets (optional)
crushed cardamom seeds (optional)

1 Grease and base-line 6 individual 150ml (¼ pint) pudding basins or ramekins and dust the sides with flour. Using a pastry cutter the same size as the base of the moulds, stamp out circles from the apple slices. Dust with sugar and fry in a preheated, non-stick frying pan until caramelised on both sides. Place an apple slice in the base of each mould.

2 Sift the flour, baking powder and salt into a bowl, then rub in the butter until the mixture resembles fine crumbs. Stir in the sugar and ground almonds. Add the apple, pineapple, egg and almond extract and stir until evenly combined.

3 Spoon the mixture into the prepared moulds and stand on a baking tray. Bake at 180°C/fan oven 170°C (350°F) Mark 4 for 35-40 minutes or until golden and firm in the centre.

4 Leave to stand for 15 minutes, then carefully run a knife around the inside of each mould to loosen the puddings and turn out on to serving plates. Decorate with mint, crystallised violets and cardamom seeds if using. Serve with homemade custard (see note).

NOTES

◆ Cardamom custard is a delicious accompaniment to this pudding. Simply infuse the milk for the custard with the seeds from 3 cardamom pods, as well as a vanilla pod.

◆ If frozen, defrost at room temperature, then reheat at 180°C/fan oven 170°C (350°F) Mark 4 for 5-10 minutes. Finish as above.

CHOCOLATE MOUSSE PUDDINGS

These rich, gooey fudge-like puddings are delicious topped with Greek yogurt flavoured with vanilla seeds and honey, or lightly whipped cream if you prefer.

SERVES 4-6 ◆ PREPARATION 25 minutes ◆ COOKING TIME 20-25 minutes
◆ FREEZING Not suitable ◆ 690-460 CALS PER SERVING

125g (4oz) good quality plain dark chocolate (70% cocoa solids), in pieces
100g (3½oz) unsalted butter
30ml (2 tbsp) rum
2 eggs, plus 1 egg yolk
150g (5oz) caster sugar
25g (1oz) plain white flour
25g (1oz) ground almonds

TO SERVE
200g (7oz) Greek yogurt, or lightly whipped cream
1 vanilla pod, split (optional)
2 tsp thin honey (optional)

TO DECORATE
50g (2oz) dark chocolate

1 Place the chocolate, butter and rum in a small pan and heat gently until melted. Remove from the heat and allow to cool slightly. Whisk the eggs, egg yolk and sugar together in a bowl until pale and creamy.

2 Sift the flour over the whisked mixture and add the ground almonds and melted chocolate mixture. Fold in carefully, using a large metal spoon.

3 Spoon the mixture into six 150ml (5fl oz), or four 200ml (7fl oz) lightly greased ramekins or non-metallic individual pudding basins and place on a baking sheet. Bake at 190°C/fan oven 180°C (375°F) Mark 5 for 20-25 minutes until just firm to the touch.

4 Meanwhile, if using yogurt, spoon into a bowl and add the honey. Scrape the vanilla seeds from the pod into the bowl and stir until evenly blended.

5 Leave the baked puddings in their moulds for 3 minutes. Meanwhile, melt the chocolate in a small bowl set over a pan of simmering water. Transfer to a small greaseproof paper piping bag. Using a small palette knife, loosen each pudding around the edge, then carefully turn out on to plates.

6 Top each pudding with a spoonful of the yogurt or whipped cream. Snip the end off the paper piping bag and drizzle melted chocolate over the puddings to decorate. Serve at once.

FRANGIPANE BAKED PEARS

Poached fresh pears are stuffed with macerated raisins and almonds, then baked in a delicious almond sponge.

SERVES 6 ◆ PREPARATION 40 minutes, plus macerating
◆ COOKING TIME 50 minutes ◆ FREEZING Suitable ◆ 575 CALS PER SERVING
◆ COLOUR INDEX Page 22

25g (1oz) blanched almonds, chopped
25g (1oz) candied peel, chopped
25g (1oz) raisins
45ml (3 tbsp) kirsch or rum
75g (3oz) flaked almonds
50g (2oz) plain white flour

900ml (1½ pints) water
225g (8oz) caster sugar
6 pears
15ml (1 tbsp) apricot jam
125g (4oz) butter
2 eggs, beaten
few drops of almond extract (optional)

1 Mix the almonds, candied peel and raisins together in a small bowl. Sprinkle with the kirsch or rum, cover and leave to soak for at least 6 hours, preferably overnight. Drain, reserving the liquor.
2 Place the flaked almonds and flour in a food processor and process until the nuts are finely ground; set aside.
3 Pour the water into a large saucepan and add half of the sugar. Heat slowly until the sugar is dissolved, then bring to the boil. Add the pears, cover with a disc of greaseproof paper and poach gently for 10-15 minutes or until tender. Remove the pears with a slotted spoon; set aside.
4 Add the apricot jam to the syrup and let bubble for 30 minutes or until well reduced and syrupy. Set aside.
5 Meanwhile, cream the butter and remaining sugar together together in a bowl until light and fluffy. Add the eggs a little at a time, beating well. Fold in the flour and almond mixture, the reserved kirsch or rum, and almond extract, if using.
6 Using a teaspoon, scoop out the base of each pear. Stir a spoonful of the creamed mixture into the raisin mixture; use to fill the pears. Place in a 900ml (1½ pint) shallow ovenproof dish and spoon the creamed mixture around them. Brush the pears with a little of the syrupy glaze.
7 Bake at 190°C/fan oven 180°C (350°F) Mark 5 for about 50 minutes or until the frangipane is golden brown and just firm to the touch, covering with foil during baking if it appears to be overbrowning. Brush with a little more glaze and serve hot, with cream.

DOUBLE LEMON PUDDING

Poppy seeds add texture to this tangy lemon pudding. On baking the mixture separates to form a light, golden sponge over a layer of zesty, thick lemon custard.

SERVES 6-8 ◆ PREPARATION 20 minutes ◆ COOKING TIME 35 minutes
◆ FREEZING Not suitable ◆ 345-260 CALS PER SERVING

100g (3½oz) unsalted butter, softened
175g (6oz) golden caster sugar
finely grated rind of 3 lemons
100ml (3½fl oz) lemon juice (3-4 lemons)

4 eggs, separated
50g (2oz) plain white flour
15-30ml (1-2 tbsp) poppy seeds (optional)
200ml (7fl oz) milk

1 Beat the butter and sugar together in a bowl until pale and fluffy. Beat in the lemon rind and juice, egg yolks, flour, poppy seeds if using, and milk. (It won't matter if the mixture curdles at this stage.)
2 Whisk the egg whites in a clean bowl until they form soft peaks, then fold into the mixture until evenly incorporated.
3 Transfer to a greased 1.5 litre (2½ pint) baking dish and stand in a roasting tin half filled with boiling water. Bake at 180°C/fan oven 170°C (350°F) Mark 4 for 35 minutes. Serve warm, with crème fraîche.

CLAFOUTIS

SERVES 6 ◆ PREPARATION 20-30 minutes ◆ COOKING TIME 45-50 minutes
◆ FREEZING Not suitable ◆ 410 CALS PER SERVING ◆ COLOUR INDEX Page 23

700g (1½lb) ripe cherries, stoned
65g (2½oz) butter
4 eggs, plus 2 egg yolks
125g (4oz) caster sugar

75g (3oz) plain white flour
600ml (1 pint) milk
vanilla sugar, for dusting

1 Grease a shallow, round ovenproof dish large enough to hold the cherries using 15g (½oz) of the butter. Scatter the cherries in the dish.
2 Melt the remaining butter and allow to cool. In a large bowl, beat the eggs and egg yolks together. Add the sugar and whisk until the mixture is pale and light. Whisk in the cooled melted butter. Gradually sift in the flour, beating well to ensure the mixture is smooth, then stir in the milk.
3 Pour the batter over the cherries and bake at 190°C (375°F) Mark 5 for 45-50 minutes, until the clafoutis is golden and lightly set. Serve warm, dusted with vanilla sugar.

VARIATION Use two 425g (15oz) cans pitted cherries instead of fresh ones, draining them thoroughly.

COCONUT AND SAFFRON RICE PUDDING

SERVES 4 ◆ PREPARATION 5 minutes, plus standing ◆ COOKING TIME 1½-1¾ hours
◆ FREEZING Not suitable ◆ 420 CALS PER SERVING ◆ COLOUR INDEX Page 23

300ml (½ pint) milk
seeds from 3 green cardamom pods, bruised
1.25ml (¼ tsp) saffron strands
50g (2oz) short-grain pudding rice
300ml (½ pint) coconut milk

30ml (2 tbsp) caster sugar
25g (1oz) pistachio nuts, toasted and chopped
25g (1oz) stoned dates, chopped
pinch of freshly grated nutmeg
15g (½oz) butter

1 Put the milk, cardamom and saffron into a saucepan and slowly bring to the boil.
2 Put all the remaining ingredients, except the butter, into a greased 1.2 litre (2 pint) pie dish. Pour over the hot milk mixture and leave to stand for 1 hour.
3 Dot the butter over the top of the rice mixture and bake in the oven at 150°C/fan oven 140°C (300°F) Mark 2 for 30 minutes. Stir once, then bake for a further 1-1¼ hours until the rice is perfectly tender. Leave to stand for 10 minutes before serving.

APRICOT EGG CUSTARD

Fresh, juicy apricots are baked in an egg-rich batter in this lighter version of a clafoutis.

SERVES 8 ◆ PREPARATION 10 minutes, plus standing
◆ COOKING TIME 40-50 minutes ◆ FREEZING Not suitable
◆ 250 CALS PER SERVING

4 eggs
100g (3½oz) caster sugar
25g (1oz) plain white flour
150ml (¼ pint) milk
150ml (¼ pint) double cream

5ml (1 tsp) vanilla extract
25g (1oz) unsalted butter, melted
16 fresh apricots, halved and stoned
icing sugar, for dusting

1 Whisk the eggs, sugar and flour together in a bowl until smooth. Pour the milk and cream into a pan and slowly bring to the boil. Pour on to the egg mixture, whisking constantly, to form a smooth batter. Strain into a bowl, then stir in the vanilla extract. Cover and leave the batter to stand for 30 minutes.
2 Liberally grease a 1.7 litre/3 pint shallow ovenproof dish with melted butter. Place the apricots in the dish, cut-side up, and drizzle with the remaining butter.
3 Carefully pour over the batter and bake at 180°C/fan oven 170°C (350°F) Mark 4 for 40-50 minutes or until puffed up and set. Dust with icing sugar and serve warm.

CARAMELISED APPLE CREAMS

This variation of crème caramel uses a reduced apple juice and honey glaze instead of caramel to coat the insides of the timbales, giving a lighter, slightly sharper result.

SERVES 8 ◆ PREPARATION 25 minutes, plus infusing ◆ COOKING TIME 1¼ hours
◆ FREEZING Not suitable ◆ 190 CALS PER SERVING

500ml (16fl oz) milk
1 vanilla pod, split
600ml (1 pint) clear apple juice

15ml (1 tbsp) thin honey
125g (4oz) caster sugar
2 eggs, plus 4 egg yolks

1 Put the milk and vanilla pod into a saucepan and slowly bring to the boil. Remove from the heat and set aside to infuse for 20 minutes.

2 Meanwhile pour the apple juice and honey into a small heavy-based pan and boil rapidly for about 15-20 minutes until reduced to a thick glaze, about 90ml (3fl oz). Pour into 8 individual 120ml (4fl oz) timbales or ramekins, rotating to coat the base and partway up the sides; set aside to cool.

3 Beat the sugar, eggs and egg yolks together in a bowl until pale and creamy. Strain in the infused milk and stir well.

4 Pour the custard into the timbales or ramekins and stand them in a roasting tin. Surround with enough boiling water to come halfway up the sides of the moulds.

5 Bake at 150°C/fan oven 140°C (300°F) Mark 2, for 1-1¼ hours until just set; they should still feel slightly soft in the centre. Leave in the bain-marie to cool for 30 minutes, then remove from the water. Leave until cold, then chill in the refrigerator for 2-3 hours.

6 To serve, carefully run a small knife around each cream and invert on to serving plates.

VARIATION For a traditional crème caramel, omit the apple glaze. Melt 175g (6oz) granulated sugar in a heavy-based pan over a low heat, then cook to a rich brown caramel. Dip base of pan into cool water, then quickly use the caramel to coat the dishes (as in stage 2).

GOLDEN CROISSANT PUDDING

SERVES 6 ◆ PREPARATION 15 minutes ◆ COOKING TIME 40 minutes
◆ FREEZING Suitable (stage 3) ◆ 645 CALS PER SERVING
◆ COLOUR INDEX Page 24

**4 large croissants
(preferably one-day old)**
**75g (3oz) unsalted butter,
softened**
50g (2oz) sultanas

CUSTARD
**300ml (½ pint) double
cream**

300ml (½ pint) milk
1 vanilla pod, split
6 egg yolks
125g (4oz) caster sugar

TO FINISH
icing sugar, for dusting

1 Slice the croissants thickly, then spread with the butter. Arrange the croissant slices, butter-side up and overlapping, in a buttered 1.7 litre (3 pint) shallow baking dish, scattering in the sultanas as you do so.

2 To make the custard, pour the cream and milk into a heavy-based saucepan. Add the vanilla pod and place over a very low heat for about 5 minutes until the mixture is almost boiling and well flavoured with vanilla.

3 Meanwhile, in a large bowl, whisk together the egg yolks and caster sugar until light and foamy. Strain the flavoured milk on to the egg mixture, whisking all the time. Pour the egg mixture evenly over the croissants.

4 Stand the dish in a large roasting tin and pour in enough boiling water to come halfway up the sides of the dish. Bake at 180°C/fan oven 170°C (350°F) Mark 4 for 40 minutes or until the custard is softly set and the top is crisp and golden.

5 Leave the pudding to stand in the bain-marie for about 5 minutes. Serve warm, dusted with icing sugar and accompanied by cream or crème fraîche.

CHOCOLATE BREAD AND BUTTER PUDDING

Use a teabread that's lightly dotted with fruits, for this pudding or it will be too heavy. Allow to stand for a full 1 hour before baking to ensure a really good texture.

SERVES 6 ◆ PREPARATION 15 minutes, plus standing ◆ COOKING TIME 45 minutes
◆ FREEZING Not suitable ◆ 500 CALS PER SERVING ◆ COLOUR INDEX Page 24

**200g (7oz) plain dark
chocolate, in pieces**
75g (3oz) unsalted butter
**225g (8oz) fruited bun loaf
or light teabread, thinly
sliced**
5ml (1 tsp) vanilla extract

**2.5ml (½ tsp) ground
cinnamon**
3 eggs
25g (1oz) caster sugar
600ml (1 pint) milk
**cocoa powder and icing
sugar, for dusting**

1 Lightly grease the sides of a 1.7 litre (3 pint) ovenproof dish. Melt the chocolate with 25g (1oz) of the butter in a heatproof bowl set over a pan of simmering water.

2 Arrange a third of the fruited bread, overlapping, in the prepared dish. Spread with half of the melted chocolate. Repeat these layers, then top with the last of the bread.

3 Melt the remaining butter. Remove from the heat and stir in the vanilla extract, cinnamon, eggs, sugar and milk. Beat thoroughly, then pour over the bread. Leave to stand for 1 hour before baking.

4 Bake the pudding at 180°C/fan oven 170°C (350°F) Mark 4 for 45 minutes or until the custard is just set and the bread is deep golden brown. Leave to stand for 5 minutes. Dust with cocoa powder and icing sugar before serving.

VARIATION Use sliced brioche or croissants instead of fruited bread and lightly scatter with raisins or sultanas as you layer the pudding in the dish.

COCONUT AND LIME SYRUP CAKE

This light coconut cake soaked in a tangy lime syrup makes a refreshing dessert. Serve with Greek yogurt or crème fraîche.

SERVES 6 ◆ PREPARATION 20 minutes ◆ COOKING TIME 30-35 minutes
◆ FREEZING Not suitable ◆ 345 CALS PER SERVING

3 limes
125g (4oz) caster sugar
4 eggs, separated
**125g (4oz) desiccated
coconut**
**50g (2oz) fresh white
breadcrumbs**

90ml (3fl oz) thin honey
1 cinnamon stick
**8 small kaffir lime leaves,
shredded (optional)**
15ml (1 tbsp) rum

1 Grease and base-line a 20cm (8 inch) cake tin. Grate the rind and squeeze the juice from 1 lime. Place in a bowl with the sugar and egg yolks and whisk until pale and creamy. Fold in the desiccated coconut and breadcrumbs.

2 Whisk the egg whites in a clean bowl until they hold peaks, then carefully fold into the creamed mixture. Turn into the prepared cake tin and bake at 180°C/fan oven 170°C (350°F) Mark 4 for 30-35 minutes until risen, golden and springy to the touch. Leave to cool in the tin for 10 minutes.

3 Meanwhile, make the syrup. Finely peel the rind from the remaining limes and cut into very thin strips; set aside. Squeeze the juice from the limes and put into a small pan with the honey, cinnamon stick and lime leaves if using. Stir, then slowly bring to the boil. Add the shredded lime rind and simmer fast for 1 minute. Allow to cool slightly, then stir in the rum.

4 Transfer the warm cake to a serving plate, prick all over with a skewer and pour over the lime syrup. Serve cut into wedges with a spoonful of Greek yogurt or crème fraîche.

TROPICAL FRUIT CAKE

This spectacular pudding has a wonderful sticky base, topped with tropical fruits and crunchy caramel.

SERVES 8 ◆ PREPARATION 40 minutes, plus cooling
◆ COOKING TIME 45-50 minutes ◆ FREEZING Not suitable
◆ 765 CALS PER SERVING

CITRUS SYRUP
2 oranges
3 lemons
125g (4oz) caster sugar
1 cinnamon stick
450ml (¾ pint) water

CAKE
125g (4oz) butter, softened
125g (4oz) caster sugar
grated rind of 1 orange
pinch of salt
2 large eggs, lightly beaten
125g (4oz) semolina
125g (4oz) desiccated coconut
200g (7oz) ground almonds
5ml (1 tsp) baking powder
45ml (3 tbsp) orange juice

FRUIT TOPPING
300ml (½ pint) double cream
icing sugar, to taste
few drops of vanilla extract
1 mango, peeled and sliced
1 medium papaya or pineapple, peeled and sliced
1 star fruit, peeled and sliced
1 banana, peeled and sliced
6 lychees, peeled and sliced
50g (2oz) shredded fresh coconut, toasted (optional)
75g (3oz) caster sugar

1 For the citrus syrup, pare the rind from 1 orange and 1 lemon; squeeze the juice from all of the citrus fruit. Put the pared citrus rind and juice in a pan with the caster sugar, cinnamon and water. Bring to the boil and allow to bubble for 15-20 minutes or until syrupy. Strain and set aside to cool.

2 Grease and base-line a 22cm (8 inch) deep fluted cake tin or a 23cm (9 inch) spring-release cake tin. Beat the butter and caster sugar together in a bowl until pale and fluffy. Add the grated orange rind and salt, then gradually beat in the eggs, a spoonful at a time. Carefully fold in the semolina, desiccated coconut, ground almonds, baking powder and 45ml (3 tbsp) orange juice.

3 Spoon the mixture into the prepared tin. Bake at 170°C/fan oven 160°C (325°F) Mark 3 for 45-50 minutes or until a skewer inserted in the centre comes out clean. Cool in the tin for 15 minutes, then turn out on to a wire rack to cool completely. Cut a 1cm (½ inch) slice from the top of the cake, crumble and reserve the crumbs.

4 Prick the cake with a fine skewer, taking care not to push right through to the base (or the syrup will run through). Spoon all but 45ml (3 tbsp) of the syrup over the cake.

5 For the topping, whisk the cream with the icing sugar and vanilla extract to taste until soft peaks form. Carefully fold in the reserved cake crumbs, a third of the prepared fruit and the reserved citrus syrup. Stir the mixture gently until well combined, taking care not to mash the fruit.

6 Spoon the cream mixture on to the cake and top with the remaining fruit and toasted coconut if using. For the caramel, dissolve the caster sugar in 50ml (2fl oz) water in a small heavy-based pan over a low heat, then bubble until the caramel turns a light brown. Carefully add 30ml (2 tbsp) cold water. Drizzle the caramel over the cake while still warm and serve immediately.

DOUBLE CHOCOLATE BAKED ALASKAS

SERVES 6 ◆ PREPARATION 20 minutes, plus freezing ◆ COOKING TIME 5 minutes
◆ FREEZING Suitable (stage 4) ◆ 665 CALS PER SERVING
◆ COLOUR INDEX Page 24

200g (7oz) plain chocolate digestive biscuits, crushed
50g (2oz) butter, melted
600ml (1 pint) good quality chocolate ice cream
2 chocolate flake bars, roughly chopped

4 egg whites
225g (8oz) caster sugar
50g (2oz) desiccated coconut
cocoa powder, for dusting
toasted coconut shavings, to decorate

1 Mix the crushed biscuits with the hot melted butter. Using a 6cm (2½ inch) round pastry cutter as a template, press the mixture into 6 rounds on a lightly greased baking sheet. Place in the freezer to firm up for 30 minutes.

2 Beat the ice cream to soften slightly, then pile in mounds on to the biscuit bases, making a shallow hollow in the middle. Fill the hollow with the chocolate flakes. Return to the freezer for at least 1 hour until firm.

3 Put the egg whites and sugar in a large heatproof bowl set over a pan of barely simmering water and beat, using an electric whisk, for 10 minutes or until thick and glossy. Take the bowl off the heat, then fold in the desiccated coconut; allow the meringue to cool for 5 minutes.

4 Cover the ice cream completely with the meringue. Return to the freezer for at least 4 hours or overnight.

5 Bake the puddings at 220°C/fan oven 210°C (425°F) Mark 7 for 5 minutes or until golden. Serve immediately, dusted with cocoa powder and decorated with toasted coconut.

HOT ORANGE SOUFFLÉ

SERVES 6 ◆ PREPARATION 20 minutes ◆ COOKING TIME 25-30 minutes
◆ FREEZING Not suitable ◆ 250 CALS PER SERVING ◆ COLOUR INDEX Page 24

65g (2½oz) unsalted butter
30ml (2 tbsp) dried breadcrumbs
40g (1½oz) plain white flour
grated rind and juice of 2 small (or 1 large) oranges
grated rind and juice of 1 lemon

200ml (7fl oz) milk
125g (4oz) caster sugar
4 eggs, separated
45ml (3 tbsp) Grand Marnier or other orange liqueur
icing sugar, for dusting

1 Melt 15g (½oz) of the butter and use to grease a 1.5 litre (2½ pint) soufflé dish. Sprinkle the breadcrumbs over the base and side of the dish to coat; set aside.

2 Melt the remaining butter in a saucepan, then add the flour, orange and lemon rind and cook for 30 seconds. Take off the heat, then gradually whisk in the milk. Return to a low heat

and cook, stirring, until the sauce is thickened and smooth. Continue to cook for a further 2 minutes.

3 Remove from the heat and stir in the sugar, orange and lemon juices and Grand Marnier, then beat in the egg yolks.

4 Whisk the egg whites in a clean bowl until stiff, then carefully fold into the sauce until evenly incorporated.

5 Spoon the mixture into the prepared soufflé dish and bake at 190°C/fan oven 180°C (375°F) Mark 5 for 25-30 minutes until risen and golden. Dust with icing sugar and serve at once.

CHOCOLATE SOUFFLÉ

SERVES 8 ◆ PREPARATION 30 minutes ◆ COOKING TIME 15 minutes
◆ FREEZING Not suitable ◆ 490 CALS PER SERVING

225g (8oz) plain chocolate
15g (½oz) butter, melted
30ml (2 tbsp) cocoa powder, sifted
150ml (¼ pint) double cream
3 eggs, separated
30ml (2 tbsp) rum or brandy
pinch of cream of tartar

30ml (2 tbsp) caster sugar
cocoa powder, for dusting

VANILLA CREAM
300ml (½ pint) double cream
½ vanilla pod, split
2 egg yolks
25g (1oz) caster sugar

1 First make the vanilla cream. Put 150ml (¼ pint) of the cream in a saucepan with the split vanilla pod and slowly bring to the boil. Remove from the heat and allow to cool slightly. Meanwhile, lightly beat the egg yolks and sugar together in a bowl. Pour on the warm cream, stirring well, then return to the rinsed-out pan. Cook, stirring, over a low heat for 4-5 minutes until the custard is thickened slightly, enough to thinly coat the back of the spoon; do not boil it will curdle. Strain into a bowl, cover and cool, then chill.

2 For the soufflé, melt 75g (3oz) of the chocolate in a bowl over a pan of gently simmering water. Pour the melted chocolate into 8 sections of an ice-cube tray, dividing it equally. Cool, then place in the freezer to set.

3 Brush the insides of 8 ramekins, each about 7.5cm (3 inches) in diameter and 5cm (2 inches) high, with the melted butter. Dust the insides with a little of the cocoa, gently tapping out any excess. Chill the ramekins.

4 Put the remaining chocolate, cocoa powder and cream in a heavy-based pan and melt over a gentle heat until the mixture is smooth. Allow to cool slightly, then beat in the egg yolks and rum.

5 Place the egg whites and cream of tartar in a clean bowl and whisk until stiff. Gradually whisk in the sugar, a spoonful at a time. Continue to whisk until the mixture is very stiff and shiny. Using a large metal spoon, fold the whisked egg whites into the chocolate mixture until evenly incorporated.

6 Turn out the frozen chocolate cubes. Half fill the chilled ramekins with the chocolate soufflé mixture and place a frozen chocolate cube in the centre of each. Cover with the remaining soufflé mixture.

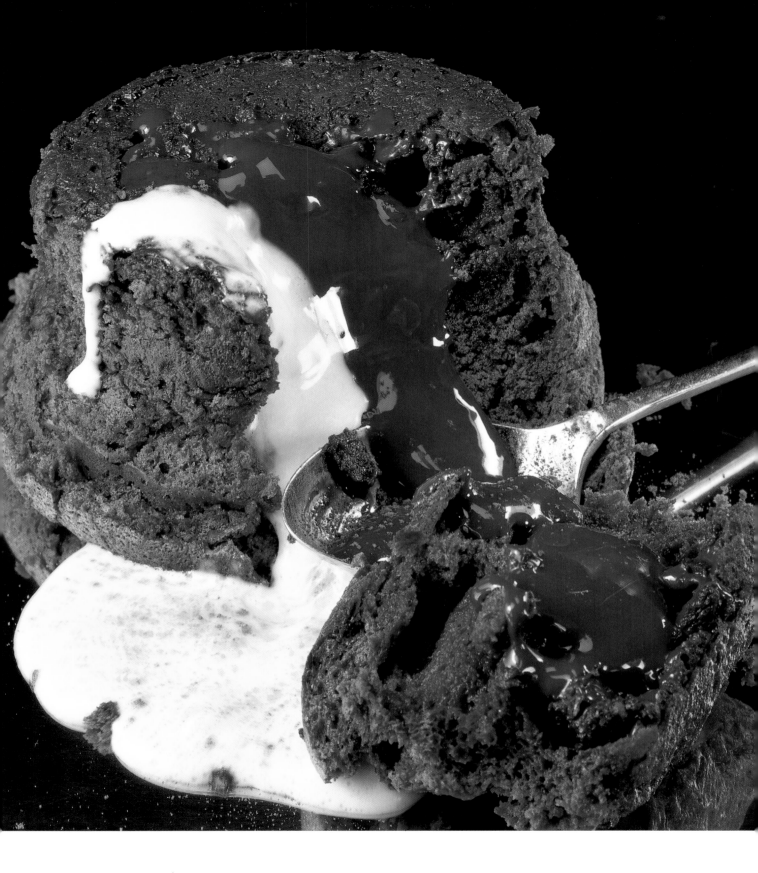

7 Preheat a baking sheet in the oven at 230°C/fan oven 220°C (450°F) Mark 8 for 1 minute. Warm the chilled vanilla cream in a large saucepan over a low heat. Using an electric whisk, whisk in the remaining cream until the custard becomes frothy; do not boil. Bake the soufflés on the hot baking sheet for 8-10 minutes or until well risen and firm to the touch. Let stand for 10 minutes.

8 To serve, run a round-bladed knife around the edge of each soufflé and turn out on to serving plates. Pour around the vanilla cream, dust with cocoa and serve immediately.

TIRAMISU TORTE

An outrageously rich cheesecake with an irresistible soft gooey texture, based on the delectable ingredients of tiramisu.

SERVES 8-10 ◆ PREPARATION 40 minutes, plus chilling
◆ COOKING TIME 45 minutes ◆ FREEZING Suitable ◆ 910-735 CALS PER SERVING

BISCUIT CASE
275g (10oz) amaretti biscuits, ratafias or macaroons
75g (3oz) unsalted butter, melted

FILLING
700g (1½lb) mascarpone or Philadelphia cream cheese (at room temperature)
150g (5oz) caster sugar
3 eggs, separated
30g (1¼oz) plain white flour

45ml (3 tbsp) dark rum
2.5ml (½ tsp) vanilla extract
175g (6oz) good quality plain dark chocolate (70% cocoa solids)
15ml (1 tbsp) finely ground espresso coffee
45ml (3 tbsp) Tia Maria or other coffee liqueur

TO FINISH
icing sugar, for dusting (optional)

1 Place the biscuits in a blender or food processor and process until finely ground. Mix with the melted butter, then spoon into a 23cm (9 inch) spring-release cake tin. Press evenly over the base with a potato masher, and 4cm (1½ inches) up the sides using the back of a spoon to form a neat shell. Chill for at least 30 minutes until firm.

2 Using a wooden spoon or electric mixer, beat the cream cheese until smooth. Add the sugar and beat again until smooth, then beat in the egg yolks. Divide the mixture in half and stir the flour, rum and vanilla extract into one half.

3 Melt the chocolate in a bowl over a pan of simmering water, cool slightly, then stir in the espresso coffee and coffee liqueur. Stir into the remaining half of the cheese mixture.

4 Whisk the egg whites until just holding soft peaks and fold half into each of the flavoured cheese mixtures.

5 Quickly fill the biscuit case with alternate large spoonfuls of the two mixtures.

6 Lightly swirl the two mixtures together to create a marbled effect. Bake at 200°C/fan oven 190°C (400°F) Mark 6 for 45 minutes, covering the top with foil if it appears to be overbrowning. At this stage the torte will be soft in the middle. Leave in the switched-off oven with the door slightly ajar, to cool completely; the filling will continue to firm up during this time. Chill for several hours before serving. Dust with icing sugar, if preferred. Serve cut into wedges, with crème fraîche if desired.

wire rack for 15 minutes; the cheesecake will sink slightly.

6 For the sauce, put the cream, ginger syrup and whisky in a small pan and heat gently; do not boil.

7 Unmould the cheesecake and serve warm, cut into wedges, with the ginger and whisky sauce.

NOTE If frozen, the cake may be baked straight from the freezer, allow an extra 15 minutes at the lower setting.

GINGER RICOTTA CAKE

An enticing cheesecake flavoured with stem ginger, served warm with a ginger and whisky cream sauce.

SERVES 6-8 ◆ PREPARATION 25 minutes ◆ COOKING TIME 1¼ hours ◆ FREEZING Suitable (stage 4) ◆ 715-475 CALS PER SERVING

225g (8oz) digestive biscuits
75g (3oz) butter, melted
200g (7oz) carton full-fat soft cheese
225g (8oz) ricotta cheese
60ml (4 tbsp) double cream
3 eggs, separated
15ml (1 tbsp) cornflour
1 piece preserved stem ginger in syrup, finely chopped

15ml (1 tbsp) ginger syrup (from the ginger jar)
125g (4oz) icing sugar, sifted

SAUCE
300ml (½ pint) single cream
10ml (2 tsp) stem ginger syrup
10ml (2 tsp) whisky

1 Line the base of a 20cm (8 inch) spring-release cake tin with non-stick baking parchment. Crush the biscuits in a blender or processor to a powder, then pour on the melted butter. Process for a further 1 minute until evenly mixed.

2 Spoon just over half of the crumb mixture into the prepared tin and press evenly over the base with a potato masher; set aside.

3 Put the cheeses, cream, egg yolks, cornflour, ginger and ginger syrup in the (clean) processor bowl and process briefly until the mixture is evenly blended. Transfer to a large bowl.

4 Whisk the egg whites in a clean bowl until stiff. Gradually whisk in the icing sugar, keeping the mixture very stiff and shiny. Fold into the ricotta mixture, using a metal spoon. Spread the ricotta mixture evenly over the biscuit base. Sprinkle the remaining biscuit crumbs over the top.

5 Bake at 200°C/fan oven 190°C (400°F) Mark 6 for 30 minutes. Cover loosely with foil and reduce the setting to 180°C/fan oven 170°C (350°F) Mark 4; bake for a further 45 minutes or until just set in the centre. Leave to cool on a

PECAN STREUSEL CHEESECAKE

SERVES 6 ◆ PREPARATION 40 minutes, plus chilling ◆ COOKING TIME 45 minutes ◆ FREEZING Not suitable ◆ 745 CALS PER SERVING

200g (7oz) shortbread-style biscuits
150g (5oz) butter
three 200g (7oz) packets half-fat soft cheese
275g (10oz) light soft brown sugar
3 eggs
300ml (½ pint) double cream

15ml (1 tbsp) vanilla extract
125g (4oz) pecan nuts, chopped
25g (1oz) caster sugar
60ml (4 tbsp) maple syrup
icing sugar, for dusting

1 Grease and base-line a 23cm (9 inch) spring-release cake tin with non-stick baking parchment. Place the shortbread biscuits in a food processor and process to fine crumbs.

2 Melt 25g (1oz) of the butter and stir in 125g (4oz) of the biscuit crumbs. Press on to the base of the cake tin. Chill for 30 minutes.

3 Place the soft cheese and 225g (8oz) brown sugar in a food processor and mix until evenly combined. Add the eggs, 60ml (2fl oz) cream and the vanilla extract. Process until evenly blended.

4 Pour the filling over the chilled biscuit base and bake at 180°C/fan oven 170°C (350°F) Mark 4 for about 45 minutes or until just set. Cool, then refrigerate for at least 6 hours.

5 For the streusel topping, melt 50g (2oz) of the remaining butter in a non-stick frying pan, add the pecan nuts and fry for about 2 minutes. Add the remaining biscuit crumbs and brown sugar; fry for about 3 minutes until the crumbs are turning golden. Add 90ml (3fl oz) cream and cook, stirring, for about 2 minutes until the mixture thickens. Spoon on to a foil-lined baking sheet and leave to cool.

6 For the sauce, melt the remaining 50g (2oz) butter with the caster sugar, maple syrup and remaining 150ml (¼ pint) cream. Bring to the boil and cook until light golden.

7 Unmould the cheesecake and transfer to a serving plate. Break the cooled pecan streusel into pieces and scatter over the top of the cheesecake. Dust with icing sugar and serve with the warm maple sauce.

BAKED CHEESECAKE WITH EXOTIC FRUITS

A traditional deep American style cheesecake, baked until just set – served topped with a medley of tropical fruits.

SERVES 8-10 ◆ PREPARATION 20 minutes ◆ COOKING TIME 1¼ hours
◆ FREEZING Not suitable ◆ 630-500 CALS PER SERVING

175g (6oz) digestive biscuits
65g (2½oz) unsalted butter, melted

FILLING
225g (8oz) ricotta cheese
225g (8oz) cream cheese
225g (8oz) crème fraîche
3 eggs, lightly beaten
225g (8oz) caster sugar

grated rind and juice of 1 lemon
15ml (1 tbsp) cornflour

TOPPING
1 ripe mango
1 ripe papaya
3 passion fruit
a little shredded coconut, toasted

1 Crush the biscuits in a blender or food processor, then mix with the melted butter. Spoon into a lightly greased 20cm (8 inch) spring-release cake tin and spread evenly. Chill while preparing the filling.

2 Put all the filling ingredients in a food processor and pulse briefly until smooth. Spoon over the biscuit base and bake at 150°C/fan oven 140°C (300°F) Mark 2 for 1¼ hours. At this stage the cheesecake will still be slightly soft in the middle. Turn off the heat but do not open the door. Leave the cheesecake to cool completely in the switched-off oven, for 3-4 hours. It will continue to firm up during this time.

3 For the topping, peel and slice the mango, discarding the stone. Peel, halve and deseed the papaya. Halve the passion fruit.

4 Unmould the cooled cheesecake on to a large plate and arrange the mango and papaya slices on top. Scoop out the passion fruit seeds and pulp, spooning them on to the fruit, then scatter over the toasted coconut. Serve at once.

SWEET TARTS
AND PASTRIES

Velvety smooth custard tarts with fragrant fruit toppings,
decadent chocolate tarts, crisp filo strudels, and a superb
collection of pâtisserie with mouth-watering appeal

PÂTE SUCRÉE

This is the classic French rich short pastry used for sweet flans; it is thin and crisp, yet melting in texture.

MAKES a 200g (7oz) quantity ◆ PREPARATION 15 minutes, plus resting
◆ FREEZING Suitable

200g (7oz) plain white flour

pinch of salt

2 egg yolks

100g (3½oz) butter (at room temperature)

90g (3¼oz) caster sugar

1 Sift the flour and salt on to a work surface. Make a well in the centre and add the egg yolks, butter and sugar.
2 Using the fingertips of one hand, work the sugar, butter and egg yolks together until well blended.
3 Gradually work in the flour to bind the mixture together.
4 Knead lightly until smooth, then wrap the pastry in cling film and rest in the refrigerator for at least 30 minutes.

SWEET FLAN PASTRY

This pastry is an enriched, sweetened version of shortcrust, which is perfect for sweet flans and easy to make.

MAKES a 225g (8oz) quantity ◆ PREPARATION 10 minutes, plus resting
◆ FREEZING Suitable

225g (8oz) plain white flour

pinch of salt

150g (5oz) firm butter, diced

30ml (2 tbsp) caster sugar

1 egg yolk

45ml (3 tbsp) cold water

1 Sift the flour and salt into a large bowl and rub in the butter using your fingertips until the mixture resembles breadcrumbs. Stir in the sugar.
2 Mix egg yolk with the water. Add to the dry ingredients and mix with a round-bladed knife to a firm dough.
3 Knead gently until just smooth. Wrap the pastry in cling film and leave to rest in the refrigerator for 30 minutes.

PÂTE BRISÉE

A quick version of this classic French pastry, prepared in minutes in the food processor.

MAKES a 225g (8oz) quantity ◆ PREPARATION 10 minutes, plus resting
◆ FREEZING Suitable

225g (8oz) plain white flour

5ml (1 tsp) salt

30ml (2 tbsp) sugar

110g (4oz) butter, softened

1 extra large egg yolk

1 Sift the flour and salt on to a sheet of greaseproof paper.

2 Place the sugar, butter and egg yolk in a food processor and blend until smooth. Shoot in the flour and process until just combined.
3 Turn the dough out on to a lightly floured surface and knead gently until smooth. Form into a ball, flatten and wrap in cling film. Chill in the refrigerator for at least 30 minutes.
4 Allow to come to room temperature before rolling out.

COCONUT AND MANGO TART

A luxurious tart of poached mangoes under a blanket of velvety smooth coconut custard. The secret to success is in the baking – the coconut custard should be quite wobbly on removing from the oven; on cooling, it slowly firms to an irresistible soft-set texture.

SERVES 10 ◆ PREPARATION 35 minutes, plus chilling ◆ COOKING TIME 50 minutes
◆ FREEZING Not suitable ◆ 415 CALS PER SERVING

PASTRY

125g (4oz) plain white flour

65g (2½oz) firm unsalted butter, diced

15ml (1 tbsp) caster sugar

40g (1½oz) desiccated coconut

1 egg yolk

30ml (2 tbsp) cold water (approximately)

FILLING

2 small ripe mangoes

75ml (2½fl oz) freshly squeezed orange juice

75g (3oz) caster sugar, plus 30ml (2 tbsp)

3 eggs

15g (½oz) cornflour

400ml (14fl oz) can coconut milk

150ml (¼ pint) double cream

TO DECORATE

toasted coconut shreds

icing sugar, for dusting

1 To make the pastry, sift the flour into a bowl, then rub in the butter, using fingertips. Stir in the sugar and desiccated coconut. Add the egg yolk and sufficient water to mix to a firm dough. Knead lightly and chill for 30 minutes.
2 Roll out the pastry thinly on a lightly floured surface and use to line a 4cm (1½ inch) deep, 24cm (9½ inch) loose-based flan tin, pressing the pastry into the tin. Line the pastry case with greaseproof paper and baking beans and bake blind at 200°C/fan oven 190°C (400°F) Mark 6 for 15 minutes. Remove paper and beans and bake for a further 5 minutes. Reduce setting to 150°C/fan oven 140°C (300°F) Mark 2.
3 Meanwhile, cut the mango into thin slices, discarding the skin and stone. Place in a heavy-based pan with the orange juice and 30ml (2 tbsp) sugar. Bring to a simmer and cook gently for 3-5 minutes until the mango slices are softened but still retaining their shape. Cool slightly.
4 Beat the eggs and remaining sugar together in a bowl. Blend the cornflour with a little of the coconut milk in a saucepan. Add the remaining coconut milk and bring to the boil, stirring until thickened. Remove from the heat and stir in the cream. Pour over the egg mixture, stirring until smooth.

5 Drain the mangoes, reserving the juice, and arrange evenly in the pastry case. Stir the reserved juice into the coconut custard and ladle it over the mangoes. Bake in the oven for about 30 minutes until the custard is just set; it will continue to firm up as it cools. Leave to cool, then chill for several hours, preferably overnight.

6 Decorate the tart with toasted coconut shreds and dust with icing sugar to serve.

VANILLA TART WITH BLUEBERRY COMPOTE

A delicately flavoured vanilla custard baked in a shallow pastry shell – served cold with a contrasting blueberry compote.

SERVES 8 ◆ PREPARATION 40 minutes, plus chilling
◆ COOKING TIME About 1 hour ◆ FREEZING Not suitable
◆ 650 CALS PER SERVING

PASTRY
200g (7oz) plain white flour
pinch of salt
100g (3½oz) firm unsalted butter, diced
25g (1oz) icing sugar, sifted
2 medium egg yolks
10-20ml (2-4 tsp) cold water

FILLING
600ml (1 pint) double cream
1 vanilla pod, split
3 eggs
1 egg yolk
75g (3oz) caster sugar

COMPOTE
450g (1lb) blueberries
60ml (4 tbsp) balsamic vinegar
60ml (4 tbsp) caster sugar
4 strips orange zest

1 To make the pastry, sift the flour and salt into a bowl and rub in the butter until the mixture resembles breadcrumbs. Stir in the icing sugar, then gradually work in the egg yolks and sufficient water to form a soft dough. Wrap the pastry in cling film and chill for 30 minutes.

2 Roll out the pastry on a lightly floured surface to a 30cm (12 inch) round and use to line a lightly greased 2.5cm (1 inch) deep, 25cm (10 inch) fluted flan tin. Lightly prick the base with a fork and chill for a further 20 minutes.

3 Line the pastry case with greaseproof paper and baking beans and bake blind at 200°C/fan oven 190°C (400°F) Mark 6 for 15 minutes. Remove the paper and beans and bake blind for a further 12-15 minutes until the pastry is golden. Set aside to cool slightly. Lower oven setting to 150°C/fan oven 140°C (300°F) Mark 2.

4 Meanwhile, prepare the filling. Put the cream and vanilla pod in a pan and bring slowly to the boil. Remove from the heat and leave to infuse until cool, then scrape the vanilla seeds from the pod into the cream; discard the pod.

5 Beat the eggs, extra egg yolk, sugar and cooled cream together in a bowl and pour into the pastry case. Bake in the oven for 30-40 minutes until very softly set; the custard will continue to firm up as it cools. Leave to cool.

6 Meanwhile, make the compote. Put all the ingredients in a pan and heat gently for 10 minutes. Transfer the blueberries to a bowl, using a slotted spoon. Boil the liquid steadily to reduce by half, then pour over the blueberries and leave to cool. Serve the vanilla tart at room temperature, accompanied by the blueberry compote.

FRENCH APPLE TART

SERVES 10 ◆ PREPARATION 40 minutes, plus chilling ◆ COOKING TIME 40 minutes
◆ FREEZING Not suitable ◆ 330 CALS PER SERVING ◆ COLOUR INDEX Page 26

PASTRY
175g (6oz) plain white flour
125g (4oz) firm unsalted butter, in pieces
10ml (2 tsp) caster sugar
1 egg

FILLING
1.8 kg (4 lb) crisp, tart dessert apples

60ml (4 tbsp) Calvados or brandy
grated rind and juice of 1 lemon
50-75g (2-3oz) caster sugar

GLAZE
15g (½oz) butter, melted
30ml (2 tbsp) caster sugar
60ml (4 tbsp) apricot jam

1 Put the flour in a food processor, add the butter and process until the mixture resembles fine breadcrumbs. Add the sugar and egg and process briefly until the mixture forms a firm dough. Wrap in cling film and chill for 30 minutes.

2 Roll out the pastry on a lightly floured surface and use to line a shallow 24cm (9½ inch) loose-based flan tin. Line the pastry case with greaseproof paper and baking beans. Bake blind at 200°C/fan oven 190°C (400°F) Mark 6 for 15 minutes. Remove paper and beans; bake for a further 5 minutes.

3 Set aside 4 apples. Roughly chop the remainder, including cores and skins, but discarding any blemished areas. Put in a heavy-based pan with 15ml (1 tbsp) water. Cover and cook very gently for 25-30 minutes, stirring occasionally, until the apples are soft. Press the pulp through a sieve into a clean pan. Add the Calvados, lemon rind and sugar to taste. Cook, uncovered, until slightly thickened; cool.

4 Peel, core and thinly slice the reserved apples; immerse in a bowl of cold water with 15ml (1 tbsp) lemon juice added.

5 Spread the apple purée in the pastry case. Drain the apple slices, pat dry on kitchen paper and arrange in overlapping circles over the apple purée. Brush with the melted butter and sprinkle with the sugar. Bake at 220°C/fan oven 210°C (425°F) Mark 7 for 20 minutes or until the apples are golden.

6 Pop the tart under a hot grill for a few minutes to brown the top if necessary. Melt jam with 15ml (1 tbsp) water, sieve, then brush over the apples to glaze. Serve warm or cold.

TARTE TATIN

SERVES 8 ◆ PREPARATION 30 minutes, plus cooling
◆ COOKING TIME 40-45 minutes ◆ FREEZING Suitable ◆ 535 CALS PER SERVING
◆ COLOUR INDEX Page 26

PASTRY
225g (8oz) plain white flour
150g (5oz) firm butter, in pieces
1.25ml (¼ tsp) salt
50g (2oz) icing sugar
1 egg

2-3 drops vanilla extract

FILLING
125g (4oz) butter
1-1.2 kg (2-2½ lb) dessert apples, preferably Cox's
200g (7oz) caster sugar
juice of ½ lemon

1 To make the pastry, put all of the ingredients in a food processor and process briefly until the mixture resembles coarse crumbs. Knead lightly to a smooth dough on a lightly floured surface. Wrap in cling film and chill for 20 minutes.

2 For the filling, melt the butter in a 25cm (10 inch) tarte tatin mould or heavy-based shallow cake tin (not a loose-based one). Meanwhile, peel, quarter and core the apples.

3 Sprinkle the sugar over the melted butter, then tightly pack the apples in the tin. Cook over a low heat for 15 minutes or until well caramelised, turning apples halfway through cooking. Sprinkle with the lemon juice. Allow to cool.

4 Roll out the pastry on a lightly floured surface to a round, 2.5cm (1 inch) larger all round than the top of the tarte tatin tin. Lay over the top of the cooked apples, tucking the edges of the pastry down the side of the tin. Prick the pastry with the tip of a sharp knife. Bake at 220°C/fan oven 210°C (425°F) Mark 7 for 25-30 minutes until golden brown.

5 Leave in the tin for 10 minutes, then turn out on to a serving plate. Serve warm, with cream, custard or ice cream.

RASPBERRY TART

SERVES 6 ◆ PREPARATION 40 minutes, plus chilling ◆ COOKING TIME 1 hour
◆ FREEZING Not suitable ◆ 510 CALS PER SERVING ◆ COLOUR INDEX Page 26

PASTRY
175g (6oz) plain white flour
125g (4oz) firm butter, in pieces
25g (1oz) vanilla sugar
5ml (1 tsp) finely grated orange rind
1 egg yolk
10-15ml (2-3 tsp) cold water

FILLING
2 eggs
2 egg yolks
40g (1½oz) caster sugar
450ml (¾ pint) single cream
½ vanilla pod, split
175g (6oz) raspberries
vanilla sugar, for dusting

1 To make the pastry, sift the flour into a bowl and rub in the butter, using fingertips. Add the vanilla sugar and orange rind, then add the egg yolk with enough water to mix to a firm dough. Knead briefly, then wrap and chill for 20 minutes.

2 Roll out the dough on a lightly floured surface and use to line a 4cm (1½ inch) deep, 20cm (8 inch) loose-based fluted flan tin. Chill again for 20 minutes.

3 Line pastry case with greaseproof paper and baking beans and bake blind at 200°C/fan oven 190°C (400°F) Mark 6 for 15 minutes. Remove paper and beans; bake for 5 minutes.

4 Meanwhile, make the custard filling. Beat the whole eggs, egg yolks and sugar together in a bowl. Put the cream and split vanilla pod in a small pan over a very low heat until the cream is well flavoured and almost boiling. Pour on to the egg mixture, whisking constantly, then strain into the pastry case.

5 Lower the oven setting to 150°C/fan oven 140°C (300°F) Mark 2 and place the tart in the oven. Bake for 45 minutes or until the centre is lightly set; it will continue to firm up as it cools. Leave until cold, then carefully remove flan from tin. Top with the raspberries and dust with vanilla sugar to serve.

CHOCOLATE AND CHERRY AMARETTI TART

Chocolate and cherries are a classic combination. Tart morello cherries give this flan a wonderful depth of flavour.

SERVES 8 ◆ PREPARATION 30 minutes, plus chilling
◆ COOKING TIME 1 hour 20 minutes ◆ FREEZING Suitable
◆ 765 CALS PER SERVING

PASTRY
150g (5oz) butter, softened
50g (2oz) icing sugar
1 small egg, beaten
225g (8oz) plain white flour

FILLING
400g (14oz) bottled or canned pitted morello cherries, drained
45ml (3 tbsp) brandy, sloe gin or amaretto liqueur
100g (3½oz) good quality plain chocolate (70% cocoa solids)

125g (4oz) butter, softened
125g (4oz) caster sugar
3 large eggs, beaten
125g (4oz) ground almonds
25g (1oz) self-raising white flour
50g (2oz) amaretti biscuits, crushed
75g (3oz) silvered or flaked almond

TO FINISH
icing sugar, for dusting

1 Put the morello cherries in a bowl, add the brandy, sloe gin or liqueur and leave to stand for 30 minutes.
2 Meanwhile, make the pastry. Put the butter, icing sugar and egg in a food processor and whizz until almost smooth. Add the flour and process until the mixture just begins to form a dough. Turn on to a floured work surface and knead lightly until smooth, then wrap in cling film and chill for 30 minutes.
3 Roll out the pastry on a floured surface and use to line a 24cm (9½ inch) loose-based flan tin. Chill for 20 minutes.
4 Line the pastry case with greaseproof paper and baking beans and bake blind at 200°C/fan oven 190°C (400°F) Mark 6 for 15 minutes. Remove paper and beans and bake for a further 5 minutes. Lower the setting to 150°C/fan oven 140°C (300°F) Mark 2.
5 For the filling, melt the chocolate in a heatproof bowl over a pan of simmering water; stir until smooth; allow to cool.
6 In a bowl, beat together the butter and sugar until pale and fluffy. Gradually beat in the eggs, alternately with the ground almonds and flour. Finally, fold in the cooled melted chocolate and crushed amaretti biscuits.
7 Spoon about one third of the mixture over the base of the pastry case. Spoon the cherries evenly over the surface, then cover with the remaining filling, spreading it carefully. Sprinkle the almonds on the top. Bake for about 1 hour until the tart forms a thin crust on top; it should be quite soft underneath.
8 Leave to stand for about 10 minutes, then carefully remove the flan from the tin. Serve warm, dusted with icing sugar.

7 Scatter the prunes in the pastry case, then pour the cream mixture around them. Bake for about 30 minutes until the custard is turning golden, and is just set in the centre.

8 Meanwhile, warm the apricot jam and brandy in a small pan to make the glaze. Brush over the tart while still warm. Serve warm or cold, with crème fraîche.

SUMMER FRUIT AND PRALINE TART

SERVES 10 ◆ PREPARATION 25 minutes, plus chilling ◆ COOKING TIME 30 minutes
◆ FREEZING Not suitable ◆ 375 CALS PER SERVING ◆ COLOUR INDEX Page 26

PASTRY
150g (5oz) plain white
flour
75g (3oz) firm unsalted
butter, in pieces
50g (2oz) caster sugar
2 egg yolks

PRALINE
75g (3oz) flaked almonds,
lightly toasted
175g (6oz) caster sugar
90ml (3fl oz) water

FILLING
3 egg yolks
25g (1oz) caster sugar
30ml (2 tbsp) cornflour
30ml (2 tbsp) plain white
flour
7.5ml (1½ tsp) vanilla
extract
30ml (½ pint) milk
150ml (¼ pint) double
cream
450g (1lb) small summer
fruits, such as redcurrants,
raspberries and
blueberries

1 To make the pastry, sift the flour into a bowl and rub in the butter, using the fingertips. Add the sugar and egg yolks and mix to a smooth dough, adding a little water if necessary. Wrap in cling film and chill for 30 minutes.

2 For the praline, scatter the almonds on to a lightly oiled baking sheet. Put the sugar and water in a small heavy-based pan and dissolve over a low heat, then boil rapidly until golden. Immediately pour the caramel over the almonds. Leave to cool and harden.

3 Roll out the pastry on a lightly floured surface and use to line a 23cm (9 inch) loose-based flan tin. Prick the base. Line with greaseproof paper and baking beans and bake blind at 200°C/fan oven 190°C (400°F) Mark 6 for 20 minutes. Remove paper and beans and bake for a further 10 minutes or until crisp.

4 Beat the egg yolks, sugar, cornflour, flour and vanilla extract together in a bowl with a little of the milk. Pour the remaining milk and the cream into a heavy-based pan and slowly bring to the boil. Pour on to the egg mixture, stirring constantly. Return to the heat and slowly bring a simmer, stirring until thickened. Transfer to a bowl, cover the surface with damp greaseproof paper and leave to cool.

5 Break half of the praline into jagged pieces and set aside for the decoration. Crush the remainder with a rolling pin, then stir into the cooled custard. Spread in the pastry case.

6 Scatter the fruit and reserved praline pieces over the custard. Serve the tart within 2-3 hours of assembling.

GLAZED PRUNE TART

SERVES 8 ◆ PREPARATION 25 minutes, plus macerating and chilling
◆ COOKING TIME 50 minutes ◆ FREEZING Suitable ◆ 450 CALS PER SERVING

PASTRY
175g (6oz) plain white
flour
75g (3oz) firm lightly
salted butter, diced
75g (3oz) caster sugar
3 egg yolks

FILLING
250g (9oz) ready-to-eat
pitted prunes
75ml (5 tbsp) brandy

1 vanilla pod, split
150ml (¼ pint) double
cream
150ml (¼ pint) single
cream
25g (1oz) caster sugar
2 eggs

TO GLAZE
60ml (4 tbsp) apricot jam,
sieved
30ml (2 tbsp) brandy

1 For the filling, soak the prunes in the brandy for several hours until the brandy is absorbed, or overnight if possible.

2 To make the pastry, sift the flour into a bowl, then rub in the butter until the mixture resembles fine breadcrumbs. Stir in the sugar, then add the egg yolks and mix to a soft dough. Knead lightly, wrap in cling film and chill for 30 minutes.

3 Roll out the pastry on a lightly floured surface and use to line a 2.5cm (1 inch) deep, 23-24cm (9-9½ inch) loose-based flan tin. Chill for 20 minutes.

4 Prick the base with a fork, then line with greaseproof paper and baking beans. Bake blind at 200°C/fan oven 190°C (400°F) Mark 6 for 15 minutes. Remove paper and beans and bake for a further 5 minutes. Lower the oven setting to 180°C/fan oven 170°C (350°F) Mark 4.

5 Meanwhile, put the vanilla pod and double cream in a saucepan and bring just to the boil, then take off the heat and set aside to infuse for 20 minutes. Discard the vanilla pod.

6 Pour the infused cream into a bowl, add the single cream, sugar and eggs, and beat well.

GOLDEN PASSION FRUIT TART

SERVES 8 ◆ PREPARATION 1 hour, plus chilling
◆ COOKING TIME 1 hour 25 minutes ◆ FREEZING Suitable (stage 6)
◆ 640 CALS PER SERVING ◆ COLOUR INDEX Page 26

PASTRY
225g (8oz) plain white flour
50g (2oz) icing sugar
finely grated rind of 1 orange
150g (5oz) butter
1 egg, lightly beaten

FILLING
8 large, ripe passion fruit
150g (5oz) caster sugar
4 eggs, beaten
200ml (7fl oz) double cream

MANGO SAUCE
2 large, ripe mangoes, peeled, stoned and chopped
1 orange, peeled and chopped
lemon juice, to taste

TO DECORATE
2 passion fruit, halved
1 mango, peeled, stoned and sliced
caster sugar, for dredging

1 To make the pastry, put the flour, icing sugar and grated orange rind in a food processor. Add the butter and process until the mixture resembles fine crumbs. Add all but 15ml (1 tbsp) of the egg and pulse until the dough comes together in a ball. Wrap in cling film and chill for 30 minutes.
2 Roll out the dough on a lightly floured surface and use to line a 23cm (9 inch) fluted, loose-based flan tin. Chill for 30 minutes.
3 Prick the pastry base and line with greaseproof paper and baking beans. Bake blind at 200°C/fan oven 190°C (400°F) Mark 6 for 10 minutes, then remove beans and paper and cook for a further 10 minutes. Brush with the reserved beaten egg and cook for a further 2 minutes to seal the base. Lower the setting to 140°C/fan oven 130°C (275°F) Mark 1.
4 To make the filling, halve the passion fruit and scoop the pulp into the (clean) food processor. Add the caster sugar and process for 1 minute. With the machine running, add the eggs and cream through the feeder tube, process briefly to mix, then strain through a fine sieve.
5 Pour the filling into the pastry case and bake for 1 hour or until it is just set in the middle; the filling will firm up further on cooling. Set aside to cool, then chill for 2 hours.
6 To make the sauce, put the mango and orange flesh into a food processor and pulse to a purée. Pass through a sieve into a bowl and add lemon juice to taste.
7 For the decoration, scoop the passion fruit pulp into a bowl, add the mango slices and turn to mix, then toss in caster sugar until heavily coated. Grill until golden; cool.
8 Decorate the tart with the grilled mango slices and serve with the mango sauce and whipped cream.

VARIATION For a special touch, decorate the tart with edible gold leaf and caramel 'bark'. To make 'bark', sprinkle a layer of caster sugar on a clean baking sheet and grill for 4-5 minutes until liquid. Cool for 10 minutes, then crack into pieces.

PEAR TARTE RENVERSÉE

This is cooked in a similar way to a tarte tatin. Halved pears are poached in a red wine syrup, then topped with pastry and baked. To serve, the tart is inverted.

SERVES 6 ◆ PREPARATION 40 minutes
◆ COOKING TIME 1 hour for filling; 35-40 minutes baking
◆ FREEZING Not suitable ◆ 495 CALS PER SERVING

225g (8oz) quantity Pâte Brisée (see page 172)

FILLING
8 slightly under-ripe pears
1 cinnamon stick
75g (3oz) caster sugar

600ml (1 pint) full-bodied red wine

TO DECORATE
toasted slivered almonds

1 Peel the pears, halve lengthwise and scoop out the cores, then arrange the pear halves in a 25cm (10 inch) heavy-based non-stick metal dish or frying pan (suitable for oven use), positioning the tapering stalk ends towards the centre.
2 Crumble the cinnamon over the top and sprinkle over the sugar. Pour on the wine and bring to the boil. Cover and simmer gently for about 1 hour or until tender.
3 Uncover and position a plate over the pears to hold them in place as you drain off the juices into a pan. Boil the juices rapidly until reduced and very syrupy. Drizzle over the pears.
4 Roll out the pastry to a round, slightly larger than the pan. Lift the pastry over the pears and tuck the edges down the side of the tin. Bake at 200°C/fan oven 190°C (400°F) Mark 6 for 35-40 minutes until the pastry is crisp and golden. Leave to stand in the tin for 5-10 minutes, or until cold (if serving cold).
5 When ready to serve, invert the tart on to a plate, sprinkle with toasted almonds and accompany with crème fraîche.

LEMON TART WITH FROSTED BERRIES

The addition of frosted seasonal berries to a classic lemon tart makes this version extra special.

SERVES 8 ◆ PREPARATION 50 minutes, plus chilling
◆ COOKING TIME About 1 hour ◆ FREEZING Suitable (stage 5)
◆ 350 CALS PER SERVING

PASTRY
150g (5oz) plain white
flour
finely grated rind of
½ lemon
65g (2½oz) caster sugar
75g (3oz) firm unsalted
butter, in pieces
25g (1oz) ground almonds,
lightly toasted
1 egg, beaten
few drops of almond
extract
15ml (1 tbsp) cold water

FILLING
25g (1oz) unsalted butter
3 large lemons
5 eggs
150g (5oz) caster sugar

TO FINISH
1 egg white, lightly
whisked
lemon balm or mint leaves
caster sugar, for coating
redcurrant sprigs
blackberries or blueberries
rose petals (optional)

1 To make the pastry, put the flour, lemon rind and sugar in a food processor, add the butter and process until the mixture resembles fine crumbs. Add the ground almonds and process for 2-3 seconds only. Add all but 10ml (2 tsp) of the beaten egg with the almond extract and water. Process until the dough just comes together, then turn out and knead lightly. Wrap in cling film and chill for 2 hours. Roll out the pastry thinly on a lightly floured surface.

2 Use the pastry to line a 33x10cm (13x4 inch) oblong loose-based tart tin (see note). Line with greaseproof paper and baking beans and bake blind at 200°C/fan oven 190°C (400°F) Mark 6 for 20 minutes until pale golden. Remove the paper and beans and return to the oven for 5 minutes. Lower the oven setting to 130°C/fan oven 120°C (250°F) Mark ½. Immediately brush the inside of the pastry case with the reserved egg to seal, then return to the oven for 5 minutes.

3 For the filling, melt the butter and allow to cool slightly. Grate the rind from the lemons and squeeze the juice; you will need about 175ml (6fl oz) in total.

4 In a bowl, whisk the eggs together lightly, then add the melted butter, lemon rind and juice, and caster sugar. Whisk together quickly until the mixture is smooth and well combined.

5 Immediately pour the lemon filling into the warm pastry case and bake for 30-40 minutes until just set. Allow to stand for 15 minutes before carefully removing from the tin and placing on a wire rack to cool.

6 To decorate, dip the herb leaves into the egg white, then into the sugar to coat, shaking off excess. Repeat with the berries and redcurrants. Leave to dry on a sheet of non-stick baking parchment. When ready to serve, decorate the lemon tart with the frosted fruit and berries, and a few rose petals if wished.

NOTE If you do not have an oblong tart tin, use a 22cm (8½ inch) round loose-based flan tin instead.

TREACLE TART

Breadcrumbs are mixed with plenty of golden syrup and lemon to cut the sweetness, then baked in a deep pastry case. Serve with melting ice cream or crème fraîche.

SERVES 8-10 ◆ PREPARATION 25 minutes, plus chilling
◆ COOKING TIME 25-50 minutes ◆ FREEZING Suitable
◆ 620-495 CALS PER SERVING ◆ COLOUR INDEX Page 27

PASTRY
225g (8oz) plain white flour
150g (5oz) firm unsalted butter, in pieces
1 egg yolk
15g (½oz) caster sugar
30ml (2 tbsp) cold water

FILLING
700g (1½lb) golden syrup
175g (6oz) fresh white breadcrumbs
grated rind of 3 lemons
2 eggs, lightly beaten

1 To make the pastry, put the flour in a food processor, add the butter and process until the mixture resembles fine breadcrumbs. Add the egg yolk, sugar and water; process briefly to a firm dough. Turn on to a lightly floured surface and knead gently, then wrap in cling film and chill for 30 minutes.
2 Roll out the pastry on a lightly floured surface and use to line a 4cm (1½ inch) deep, 25cm (10 inch) fluted flan tin. Prick the base with a fork.
3 For the filling, lightly heat the golden syrup in a saucepan until thinned in consistency. Remove from the heat and mix with the breadcrumbs and lemon rind. Stir in the beaten eggs.
4 Pour the filling into the pastry case and bake at 180°C/fan oven 170°C (350°F) Mark 4 for 45-50 minutes or until the filling is lightly set and turning golden. Allow to cool slightly. Serve warm, with ice cream or crème fraîche.

PECAN, MAPLE AND WHISKY PIE

SERVES 6-8 ◆ PREPARATION 30 minutes, plus chilling ◆ COOKING TIME 1¼ hours
◆ FREEZING Suitable ◆ 890-665 CALS PER SERVING ◆ COLOUR INDEX Page 28

PASTRY
225g (8oz) plain white flour
150g (5oz) butter
45ml (3 tbsp) iced water

FILLING
75g (3oz) butter, in pieces
75g (3oz) dark soft brown or molasses sugar
3 eggs, beaten

5ml (1 tsp) cornflour
60ml (2fl oz) maple syrup
250ml (8fl oz) golden syrup
60ml (4 tbsp) whisky
5ml (1 tsp) vanilla extract
200g (7oz) pecan nuts, toasted and roughly chopped
maple syrup, to serve

1 To make the pastry, put the flour and butter in a food processor and pulse until the mixture resembles fine crumbs. Add the water and pulse until the mixture comes together in a ball. Wrap in cling film and chill for 30 minutes.

2 Roll out the pastry on a lightly floured surface and use to line a 23cm (9 inch) loose-based flan tin. Chill for 30 minutes.
3 Prick the pastry base, line with greaseproof paper and baking beans and bake blind at 200°C/fan oven 190°C (400°F) Mark 6 for 15 minutes. Remove paper and beans and bake for a further 10 minutes or until the base is firm. Brush the pastry case with a little beaten egg (from the filling) and return to the oven for 3-4 minutes to seal. Set aside. Lower setting to 180°C/fan oven 170°C (350°F) Mark 4.
4 To make the filling, beat the butter and sugar together in a bowl until light, then slowly add the beaten eggs and cornflour. Stir in the maple and golden syrups, whisky and vanilla extract; don't worry if the mixture appears curdled. Mix in the toasted pecan nuts and pour into the pastry case.
5 Bake for about 45 minutes until the filling is just set. Leave to cool slightly. Serve warm, drizzled with maple syrup. Accompany with ice cream or whipped cream.

CHOCOLATE TART WITH HAZELNUT AND ORANGE SYRUP

A sensational smooth, slightly bitter, dark chocolate tart contrasted by a sweet, tangy hazelnut syrup. Both the tart and syrup can be made a day in advance.

SERVES 10 ◆ PREPARATION 25 minutes, plus chilling ◆ COOKING TIME 35 minutes
◆ FREEZING Not suitable ◆ 525 CALS PER SERVING

PASTRY
150g (5oz) plain white flour
15g (½oz) cocoa powder
75g (3oz) unsalted butter, in pieces
30ml (2 tbsp) icing sugar
1 egg yolk
15-20ml (3-4 tsp) cold water

FILLING
200g (7oz) good quality plain, dark chocolate (70% cocoa solids)
125g (4oz) unsalted butter
75g (3oz) cocoa powder

150ml (¼ pint) hot water
2 eggs
2 egg yolks
50g (2oz) caster sugar

SYRUP
150g (5oz) caster sugar
100ml (3½fl oz) water
finely grated rind of 1 orange
150ml (¼ pint) fresh orange juice
75g (3oz) blanched hazelnuts, roughly chopped
15g (½oz) unsalted butter

1 To make the pastry, put the flour, cocoa powder and butter in a food processor and work until the mixture resembles breadcrumbs. Add the icing sugar, egg yolk and 15ml (3 tsp) cold water. Blend briefly to a dough, adding a little extra water if necessary. Knead gently on a lightly floured surface, then wrap in cling film and chill for 30 minutes.
2 Roll out the pastry on a lightly floured surface and use to line a 2cm (¾ inch) deep, 24cm (9½ inch) loose-based fluted flan tin. Line with greaseproof paper and baking beans.

3 Bake blind at 200°C/fan oven 190°C (400°F) Mark 6 for 15 minutes. Remove the paper and beans and bake for a further 5 minutes. Reduce the oven setting to 150°C/fan oven 140°C (300°F) Mark 2.

4 For the filling, put the chocolate in a heatproof bowl with the butter. Place over a pan of gently simmering water and leave until melted. In another bowl, blend the cocoa powder with the water until smooth.

5 Whisk the eggs, egg yolks and sugar together in a bowl. Stir in the cocoa mixture, then fold in the chocolate mixture until

smooth. Pour the filling into the pastry case and bake for about 10 minutes until just beginning to set around the edges.

6 For the syrup, put the sugar and water in a small heavy-based pan and heat gently until dissolved. Bring to the boil and boil rapidly for about 5 minutes until the syrup turns to a pale caramel. Add the orange rind and juice (standing back as it will splutter) and heat gently until the caramel softens to form a smooth syrup. Stir in the hazelnuts and butter.

7 Serve the chocolate tart warm or cold, with the hazelnut and orange syrup spooned over.

RATAFIA BAKEWELL TART

A deep almondy sponge set on a layer of apricot conserve in a crisp pastry case. Caramel oranges are an ideal accompaniment.

SERVES 8 ◆ PREPARATION 30 minutes, plus chilling
◆ COOKING TIME About 50 minutes ◆ FREEZING Suitable
◆ 500 CALS PER SERVING ◆ COLOUR INDEX Page 27

Shortcrust Pastry, made with 225g (8oz) flour (see page 76)
60ml (4 tbsp) apricot conserve

FILLING
75g (3oz) unsalted butter
3 eggs
125g (4oz) caster sugar
5ml (1 tsp) almond extract

125g (4oz) ground almonds
50g (2oz) ratafia biscuits, halved

TO SERVE
caramelised oranges (optional, see below)
icing sugar, for dusting

1 Preheat a baking sheet in the oven at 200°C/fan oven 190°C (400°F) Mark 6. Roll out the pastry on a lightly floured surface and use to line a 23cm (9 inch) spring-release cake tin. Spread the apricot conserve over the base.
2 Melt the butter and set aside to cool slightly. Place the eggs and sugar in a large bowl and whisk until the mixture is thick enough to leave a trail when the whisk is lifted from the bowl. Pour in the melted butter, around the edge of the bowl. Add the almond extract and scatter over the ground almonds and ratafia biscuits. Fold in carefully, using a large metal spoon, until just combined.
3 Turn the mixture into the pastry-lined tin. Place on the preheated baking sheet and bake for 10 minutes. Reduce the setting to 180°C/fan oven 170°C (350°F) Mark 4 and bake for a further 40 minutes or until the filling is firm and set.
4 Allow the tart to cool slightly, then remove from the tin and place on a serving plate. Dust the edges with icing sugar and serve warm or cold. Accompany with cream or crème fraîche, and caramelised oranges if you wish.

◆ CARAMELISED ORANGES Pare strips of zest from 1 orange; peel and thinly slice 3 oranges, discarding all white pith. Dissolve 175g (6oz) sugar in 600ml (1 pint) water in a heavy-based pan over a low heat. Increase heat and boil steadily for 5 minutes. Add the orange slices and zest strips. Bring to the boil, then simmer gently for 15 minutes. Transfer the orange slices and zest to a bowl with a slotted spoon. Cook the syrup for a further 20 minutes or until pale golden. Pour over the fruit and allow to cool.

PLUM AND ALMOND TART

Plums have a natural affinity with almonds and make a flavourful winter tart. This one uses an easy sourdough pastry.

SERVES 6-8 ◆ PREPARATION 30 minutes, plus chilling
◆ COOKING TIME 35-40 minutes ◆ FREEZING Suitable (stage 5)
◆ 710-535 CALS PER SERVING ◆ COLOUR INDEX Page 28

PASTRY
175g (6oz) plain white flour
150g (5oz) chilled butter, diced
105ml (7 tbsp) soured cream

FILLING
50g (2oz) butter
50g (2oz) caster sugar
2 eggs, lightly beaten
100g (4oz) ground almonds

15ml (1 tbsp) kirsch or 3-4 drops almond extract
900g (2lb) plums or apricots, quartered and stoned
caster sugar, for dusting

TO FINISH
50g (2oz) blanched almonds
175g (6oz) redcurrant jelly

1 First, make the pastry. Put the flour in a food processor, add the butter and process for 1-2 seconds (pieces of butter should still be visible). Add the soured cream and process for a further 1-2 seconds until the dough just begins to come together.
2 Turn the sourdough pastry out on to a lightly floured surface and knead very lightly for about 30 seconds or until the pastry just comes together (it should look crumbly). Wrap in cling film and chill for about 30 minutes.
3 Meanwhile, prepare the filling. Beat the butter in a bowl until soft, then add the caster sugar and beat until light and fluffy. Beat in the eggs, alternately with the ground almonds. Add the kirsch or almond extract, then cover and set aside.
4 Roll out the pastry thinly on a lightly floured surface to a 30cm (12 inch) round, then transfer to a large baking sheet and prick all over with a fork. Spread the almond mixture over the pastry, leaving a 3cm (1¼ inch) border around the edge. Scatter the quartered plums or apricots over the almond filling and fold the edges of the pastry up over the fruit.
5 Dust with sugar, then chill for 20 minutes. Preheat another large baking sheet in the oven at 220°C/fan oven 210°C (425°F) Mark 7. Slide the tart on its baking sheet on top of the hot sheet. Cook for 35-40 minutes until deep golden brown.
6 Leave the tart on the baking sheet for 10 minutes, then slide on to a wire rack. Arrange the almonds among the fruit. Warm the redcurrant jelly in a small pan until melted and smooth. Brush generously over the tart and allow to set. Serve with crème fraîche or vanilla custard.

NOTE If frozen, reheat tart from frozen at 200°C/fan oven 190°C (400°F) Mark 6 for 20 minutes. Complete step 6.

LEMON AND LIME PAVLOVA PIE

SERVES 6 ◆ PREPARATION 1 hour, plus chilling ◆ COOKING TIME 1 hour ◆ FREEZING Not suitable ◆ 815 CALS PER SERVING

PASTRY
225g (8oz) plain white flour
150g (5oz) butter, diced
15ml (1 tbsp) caster sugar
grated rind of 1 lime
1 egg, lightly beaten
15ml (1 tbsp) water

FILLING
finely grated rind of 4 limes
juice of 5 limes

juice of 2 large lemons
175g (6oz) caster sugar
65ml (4 tbsp, plus 1 tsp) cornflour
50g (2oz) butter
8 egg yolks

MERINGUE
5 egg whites
5ml (1 tsp) distilled vinegar
275g (10oz) icing sugar, plus extra for dusting

1 To make the pastry, put the flour, butter, sugar and lime rind in a food processor and process until the mixture resembles fine breadcrumbs. Add all but 10ml (2 tsp) of the beaten egg with the 15ml (1 tbsp) water. Pulse until the dough comes together. Wrap the pastry in cling film and chill in the refrigerator for 30 minutes.

2 Roll out the pastry on a lightly floured surface and use to line a 4cm (1½ inch) deep, 23cm (9 inch) loose-based flan tin. Prick the base, then chill for 30 minutes.

3 Line the pastry case with greaseproof paper and baking beans and bake blind at 200°C/fan oven 190°C (400°F) Mark 6 for 15 minutes. Remove paper and beans; cook for a further 10 minutes until the base is golden. Brush with the reserved egg to seal, then return to the oven for 1 minute.

4 Measure the lime and lemon juice; you need 200ml (7fl oz) in total. Place in a pan with the lime rind, caster sugar and 400ml (14fl oz) water; heat gently until the sugar is dissolved.

5 Mix 60ml (4 tbsp) cornflour with 90ml (6 tbsp) water to a paste; stir into the lime mixture with the butter and egg yolks. Slowly bring to the boil, stirring. Cook, stirring, for 1-2 minutes until slightly thickened. Let cool, then pour into the pastry case.

6 Put the egg whites, vinegar, icing sugar and 5ml (1 tsp) cornflour in a bowl over a pan of barely simmering water and whisk, using an electric whisk, for 10 minutes until very thick and shiny. Off the heat, continue to whisk the meringue on the lowest setting for 5-10 minutes until the bowl is cool.

7 Pile the meringue on top of the pie filling to form rough peaks. Bake at 150°C/fan oven 140°C (300°F) Mark 2 for 35 minutes or until golden. Allow to cool for 20 minutes, then serve dusted with icing sugar.

FREE-FORM FIG TART

Glazed fresh figs baked on a sweet flan pastry base, and served with a delicious honey ice cream. For convenience, you could use a 350g packet ready-made sweet shortcrust pastry rather than make your own.

SERVES 6-8 ◆ PREPARATION 1 hour, plus freezing ◆ COOKING TIME 30-35 minutes ◆ FREEZING Suitable (ice cream only) ◆ 715-535 cals per serving

Sweet Flan Pastry, made with 225g (8oz) flour (see page 172)
30-45ml (2-3tbsp) raspberry jam
40g (1½oz) fresh white breadcrumbs
350g (12oz) fresh figs
15ml (1 tbsp) caster sugar
25g (1oz) firm unsalted butter, in pieces

HONEY ICE CREAM
300ml (½ pint) double cream
300ml (½ pint) milk
1 vanilla pod, split
4 egg yolks
125g (4oz) thin honey (preferably acacia or Greek honey)

1 First make the ice cream. Put the cream, milk and vanilla pod in a small pan and heat slowly until it just comes to the boil. Remove from the heat and set aside to infuse for 20 minutes. Remove the pod and scrape the vanilla seeds into the cream; discard the pod.

2 Whisk the egg yolks and honey together in a bowl, then gradually beat in the infused cream. Pour into a clean pan and heat gently, stirring constantly, until the mixture thickens enough to lightly coat the back of a wooden spoon. Set aside to cool, then freeze in an ice-cream maker according to the manufacturer's instructions. Alternatively, freeze in a plastic container for 3-4 hours until firm, beating at hourly intervals to break down the ice crystals and ensure a smooth texture.

3 Roll out the pastry on a lightly floured surface to a 25cm (10 inch) round. Transfer to a baking sheet and leave to rest in the refrigerator for 30 minutes.

4 Spread the raspberry jam evenly over the pastry, leaving a 5cm (2 inch) border, then scatter over the breadcrumbs.

5 Slice the figs into quarters and arrange over the breadcrumbs. Carefully fold the pastry border up and over the edge of the fruit filling to form a rim, pleating the folds.

6 Scatter the sugar and butter over the filling, then chill for a further 20 minutes. Preheat a baking sheet in the oven at 190°C/fan oven 180°C (375°F) Mark 5. Bake the tart on the hot baking sheet for 30-35 minutes until the pastry is crisp and the fruit is tender. Allow to cool slightly. Serve the fig tart warm, with scoops of honey ice cream.

VARIATION Stir 50g (2oz) roughly crushed honeycomb into the ice cream mixture before freezing.

PLUM AND MARZIPAN KUCHEN

SERVES 6-8 ◆ PREPARATION 20 minutes, plus chilling
◆ COOKING TIME 45-50 minutes ◆ FREEZING Suitable
◆ 490-370 CALS PER SERVING ◆ COLOUR INDEX Page 28

PASTRY
160g (5½oz) self-raising white flour
125g (4oz) unsalted butter, in pieces
grated rind of 2 lemons
50g (2oz) light muscovado sugar
50g (2oz) ground almonds

5ml (1 tsp) almond extract
1 egg

TO ASSEMBLE
175g (6oz) white almond paste
350g (12oz) red plums, halved and stoned
icing sugar, for dusting

1 To make the pastry, sift the flour into a bowl, then rub in the butter, using the fingertips. Stir in the lemon rind, sugar, almonds and extract. Set aside 50g (2oz) of the mixture; beat the egg into the remainder to make a moist paste.
2 Use the paste to line a 35x10cm (14x4 inch) loose-based oblong flan tin, pressing it on to the base and sides. (Or use a 23cm (9 inch) round tin.) Chill for 30 minutes.
3 Roll out the almond paste on a lightly floured surface until slightly smaller than the tin dimensions. Lay in the flan tin.
4 Arrange the plums over the almond paste and scatter the reserved pastry mixture on top. Bake at 180°C/fan oven 170°C (350°F) Mark 4 for about 45-50 minutes until slightly risen and golden. Leave in the tin for 10 minutes, then carefully unmould. Serve cold, dusted with icing sugar.

PITHIVIERS

SERVES 10 ◆ PREPARATION 30 minutes, plus overnight soaking
◆ COOKING TIME About 35 minutes ◆ FREEZING Suitable (stage 5)
◆ 530 CALS PER SERVING ◆ COLOUR INDEX Page 28

450g (1lb) packet ready-made puff pastry

FRUIT FILLING
450g (1lb) dried fruit salad
grated rind of ½ orange
150ml (¼ pint) freshly squeezed orange juice
25g (1oz) caster sugar
2.5ml (½ tsp) cornflour
60ml (4 tbsp) orange liqueur

ALMOND FILLING
125g (4oz) unsalted butter, softened
1 egg
30ml (2 tbsp) orange liqueur
75g (3oz) caster sugar
juice of 1 lemon
200g (7oz) ground almonds

TO FINISH
beaten egg, to glaze
icing sugar, for dusting

1 For the filling, soak the dried fruit and orange rind in the orange juice overnight.
2 Transfer the fruit and juice to a saucepan and add the sugar. Blend the cornflour with a little water and add to the pan. Cook, stirring, until the fruit is coated in the glossy juice. Stir in the liqueur and leave to cool.
3 For the almond filling, beat the butter in a bowl, then beat in the egg, liqueur, sugar, lemon juice and ground almonds.
4 Roll out half of the puff pastry on a lightly floured surface. Cut out a 27cm (10½ inch) circle, using a plate as a guide. Lay on a dampened baking sheet. Spread with the fruit mixture to 2.5cm (1 inch) from the edge. Top with the almond mixture.
5 Roll out the remaining pastry to a 28cm (11 inch) round. Brush the edge of the pastry base with beaten egg, then carefully lay the pastry lid over the filling. Press the edges firmly to seal and scallop the edge of the pie decoratively.
6 Brush with egg to glaze. Using the tip of a knife, mark feint lines, radiating out from the centre to the edge. Bake at 220°C/fan oven 210°C (425°F) Mark 7 for about 30 minutes until well risen and golden. Remove from oven and increase the setting to 230°C/fan oven 220°C (450°F) Mark 8.
7 Dust generously with icing sugar and bake for a further 3-4 minutes, until glazed. Serve warm or cold, with pouring cream.

ITALIAN EASTER TART

SERVES 6-8 ◆ PREPARATION 50 minutes, plus chilling ◆ COOKING TIME 1 hour
◆ FREEZING Not suitable ◆ 715-535 CALS PER SERVING

PASTRY
250g (9oz) plain white flour
100g (3½oz) chilled butter, diced
100g (3½oz) icing sugar, sifted
grated rind of 1 orange
1 egg yolk
1.25ml (¼ tsp) vanilla extract

FILLING
75g (3oz) arborio or carnaroli (risotto) rice
750ml (1¼ pints) milk
15g (½oz) butter
50ml (2fl oz) brandy

30ml (2 tbsp) orange flower water
grated rind and juice of 1 orange
75g (3oz) raisins
2.5ml (½ tsp) ground cinnamon
1 vanilla pod, split
500g (1lb 2oz) ricotta cheese
125g (4oz) caster sugar
2 eggs, separated

TO SERVE
icing sugar, for dusting
caramelised oranges (optional, see page 184)

1 To make the pastry, put the flour, butter, icing sugar and orange rind in a food processor and whizz until the mixture resembles coarse crumbs. Add the egg yolk, vanilla extract and a few drops of cold water and pulse until the mixture forms a dough. Wrap in cling film and chill for 30 minutes.
2 Roll out two thirds of the pastry on a lightly floured surface and use to line a deep 23cm (9 inch) loose-based fluted flan tin. Prick the base and line with greaseproof paper and baking beans. Bake blind at 200°C/fan oven 190°C (400°F) Mark 6 for 15 minutes. Remove paper and beans and bake for a further 5-10 minutes until the base is cooked.
3 Meanwhile, make the filling. Put the rice in a saucepan with 600ml (1 pint) milk. Add the butter, brandy, orange flower

water, orange rind and juice, raisins, cinnamon and vanilla pod. Bring slowly to the boil and simmer, stirring occasionally, for 20 minutes or until the rice is cooked and creamy. Take off the heat and stir in the remaining milk; discard the vanilla pod.

4 Beat the ricotta cheese, caster sugar and egg yolks together in a bowl until light and fluffy, then fold into the rice.

5 Whisk the egg whites in a clean bowl to stiff peaks, then gently fold into the rice and ricotta mixture. Spoon the filling into the pastry case and level the surface.

6 Roll out the remaining pastry, cut into 5mm (¼ inch) strips and arrange in a lattice on top of the tart. Bake at 180°C/fan oven 170°C (350°F) Mark 4 for 20 minutes, then increase the temperature to 190°C/fan oven 180°C (375°F) Mark 5 and cook for a further 15 minutes. The pastry should be golden and the filling just set. Leave to cool slightly in the tin for 10-15 minutes, then carefully remove.

7 Dust the tart with icing sugar and serve warm, accompanied by caramelised oranges if you like.

BERRY MILLE FEUILLES

Mille feuilles of crisp pastry and creamy custard are a pâtisserie classic. Summer fruits add irresistible appeal.

SERVES 8-10 ◆ PREPARATION 40 minutes, plus chilling
◆ COOKING TIME 40 minutes ◆ FREEZING Not suitable
◆ 689-550 CALS PER SERVING

550g (1¼lb) packet ready-made puff pastry

45ml (3 tbsp) caster sugar

50g (2oz) almonds or hazelnuts, lightly toasted and roughly chopped

CUSTARD
1 vanilla pod, split

450ml (¾ pint) milk

4 egg yolks

125g (4oz) caster sugar

50g (2oz) plain white flour, sifted

225g (8oz) raspberries, or mixed summer berries

15ml (1 tbsp) lemon juice

300ml (½ pint) double cream

125g (4oz) icing sugar, sifted

STRAWBERRY SAUCE
450g (1lb) strawberries, halved

50g (2oz) icing sugar, sifted

5ml (1 tsp) lemon juice

TO DECORATE
mixed berries

1 Cut the pastry into 3 equal portions. Roll each one out on a lightly floured surface to a 35x18cm (14x7 inch) rectangle. Place each pastry rectangle on a baking sheet, prick with a fork and chill for 30 minutes. Bake at 220°C/fan oven 210°C (425°F) Mark 7 for 10 minutes, then carefully turn over and cook for a further 3 minutes.

2 Sprinkle each of the pastry sheets with 15ml (1 tbsp) sugar and one third of the nuts. Bake in the oven for 8 minutes or until the sugar melts to form a crisp glaze. Leave to cool slightly, then transfer the pastry sheets to wire racks and leave to cool completely.

3 Put the milk in a heavy-based pan. Scrape the seeds from the vanilla pod into the milk; add the pod, too. Bring slowly to the boil; set aside to infuse for 30 minutes. Whisk the egg yolks with 75g (3oz) sugar in a bowl until pale; whisk in the flour. Strain a quarter of the milk on to the mixture, mix to a paste, then stir in the remainder; return to the pan. Slowly bring to the boil, stirring constantly. Pour the custard into a bowl and cover the surface closely with dampened greaseproof paper. Cool, then chill for 3-4 hours or overnight until firm.

4 Put the raspberries in a bowl and sprinkle with the remaining sugar and lemon juice. Beat the chilled custard until smooth. In another bowl, whip the cream to a similar consistency. Fold the cream into the custard, then fold in the raspberries with their juice. Cover and chill.

5 If preferred, trim each cooked pastry sheet to neaten. Mix the icing sugar with 30ml (2 tbsp) water until smooth. Drizzle the icing over each pastry sheet. Set aside for about 15 minutes to allow the icing to harden. To make the strawberry sauce, purée the ingredients in a blender or food processor until smooth. Pass through a sieve into a bowl; cover and chill until required.

6 Spoon half of the custard mixture over one sheet of pastry. Place another sheet of pastry on top and spoon over the remaining custard. Top with the final pastry sheet and press down lightly. Leave to stand for 30 minutes before slicing, to allow the pastry to soften a little. Decorate with berries and serve with the strawberry sauce.

NOTE Covering the custard with dampened greaseproof paper as it cools will prevent a skin forming.

MAPLE AND WALNUT MILLE FEUILLES

SERVES 8 ◆ PREPARATION 30 minutes, plus cooling ◆ COOKING TIME 6-8 minutes
◆ FREEZING Not suitable ◆ 455 CALS PER SERVING ◆ COLOUR INDEX Page 29

4 large sheets filo pastry
25g (1oz) unsalted butter, melted
3 egg yolks
50g (2oz) caster sugar
5ml (1 tsp) vanilla extract
60ml (4 tbsp) cornflour
pinch of freshly grated nutmeg
300ml (½ pint) milk

150ml (¼ pint) double cream
50g (2oz) pistachio nuts
150g (5oz) walnut pieces, finely chopped
75g (3oz) dried dates or figs, finely chopped
pinch of ground cloves
125ml (4fl oz) maple syrup
icing sugar, for dusting

1 Cut each filo sheet crosswise into 3 rectangles. Arrange 3 rectangles on lightly greased baking sheets, crumpling them a little to make slightly narrower rectangles. Sprinkle with a little melted butter. Layer the other rectangles on top, again crumpling slightly and sprinkling with more butter.

2 Bake at 200°C/fan oven 190°C (400°F) Mark 6 for 6-8 minutes until golden. Leave to cool on the baking sheets.

3 For the filling, beat the egg yolks, sugar, vanilla extract, cornflour, nutmeg and a little of the milk together in a bowl until smooth. Put the remaining milk and cream in a heavy-based pan and slowly bring to the boil. Pour on to the egg mixture, beating well. Return to the pan and cook over a low heat, stirring, until thickened enough to coat the back of the spoon. Pour into a bowl, cover the surface and leave to cool.

4 Put the pistachio nuts in a small bowl, cover with boiling water, leave for 3 minutes, then drain. Rub the nuts between sheets of kitchen paper to remove the skins, then chop finely. Put the pistachios, walnuts, dates or figs and cloves in a bowl. Add all but 30ml (2 tbsp) of the maple syrup and stir to mix.

5 Lay one filo layer on a serving plate and sprinkle with 15ml (1 tbsp) maple syrup. Spoon over half of the walnut mixture, then cover with half of the custard. Repeat these layers and top with the remaining filo. Refrigerate for up to 2 hours.

6 Dust generously with icing sugar to serve.

APPLE AND ALMOND MILLE FEUILLES

SERVES 6 ◆ PREPARATION 30 minutes, plus cooling ◆ COOKING TIME 15 minutes
◆ FREEZING Not suitable ◆ 425 CALS PER SERVING ◆ COLOUR INDEX Page 29

150g (5oz) caster sugar
2 dessert apples, peeled, cored and sliced
100g (3½oz) cranberries
75g (3oz) unsalted butter, softened
finely grated rind of 1 lemon

1 egg
150g (5oz) ground almonds
6 sheets filo pastry
25g (1oz) butter, melted
15ml (1 tbsp) flaked almonds
icing sugar, for dusting

1 Put 100g (3½oz) of the sugar and 100ml (3½fl oz) water in a heavy-based pan and heat gently until the sugar is dissolved. Add the apples and simmer gently for 2 minutes until slightly softened. Add the cranberries and simmer gently until softened and their juices start to run into the syrup. Drain, reserving the syrup; leave to cool.

2 Beat the butter, lemon rind, egg, ground almonds and remaining sugar together in a bowl to make a smooth paste.

3 Lightly grease 2 baking sheets. Unroll the filo sheets and cut through all thicknesses into 33x18cm (13x7inch) rectangles. Lay one rectangle on a baking sheet and crumple up slightly to reduce the rectangle to about 24x12cm (9½x5 inches). Brush lightly with melted butter. Cover with another crumpled rectangle, brushing again with butter. Spread almost to the edges with half of the almond paste.

4 Assemble another layered rectangle in exactly the same way, spreading with the remaining almond paste. Make a third one on the second baking sheet, scattering with flaked almonds (this will form the top layer). Bake at 200°C/fan oven 190°C (400°F) Mark 6 for about 12 minutes until each of the layers is golden. Leave to cool.

5 Place one almond covered layer on a serving plate and spread with half of the apples and cranberries. Drizzle with 30ml (2 tbsp) of the reserved syrup. Cover with the other almond layer and the remaining fruit. Drizzle again with syrup then top with the final filo layer.

6 Dust the mille feuille with icing sugar. Serve with lightly whipped cream and the reserved syrup.

PISTACHIO BAKLAVA

SERVES 6-8 ◆ PREPARATION 30 minutes ◆ COOKING TIME 40-45 minutes
◆ FREEZING Not suitable ◆ 540-405 CALS PER SERVING

175g (6oz) skinned pistachio nuts
125g (4oz) pine nuts
5ml (1 tsp) ground cinnamon
2.5ml (½ tsp) ground cloves
pinch of freshly grated nutmeg
30ml (2 tbsp) caster sugar
225g (8oz) filo pastry sheets

75g (3oz) unsalted butter, melted

SYRUP
grated rind and juice of ½ lemon
225g (8oz) thin honey
150ml (¼ pint) water
2 cardamom pods, bruised
30ml (2 tbsp) rosewater

1 Put the pistachios, pine nuts and spices in a food processor and pulse briefly until coarsely ground. Stir in the sugar.

2 Brush a sheet of filo pastry with butter and press into an 18x25cm (10x7 inch) baking tin. Continue to brush and layer half of the filo sheets. Scatter over the nut mixture, then top with the remaining filo sheets, brushing with butter each time.

3 Score the pastry in a diamond pattern, cutting through the layers to the base. Drizzle over any remaining butter and bake at 180°C/fan oven 170°C (350°F) Mark 4 for 20 minutes.

4 Lower the setting to 170°C/fan oven 160°C (325°F) Mark 3 and bake for a further 20-25 minutes until crisp and golden.
5 Meanwhile, make the syrup. Put the lemon rind and juice, honey, water and cardamom in a pan and heat gently. Simmer for 5 minutes, then take off the heat and stir in the rosewater.
6 On removing the baklava from the oven, pour over half of the honey syrup. Leave in the tin until cold. Serve cut into diamonds and drizzled with the remaining syrup.

edges and scatter the trimmings into the tin (see note).

4 Pour the mascarpone mixture into the filo case, then bake at 200°C/fan oven 190°C (400°F) Mark 6 for 12 minutes until the filling is just setting. Meanwhile, drain the cranberries and ginger, reserving the syrup.

5 Scatter the cranberries and ginger over the filling and bake for a further 10-12 minutes. Allow to stand for 20-30 minutes. Serve sliced, with the reserved syrup spooned over.

NOTE There is no need to trim off the excess pastry neatly – raised jagged edges give an interesting finish.

APPLE STRUDEL WITH MAPLE FUDGE SAUCE

SERVES 6-8 ◆ PREPARATION 30 minutes ◆ COOKING TIME 40 minutes
◆ FREEZING Not suitable ◆ 245-220 CALS PER SERVING
◆ COLOUR INDEX Page 29

grated rind and juice of 1 lemon
25g (1oz) fresh white breadcrumbs
30ml (2 tbsp) caster sugar
700g (1½lb) cooking apples
6 sheets filo pastry, about 50g (2oz)
40g (1½oz) butter, melted
icing sugar, for dusting

SAUCE
75g (3oz) butter
150g (5oz) light brown (muscovado) sugar
30ml (2 tbsp) maple syrup
90ml (3fl oz) double cream

1 Mix the lemon rind with the breadcrumbs and 15ml (1 tbsp) of the caster sugar. Peel, quarter, core, and thickly slice the apples; toss in lemon juice to prevent browning. Mix the apple with the breadcrumb mixture.

2 Lay 3 sheets of filo pastry side by side on a clean tea-towel, overlapping the longest edges by 5cm (2 inches). Brush with a little melted butter. Cover with the remaining sheets of filo, overlapping them as before; brush with butter.

3 Spoon the apple mixture on to the filo pastry. Using the tea-towel to help, roll the filo from the longest edge to form a thick roll. Roll it on to a non-stick baking sheet, positioning it seam-side down and curling slightly, if necessary, to fit on the baking sheet. Brush with the remaining butter and sprinkle with the remaining sugar.

4 Bake the strudel at 190°C/fan oven 180°C (375°F) Mark 5 for 40 minutes or until the pastry is golden brown and the apples are soft. If necessary, cover the pastry loosely with foil halfway through baking to prevent overbrowning.

5 Meanwhile, make the sauce. Melt the butter in a small heavy-based pan, add the sugar and maple syrup and cook gently until the sugar is dissolved. Stir in the cream and bring to the boil. Let cool slightly.

6 Dust the strudel with icing sugar, cut into slices and serve with the maple sauce.

CRANBERRY AND GINGER SLICE

Tart cranberries and silky smooth mascarpone complement each other in this smart, wintry dessert. Serve warm or chilled with the accompanying ginger syrup.

SERVES 6-8 ◆ PREPARATION 20 minutes, plus standing
◆ COOKING TIME 25 minutes ◆ FREEZING Not suitable
◆ 410-305 CALS PER SERVING

115g (4oz) caster sugar
75ml (5 tbsp) water
175g (6oz) fresh cranberries
2 pieces preserved stem ginger in syrup, about 40g (1½oz), thinly sliced
250g (9oz) mascarpone
5ml (1 tsp) vanilla extract
1 egg
150ml (¼ pint) double cream
3 large sheets filo pastry, about 100g (3½oz)
15g (½oz) unsalted butter, melted

1 Put 90g (3oz) of the sugar in a small heavy-based saucepan with the water and heat gently until the sugar dissolves, then bring to the boil. Lower the heat, add the cranberries and simmer very briefly until they pop and start to split. Transfer to a bowl, stir in the ginger and leave to cool.

2 Beat the mascarpone, vanilla extract, egg, cream and remaining sugar together in a bowl.

3 Line the base and sides of a 35x10cm (14x4inch) loose-based oblong flan tin with the sheets of filo pastry, crumpling them slightly and brushing each layer with melted butter. Roughly cut off the excess filo pastry from the overhanging

edges of the pastry over the filling. Loosely roll up like a Swiss roll to enclose the filling.

6 Carefully transfer to a baking sheet, placing the strudel seam-side down. Brush lightly with melted butter. Cut the remaining filo pastry into strips. Crumple the filo strips and lay on top of the strudel to decorate.

7 Brush with the remaining butter and bake at 190°C (375°F) Mark 5 for about 30 minutes until deep golden brown. Drizzle a little extra maple syrup over the strudel and serve warm, with pouring cream or ice cream.

VARIATION Replace the glacé cherries with chopped preserved stem ginger in syrup.

FESTIVE MINCE PIES

MAKES 12 ◆ PREPARATION 30 minutes, plus standing
◆ COOKING TIME 20 minutes ◆ FREEZING Suitable (stage 4) ◆ 260 CALS PER PIE
◆ COLOUR INDEX Page 29

PASTRY
225g (8oz) plain white flour
pinch of salt
150g (5oz) butter
30ml (2 tbsp) caster sugar
1 egg yolk
45ml (3 tbsp) cold water

FILLING
225-300g (8-10oz) luxury mincemeat (preferably homemade)

TO FINISH
1 egg white, lightly beaten
caster sugar, for sprinkling
icing sugar, for dusting

1 To make the pastry, sift the flour and salt into a large bowl and rub in the butter using your fingertips until the mixture resembles coarse breadcrumbs. Stir in the sugar.

2 Mix the egg yolk with the water, then add to the dry ingredients and mix to a dough. Knead gently until smooth, wrap in cling film and chill for 30 minutes.

3 On a lightly floured surface, roll out half of the pastry to a 3mm (⅛ inch) thickness. Using a 7.5-9cm (3-3½ inch) fluted cutter, stamp out 12 circles of pastry. Gently press these into patty tins or individual tartlet tins – the pastry should just protrude above the tins to allow for shrinkage when cooked. Spoon the mincemeat into the pastry cases; do not overfill.

4 Roll out the remaining pastry and stamp out 12 circles or stars, using a 6cm (2½ inch) fluted or star cutter. Dampen the edges of the pastry in the patty tins, then top with the smaller pastry circles or stars. Press the edges together to seal. Decorate plain tops with holly leaves cut from the trimmings, if wished.

5 Brush the tops with egg white, then sprinkle lightly with caster sugar. Bake at 190°C/fan oven 180°C (375°F) Mark 5 for about 20 minutes. Leave in the tins for 5 minutes, then transfer to a wire rack. Serve warm, dusted with icing sugar and accompanied by brandy butter or cream if desired.

NOTE The uncooked mince pies can be glazed and baked from frozen, as above. Allow an extra 10-15 minutes in oven.

SPICED NUT STRUDEL

SERVES 8-10 ◆ PREPARATION 20 minutes ◆ COOKING TIME 30 minutes
◆ FREEZING Suitable ◆ 365-290 CALS PER SERVING

8 large sheets filo pastry
25g (1oz) unsalted butter, melted

FILLING
50g (2oz) glacé cherries, chopped
200g (7oz) mixed roughly chopped nuts, such as walnuts, hazelnuts and almonds
50g (2oz) soft white breadcrumbs
25g (1oz) dark muscovado sugar

25g (1oz) chopped candied peel
50g (2oz) raisins
5ml (1 tsp) ground cinnamon
5ml (1 tsp) ground ginger
50g (2oz) unsalted butter, melted
90ml (6 tbsp) maple syrup
1 egg

TO FINISH
a little extra maple syrup

1 For the filling, place all of the ingredients in a bowl and mix well until evenly combined.

2 Lay one sheet of filo pastry on a clean surface; brush lightly with melted butter. Take a second sheet of pastry and place it overlapping the first sheet by 5cm (2 inches). Brush lightly with melted butter.

3 Spoon half of the filling over the pastry, leaving a 5cm (2 inch) border free around the edges.

4 Lay another two sheets of filo pastry over the filling, again overlapping them slightly. Brush lightly with butter.

5 Spoon the remaining filling on top. Fold the two opposite

WHITE CHOCOLATE TARTLETS

These spectacular, satin-textured white chocolate tarts are the ultimate indulgence.

SERVES 8 ◆ PREPARATION 40 minutes, plus chilling ◆ COOKING TIME 40 minutes ◆ FREEZING Suitable (stage 5) ◆ 660 CALS PER SERVING

PASTRY
225g (8oz) plain white flour
150g (5oz) butter, diced
50g (2oz) icing sugar
1 egg, lightly beaten
2-3 drops vanilla extract

FILLING
300ml (½ pint) double cream
1 vanilla pod, split
275g (10oz) white chocolate, chopped
2 eggs, separated
30ml (2 tbsp) kirsch
450g (1lb) fresh fruit, such as raspberries, or mango or pear slices

TO FINISH
icing sugar, for dusting
mint sprigs, to decorate

1 To make the pastry, put the flour, butter and icing sugar in a food processor; pulse until the mixture resembles fine crumbs. Add all but 10ml (2 tsp) of the beaten egg and the vanilla extract. Pulse until the dough comes together in a ball. Wrap in cling film and refrigerate for at least 30 minutes.

2 Roll out the pastry thinly on a lightly floured surface and use to line eight 3cm (1½ inch) deep, 9cm (3½ inch) loose-based tartlet tins. Prick with a fork and chill for 30 minutes. Line the tartlet cases with greaseproof paper and baking beans and bake blind at 200°C/fan oven 190°C (400°F) Mark 6 for 10 minutes. Remove the paper and beans and cook for a further 5-10 minutes. Brush with the reserved 10ml (2 tsp) egg and return to the oven for 1 minute to seal. Cool slightly.

3 To make the filling, pour the cream into a small heavy-based saucepan, add the vanilla pod and slowly bring to the boil. Remove from the heat and take out the vanilla pod. Pour the hot cream on to the chocolate and stir until the chocolate is completely melted. Allow to cool.

4 Mix the egg yolks and kirsch into the cooled chocolate and cream mixture. Whisk the egg whites in a clean bowl until they form soft peaks, then fold carefully into the chocolate mixture until evenly incorporated.

5 Pour the mixture into the pastry cases and cook at 190°C/fan oven 180°C (375°F) Mark 5 for 10-15 minutes until just set. Cover loosely with foil during baking if the filling appears to be colouring too quickly. Leave the tartlets to cool in their tins, then refrigerate for 5 hours or overnight; the filling will firm up as it is chilled.

6 Remove from the refrigerator 30 minutes before serving. Unmould the tartlets and arrange the fresh fruit on top. Dust liberally with icing sugar and decorate with mint sprigs to serve. Accompany with chilled pouring cream.

NOTE Don't worry if the pastry cracks when you're lining the tins – it's easy to patch together.

3 To prepare the filling, beat the butter until soft, then gradually beat in the caster sugar until the mixture is light and fluffy. Gradually beat in 2 eggs. Beat in the remaining egg together with a third of the ground almonds. Fold in the remaining ground almonds and almond extract.

4 Melt the redcurrant jelly in a small pan and brush generously over the insides of the pastry cases. Spoon in the almond filling. Place the tarts on a baking sheet and bake at 190°C/fan oven 180°C (375°F) Mark 5 for 20-25 minutes until golden and just firm. Leave in the tins for 10 minutes, then unmould and cool on a wire rack.

5 To make the plum sauce, put all the ingredients in a pan and bring to the boil. Take out 3 plum halves; reserve for decoration. Cook remaining plums for about 15 minutes until soft, then purée in a food processor until smooth. Sieve, and taste for sweetness. Allow to cool.

6 For the crumble topping, put the ingredients in the (clean) food processor and pulse to a crumble texture. Spread evenly on a baking sheet and grill until golden. Allow to cool.

7 Sprinkle the crumble on to the tarts. Top with the reserved plums, cut into strips, and serve with the sauce.

BAKEWELL TARTLETS WITH PLUM SAUCE

SERVES 6 ◆ PREPARATION 35 minutes, plus chilling ◆ COOKING TIME 40 minutes
◆ FREEZING Suitable (before decorating) ◆ 935 CALS PER SERVING

PASTRY
200g (7oz) plain white flour
100g (3½oz) butter, diced
75g (3oz) caster sugar
3 egg yolks
2.5ml (½ tsp) vanilla extract

FILLING
125g (4oz) butter
125g (4oz) caster sugar
3 eggs
125g (4oz) ground almonds
2-3 drops almond extract

90ml (6 tbsp) redcurrant jelly

PLUM SAUCE
450g (1lb) ripe plums, halved and stoned
50-75g (2-3oz) soft brown sugar
150ml (¼ pint) sweet white wine
150ml (¼ pint) water

CRUMBLE TOPPING
25g (1oz) butter
75g (3oz) plain white flour
25g (1oz) caster sugar

1 To make the pastry, place the flour and butter in a processor and process until it resembles fine breadcrumbs. Add the sugar, egg yolks and vanilla extract and process until the dough comes together. Turn out on to a floured surface and knead lightly until smooth. Divide into 6 balls, flatten slightly, wrap and chill for 30 minutes.

2 On a floured surface, roll out the pastry thinly and use to line six 3cm (1¼ inch) deep, 10cm (4 inch) individual flan tins. Prick the pastry bases and line with greaseproof paper and baking beans. Bake blind at 190°C/fan oven 180°C (375°F) Mark 5 for 15-20 minutes until lightly coloured. Remove the paper and beans and return to the oven for 2 minutes. Cool.

PEACH CINNAMON TARTLETS

SERVES 4 ◆ PREPARATION 20 minutes ◆ COOKING TIME 12-15 minutes
◆ FREEZING Not suitable ◆ 360 CALS PER SERVING ◆ COLOUR INDEX Page 30

225g (8oz) ready-made puff pastry
40g (1½oz) unsalted butter
15g (½oz) ground almonds
15ml (1 tbsp) caster sugar
5ml (1 tsp) ground cinnamon

2 large ripe peaches

GLAZE
1 egg yolk
15ml (1 tbsp) milk
pinch of sugar
icing sugar, for dusting

1 Preheat a baking sheet on the middle shelf of the oven at 220°C/fan oven 210°C (425°F) Mark 7. Divide the pastry into 4 equal pieces. Roll each one out thinly on a lightly floured surface and cut out a 13cm (5 inch) round, using a fluted cutter. Prick the base, leaving a 1cm (½ inch) border.

2 Cream the butter, ground almonds, sugar and cinnamon together in a bowl until smooth.

3 Halve the peaches and carefully cut out the stone. Stand the peach halves rounded-side up and slice each one into 6-8 wedges, holding them in shape.

4 For the glaze, whisk the egg yolk, milk and sugar together.

5 Spread the cinnamon butter evenly over the pastry rounds, to within 1cm (½ inch) from the edges. Arrange a sliced peach half in the middle of each one, fanning it out slightly.

6 Brush the pastry edges with the egg glaze and dust the peaches with icing sugar. Transfer the pastries to the hot baking sheet and bake for 12-15 minutes until puffed and golden and the peaches are tender. Serve hot, with cream.

RHUBARB CRUMBLE TARTS

These attractive filo tarts are an excellent way to serve fresh rhubarb. An orange syrup sauce is the perfect complement.

SERVES 6 ◆ PREPARATION 25 minutes, plus overnight standing and chilling
◆ COOKING TIME 35 minutes ◆ FREEZING Not suitable ◆ 370 CALS PER SERVING
◆ COLOUR INDEX Page 30

450g (1lb) rhubarb,
trimmed
125g (4oz) caster sugar
75g (3oz) filo pastry
25g (1oz) butter, melted
150g (5oz) plain white
flour
125g (4oz) unsalted
butter, in pieces

ORANGE SAUCE
grated rind of 1 orange
juice of 3 oranges
200ml (7fl oz) water
45ml (3 tbsp) golden syrup
45ml (3 tbsp) double
cream (optional)

TO FINISH
icing sugar, for dusting

1 Cut the rhubarb into short lengths and place in a bowl with 50g (2oz) caster sugar. Toss to mix, cover and leave in a cool place overnight.

2 Cut twelve 15cm (6 inch) squares from the filo pastry. Brush 6 filo squares with melted butter and press firmly into six 3cm (1¼ inch) deep, 8cm (3¼ inch) loose-based tartlet tins, allowing the edges to protrude above the rim. Brush the remaining filo squares with butter and position on top, at an angle so the points form a star; press into the edges of the tin. Chill for 30 minutes.

3 Bake the filo cases at 190°C/fan oven 180°C (375°F) Mark 5 for 5 minutes or until golden and crisp. Leave in the tins for 5 minutes, then ease out on to a baking sheet.

4 Put the flour, unsalted butter and remaining sugar in a food processor and pulse to a crumble texture.

5 Drain the rhubarb, reserving any juice. Spoon 15ml (1 tbsp) of the crumble mixture over each pastry base. Spoon in the rhubarb, then top with the remaining crumble. Bake at 200°C/fan oven 190°C (400°F) Mark 6 for 30 minutes or until the crumble is golden.

6 Meanwhile, make the sauce. Put the orange rind and juice, water and golden syrup into a pan with the reserved rhubarb juice. Slowly bring to the boil, then let bubble for 10-15 minutes until syrupy. Remove from the heat and stir in the cream if using.

7 Dust the rhubarb tarts with icing sugar and serve on a pool of orange sauce.

PEAR GALETTES WITH CHOCOLATE SAUCE

Easy, attractive pastries, made with ready-to-bake dough.

SERVES 6 ◆ PREPARATION 15 minutes ◆ COOKING TIME 6-8 minutes
◆ FREEZING Not suitable ◆ 220 CALS PER SERVING

1 tube ready-to-bake pain
au chocolat dough with
chocolate pieces (eg
Kool's)
2 firm ripe pears, cored
and cut into thick slices
ground cinnamon, for
sprinkling

30ml (6 tsp) dark soft
brown sugar
150ml (¼ pint) semi-
skimmed milk

TO FINISH
cinnamon and icing sugar,
for dusting

1 Preheat a baking sheet in the oven at 200°C/fan oven 190°C (400°F) Mark 6. Unroll the dough on a lightly floured surface; set aside the chocolate pieces. Using a saucer as a guide, cut out six 10cm (4 inch) rounds; place on a second baking sheet.

2 Halve, core and thickly slice the pears; arrange on the dough rounds. Sprinkle with a little cinnamon and the brown sugar.

3 Slide the second baking sheet on to the hot baking sheet and bake the galettes for 6-8 minutes or until golden brown.

4 Meanwhile, to make the chocolate sauce, bring the milk to the boil, then whisk in the reserved chocolate pieces. Bubble for about 3 minutes or until the sauce is syrupy.

5 Dust the galettes with a little cinnamon and icing sugar. Serve with the warm chocolate sauce.

BISCUITS
AND COOKIES

A tempting collection of crisp, light, melt-in-the-mouth
treats which are quick to make and taste far superior
to those you can buy

SHORTBREAD

MAKES 18-20 ◆ PREPARATION 20 minutes, plus chilling
◆ COOKING TIME 15-20 minutes ◆ FREEZING Not suitable
◆ 270-180 CALS PER PIECE ◆ COLOUR INDEX Page 31

225g (8oz) butter
125g (4oz) caster sugar
225g (8oz) plain white flour
125g (4oz) ground rice or rice flour

pinch of salt
golden or coloured granulated sugar, for coating
caster sugar, for sprinkling

1 Make sure all of the ingredients are at room temperature. Cream the butter and sugar together in a bowl until pale and fluffy. Sift the flour, rice flour and salt together on to the creamed mixture and stir in, using a wooden spoon, until the mixture resembles breadcrumbs.

2 Gather the dough together with your hand and turn on to a clean surface. Knead very lightly until it forms a ball, then lightly roll into a sausage, about 5cm (2 inches) thick. Wrap in cling film and chill in the refrigerator until firm.

3 Unwrap the roll and slice into discs, about 7-10 mm (⅓-½ inch) thick. Pour golden or coloured granulated sugar on to a plate and roll the edge of each disc in the sugar. Place the biscuits, cut-side up, on 2 baking sheets, lined with greaseproof paper.

4 Bake at 190°C/fan oven 180°C (375°F) Mark 5 for 15-20 minutes, depending on thickness, until very pale golden. On removing from the oven, sprinkle with caster sugar. Leave on the baking sheet for 10 minutes to firm up, then transfer to a wire rack to cool.

NOVELTY BISCUITS

Children will enjoy making and decorating these biscuits.

MAKES 18-20 ◆ PREPARATION 40 minutes ◆ COOKING TIME 7-10 minutes
◆ FREEZING Suitable (uniced) ◆ 90-80 CALS PER BISCUIT
◆ COLOUR INDEX Page 31

175g (6oz) self-raising white flour
2.5ml (½ tsp) bicarbonate of soda
2.5ml (½ tsp) ground cinnamon
15ml (1 tbsp) caster sugar
50g (2oz) butter

45ml (3 tbsp) golden syrup
30-45ml (2-3 tbsp) milk
few drops of food colouring (optional)
125g (4oz) icing (see note)
sweets, such as Smarties and Dolly Mixtures, to decorate

1 Sift the flour, bicarbonate of soda and cinnamon together into a bowl. Stir in the caster sugar.

2 Melt the butter and syrup together in a small pan over a low heat. Pour on to the flour mixture. Add 30ml (2 tbsp) milk then, using a fork, stir the mixture until it starts to come together to form a dough; add another 15ml (1 tbsp) milk if the mixture seems too dry. Allow to cool a little.

3 Roll the dough out on a lightly floured surface until it's about 3 mm (⅛ inch) thick — you may need to sprinkle the mixture with flour as you're doing this to stop it from sticking to the surface.

4 Cut the dough into shapes using fancy biscuit cutters (see note). Carefully lift the biscuits on to a baking sheet. Gather the remaining dough into a ball, roll it out again and cut out some more shapes. Continue to do this until all of the dough is used up.

5 Bake at 190°C/fan oven 180°C (375°F) Mark 5 for 7-10 minutes or until lightly browned. Allow to cool slightly on the baking sheet. When firm, lift them on to a cooling rack using a round-bladed knife.

6 If you wish, mix 1-2 drops of colouring into the icing. Using a round-bladed knife, spread the icing on to the biscuits and decorate with sweets. Leave to set. Store in an airtight container for up to 4 days.

NOTES
◆ Tubs of spreadable soft icing and tubes of writing icing are ideal for decorating. These are available in assorted flavours and colours from most large supermarkets.
◆ Try to cut out biscuit shapes as close together as possible, as those cut from the second and subsequent rollings are never as good as the first.

MACADAMIA NUT COOKIES

MAKES 24-26 ◆ PREPARATION 15 minutes ◆ COOKING TIME 20 minutes
◆ FREEZING Suitable ◆ 110-100 CALS PER COOKIE

125g (4oz) unsalted butter, softened
25g (1oz) caster sugar
165g (5½oz) plain white flour

pinch of salt
150g (5oz) macadamia nuts, finely ground
icing sugar, for dusting

1 Beat the butter and sugar together in a bowl until pale and fluffy, then beat in the flour, salt and ground nuts to form a soft dough.

2 Break off small pieces of the dough and roll lightly to form a short log, about 5cm (2 inches) long, curling each one into a crescent. Flatten slightly and transfer to an oiled non-stick baking sheet.

3 Bake at 170°C/fan oven 160°C (325°F) Mark 3 for 20 minutes until pale golden and firm. Transfer to a wire rack to cool. Store in an airtight tin for up to 4 days. Dust generously with icing sugar to serve.

DOUBLE CHOCOLATE COOKIES

MAKES 18 ◆ PREPARATION 15 minutes ◆ COOKING TIME 12-15 minutes
◆ FREEZING Suitable ◆ 215 CALS PER COOKIE ◆ COLOUR INDEX Page 31

125g (4oz) white chocolate
125g (4oz) plain dark chocolate
125g (4oz) unsalted butter, softened
125g (4oz) caster sugar
1 egg

5ml (1 tsp) vanilla extract
125g (4oz) porridge oats
150g (5oz) plain white flour
2.5ml (½ tsp) baking powder

1 Chop the white and plain chocolate into small chunks, no larger than 1cm (½ inch).
2 Cream the butter and sugar together in a bowl until pale and creamy. Add the egg, vanilla extract and oats. Sift in the flour and baking powder and mix until evenly combined. Stir in the chocolate chunks.
3 Place dessertspoonfuls of the mixture on 2 lightly greased baking sheets, spacing well apart. Flatten each one slightly with the back of a fork.
4 Bake at 180°C/fan oven 170°C (350°F) Mark 4 for 12-15 minutes until risen and turning golden. Leave on the baking sheets for 5 minutes, then transfer to a wire rack to cool. Store in an airtight tin for up to 1 week.

ORANGE FLOWER BISCUITS

MAKES 20-24 ◆ PREPARATION 10 minutes, plus chilling
◆ COOKING TIME 8 minutes ◆ FREEZING Not suitable ◆ 65 CALS PER BISCUIT
◆ COLOUR INDEX Page 31

125g (4oz) plain white flour
15g (½oz) cornflour
100g (3½oz) firm lightly salted butter, diced

50g (2oz) icing sugar
20ml (4 tsp) orange flower water
icing sugar, for dusting

1 Sift the flour and cornflour together into a bowl and rub in the butter.
2 Add the icing sugar and orange flower water and mix to a firm dough, using a round-bladed knife. Knead lightly and chill for 30 minutes.
3 Roll out the dough thinly on a lightly floured surface and cut out rounds using a 6cm (2½ inch) cutter.
4 Place on a lightly greased baking sheet and bake at 200°C/fan oven 190°C (400°F) Mark 6 for about 8 minutes until beginning to colour around the edges.
5 Leave on the baking sheet for a few minutes, then transfer to a wire rack to cool. Dust generously with icing sugar to serve.

VARIATIONS Use rosewater instead of orange flower water, or add the finely grated rind of 1 orange or lemon.

GINGER CHOCOLATE CHIP COOKIES

MAKES 32-34 ◆ PREPARATION 15 minutes ◆ COOKING TIME 12-15 minutes
◆ FREEZING Suitable ◆ 95-85 CALS PER COOKIE

175g (6oz) butter, softened
175g (6oz) caster sugar
1 egg, beaten
90ml (6 tbsp) milk
75g (3oz) plain white flour
75g (3oz) self-raising white flour

25g (1oz) dark chocolate, finely grated
125g (4oz) crystallised ginger, chopped
40g (1½oz) plain chocolate chips

1 Beat the butter and sugar together in a bowl until pale and fluffy. Gradually beat in the egg and milk, then fold in the remaining ingredients to form a soft dough.
2 Drop heaped teaspoonfuls of the mixture, spaced well apart, on to oiled non-stick baking sheets. Bake at 180°C/fan oven 170°C (350°F) Mark 4 for 12-15 minutes until golden.
3 Leave on the baking sheets for 5 minutes, then transfer to wire racks to cool. These cookies are best eaten on the day they are made.

ALMOND FUDGE CRUMBLES

MAKES 24 ◆ PREPARATION 15 minutes ◆ COOKING TIME 12 minutes
◆ FREEZING Suitable ◆ 130 CALS PER BISCUIT ◆ COLOUR INDEX Page 32

200g (7oz) plain white flour
pinch of salt
2.5ml (½ tsp) bicarbonate of soda
125g (4oz) unsalted butter, in pieces
125g (4oz) light muscovado sugar
1 egg
5ml (1 tsp) almond extract

75g (3oz) flaked almonds, broken into small flakes
50g (2oz) vanilla fudge (see note), finely diced

TOPPING
25g (1oz) flaked almonds, lightly crumbled
25g (1oz) vanilla fudge, chopped
icing sugar, for dusting

1 Sift the flour, salt and bicarbonate of soda into a bowl. Rub in the butter, using the fingertips. Add the sugar, egg, almond extract, flaked almonds and diced fudge and mix to a fairly firm dough.
2 Turn on to a lightly floured surface and roll into a cylinder, 23cm (9 inches) long. Cut the dough into 24 slices. Place the rounds, slightly apart, on 2 lightly greased baking sheets.
3 For the topping, scatter the crumbled almonds and chopped fudge on top of the biscuits and press down lightly to adhere. Bake at 190°C/fan oven 180°C (375°F) Mark 5 for about 12 minutes until turning golden around the edges.
4 Leave on the baking sheets for 5 minutes, then transfer to a wire rack to cool. Store in an airtight tin for up to 1 week. Serve dusted with icing sugar.

NOTE Either use a slab of vanilla or 'cream' fudge, or individually wrapped sweets.

LEMON ZESTIES

MAKES 16-18 ◆ PREPARATION 10 minutes ◆ COOKING TIME 10-15 minutes
◆ FREEZING Suitable ◆ 100-90 CALS PER BISCUIT ◆ COLOUR INDEX Page 32

125g (4oz) butter, softened
50g (2oz) caster sugar
grated rind of ½ lemon

150g (5oz) self-raising white flour
10ml (2 tsp) lemon juice

1 Beat the butter, sugar and lemon rind together in a bowl until pale and fluffy. Gradually sift in the flour, then add the lemon juice and beat to form a stiff dough.
2 Break off small pieces of the dough and roll into balls, about 4cm (1½ inches) in diameter.
3 Place on oiled baking sheets, spacing well apart, and flatten to 7cm (2¾ inch) rounds. Score the surface with a fork and bake at 180°C/fan oven 170°C (350°F) Mark 4 for 10-15 minutes until lightly golden. Cool on a wire rack.

ORANGE CINNAMON SABLÉS

These delicious biscuits are crisp, yet melt-in-the-mouth.

MAKES 20 ◆ PREPARATION 10 minutes, plus chilling
◆ COOKING TIME 8-10 minutes ◆ FREEZING Suitable ◆ 70 CALS PER BISCUIT

125g (4oz) plain white flour
2.5ml (½ tsp) ground cinnamon
50g (2oz) icing sugar
finely grated rind of 1 large orange

100g (3½oz) butter, softened
1 egg yolk
15ml (1 tbsp) orange juice

1 Sift the flour, cinnamon and icing sugar together into a bowl. Stir in the orange rind, then add the butter, egg yolk and orange juice, and beat well to form a soft dough. Wrap in cling film and chill for 30 minutes.
2 Roll out the dough on a lightly floured surface to a 3mm (⅛ inch) thickness. Stamp out 7.5cm (3 inch) rounds using a pastry cutter and transfer to oiled baking sheets.
3 Bake at 190°C/fan oven 180°C (375°F) Mark 5, for 8-10 minutes until golden. Cool on a wire rack.

FLORENTINES

These elegant biscuits are rich with nuts, fruit and sunflower seeds. After baking, the edges are rolled in melted chocolate.

MAKES 12 ◆ PREPARATION 15 minutes ◆ COOKING TIME 8-10 minutes
◆ FREEZING Not suitable ◆ 170 CALS PER BISCUIT

65g (2½oz) unsalted butter
50g (2oz) caster sugar
30ml (2 tbsp) double cream
25g (1oz) sunflower seeds
20g (¾oz) chopped mixed candied peel
20g (¾oz) sultanas

25g (1oz) glacé cherries, roughly chopped
40g (1½oz) flaked almonds, lightly crushed
15g (½oz) plain white flour

TO FINISH
125g (4oz) plain dark chocolate, in pieces

1 Melt the butter in a small heavy-based pan. Add the sugar and heat gently until dissolved, then bring to the boil. Take off the heat and stir in the cream, sunflower seeds, candied peel, sultanas, cherries, almonds and flour. Mix well until evenly combined.

2 Placed heaped teaspoonfuls of the mixture on 2 lightly greased baking sheets, spacing well apart.

3 Bake, one sheet at a time, at 180°C/fan oven 170°C (350°F) Mark 4 for about 6-8 minutes until the biscuits have spread considerably and the edges are golden brown.

4 Immediately push the edges into the centre, using a large plain metal biscuit cutter, to create neat rounds. Bake for a further 2 minutes or until deep golden.

5 Leave the florentines on the baking sheet for 2 minutes, then transfer to a wire rack to cool.

6 Melt the chocolate in a heatproof bowl over a pan of simmering water; stir until smooth. Roll the edges of the biscuits in the chocolate and place on a sheet of non-stick baking parchment until set.

NOTE If the biscuits solidify before you use the cutter, return to the oven for 30 seconds.

CHOCOLATE SOFT CENTRES

These crackled, crumbly biscuits conceal a velvet smooth chocolate centre. Serve freshly baked and the filling literally melts in-the-mouth; if served cool it hardens slightly to an equally delicious fudge-like texture.

MAKES 18 ◆ PREPARATION 20 minutes, plus chilling
◆ COOKING TIME 10 minutes ◆ FREEZING Suitable ◆ 180 CALS PER BISCUIT
◆ COLOUR INDEX Page 32

150g (5oz) unsalted butter, softened
150g (5oz) caster sugar
1 egg yolk
250g (9oz) self-raising white flour
25g (1oz) cocoa powder

18-20 squares plain chocolate, about 125g (4oz) in total

TO FINISH
cocoa powder, for dusting

1 Cream the butter and sugar together in a bowl until pale and fluffy. Beat in the egg yolk. Sift the flour and cocoa powder into the bowl and mix to a firm dough, using a round-bladed knife.
2 Turn out on to a lightly floured surface and knead lightly. Chill in the refrigerator for 30 minutes.
3 Roll a third of the dough out thinly on a floured surface and cut out 18 circles, using a 4cm (1½ inch) cutter. Place on a lightly greased baking sheet and press a chocolate square into the centre of each one.
4 Roll out the remaining dough and cut out 18 larger circles, using a 5cm (2 inch) cutter. Lay these over the chocolate bases, pressing the edges together to seal in the chocolate filling.
5 Bake at 190°C/fan oven 180°C (375°F) Mark 5 for about 10 minutes until the biscuits have spread and risen. Leave on the baking sheet for 5 minutes, then transfer to a wire rack to cool. Serve dusted with cocoa powder.

NOTE The larger circles of dough will crack slightly as you position them over the bases.

VARIATION Use milk or white chocolate squares to fill the biscuits instead of plain chocolate.

PANFORTE DE SIENA

This rich, spicy, thin 'cake' is packed with candied peel, honey and nuts. Served in thin slices, after dinner or with coffee, panforte is a traditional Christmas treat throughout Italy.

MAKES 12 SLICES ◆ PREPARATION 45 minutes ◆ COOKING TIME 35 minutes
◆ FREEZING Not suitable ◆ 265 CALS PER SLICE ◆ COLOUR INDEX Page 32

125g (4oz) whole blanched almonds
125g (4oz) whole skinned hazelnuts
125g (4oz) candied orange peel, finely chopped
125g (4oz) candied citron peel, finely chopped
50g (2oz) plain white flour
1.25ml (¼ tsp) ground coriander
1.25ml (¼ tsp) ground white pepper

1.25ml (¼ tsp) ground nutmeg
1.25ml (¼ tsp) ground cloves
5ml (1 tsp) ground cinnamon
125g (4oz) granulated sugar
225g (8oz) thin honey
25g (1oz) butter
icing sugar, for dusting

1 Grease and line a 20cm (8 inch) spring-release cake tin with non-stick baking parchment (see note). Spread the almonds and hazelnuts on a baking tray and bake at 180°C/fan oven 170°C (350°F) Mark 4 for 10-15 minutes until golden brown. Allow to cool slightly, then chop roughly and place in a bowl.
2 Lower the oven setting to 150°C/fan oven 140°C (300°F) Mark 2.
3 Add the orange and citron peel to the nuts. Sift the flour and spices together into the bowl. Stir to mix.
4 Put the sugar, honey and butter in a heavy-based pan and heat gently, stirring occasionally, until dissolved. Bring to the boil and boil steadily until the syrup registers 117°C (242°F) on a sugar thermometer (the soft ball stage). Quickly stir in the nut mixture, pour into the prepared tin and smooth the surface with an oiled potato masher; work quickly otherwise the mixture will set.
5 Bake in the oven for 35 minutes; the cake won't be brown or set at this stage. Transfer the tin to a wire rack; the cake will harden as it cools. When cold, carefully remove the tin and baking parchment.
6 Dredge the panforte with icing sugar. Store in an airtight tin for up to 1 month. Serve cut into thin slices.

NOTE You can line the cake tin with edible rice paper if you prefer; this makes it easier to turn the cake out.

VARIATION Use walnuts instead of almonds. Add 50g (2oz) chopped dried figs (not ready-to-eat) with the candied peel. Sift 30ml (2 tbsp) cocoa powder together with the flour and spices.

PAMPERATO

This variation of panforte is richly flavoured with brandy-soaked raisins, nuts, chocolate and candied peel. Freshly ground pepper gives a warm, spicy flavour without being too overpowering. Serve with coffee.

MAKES 3; EACH 4 SLICES ◆ PREPARATION 20 minutes
◆ COOKING TIME 20 minutes ◆ FREEZING Not suitable ◆ 305 CALS PER SLICE

150g (5oz) raisins
60ml (4 tbsp) brandy or orange juice
100g (3½oz) walnuts
100g (3½oz) flaked almonds
50g (2oz) candied peel, chopped
100g (3½oz) plain chocolate, chopped
60ml (4 tbsp) thin honey

120ml (8 tbsp) redcurrant jelly
finely grated rind of 1 orange
1 egg, beaten
200g (7oz) self-raising white flour
freshly ground black pepper
icing sugar, for dusting

1 Put the raisins in a saucepan with the brandy or orange juice and warm gently until the liquid is absorbed.
2 Put the walnuts, almonds and candied peel in a food processor and chop coarsely. Add the raisins and chocolate and process briefly until the raisins are slightly broken up. Transfer to a bowl.
3 Warm the honey with half of the redcurrant jelly until smooth. Add to the nut mixture with the orange rind, egg, flour and about 12 generous twists of pepper from the mill. Mix the ingredients together to make a firm dough.

4 Divide the dough into 3 portions. Shape each into a flat round, about 20cm (8 inches) in diameter. Transfer to a greased large baking sheet and bake at 180°C/fan oven 170°C (350°F) Mark 4 for 20 minutes or until just firm. Transfer to a wire rack to cool.
5 Melt the remaining redcurrant jelly with 15ml (1 tbsp) water. Brush over the cakes, then dust generously with icing sugar. Store in an airtight container for up to 1 week.

VARIATION Divide the pamperato dough into 15 pieces and shape into flat rounds, like biscuits. Bake as above, reducing the cooking time to 12-15 minutes.

BISCOTTI

These light, crunchy biscuits studded with toasted almonds and flavoured with a hint of orange are traditionally served with a glass of vin santo, a sweet dessert wine from Tuscany.

MAKES ABOUT 50 ◆ PREPARATION 25 minutes
◆ COOKING TIME 45 minutes, plus cooling ◆ FREEZING Not suitable
◆ 90 CALS PER BISCUIT ◆ COLOUR INDEX Page 33

175g (6oz) whole blanched almonds
125g (4oz) unsalted butter, softened
200g (7oz) granulated sugar
2 eggs, beaten
finely grated rind of 1 orange
15ml (1 tbsp) Grand Marnier or other orange liqueur

7.5ml (1½ tsp) baking powder
2.5ml (½ tsp) salt
350g (12oz) plain white flour (approximately)
75g (3oz) coarse-grain polenta (ordinary or quick-cook)
15ml (1 tbsp) coriander seeds, lightly crushed

1 Spread the almonds on a baking sheet and toast in the oven at 170°C/fan oven 160°C (325°F) Mark 3 for 5-10 minutes until golden. Allow to cool, then coarsely chop one third; mix with the whole nuts.
2 Cream the butter and sugar together in a bowl. Beat in the eggs, orange rind, liqueur, baking powder and salt. Stir in 300g (10oz) of the flour, the polenta, almonds and coriander.
3 Turn the dough on to a floured work surface and knead until smooth, adding the remaining flour little by little as necessary, until the dough is soft but not sticky.
4 Divide dough into 4 pieces. Roll each into a 5cm (2 inch) wide, 2cm (¾ inch) deep log. Place on 2 greased baking sheets and bake for about 35 minutes until golden around the edges.
5 Carefully transfer to a wire rack. Allow to cool slightly, for 10 minutes, then cut diagonally into 1cm (½ inch) thick slices, using a large sharp knife. Place, cut-side down, on the baking sheets and bake for a further 10 minutes until golden brown. Transfer to a wire rack to cool completely. Store in an airtight tin for up to 1 week.

VARIATION Replace the almonds with pine nuts.

BRANDY SNAPS

MAKES 12-16 ◆ PREPARATION 25 minutes, plus cooling
◆ COOKING TIME 8-10 minutes ◆ FREEZING Suitable
◆ 165-125 CALS PER BISCUIT ◆ COLOUR INDEX Page 33

75g (3oz) butter
75g (3oz) caster sugar
45ml (3 tbsp) golden syrup
75g (3oz) plain white flour
5ml (1 tsp) ground ginger

30ml (2 tbsp) brandy
15ml (1 tbsp) lemon juice

TO SERVE
150ml (¼ pint) double cream, whipped (optional)

1 Lightly oil the handles of several wooden spoons.
2 Place the butter, sugar and golden syrup in a heavy-based pan and warm gently until evenly blended. Let cool for 2-3 minutes. Sift in the flour and ginger, and add the brandy and lemon juice. Mix until smooth.
3 Taking 15ml (1 tbsp) of mixture at a time, spoon on to baking sheets lined with non-stick baking parchment, allowing plenty of room for spreading, and no more than three per baking sheet.
4 Bake, one sheet at a time, at 190°C/fan oven 180°C (375°F) Mark 5 for about 8-10 minutes or until golden brown – the texture will be open and lacy. Remove from the oven and leave for about 15 seconds to firm up slightly. Loosen with a palette knife and roll them around the spoon handles.
5 Place on a wire rack and leave until set, then twist gently to remove and leave to cool completely and crisp up. Just before serving, fill with whipped cream if desired, using a piping bag fitted with a 1cm (½ inch) nozzle.

NOTE If the biscuits set too hard to roll while on the baking sheet, return to the oven for a few moments to soften.

VARIATIONS
◆ LACY TUILES Instead of using wooden spoon handles, curve the brandy snap rounds over a lightly oiled large rolling pin.
◆ BRANDY SNAP BASKETS Bake heaped tablespoonfuls of the mixture to make larger rounds. Once cooked, mould over upturned ramekins to form baskets. Lift off once set.

GINGER GLASS BISCUITS

MAKES 18 ◆ PREPARATION 15 minutes, plus chilling
◆ COOKING TIME 5-6 minutes ◆ FREEZING Suitable ◆ 55 CALS PER BISCUIT
◆ COLOUR INDEX PAGE 33

50g (2oz) unsalted butter
40g (1½oz) liquid glucose
100g (3½oz) caster sugar

40g (1½oz) plain white flour
5ml (1 tsp) ground ginger

1 Melt the butter and glucose together in a bowl over a pan of gently simmering water.

2 Mix the sugar, flour and ginger together in a bowl. Pour on the glucose mixture and beat well. Cover and refrigerate for about 20 minutes or until firm.
3 Roll teaspoonfuls of mixture into balls and place them, well apart, on a baking sheet lined with non-stick baking parchment to allow room for spreading. Cover with another sheet of baking parchment and flatten with a rolling pin; peel off the top sheet.
4 Bake the biscuits at 180°C/fan oven 170°C (350°F) Mark 4 for 5-6 minutes or until golden. Remove from oven and press a 7.5cm (3 inch) plain cutter into each biscuit to neaten.
5 Peel off the paper, break off excess and gently curl each biscuit over. Interleave with baking parchment or greaseproof paper. Store in an airtight container for up to 3 days. Serve as dessert biscuits, with ices or creamy desserts.

PISTACHIO THINS

MAKES ABOUT 30 ◆ PREPARATION 10 minutes
◆ COOKING TIME 50-55 minutes, plus cooling ◆ FREEZING Not suitable
◆ 35 CALS PER BISCUIT

3 egg whites
95g (3¼oz) golden caster sugar
95g (3¼oz) plain white flour, sifted

50g (2oz) shelled pistachio nuts, chopped
10ml (2 tsp) anise seeds (optional)

1 Whisk the egg whites in a clean bowl until stiff, then gradually whisk in the sugar, a little at a time, until the mixture is once again stiff. Carefully fold in the flour, pistachio nuts, and anise seeds if using, until evenly incorporated.
2 Spoon into an oiled and lined shallow 18cm (7 inch) square baking tin. Bake at 170°C/fan oven 160°C (325°F) Mark 3 for 25 minutes or until a skewer inserted into the centre comes out clean. Turn on to a baking sheet, remove the paper and bake for a further 15 minutes.
3 Transfer to a wire rack and leave until cold. Reduce the oven setting to 150°C/fan oven 140°C (300°F) Mark 2.
4 Using a sharp knife, cut the cooled mixture into very thin, long slices. Place on non-stick baking sheets and bake for 10-15 minutes until they just start to turn golden at the edges. Transfer to a wire rack to cool. Store in an airtight container for up to 1 month. Serve as dessert biscuits, with ice creams or sorbets.

NOTE Don't worry if some of the biscuits break as you slice them – they will taste just as good.

VARIATION Replace the pistachios with blanched almonds.

ROSEMARY TUILES

Serve these delicious biscuits with ice creams, sorbets or creamy desserts. To make plain tuiles, simply omit the rosemary and lemon rind.

MAKES 20-24 ◆ PREPARATION 10 minutes ◆ COOKING TIME 5-6 minutes
◆ FREEZING Not suitable ◆ 55-45 CALS PER TUILLE

50g (2oz) unsalted butter
2 egg whites
125g (4oz) caster sugar
15ml (1 tbsp) finely
chopped fresh rosemary
leaves

finely grated rind of
1 lemon
50g (2oz) plain white flour

1 Melt the butter in a small pan and allow to cool slightly. In a bowl, whisk the egg whites until stiff, then gradually whisk in the sugar until it is all incorporated and the mixture is stiff.

2 Fold in the rosemary, lemon rind, melted butter and flour until evenly incorporated.

3 Place 2 heaped teaspoonfuls of the mixture, well spaced apart, on a lightly oiled non-stick baking sheet.

4 Using a palette knife, spread each one into a small oval, measuring about 10x5cm (4x2 inches). Bake at 190°C/fan oven 180°C (375°F) Mark 5 for 5-6 minutes until golden around the edges.

5 Immediately transfer the tuiles to a lightly oiled rolling pin, curling them around the rolling pin. Leave to cool and crisp up while cooking another 2 biscuits.

6 Carefully remove the tuiles from the rolling pin and place on a wire rack. Repeat with the remaining mixture.

VARIATION

TUILE BASKETS Drop 2 heaped tablespoonfuls of mixture, well apart, on to the baking sheet, spreading out to 12cm (5 inch) rounds. Bake until golden, then drape over upturned and oiled timbales. Leave to set, then carefully unmould. Use as containers to serve ice cream, sorbets or mousses.

SCONES, TRAYBAKES AND TEABREADS

Traditional favourites and original fresh fruit bakes
are included in this collection of effortless recipes, many
of which keep exceptionally well

TRADITIONAL SCONES

Serve scones fresh from the oven with lightly whipped cream or crème fraîche, or make them several hours ahead and warm through in the oven.

MAKES 8 ◆ PREPARATION 15 minutes ◆ COOKING TIME 12-15 minutes
◆ FREEZING Suitable ◆ 140 CALS PER SCONE ◆ COLOUR INDEX Page 34

225g (8oz) self-raising white flour
pinch of salt
5ml (1 tsp) baking powder
40g (1½oz) firm butter or margarine, cut into pieces

150ml (¼ pint) milk (approximately)
beaten egg or milk, to glaze

TO SERVE
whipped cream, or butter and jam

1 Sift the flour, salt and baking powder together into a bowl. Rub in the butter using the fingertips until the mixture resembles fine breadcrumbs. Mix in enough milk to give a fairly soft dough.
2 Turn the dough on to a lightly floured surface and lightly roll out to a 2cm (¾ inch) thickness. Cut out rounds, using a 6cm (2½ inch) plain cutter. (Re-roll trimmings to cut more.)
3 Place on a greased baking sheet and brush the tops with beaten egg or milk. Bake at 220°C/fan oven 210°C (425°F) Mark 7 for about 12-15 minutes until golden brown and well risen. Transfer to a wire rack to cool.
4 Serve warm, split and filled with cream or butter and jam.

NOTE To ensure a good rise, avoid heavy handling and make sure the rolled-out dough is at least 2 cm (¾ inch) thick.

VARIATIONS
◆ WHOLEMEAL SCONES Replace half of the white flour with wholemeal self-raising flour.
◆ FRUIT SCONES Add 50g (2oz) currants, sultanas, raisins or chopped dates (or a mixture) to the dry ingredients.
◆ CHEESE AND HERB SCONES Sift 5ml (1 tsp) mustard powder with the dry ingredients. Stir 50g (2oz) finely grated Cheddar cheese into the mixture before adding the milk. After glazing, sprinkle the tops with a little extra cheese.

BLUEBERRY SCONES

MAKES 10-12 ◆ PREPARATION 15 minutes ◆ COOKING TIME 12-15 minutes
◆ FREEZING Suitable ◆ 145-125 CALS PER SCONE ◆ COLOUR INDEX Page 34

225g (8oz) self-raising white flour
large pinch of salt
7.5ml (1½ tsp) baking powder
50g (2oz) firm butter or margarine, cut into pieces
50g (2oz) caster sugar
150g (5oz) fresh blueberries

150ml (¼ pint) milk (approximately)
10ml (2 tsp) vanilla extract
beaten egg or milk, to glaze

TO SERVE
whipped cream or crème fraîche

1 Sift the flour, salt and baking powder into a bowl. Add the butter and rub in using the fingertips until the mixture resembles fine breadcrumbs. Stir in the sugar and blueberries.
2 Mix 125ml (4fl oz) of the milk with the vanilla extract and add to the bowl. Mix to a soft dough, adding more of the milk if necessary.
3 Turn out on to a floured surface and lightly roll out to a 2cm (¾ inch) thickness. Cut out rounds, using a 6cm (2½ inch) cutter. (Re-roll the trimmings to cut more scones.)
4 Place on a greased baking sheet and brush the tops with beaten egg or milk. Bake at 220°C/fan oven 210°C (425°F) Mark 7 for about 12-15 minutes until risen and golden.
5 Transfer to a wire rack to cool. Serve warm, with whipped cream or crème fraîche.

VARIATION
WHOLEMEAL APPLE SCONES Substitute half the flour with wholemeal self-raising flour and sift 2.5ml (½ tsp) ground cinnamon with the dry ingredients. Replace the blueberries with 2 peeled, cored and chopped dessert apples.

CARROT AND RAISIN SCONES

MAKES 9 ◆ PREPARATION 15 minutes ◆ COOKING TIME 12-15 minutes
◆ FREEZING Not suitable ◆ 180 CALS PER SCONE

225g (8oz) self-raising white flour
good pinch of salt
7.5ml (1½ tsp) baking powder
5ml (1 tsp) ground mixed spice
50g (2oz) firm unsalted butter or margarine, cut into pieces
40g (1½oz) light muscovado sugar

200g (7oz) small carrots, peeled and finely grated (see note)
75g (3oz) raisins
50-75ml (2-2½fl oz) milk
extra milk, to glaze
oatmeal, for dusting

TO SERVE
lightly whipped mascarpone or cream cheese

1 Sift the flour, salt, baking powder and spice into a bowl. Add the butter and rub in using the fingertips until the mixture resembles fine breadcrumbs.
2 Stir in the sugar, grated carrots and raisins. Add sufficient milk to mix to a soft dough.
3 Turn out on to a floured surface and lightly roll out to a 19cm (7½inch) square, about 2cm (¾inch) thick. Using a floured, sharp knife, cut the dough into 9 squares and transfer to a greased baking sheet.
4 Brush with milk to glaze and scatter with oatmeal. Bake at 220°C/fan oven 210°C (425°F) Mark 7 for 12-15 minutes or until risen and pale golden. Transfer to a wire rack to cool.
5 Serve warm, with mascarpone or cream cheese.

NOTE If the carrots are wet once you have grated them, pat dry on kitchen paper before adding to the flour.

POPPY SEED, ORANGE AND ALMOND SCONE RING

MAKES 8 LARGE SCONES ◆ PREPARATION 20 minutes
◆ COOKING TIME About 20 minutes ◆ FREEZING Suitable
◆ 320 CALS PER SCONE

15ml (1 tbsp) poppy seeds

**finely grated rind of
1 orange**

**150g (5oz) fine-cut orange
marmalade**

**40g (1½oz) flaked
almonds, lightly toasted**

**350g (12oz) self-raising
white flour**

pinch of salt

**7.5ml (1½ tsp) baking
powder**

**75g (3oz) firm butter or
margarine, cut into pieces**

15ml (1 tbsp) caster sugar

**45ml (3 tbsp) light
muscovado sugar**

**150ml (¼ pint) milk
(approximately)**

beaten egg, to glaze

1 Mix together the poppy seeds, orange rind, marmalade and all but 30ml (2tbsp) of the toasted almonds.

2 Sift the flour, salt and baking powder together into a bowl. Add the butter and rub in using the fingertips until the mixture resembles fine breadcrumbs. Stir in the sugars. Add sufficient milk to mix to a soft dough.

3 Turn the dough on to a floured surface and lightly roll out to a 30×20cm (12×8 inch) rectangle.

4 Spread the poppy seed mixture on top of the dough to within 2cm (¾ inch) of the edges. Starting from a long side, roll up the dough, enclosing the filling.

5 Using a floured knife, cut the rolled dough into 8 slices. Arrange the slices, cut side up, in a ring on a greased baking sheet, leaving a 3mm (⅛ inch) space between each.

6 Brush the tops with beaten egg and sprinkle with the reserved almonds. Bake at 220°C/fan oven 210°C (425°F) Mark 7 for 10 minutes, then bush the sides with more egg. Bake for a further 8-12 minutes until deep golden. Serve warm with butter.

PLUM AND HAZELNUT SLICE

Puréed plums give this traybake a deliciously moist texture. Served warm with spoonfuls of whipped cream or thick yogurt, it doubles up as a simple dessert.

MAKES 10 SLICES ◆ PREPARATION 20 minutes ◆ COOKING TIME 35 minutes
◆ FREEZING Suitable ◆ 400 CALS PER SLICE

480g (1lb 1oz) red plums
150g (5oz) unsalted butter or margarine, softened
150g (5oz) light muscovado sugar
3 eggs, beaten
175g (6oz) ground hazelnuts (see note)

175g (6oz) self-raising white flour
5ml (1 tsp) baking powder
25g (1oz) hazelnuts, toasted and roughly chopped
caster sugar, for dusting

1 Grease and base-line a 27x19cm (10½x7½ inch) shallow baking tin (or a tin with similar dimensions). Set aside 3 plums. Stone the remainder, then purée in a food processor.
2 Cream the butter and sugar together in a bowl. Add the plum purée, eggs and ground hazelnuts. Sift in the flour and baking powder. Mix thoroughly until smooth.
3 Turn the mixture into the prepared tin and level the surface. Stone and slice the remaining plums. Scatter the chopped hazelnuts and plum slices over the surface of the mixture. Bake at 180°C/fan oven 170°C (350°F) Mark 4 for about 35 minutes until risen and just firm in the centre.
4 Leave to cool in the tin. Dust with caster sugar and serve warm or cold, cut into fingers.

NOTE If you cannot buy ground hazelnuts, grind toasted hazelnuts in the food processor, or use ground almonds.

ORANGE FLAPJACKS

MAKES 18 ◆ PREPARATION 15 minutes ◆ COOKING TIME 25-30 minutes
◆ FREEZING Suitable ◆ 300 CALS PER FLAPJACK ◆ COLOUR INDEX Page 34

2 small oranges
250g (9oz) unsalted butter, in pieces
250g (9oz) caster sugar
175g (6oz) golden syrup

425g (15oz) rolled oats
30ml (2 tbsp) sunflower seeds
45ml (3 tbsp) fine-cut orange marmalade

1 Grease a 28x20cm (11x8 inch) shallow baking tin (or a tin with similar dimensions).
2 Using a citrus zester, finely pare the zest from the oranges in fine strips.
3 Put the orange zest in a large heavy-based saucepan with the butter, sugar and syrup. Stir over a moderate heat until the butter is melted. Remove from the heat and stir in the rolled oats to coat evenly with the syrup mixture.
4 Turn the mixture into the prepared tin, level the surface and sprinkle with the sunflower seeds. Bake at 180°C/fan oven 170°C (350°F) Mark 4 for 25-30 minutes until deep golden around the edges; the mixture will still be very soft in the centre. Leave in the tin until almost cold.
5 Heat the marmalade in a small pan with 15ml (1 tbsp) water until syrupy. Brush this glaze evenly over the flapjack and leave to set. Remove flapjack from the tin, place on a board and cut into 18 bars. Store in an airtight container for up to 1 week.

VARIATION

FRUIT AND NUT FLAPJACKS Omit the orange zest, sunflower seeds and marmalade. Add 125g (4oz) luxury mixed dried fruit and 75g (3oz) chopped and toasted mixed nuts with the oats.

GINGER FLAPJACKS

MAKES 18 ◆ PREPARATION 10 minutes ◆ COOKING TIME 30-35 minutes
◆ FREEZING Suitable ◆ 340 CALS PER FLAPJACK ◆ COLOUR INDEX Page 35

350g (12oz) unsalted butter
300g (10oz) caster sugar
225g (8oz) golden syrup

450g (1lb) rolled oats
15ml (1 tbsp) ground ginger

1 Grease and base-line a 28x18cm (11x7 inch), 5cm (2 inch) deep cake tin with non-stick baking parchment.
2 Put the butter, sugar and syrup in a large heavy-based saucepan and heat together gently until melted. Mix in the rolled oats and ground ginger until thoroughly combined.
3 Turn the mixture into the tin, level the surface and bake at 180°C/fan oven 170°C (350°F) Mark 4 for 30-35 minutes or until golden brown at the edges but still soft in the middle.
4 Leave to cool in the tin for 15 minutes, then while still warm, score into bars with a sharp knife. Leave in the tin to cool completely, then turn out and cut into bars.

WHITE CHOCOLATE HAZELNUT BROWNIES

MAKES 12 ◆ PREPARATION 20 minutes ◆ COOKING TIME 30-35 minutes
◆ FREEZING Suitable ◆ 490 CALS PER BROWNIE

500g (1lb 2oz) white
chocolate
75g (3oz) butter
3 eggs
175g (6oz) caster sugar
175g (6oz) self-raising
white flour

pinch of salt
175g (6oz) hazelnuts,
roughly chopped
5ml (1 tsp) vanilla extract

1 Grease and line a 27x19cm (10½x7½ inch) shallow baking tin (or a tin with similar dimensions). Roughly chop 400g (14oz) of the chocolate; set aside.
2 Melt the remaining chocolate and butter in a heatproof bowl over a pan of simmering water. Let cool slightly.
3 Whisk the eggs and sugar together in a large bowl until smooth, then gradually beat in the melted chocolate mixture.
4 Sift the flour and salt over the mixture, then fold in together with the hazelnuts, chopped chocolate and vanilla.
5 Turn the mixture into the prepared tin and level the surface. Bake at 190°C/fan oven 180°C (375°F) Mark 5 for 30-35 minutes until risen and golden, and the centre is just firm to the touch. Leave to cool in the tin.
6 Turn the mixture out on to a board and cut into squares. Store in an airtight container for up to 1 week.

NOTE When cooked, the mixture will still be soft under the crust; it firms up on cooling.

RICH CHOCOLATE BROWNIES

MAKES 24 ◆ PREPARATION 20 minutes ◆ COOKING TIME 40-45 minutes
◆ FREEZING Suitable ◆ 300 CALS PER BROWNIE

575g (1¼lb) plain
chocolate
225g (8oz) butter
3 eggs
225g (8oz) caster sugar
30ml (2 tbsp) freshly made
strong black coffee

75g (3oz) self-raising white
flour
1.25ml (¼ tsp) salt
175g (6oz) walnut halves,
chopped
5ml (1 tsp) vanilla extract

1 Grease and line a 27x19cm (10½x7½ inch) shallow baking tin (or a tin with similar dimensions). Roughly chop 225g (8oz) of the chocolate and set aside.
2 Melt the remaining chocolate and butter in a heatproof bowl over a pan of simmering water. Let cool slightly.
3 Beat the eggs, sugar and coffee together in a large bowl until smooth, then gradually beat in the melted mixture.
4 Sift the flour and salt over the mixture, then fold in together with the walnuts, vanilla and chopped chocolate.
5 Turn the mixture into the prepared tin and bake at 190°C/fan oven 180°C (375°F) Mark 5 for 40-45 minutes or until just firm to the touch in the centre.
6 Leave to cool in the tin, then turn out on to a board. Trim off the crusty edges and cut into squares. Store in an airtight container for up to 1 week.

NOTE Do not overcook or the characteristic gooey texture will be ruined.

COCONUT SQUARES

MAKES 12 ◆ PREPARATION 10 minutes ◆ COOKING TIME 35 minutes
◆ FREEZING Suitable ◆ 415 CALS PER SQUARE ◆ COLOUR INDEX Page 35

75g (3oz) butter
200g (7oz) demerara sugar
175g (6oz) ground rice
2 eggs
pinch of salt
1-2 drops vanilla extract
75g (3oz) desiccated coconut

75g (3oz) chopped hazelnuts
45ml (3 tbsp) apricot or raspberry jam
extra jam, warmed, to glaze

1 Grease a 28x18cm (11x7 inch) baking tin (or a tin with similar dimensions).
2 Cream the butter and 75g (3oz) of the sugar together in a bowl until light and fluffy. Stir in 150g (5oz) of the ground rice. Spread the mixture into the prepared tin and bake at 180°C/fan oven 170°C (350°F) Mark 4 for 15 minutes. Leave in the tin to cool for a few minutes.
3 Lightly beat the eggs in a bowl. Add the remaining sugar and ground rice, the salt, vanilla extract, desiccated coconut and chopped hazelnuts; mix well.
4 Spread the jam over the cooked base, then cover with the coconut mixture. Bake in the oven for 20 minutes.
5 Allow to cool slightly, then brush with a little warmed jam. Cut the cake into squares. Leave in the tin to cool completely before removing. Store wrapped in greaseproof paper in an airtight container for up to 5 days.

APPLE AND GINGER TEABREAD

MAKES 8-10 SLICES ◆ PREPARATION 20 minutes ◆ COOKING TIME 1-1¼ hours
◆ FREEZING Suitable ◆ 410-330 CALS PER SLICE ◆ COLOUR INDEX Page 35

4 crisp, tart dessert apples, such as Granny Smith's
15ml (1 tbsp) lemon juice
125g (4oz) unsalted butter
75g (3oz) light muscovado sugar
200g (7oz) golden syrup
300g (10oz) self-raising white flour
2.5ml (½ tsp) baking powder

2.5ml (½ tsp) ground cinnamon
2.5ml (½ tsp) ground cloves
1 egg
75g (3oz) preserved stem ginger in syrup, drained and finely chopped
45ml (3 tbsp) golden syrup, warmed, to serve (optional)

1 Grease and line a 900g (2lb) loaf tin. Peel, core and thinly slice the apples and immerse in a bowl of cold water with the lemon juice added to prevent discoloration.
2 Put the butter, sugar and syrup in a saucepan and heat until melted. Allow to cool slightly.
3 Sift the flour, baking powder and spices together into a bowl. Add the syrup mixture and egg; stir until well combined.
4 Thoroughly drain the apple slices on kitchen paper. Add three quarters of them and all but 15ml (1 tbsp) of the chopped ginger to the cake mixture; stir until evenly combined.
5 Turn the mixture into the prepared loaf tin and scatter over the reserved apple slices and ginger. Bake at 170°C/fan oven 160°C (325°F) Mark 3 for 1-1¼ hours until just firm and a skewer inserted into the centre comes out clean.
6 Leave in the tin for 15 minutes, then spoon over the syrup. Allow to cool completely before slicing. Eat within 4-5 days.

APRICOT TEABREAD WITH MARMALADE

MAKES 10 SLICES ◆ PREPARATION 15 minutes ◆ COOKING TIME 1¼ hours
◆ FREEZING Suitable ◆ 390 CALS PER SERVING ◆ ILLUSTRATED Opposite

200g (7oz) ready-to-eat dried apricots, roughly chopped
150ml (¼ pint) apricot or orange juice
225g (8oz) self-raising white flour
5ml (1 tsp) baking powder
125g (4oz) light muscovado sugar

225g (8oz) unsalted butter, softened
75g (3oz) fine-cut orange marmalade
3 eggs
60ml (4 tbsp) orange marmalade, to glaze

1 Grease a 900g (2lb) loaf tin and line the base and long sides with greaseproof paper. Put the apricots and fruit juice in a pan and bring to the boil. Lower the heat and simmer gently until most of the juice is absorbed. Allow to cool slightly.
2 Sift the flour and baking powder into a bowl. Add the sugar, butter, marmalade and eggs. Beat thoroughly until smooth and creamy. Stir in three quarters of the apricots.
3 Turn the mixture into the prepared tin and level the surface. Scatter the reserved apricots on top. Bake at 180°C/fan oven 170°C (350°F) Mark 4 for about 1¼ hours until risen and firm, covering loosely with foil after about 20 minutes to prevent overbrowning if necessary. Leave in the tin for 10 minutes, then transfer to a wire rack to cool.
4 Heat the marmalade gently in a pan with 15ml (1 tbsp) water until slightly thinned, then brush over the top of the teabread to glaze. Serve cut into slices. Store in an airtight container for up to 1 week.

RIPPLED DATE AND BANANA LOAF

MAKES 8-10 SLICES ◆ PREPARATION 20 minutes ◆ COOKING TIME 1-1¼ hours
◆ FREEZING Suitable ◆ 495-395 CALS PER SLICE ◆ COLOUR INDEX Page 35

250g (9oz) pitted dried dates
90ml (3fl oz) water
grated rind and juice of 1 lemon
2 ripe bananas
175g (6oz) unsalted butter, softened

175g (6oz) caster sugar
3 eggs
225g (8oz) self-raising white flour
2.5ml (½ tsp) baking powder
2.5ml (½ tsp) ground cinnamon (optional)

1 Grease and line a 900g (2lb) loaf tin. Set aside 4 dates; place the rest in a small heavy-based saucepan with the water, lemon rind and juice. Bring to the boil, reduce the heat and simmer gently for 5 minutes until the dates are soft and pulpy. Purée the mixture in a food processor or blender until smooth; alternatively mash together in a bowl, using a fork.
2 Mash the bananas until smooth.
3 Cream the butter and sugar together in a bowl until pale and fluffy. Add the banana purée and eggs. Sift the flour, baking powder, and cinnamon if using, into the bowl. Beat until thoroughly combined.
4 Spoon a third of the banana mixture into the prepared loaf tin and level the surface. Spread half of the date purée over the surface. Repeat these layers, then cover with the remaining banana mixture.
5 Cut the reserved dates into slivers and scatter over the surface. Bake at 170°C/fan oven 160°C (325°F) Mark 3 for 1-1¼ hours until well risen and firm to the touch.
6 Leave in the tin for 15 minutes, then transfer to a wire rack to cool. Store in an airtight container for up to 1 week.

NOTE The date purée needs to be similar in consistency to the banana mixture. If too thick, beat in a little water.

CHOCOLATE AND SWEET POTATO LOAF

MAKES 8-10 SLICES ◆ PREPARATION 20 minutes ◆ COOKING TIME 1-1¼ hours
◆ FREEZING Suitable ◆ 435-350 CALS PER SLICE ◆ COLOUR INDEX Page 35

225g (8oz) sweet potatoes
125g (4oz) soft margarine
125g (4oz) light muscovado sugar
5ml (1 tsp) vanilla extract
2 eggs
160g (5½oz) self-raising white flour
5ml (1 tsp) ground mixed spice

2.5ml (½ tsp) bicarbonate of soda
15g (½oz) cocoa powder
30ml (2 tbsp) milk
125g (4oz) milk or plain chocolate, roughly chopped
75g (3oz) flaked almonds, lightly toasted
icing sugar, for dusting

1 Peel the sweet potatoes and cut into chunks. Add to a pan of cold water, bring to the boil and cook for 15 minutes or until softened. Drain and mash well.
2 Grease a 900g (2lb) loaf tin and line the base and long sides with a strip of greaseproof paper.
3 Put the margarine, sugar, vanilla extract and eggs into a bowl. Sift the flour, spice, bicarbonate of soda and cocoa into the bowl. Add the milk and beat well until the mixture is smooth and creamy.
4 Stir in the mashed sweet potato, chopped chocolate and 50g (2oz) of the toasted almonds. Turn the mixture into the prepared tin and level the surface. Sprinkle with the remaining almonds.
5 Immediately bake in the oven at 170°C/fan oven 160°C (325°F) mark 3 for 1-1¼ hours until well risen and just firm to touch. Leave in the tin for 10 minutes, then transfer to a wire rack to cool. Serve dusted with icing sugar. Store in an airtight container for up to 5 days.

FRUIT AND SPICE PARKIN

MAKES 12 SLICES ◆ PREPARATION 10 minutes ◆ COOKING TIME 1¼-1½ hours
◆ FREEZING Suitable ◆ 440 CALS PER SLICE ◆ COLOUR INDEX Page 36

225g (8oz) dried figs, thinly sliced
125g (4oz) sultanas
200ml (7fl oz) apple or orange juice
175g (6oz) black treacle
175g (6oz) golden syrup
125g (4oz) unsalted butter
250g (9oz) plain white flour

15ml (1 tbsp) ground mixed spice
10ml (2 tsp) baking powder
65g (2½oz) light muscovado sugar
250g (9oz) medium oatmeal
1 egg

1 Grease and line a 20cm (8 inch) square cake tin. Put the figs and sultanas in a saucepan with the fruit juice. Bring to the boil, then take off the heat and leave to cool.
2 Put the treacle, syrup and butter in another saucepan and heat until the butter is melted; cool slightly.
3 Sift the flour, spice and baking powder together into a bowl, then stir in the sugar and oatmeal. Add half of the dried fruits with any remaining fruit juice, the syrup mixture and egg; stir until well combined. Turn into the prepared tin and scatter the reserved fruit over the top.
4 Bake at 170°C/fan oven 160°C (325°F) Mark 3 for 1¼-1½ hours until just firm and a skewer inserted into the centre comes out clean. Leave to cool in the tin.
5 Once cold, wrap in greaseproof paper and store in an airtight container for 1-2 weeks to mature before eating. Serve cut into slices.

VARIATION Use prunes or dried dates instead of the figs.

FRUITED TEABREAD

MAKES 10 SLICES ◆ PREPARATION 10 minutes, plus overnight soaking
◆ COOKING TIME 1-1¼ hours ◆ FREEZING Suitable ◆ 320 CALS PER SLICE
◆ COLOUR INDEX Page 36

50g (2oz) ready-to-eat dried apricots, roughly chopped

50g (2oz) ready-to-eat prunes, roughly chopped

225g (8oz) raisins

150g (5oz) dark muscovado sugar

300ml (½ pint) strong black tea, strained

125g (4oz) plain wholemeal flour

125g (4oz) self-raising white flour

5ml (1 tsp) baking powder

5ml (1 tsp) ground cinnamon

75g (3oz) brazil nuts, roughly chopped

2 eggs

125g (4oz) thin honey

extra honey, warmed, to glaze (optional)

1 Mix the apricots, prunes, raisins and sugar together in a bowl. Pour on the tea, cover and leave to soak overnight.

2 Grease and line a 900g (2lb) loaf tin. Sift the flours, baking powder and cinnamon together into a bowl. Add the soaked fruits and liquid, brazil nuts, eggs and honey. Mix well.

3 Turn into the prepared tin and bake at 180°C/fan oven 170°C (350°F) Mark 4 for 1-1¼ hours, or until a skewer inserted into the centre comes out clean, covering loosely with foil after 20 minutes to prevent overbrowning.

4 Leave to cool in the tin. Drizzle with a little extra honey to glaze if liked. Store in an airtight container for up to 1 week.

BANANA TEABREAD

MAKES 8-10 SLICES ◆ PREPARATION 15 minutes ◆ COOKING TIME 1-1¼ hours
◆ FREEZING Not suitable ◆ 420-335 CALS PER SLICE ◆ COLOUR INDEX Page 36

225g (8oz) self-raising white flour

1.25ml (¼ tsp) bicarbonate of soda

2.5ml (½ tsp) salt

75g (3oz) butter

150g (5oz) caster sugar

450g (1lb) ripe bananas

2 eggs

125g (4oz) chopped mixed nuts, such as hazelnuts, walnuts and brazil nuts

apricot jam, warmed, to glaze

dried banana chips and toasted walnuts, to decorate

1 Grease and base-line a 450g (1lb) loaf tin. Sift the flour, bicarbonate of soda and salt together into a bowl. Rub in the butter, then stir in the sugar.

2 Mash the bananas, then add to the flour mixture with the eggs and chopped nuts and beat well.

3 Turn the mixture into the prepared tin and bake at 180°C/fan oven 170°C (350°F) Mark 4 for 1-1¼ hours or until a skewer inserted into the centre comes out clean.

4 Leave in the tin for 10 minutes, then transfer to a wire rack to cool completely. Brush with warmed apricot jam to glaze and decorate with banana chips and walnut halves. Store in an airtight tin for up to 1 week.

MOLASSES, PRUNE AND WALNUT TEABREAD

MAKES 10 SLICES ◆ PREPARATION 10 minutes ◆ COOKING TIME 40-45 minutes
◆ FREEZING Suitable ◆ 250 CALS PER SLICE

150g (5oz) self-raising white flour

150g (5oz) plain wholemeal flour

5ml (1 tsp) bicarbonate of soda

225g (8oz) ready-to-eat prunes, roughly chopped

75g (3oz) walnut pieces

75g (3oz) sultanas

40g (1½oz) caster sugar

60ml (4tbsp) molasses or black treacle

1 egg

284ml (9½fl oz) buttermilk

15ml (1 tbsp) demerara sugar, for sprinkling

1 Grease and line the base and long sides of a 900g (2 lb) loaf tin with a strip of greaseproof paper.

2 Sift the flours and bicarbonate of soda into a bowl, tipping in the wholemeal grain that's left in the sieve. Stir in the prunes, walnuts, sultanas and sugar.

3 Mix together the molasses, egg and buttermilk and add to the flour mixture. Mix lightly until the ingredients are just combined.

4 Turn into the prepared tin. Sprinkle with the demerara sugar and bake at 190°C/fan oven 180°C (375°F) Mark 5 for 40-45 minutes until risen and just firm, and a skewer inserted into the centre comes out clean.

5 Transfer to a wire rack to cool. Serve sliced and buttered.

PEAR AND CARDAMOM TEABREAD

MAKES 10 SLICES ◆ PREPARATION 20 minutes
◆ COOKING TIME About 1¼ hours ◆ FREEZING Suitable ◆ 350 CALS PER SERVING

5-10ml (1-2 tsp) green cardamom pods

3 firm pears

1 tbsp lemon juice

250g (9oz) self-raising white flour

2.5ml (½ tsp) baking powder

175g (6oz) unsalted butter or margarine, softened

175g (6oz) light muscovado sugar

3 eggs

TO GLAZE

75g (3oz) icing sugar

15ml (1 tbsp) water

1 Grease and line the base and long sides of a 900g (2 lb) loaf tin.

2 Snip open the cardamom pods with scissors and tip the seeds into a pestle and mortar; crush the seeds. Quarter, core and thinly slice the pears. Put in a bowl with the lemon juice.

3 Sift the flour and baking powder into a bowl. Add the butter, sugar, eggs and cardamom seeds and beat until smooth and creamy.

4 Thoroughly drain the pears and pat dry on kitchen paper. Stir two thirds of them into the mixture. Turn into the prepared tin and level the surface.

5 Decorate the surface with the remaining pears, arranging them in an overlapping line down the centre. Bake at 180°C/fan oven 170°C (350°F) Mark 4 for about 1¼ hours until firm, covering loosely with foil after about 25 minutes to prevent overbrowning. To test if the cake is cooked, insert a skewer into the centre – it should comes out clean.

6 Leave the teabread in the tin for 10 minutes, then transfer to a wire rack to cool. Beat together the icing sugar and water to make a smooth icing. Spoon the icing over the teabread while it is still warm, then leave to cool completely. Store in an airtight container for up to 5 days.

SMALL CAKES AND PASTRIES

Ideas range from moist, fruity muffins, sticky buns and delicate madeleines to elegant tartlets and continental pastries with delectable fillings

MADELEINES

MAKES 24 ◆ PREPARATION 20 minutes, plus chilling
◆ COOKING TIME 10-12 minutes ◆ FREEZING Suitable ◆ 85 CALS PER CAKE
◆ COLOUR INDEX Page 37

4 eggs
125g (4oz) caster sugar
finely grated rind of
1 lemon
125g (4oz) plain white
flour

5ml (1 tsp) baking powder
pinch of salt
125g (4oz) unsalted
butter, melted and cooled
until tepid
icing sugar, for dusting

1 Brush 2 Madeleine trays with a little melted butter. Allow to set, then dust with flour, shaking out any excess.
2 Whisk the eggs, sugar and lemon rind together in a bowl until pale, creamy and thick enough to leave a trail when the whisk is lifted.
3 Sift in half of the flour, with the baking powder and salt. Carefully pour half of the melted butter around the edge of the bowl and gently fold in. Repeat with remaining flour and butter. Cover and refrigerate for 45 minutes.
4 Two-thirds fill the Madeleine moulds with the mixture and bake at 220°C/fan oven 210°C (425°F) Mark 7 for 10-12 minutes or until well risen and golden. Ease out of the tins and cool on a wire rack. Serve dusted with icing sugar.

NOTES
◆ Resting the mixture in the refrigerator gives the Madeleines their characteristic dense texture.
◆ If you have only one Madeleine tray, bake in two batches.

PEAR AND CINNAMON BUNS

MAKES 14 ◆ PREPARATION 10 minutes ◆ COOKING TIME About 15 minutes
◆ FREEZING Suitable (stage 2) ◆ 215 CALS PER BUN ◆ COLOUR INDEX Page 37

225g (8oz) self-raising
white flour
2.5ml (½ tsp) ground
cinnamon
125g (4oz) unsalted
butter, in pieces
75g (3oz) caster sugar
125g (4oz) dried pears,
roughly chopped
150g (5oz) sultanas
1 egg

90ml (3fl oz) milk
finely grated rind of
1 lemon

TO GLAZE
juice of 1 lemon
50g (2oz) caster sugar
15ml (1 tbsp) preserving
sugar or crushed sugar
cubes

1 Sift the flour and cinnamon together into a bowl. Rub in the butter, using fingertips, until the mixture resembles fine breadcrumbs. Add the sugar, pears, sultanas, egg, milk and lemon rind; mix to a soft dough.
2 Spoon into about 14 small mounds on a greased large baking sheet.

3 Bake at 190°C/fan oven 180°C (375°F) Mark 5 for about 15 minutes until risen and golden.
4 Meanwhile make the glaze. Heat the lemon juice in a small, heavy-based saucepan with the sugar and 30ml (2 tbsp) water until the sugar has dissolved. Bring to the boil and boil for 3 minutes until syrupy.
5 On removing the buns from the oven, spoon on the glaze and sprinkle with the preserving sugar or crushed sugar cubes. Transfer to a wire rack to cool. Eat within 1-2 days.

GREEK EASTER CAKES

MAKES 8 ◆ PREPARATION 25 minutes, plus standing
◆ COOKING TIME 15-20 minutes ◆ FREEZING Not suitable
◆ 430 CALS PER SERVING

125g (4oz) unsalted
butter, softened
100g (3½oz) caster sugar
finely grated rind of
1 lemon
60ml (4 tbsp) lemon juice
2 eggs
125g (4oz) semolina
10ml (2 tsp) baking
powder
100g (3½oz) ground
almonds

SYRUP
10 cardamom pods
1 orange
300g (10oz) caster sugar
200ml (7fl oz) water
juice of ½ lemon
1 cinnamon stick, halved
5ml (1 tsp) whole cloves
30ml (2 tbsp) orange
flower water

1 Grease eight 150ml (¼ pint) dariole moulds.
2 Cream the butter and sugar together in a bowl until pale and fluffy. Beat in the lemon rind and juice, eggs, semolina, baking powder and ground almonds until the mixture is smooth.
3 Divide between the prepared moulds, level the surfaces and stand on a baking sheet. Bake at 200°C/fan oven 190°C (400°F) Mark 6 for about 15 minutes until just firm. Leave in the tins for 5 minutes then loosen with a knife, turn out and stand on a small tray.
4 For the syrup, lightly bruise the cardamom pods using a pestle and mortar or rolling pin. Pare thin strips of rind from the orange, then cut into fine shreds. Squeeze the juice.
5 Put the sugar and water in a small, heavy-based saucepan and heat gently until the sugar dissolves. Add the lemon juice, bring to the boil and boil rapidly for 3 minutes until syrupy. Stir in the orange shreds, orange juice, cardamom, cinnamon and cloves and heat gently for 5 minutes. Remove from the heat and stir in the orange flower water.
6 Spoon the syrup over the cakes, so each one becomes evenly steeped in syrup and the excess flows into the tray. Leave to cool, then chill until ready to serve. Serve the cakes with some of the strained syrup spooned over. Accompany with Greek yogurt or lightly whipped cream.

NOTE If you haven't any dariole moulds, use 6 individual pudding moulds instead to make slightly larger cakes.

NOTE If you don't have a muffin tray and paper cases, make 'mini' muffins using ordinary paper cake cases in a sectioned tartlet tray, reducing the cooking time by a few minutes.

CRANBERRY MUFFINS

MAKES 12 ◆ PREPARATION 15 minutes ◆ COOKING TIME 15-18 minutes
◆ FREEZING Suitable ◆ 190 CALS PER MUFFIN ◆ COLOUR INDEX Page 37

125g (4oz) fresh or frozen cranberries (see note)

25g (1oz) icing sugar, sifted

300g (10oz) plain white flour

10ml (2 tsp) baking powder

150g (5oz) light muscovado sugar

grated rind of 1 large orange

1 egg

5ml (1 tsp) vanilla extract

250ml (8fl oz) milk

50g (2oz) unsalted butter, melted

icing sugar, for dusting

1 Line a 12-hole muffin or deep bun tin tray with paper muffin cases (or simply grease if using a non-stick tray). Toss the cranberries in the icing sugar to coat.
2 Sift the flour and baking powder together into a bowl. Stir in the sugar, orange rind and cranberries.
3 In another bowl, beat together the egg, vanilla, milk and butter. Add to the dry ingredients and stir until the ingredients are just mixed together; do not over-mix.
4 Spoon into the prepared muffin tins and bake at 200°C/fan oven 190°C (400°F) Mark 6 for 15-18 minutes until risen and just firm. Transfer to a wire rack to cool. Serve warm or cold, dusted with icing sugar.

NOTE If using frozen cranberries, thaw and dry thoroughly on kitchen paper before tossing in the icing sugar.

FIG AND OATMEAL MUFFINS

These muffins are best eaten on the day they are made, or warmed through the following day in the oven or microwave.

MAKES 12 ◆ PREPARATION 15 minutes ◆ COOKING TIME 15 minutes
◆ FREEZING Suitable ◆ 210 CALS PER MUFFIN

225g (8oz) self-raising white flour

15ml (1 tbsp) baking powder

75g (3oz) medium oatmeal

175g (6oz) dried figs, chopped

125g (4oz) sultanas

75g (3oz) light muscovado sugar

75g (3oz) unsalted butter, melted

1 egg

finely grated rind of ½ orange

150ml (¼ pint) milk

extra oatmeal, for dusting

1 Line a 12-hole muffin or deep bun tin tray with paper muffin cases. Sift the flour and baking powder into a bowl. Stir in the oatmeal, figs, sultanas and sugar.
2 Mix together the butter, egg, orange rind and milk and pour into the bowl. Using a large metal spoon, fold the ingredients together lightly until just mixed.
3 Pile the mixture equally into the paper cases. Sprinkle with a little extra oatmeal and bake at 200°C/fan oven 190°C (400°F) Mark 6 for about 15 minutes until well risen and just firm to the touch. Transfer to a wire rack to cool. Serve warm.

WHOLEMEAL BANANA MUFFINS

MAKES 6 ◆ PREPARATION 15 minutes, plus soaking
◆ COOKING TIME 20-25 minutes ◆ FREEZING Suitable ◆ 370 CALS PER MUFFIN
◆ COLOUR INDEX Page 37

50g (2oz) raisins

grated rind and juice of 1 orange

125g (4oz) plain wholemeal flour

25g (1oz) wheatgerm

45ml (3 tbsp) caster sugar

10ml (2 tsp) baking powder

pinch of salt

1 egg, beaten

50ml (2fl oz) milk

50ml (2fl oz) sunflower oil

2 ripe bananas, about 225g (8oz) peeled weight

TOPPING

75ml (5 tbsp) orange marmalade

50g (2oz) dried banana chips

50g (2oz) roughly chopped walnuts

1 Line 6 muffin tins with paper muffin cases, or grease non-stick muffin tins well. Place the raisins in a bowl, add the orange juice and leave to soak for 1 hour.

2 Mix the flour, wheatgerm, sugar, baking powder, salt and orange rind together in a bowl. Make a well in the centre.

3 In a separate bowl, combine the egg, milk and oil. Pour into the flour mixture and stir until just blended. Drain the raisins, reserving 15ml (1 tbsp) juice. Roughly mash the bananas and stir into the mixture with the raisins, don't over-mix.

4 Two-thirds fill each muffin case with the mixture. Bake at 200°C/fan oven 190°C (400°F) Mark 6 for 20-25 minutes or until a skewer inserted into the centre comes out clean. Transfer the muffins to a wire rack to cool slightly.

5 For the topping, gently heat the orange marmalade with the reserved orange juice until melted. Simmer for 1 minute, then add the banana chips and chopped walnuts. Spoon on top of the muffins. Serve while still warm.

DOUBLE CHOCOLATE MUFFINS

MAKES 14 ◆ PREPARATION 15 minutes ◆ COOKING TIME 25 minutes
◆ FREEZING Suitable ◆ 370 CALS PER MUFFIN ◆ COLOUR INDEX Page 37

300g (10oz) plain chocolate
125g (4oz) white chocolate
375g (13oz) self-raising white flour
15ml (1 tbsp) baking powder
65g (2½oz) cocoa powder
75g (3oz) light muscovado sugar

1 egg
1 egg yolk
10ml (2 tsp) vanilla extract
90ml (6 tbsp) sunflower oil
375ml (13fl oz) milk
icing sugar or cocoa powder, for dusting (optional)

1 Line 14 deep bun tins or muffin tins with paper muffin cases. Break up 175g (6oz) of the plain chocolate and melt in a heatproof bowl set over a saucepan of simmering water.

2 Roughly chop the remaining plain and white chocolate. Sift the flour, baking powder and cocoa powder into a bowl. Stir in the sugar.

3 In another bowl, beat together the egg, egg yolk, vanilla extract, sunflower oil, milk and melted chocolate. Add to the dry ingredients with the chopped chocolate and stir together quickly until the flour is only just incorporated; do not over-mix.

4 Spoon the mixture into the paper cases, piling it up in the centre. Bake at 220°C/fan oven 210°C (425°F) Mark 7 for 25 minutes or until the muffins are well risen and craggy in appearance.

5 Transfer to a wire rack and dust lightly with icing sugar or cocoa powder, if desired. Serve warm or cold.

VARIATION Sift 5ml (1 tsp) ground cinnamon or mixed spice with the dry ingredients.

APRICOT PATTIES

These quick and easy patty cakes are irresistibly moist. They can be served warm with crème fraîche as a dessert.

MAKES 12 ◆ PREPARATION 15 minutes ◆ COOKING TIME 15-20 minutes
◆ FREEZING Suitable ◆ 270 CALS PER CAKE

410g (14½oz) can apricot halves in natural juice
175g (6oz) unsalted butter
175g (6oz) ground almonds
175g (6oz) caster sugar

75g (3oz) self-raising white flour, sifted
4 egg whites
icing sugar, for dusting

1 Lightly grease a non-stick 12-hole muffin or deep bun tin tray. Drain the apricots and leave to dry on kitchen paper. Melt the butter and leave to cool slightly.

2 Mix the ground almonds, sugar and flour together in a bowl. Add the egg whites and melted butter and stir until evenly mixed. Divide the mixture evenly between the tray sections and place an apricot half on each.

3 Bake at 200°C/fan oven 190°C (400°F) Mark 6 for 15-20 minutes until risen and golden. Leave in the tray for about 10 minutes to firm up slightly, then run a knife around the edges of the patties to loosen them. Transfer to a wire rack to cool. Serve dusted with icing sugar.

NOTE If your muffin tray isn't non-stick, line with paper cases or baking parchment.

PECAN AND ORANGE PUFFS

Melt-in-the mouth pastries with a delicious caramelised pecan filling. Don't be put off by the idea of making your own rough puff pastry – this recipe is very easy.

MAKES 9 ◆ PREPARATION 30 minutes, plus chilling
◆ COOKING TIME 25 minutes ◆ FREEZING Not suitable
◆ 475 CALS PER PUFF

ROUGH PUFF PASTRY
225g (8oz) plain white flour
pinch of salt
175g (6oz) unsalted butter, chilled and diced
100ml (3½fl oz) cold water
5ml (1 tsp) lemon juice
beaten egg yolk, to glaze

FILLING
75g (3oz) caster sugar
90ml (3fl oz) water
finely grated rind of ½ orange
75ml (3fl oz) orange juice (1-1½ oranges)
40g (1½oz) unsalted butter
175g (6oz) pecan halves
90ml (3fl oz) double cream

1 To make the pastry, sift the flour and salt into a bowl. Add the butter and mix lightly. Using a round-bladed knife, stir in the water and lemon juice to make a soft dough, adding a little extra water if the dough is too dry.

2 Turn out on to a floured surface and roll out to a 30x10cm (12x4 inch) rectangle. Fold the bottom third up and the top third down, then give the pastry a quarter turn so the folded edges are at the sides.

3 Seal the edges with a rolling pin. Repeat the rolling, folding and turning sequence 4 more times. Wrap in cling film and chill for 30 minutes.

4 To make the filling, put the sugar in a small heavy-based saucepan with the water and heat gently until the sugar dissolves. Bring to the boil and boil rapidly until the syrup is turning golden around the edges. Add the orange rind and juice, taking care as the syrup will splutter. Add the butter and stir over a gentle heat until smooth.

5 Roll out the pastry to a 24cm (9¾ inch) square. Cut out nine 8cm (3¼ inch) squares and place on a lightly greased large baking sheet. With the tip of a sharp knife, make a shallow cut on all sides of the squares, about 8mm (⅜ inch) in from the edge. Brush pastry edges with beaten egg to glaze.

6 Bake at 220°C/fan oven 210°C (425°F) Mark 7 for about 15 minutes until well risen. Scoop out the risen centres of the pastries, then arrange the pecans in the pastry cases. Stir the cream into the syrup and pour over the pecans. Bake for a further 8 minutes, then transfer to a wire rack to cool. Serve with yogurt or crème fraîche if liked.

4 Roll out the almond paste to a 30×18cm (12×7 inch) rectangle and place on top of the dough, positioning one long edge exactly on the nearest long edge of the dough. Roll up from this edge, then cut into 12 slices. Place on a lined and greased large baking sheet, spacing apart. Cover with lightly oiled cling film and leave until doubled in size.

5 Brush with beaten egg and scatter with the almonds. Bake at 200°C/fan oven 190°C (400°F) Mark 6 for 15-20 minutes until golden. Melt the jam with 15ml (1 tbsp) water, then sieve and brush over the hot pastries. Serve warm or cold.

MOROCCAN ALMOND CRESCENTS

MAKES 18 ◆ PREPARATION 40 minutes, plus resting
◆ COOKING TIME 15-20 minutes ◆ FREEZING Not suitable
◆ 160 CALS PER PASTRY ◆ COLOUR INDEX Page 38

ALMOND PASTE
225g (8oz) ground almonds
2.5ml (½ tsp) almond extract
45ml (3 tbsp) icing sugar
45ml (3 tbsp) orange flower water
50g (2oz) butter, melted and cooled

PASTRY
225g (8oz) plain white flour
pinch of salt
15g (½oz) butter, melted
100ml (3½fl oz) cold water
45ml (3 tbsp) orange flower water

TO DECORATE
orange flower water, for sprinkling
icing sugar, for coating

1 For the almond paste, mix together the ground almonds, almond extract, icing sugar and orange flower water in a bowl. Mix in the butter, then knead until the almond paste holds together; do not overwork. Cover and refrigerate.

2 For the pastry, sift the flour and salt into a bowl and make a well in the centre. Add the butter, water and orange flower water. Mix together, using a round-bladed knife, until the dough holds together, adding a little more water if necessary.

3 Knead on a floured surface for about 20 minutes until smooth and elastic. (Or knead in a food processor or electric mixer.) Wrap in cling film and leave to rest for 15 minutes.

4 Roll out the pastry as thinly as possible on a floured surface. Using a 7.5-9cm (3-3½ inch) fluted cutter, cut out 18 rounds.

5 Divide the almond paste into 18 pieces. Shape each into a roll, about 6cm (2½ inches) long, tapering at the ends. Lay one in the middle of each pastry round, brush pastry edges with water and fold in half over the almond paste. Press the edges to seal and bend into a curve. Prick twice with a skewer.

6 Place the crescents on a baking sheet. Bake at 160°C/fan oven 150°C (325°F) Mark 3 for 15-20 minutes until very pale golden; do not overcook or the pastry will be hard. Sprinkle with orange flower water whilst still warm and roll in icing sugar to coat generously. Transfer to a wire rack to cool. Serve warm, if possible, or keep in an airtight tin for up to 2 days.

MARZIPAN AND RAISIN WHIRLS

MAKES 12 ◆ PREPARATION 25 minutes, plus rising
◆ COOKING TIME 15-20 minutes ◆ FREEZING Suitable ◆ 255 CALS PER PASTRY

250g (9oz) strong plain white flour
7g sachet fast-action dried yeast
finely grated rind of 1 lemon
30ml (2 tbsp) caster sugar
25g (1oz) unsalted butter, melted
1 egg
90ml (3fl oz) warm milk

FILLING
15g (½oz) unsalted butter, melted
5ml (1 tsp) ground mixed spice
125g (4oz) raisins
225g (8oz) ready-made white almond paste

TO FINISH
beaten egg, to glaze
25g (1oz) slivered or flaked almonds
45ml (3 tbsp) apricot jam

1 Sift the flour into a bowl. Stir in the yeast, lemon rind and sugar; make a well in the centre. Combine the melted butter, egg and milk in another bowl, then add to the well. Mix to a soft dough, adding a little more milk if the mixture feels dry.

2 Turn on to a floured surface and knead for about 5 minutes until the dough is smooth and elastic. Transfer to a lightly oiled bowl, cover with cling film and leave to rise in a warm place for 1-1½ hours until doubled in size.

3 Knead the dough lightly, then roll out on a lightly floured surface to a 30×23cm (12×9 inch) rectangle. Brush with melted butter and sprinkle with the spice and raisins.

CITRUS ECCLES CAKES

MAKES 20 ◆ PREPARATION 35 minutes ◆ COOKING TIME 12-15 minutes
◆ FREEZING Suitable ◆ 160 CALS PER CAKE ◆ COLOUR INDEX Page 38

1 quantity Rough Puff Pastry (see page 234)

FILLING
175g (6oz) currants
50g (2oz) chopped mixed candied peel
50g (2oz) muscovado sugar

finely grated rind of 2 lemons

TO FINISH
beaten egg, to glaze
caster sugar, for sprinkling
50g (2oz) unsalted butter, melted

1 For the filling, mix all the ingredients together in a bowl.
2 Roll out half of the pastry on a lightly floured surface to a 50x20cm (20x8 inch) rectangle, then cut in half lengthwise. Cut each strip into 5 equal pieces.
3 With the tip of a knife, make rows of 2cm (¾ inch) cuts on each piece of pastry, 5mm (¼ inch) apart and staggering alternate rows so that the pastry forms a lattice when eased apart. (Or use a lattice roller.) Brush edges with beaten egg.
4 Divide half the filling between the latticed pastries, placing it in the centre of each. Bring the edges of the pastry up over the filling and pinch together to seal. Invert on to a lightly greased baking sheet, so the neat sides are uppermost. Repeat with remaining pastry and filling. Brush with egg.
5 Dust lightly with sugar and bake at 220°C/fan oven 210°C (425°F) Mark 7 for 12-15 minutes until puffed and golden. Drizzle a little melted butter through each lattice. Serve warm.

RASPBERRY PALMIERS

MAKES 16 ◆ PREPARATION 20 minutes, plus chilling ◆ COOKING TIME 15 minutes
◆ FREEZING Not suitable ◆ 145 CALS PER PALMIER ◆ COLOUR INDEX Page 38

225g (8oz) ready-made puff pastry
30ml (2 tbsp) raspberry jam

25g (1oz) caster sugar
125g (4oz) raspberries
icing sugar, for dusting

1 Roll out the pastry to a 30cm (12 inch) square on a surface dusted with icing sugar. Cut the pastry into two long strips, each measuring 15x30cm (6x12 inches).
2 Spread the pastry strips with the jam, then sprinkle with the caster sugar. Scatter the fresh raspberries evenly on top, crushing them slightly. Roll up each end of one strip tightly, towards the centre until the rolls meet in the middle; press down lightly. Repeat with the other strip. Chill for 30 minutes.
3 Place the pastry rolls on the surface with the long edges towards you, then cut into 5mm (¼ inch) slices. Place on non-stick baking trays, spacing at least 7.5cm (3 inches) apart.
4 Dust liberally with icing sugar and bake at 200°C/fan oven 190°C (400°F) Mark 6 for 15 minutes or until golden. Transfer to a wire rack to cool. Dust with icing sugar and serve with mixed berry fruits and clotted cream if you like.

CHERRY TARTLETS

MAKES 8 ◆ PREPARATION 25 minutes, plus chilling ◆ COOKING TIME 20 minutes
◆ FREEZING Not suitable ◆ 405 CALS PER TARTLET

PASTRY
225g (8oz) plain white flour
pinch of salt
150g (5oz) firm unsalted butter, diced
30ml (2 tbsp) caster sugar
1 egg yolk, mixed with 45ml (3 tbsp) cold water

FILLING
400g (14oz) can pitted black cherries
125g (4oz) medium-fat soft cheese
90ml (6 tbsp) single cream
1 egg yolk
5ml (1 tsp) vanilla extract
30ml (2 tbsp) caster sugar
icing sugar, for dusting

1 Sift the flour and salt into a bowl, rub in the butter, then stir in the sugar. Add the egg yolk and mix to a dough. Knead gently until smooth, wrap and chill for 30 minutes. Drain the cherries and dry on kitchen paper.
2 Beat the soft cheese lightly in a bowl to soften, then beat in the cream, egg yolk, vanilla extract and sugar.
3 Roll out the pastry thinly on a lightly floured surface and use to line eight 9cm (3½ inch) loose-based tartlet tins, which are 2.5cm (1 inch) deep. Line the pastry cases with grease-proof paper and baking beans. Bake at 200°C/fan oven 190°C (400°F) Mark 6 for 10 minutes. Remove paper and beans, then bake for a further 5 minutes.
4 Raise setting to 220°C/fan oven 210°C (425°F) Mark 7. Pour the cream mixture into the pastry cases, then divide the cherries between them. Bake for 7-10 minutes until softly set. Serve warm or cold, dusted with icing sugar.

CARAMELISED STRAWBERRY TARTLETS

These simple, light pastries are delicious made in the summer with firm, sweet homegrown strawberries. Avoid using large fruit which will make the filling too watery.

MAKES 12 ◆ PREPARATION 20 minutes ◆ COOKING TIME 15-20 minutes
◆ FREEZING Not suitable ◆ 150 CALS PER TARTLET

6 sheets filo pastry, 100-125g (3½-4oz) total weight

FILLING
250g (9oz) mascarpone
finely grated rind of 1 lemon
15ml (1 tbsp) lemon juice

30ml (2 tbsp) caster sugar
1 egg

TO ASSEMBLE
25g (1oz) unsalted butter, melted
350g (12oz) small strawberries
icing sugar, for dusting

1 To make the filling, beat the mascarpone, lemon rind and juice, sugar and egg together in a bowl until smooth. Cut 9-10cm (3½-4 inch) squares through all the sheets of filo pastry; you will need 36 filo squares in total.

2 Lightly grease a non-stick 12-hole muffin or deep bun tin tray. Press a filo square into each of the sections, to extend above the edge and form an irregular shaped case. Brush lightly with butter.

3 Add a second layer of filo, adjusting the angle so the points are in a different place. Brush with more butter, then apply the remaining filo squares in the same way. Bake at 190°C/fan oven 180°C (375°F) Mark 5 for 5-8 minutes until just beginning to colour.

4 Spoon the mascarpone mixture into the filo cases and return to the oven for about 8 minutes until the filling is just beginning to set and the pastry is golden. Transfer to a wire rack and leave to cool.

5 Slice the strawberries. Press the slices gently between sheets of kitchen paper to dry slightly. Heat a griddle or heavy based frying pan and sprinkle with half of the sugar. Add half of the strawberries and cook quickly until the sugar is bubbling and beginning to caramelise, then remove and leave to cool. Wipe pan clean, then repeat with remaining strawberries.

6 Arrange the strawberries over the filling. Sprinkle the edges of the tartlets with icing sugar to decorate.

FLORENTINE TARTLETS

MAKES 12 ◆ PREPARATION 25 minutes, plus chilling
◆ COOKING TIME 13-15 minutes ◆ FREEZING Suitable ◆ 225 CALS PER TARTLET
◆ COLOUR INDEX Page 38

PASTRY
125g (4oz) plain white flour
50g (2oz) firm unsalted butter, in pieces
50g (2oz) caster sugar
2 egg yolks

FILLING
25g (1oz) butter, melted
2 egg yolks

90ml (6 tbsp) golden syrup
50g (2oz) ground almonds
finely grated rind of 2 lemons
50g (2oz) glacé cherries, chopped
50g (2oz) flaked almonds
45ml (3 tbsp) pumpkin seeds
icing sugar, for dusting

1 To make the pastry, sift the flour into a bowl, then rub in the butter, using your fingertips. Stir in the sugar. Add the egg yolks and mix to a smooth dough. Knead lightly, wrap and chill for 30 minutes.

2 Roll out the pastry very thinly and use to line a 12-hole shallow bun tin or tartlet tray.

3 To make the filling, beat the butter in a bowl with the egg yolks, syrup, ground almonds and lemon rind. Divide between the pastry cases, spreading evenly. Bake at 200°C/fan oven 190°C (400°F) Mark 6 for 7-8 minutes until the filling is beginning to set.

4 In the meantime, mix together the cherries, flaked almonds, and pumpkin seeds. Scatter the mixture over the tartlets and bake for a further 6-7 minutes until risen and golden.

5 Leave to cool slightly, then ease tartlets out of the tins with the tip of a knife. Serve warm or cold, dusted with icing sugar.

LEMON SHORTBREAD TARTLETS

MAKES 10 ◆ PREPARATION 25 minutes, plus chilling
◆ COOKING TIME 12-15 minutes ◆ FREEZING Not suitable
◆ 495 CALS PER TARTLET ◆ COLOUR INDEX Page 38

PASTRY
250g (9oz) plain white flour
175g (6oz) unsalted butter, in pieces
75g (3oz) caster sugar
finely grated rind of 2 lemons
10ml (2 tsp) water

FILLING
450ml (¾ pint) double cream
125g (4oz) caster sugar
100ml (3½fl oz) lemon juice (about 3 lemons)
icing sugar, for dusting

1 To make the pastry, put the flour in a food processor, add the butter and process until the mixture resembles breadcrumbs. Add the sugar, lemon rind and water. Process briefly to a firm dough. Wrap and chill for 30 minutes.

2 Roll out the shortbread on a lightly floured surface and use to line 10 greased loose-based 9cm (3½ inch) tartlet tins, which are 2.5 cm (1 inch) deep. Bake at 200°C/fan oven 190°C (400°F) Mark 6 for 12-15 minutes until pale golden. Leave to cool, then carefully remove from the tins.

3 For the filling, pour the cream into a saucepan, add the sugar and lemon juice and heat gently until the sugar is dissolved. Bring to the boil and let bubble around the edges for about 1 minute. Remove from the heat and transfer to a bowl. Cover the surface with greaseproof paper to prevent a skin forming; leave until cool.

4 Pour the filling into the shortbread cases. Chill for at least 2 hours until set. Serve dusted with icing sugar.

PEACH FILOS

MAKES 8 ◆ PREPARATION 30 minutes, plus soaking ◆ COOKING TIME 20 minutes
◆ FREEZING Not suitable ◆ 300 CALS PER RING ◆ COLOUR INDEX Page 38

3 sheets filo pastry, each about 50x28cm (20x11 inches)
25g (1oz) unsalted butter, melted
beaten egg, to glaze
30ml (2 tbsp) slivered almonds

FILLING
15ml (1 tbsp) cardamom pods, seeds extracted
50g (2oz) chopped almonds, lightly toasted
250g (9oz) ready-to-eat dried peaches, finely chopped

75g (3oz) ground almonds
1.25ml (¼ tsp) ground cloves
1.25ml (¼ tsp) ground cinnamon
15ml (1 tbsp) orange flower water
60ml (4 tbsp) thin honey

SYRUP
150g (5oz) caster sugar
120ml (4fl oz) water
45ml (3 tbsp) lemon juice
45ml (3 tbsp) orange flower water

1 For the filling, mix all the ingredients together in a bowl to a paste.

2 Lay one sheet of pastry on a clean surface and brush lightly with melted butter. Cut crosswise into 8 thin strips. Spoon a little of the paste down each strip to within 2cm (¾ inch) of the ends. Roll up each one, then bring the ends round and push together to form rings. Transfer to a lightly greased baking sheet and brush lightly with butter.

3 Cut remaining filo into 5cm (2 inch) wide strips. Wrap around the rings, crumpling them up and tucking the edges underneath, until each ring is wrapped in several layers of filo. Brush with egg and sprinkle with the almonds. Bake at 200°C/fan oven 190°C (400°F) Mark 6 for 20 minutes or until golden. Leave to cool on the baking sheet.

4 For the syrup, dissolve the sugar in the water in a small pan over a low heat, then boil for 3 minutes until syrupy. Off the heat, stir in the lemon juice and orange flower water.

5 Transfer the pastries to a shallow dish in which they fit snugly. Spoon over the syrup. Chill or leave in a cool place for several hours until most of the syrup is absorbed.

REDCURRANT AND RASPBERRY MERINGUE SHORTBREADS

These pastries are equally good as a dessert, or at teatime.

MAKES 12 ◆ PREPARATION 30 minutes, plus chilling
◆ COOKING TIME About 20 minutes ◆ FREEZING Not suitable
◆ 210 CALS PER TARTLET

SHORTBREAD
125g (4oz) plain white flour
50g (2oz) ground almonds
1.25ml (¼ tsp) freshly grated nutmeg
125g (4oz) firm unsalted butter, diced
50g (2oz) caster sugar

FILLING
125g (4oz) redcurrants

125g (4oz) raspberries
45ml (3 tbsp) redcurrant jelly
15ml (1 tbsp) water
30ml (2 tbsp) Grand Marnier or other orange liqueur

MERINGUE
2 medium egg whites
115g (4oz) caster sugar

1 To make the shortbread, put the flour, ground almonds and nutmeg in a food processor with the butter and process until the mixture resembles breadcrumbs. Add the sugar, then work briefly until the mixture comes together in a dough. Knead lightly into a ball. Wrap and chill for 30 minutes.

2 Lightly grease a 12-hole shallow bun tin or tartlet tray. Roll out the pastry on a lightly floured surface and use to line the tins, trimming off the excess. Bake at 200°C/fan oven 190°C (400°F) Mark 6 for 12-15 minutes until pale golden, then leave to cool. Raise the oven setting to 230°C/fan oven 220°C (450°F) Mark 8.

3 Divide the fruit equally between the shortbread cases, piling it up in the middle. Heat the redcurrant jelly with the water in a small pan until melted. Stir in the liqueur. Leave to cool slightly, then spoon the mixture over the fruit.

4 For the meringue, whisk the egg whites in a clean bowl until stiff. Gradually whisk in the sugar, a tablespoonful at a time, until the meringue is stiff and glossy. Spoon into a piping bag fitted with a large star nozzle. Pipe a swirl of meringue on each tartlet, starting at the edge and building up to a peak in the middle.

5 Return to the oven for about 3-4 minutes until the meringue is tinged golden, watching closely as it will suddenly colour. Serve warm or cold.

NOTE The shortbread cases can be made 1-2 days in advance, but the filling and meringue should be prepared on the day.

PASSION FRUIT ÉCLAIRS

Flavoured with passion fruit juice and kirsch, these éclairs are a lighter, refreshing alternative to the more familiar chocolate ones. The pastry can be made and baked a day ahead (or frozen) but, for best results, fill and ice shortly before serving.

MAKES 12-15 ◆ PREPARATION 30 minutes ◆ COOKING TIME 20-25 minutes
◆ FREEZING Suitable (unfilled éclairs only) ◆ 185-150 CALS PER SERVING

65g (2½oz) plain white flour
50g (2oz) unsalted butter
150ml (¼ pint) water
2 eggs, lightly beaten

FILLING
4 passion fruit
300ml (½ pint) double cream

45ml (3 tbsp) kirsch
15ml (1 tbsp) icing sugar

ICING
2 passion fruit
150g (5oz) icing sugar
15-20ml (3-4 tsp) water

1 Sift the flour on to a sheet of greaseproof paper. Put the butter and water in a saucepan and heat gently until the butter is melted, then bring to the boil. Remove from the heat and immediately shoot in the flour, beating well with a wooden spoon until the mixture forms a ball in the centre of the pan. Leave to cool slightly, for 3 minutes.

2 Add the eggs, a little at a time, beating well after each addition, until the pastry is smooth, shiny, and a piping consistency. (It may not be necessary to add all of the egg.)

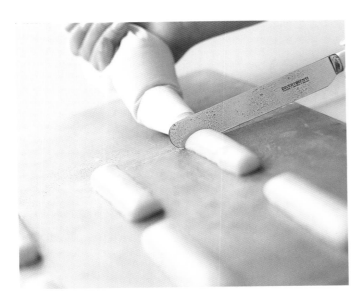

3 Place in a piping bag fitted with a 1.5cm (⅝ inch) plain nozzle. Sprinkle a lightly greased large baking sheet with water. Pipe 8cm (3¼ inch) lengths on to the baking sheet, using a wet knife to cut off the pastry neatly at the nozzle.

4 Bake at 200°C/fan oven 190°C (400°F) Mark 6 for 18-20 minutes until well risen and golden. Remove from the oven and make a slit along the side of each éclair with a knife to let the steam escape. Return to the oven for a further 2 minutes to dry out the pastry. Transfer to a wire rack to cool.

5 For the filling, halve the passion fruit and press the pulp through a sieve into a bowl to extract the juice. Add the cream, kirsch and icing sugar to the fruit juice and whip until softly peaking. Spoon or pipe the cream into the éclairs.

6 For the icing, halve the passion fruit and scoop the pulp into a bowl. Mix the icing sugar and water to a smooth icing that thickly coats the back of the spoon. Spread over the top of the éclairs, then spoon a little of the pulp on to each. Chill until ready to serve.

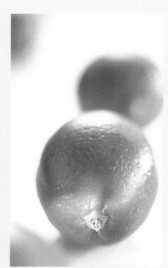

EVERYDAY CAKES

Tangy citrus sponges, crumbly moist fruit cakes and innovative flavour combinations are presented in this chapter of quick and easy cakes, most of which have excellent keeping qualities

COFFEE AND PECAN LAYER CAKE

MAKES 10 SLICES ◆ PREPARATION 30 minutes ◆ COOKING TIME 20-25 minutes
◆ FREEZING Suitable (stage 2) ◆ 570 CALS PER SLICE
◆ COLOUR INDEX Page 40

175g (6oz) self-raising white flour

7.5ml (1½ tsp) baking powder

175g (6oz) unsalted butter, softened

175g (6oz) light muscovado sugar

3 eggs

30ml (2 tbsp) instant coffee, dissolved in 15ml (1 tbsp) hot water

100g (3½oz) pecan halves, chopped

FILLING

75g (3oz) unsalted butter, softened

175g (6oz) icing sugar

2.5ml (½ tsp) vanilla extract

FROSTING

225g (8oz) caster sugar

pinch of cream of tartar

1 large egg white

15ml (1 tbsp) instant coffee, dissolved in 10ml (2 tsp) hot water

TO DECORATE

pecan halves

1 Grease and base-line three 18cm (7 inch) sandwich tins.
2 Sift the flour and baking powder into a bowl. Add the butter, sugar, eggs and coffee mixture and whisk until pale and creamy. Stir in the pecans.
3 Divide between the tins and level each surface. Bake at 180°C/fan oven 170°C (350°F) Mark 4 for 20-25 minutes until just firm to the touch. Transfer to a wire rack to cool.
4 To make the filling, beat the butter, icing sugar and vanilla together in a bowl with 5ml (1 tsp) boiling water until pale and creamy. Use to sandwich the cake layers on a plate.
5 To make the frosting, heat the sugar and cream of tartar in a small heavy-based saucepan with 60ml (4 tbsp) water until dissolved. Bring to the boil and boil, without stirring, until the syrup registers 116°C (240°F) on a sugar thermometer.
6 Meanwhile, whisk the egg white in a bowl until stiff. Pour on the sugar syrup in a thin stream, whisking all the time until the frosting is glossy and peaking. Stir in the coffee. Spread over the top and sides of the cake. Decorate with pecans.

WALNUT TORTE

MAKES 8-10 SLICES ◆ PREPARATION 25 minutes ◆ COOKING TIME 30 minutes
◆ FREEZING Not suitable ◆ 530-425 CALS PER SLICE ◆ COLOUR INDEX Page 40

165g (5½oz) walnuts, lightly toasted and roughly chopped

150g (5oz) unsalted butter

150g (5oz) caster sugar

5 eggs, separated

grated rind of 1 orange

150g (5oz) ricotta cheese

40g (1½oz) plain white flour

TO FINISH

90ml (6 tbsp) apricot jam

10ml (2 tsp) orange juice

25g (1oz) dark, bitter chocolate, in one piece

1 Grease and base-line a 23cm (9 inch) spring-release cake tin. Set aside 40g (1½oz) toasted walnuts for the decoration.
2 Cream the butter and 125g (4oz) of the sugar together in a bowl until pale and fluffy. Add the egg yolks, orange rind, ricotta cheese, flour and chopped walnuts. Mix gently until evenly combined.
3 Whisk the egg whites in another large bowl until stiff but not dry. Gradually whisk in the remaining sugar. Using a large metal spoon, fold a quarter into the cheese mixture to loosen slightly, then carefully fold in the remainder.
4 Turn mixture into prepared tin and gently level the surface. Bake at 190°C/ fan oven 180°C (375°F) Mark 5 for about 30 minutes until risen and just firm. Leave to cool in the tin.
5 Heat the apricot jam in a pan until melted, then sieve into a bowl and stir in the orange juice to make a glaze. Brush the side of the cake with half of the glaze and coat with the reserved walnuts, pressing them on with a palette knife.
6 Brush the remaining apricot glaze over the top of the cake. Using a swivel vegetable peeler, shave curls from the chocolate and scatter over the top of the cake to finish.

FROSTED LIME SPONGE

This variation on a classic Victoria Sandwich has a delicious cream cheese frosting. For a traditional sandwich cake, omit the lime and frosting. Sandwich the cake with strawberry or raspberry jam, then dust the top with icing sugar.

MAKES 10 SLICES ◆ PREPARATION 20 minutes ◆ COOKING TIME 20-25 minutes
◆ FREEZING Suitable (stage 5) ◆ 465 CALS PER SLICE

175g (6oz) unsalted butter or margarine, softened

175g (6oz) caster sugar

finely grated rind of 2 limes

3 medium eggs, lightly beaten

175g (6oz) self-raising white flour

TO FINISH

300g (10oz) full-fat cream cheese

30-45ml (2-3 tbsp) lime juice (1½-2 limes)

125g (4oz) icing sugar, sifted

lime zest, to decorate

1 Grease two 18cm (7inch) sandwich tins and dust with flour, shaking out the excess.
2 Beat the butter or margarine, sugar and lime rind together in a bowl until very pale and creamy.
3 Add the eggs gradually, beating well after each addition, and adding a little of the flour if the mixture starts to curdle.
4 Sift the flour over the mixture, then fold in using a large metal spoon.
5 Divide the mixture between the tins and level the surface. Bake at 180°C/fan oven 170°C (350°F) Mark 4 for 20-25 minutes until risen and just firm to the touch. Transfer to a wire rack and leave to cool.
6 To make the frosting, beat the cream cheese in a bowl to soften. Add the lime juice and icing sugar and beat until smooth and creamy.

7 Sandwich the cakes together with about half of the frosting and place on a serving plate. Using a palette knife spread with the rest of the cream cheese frosting. Decorate with strips of lime zest. Store in a cool place and eat within 1-2 days.

VARIATION Flavour the cake mixture with the grated rind of 1 large orange instead of lime rind, and use orange juice rather than lime juice for the glaze.

LAVENDER MADEIRA CAKE

Fresh lavender gives a subtle, summery flavour to a buttery Madeira cake. Dried lavender can be used successfully when fresh is out of season. Allow the cake to stand for 2-3 hours before eating to let the flavours develop.

MAKES 10 SLICES ◆ PREPARATION 20 minutes ◆ COOKING TIME 50 minutes ◆ FREEZING Suitable ◆ 370 CALS PER SLICE

3 fresh (or dried) lavender sprigs
225g (8oz) self-raising white flour
5ml (1 tsp) baking powder
finely grated rind of 1 lemon
175g (6oz) unsalted butter, softened
175g (6oz) caster sugar
3 eggs

ICING
3 sprigs fresh (or dried) lavender
175g (6oz) icing sugar
15ml (1 tbsp) lemon juice
10-15ml (2-3tsp) water

TO DECORATE
lavender sprigs (optional)

1 Grease a 900g (2lb) loaf tin. Line the base and long sides with one continuous strip of paper, which overhangs the edges so the cake can easily be lifted out of the tin. Line the ends of the tin with more paper.

2 Remove the lavender flowers from their stalks. Sift the flour and baking powder into a bowl.

3 Add the lemon rind, lavender, softened butter, sugar and eggs to the flour and beat well until the mixture is smooth and creamy.

4 Turn the mixture into the prepared tin and level the surface. Bake at 180°C/fan oven 170°C (350°F) Mark 4 for 30 minutes, then lower the setting to 170°C/fan oven 160°C (325°F) Mark 3. Bake for a further 20 minutes or until firm and a skewer inserted into the centre comes out clean. Leave to cool in the tin.

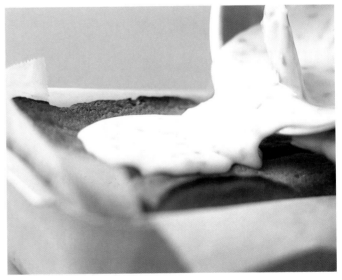

5 To make the icing, strip the lavender flowers from their stalks and put them in a bowl with the icing sugar, lemon juice and 10ml (2 tsp) of the water. Mix until smooth. The icing should thickly coat the back of the spoon; add a little extra water if it is too stiff.

6 Pour the icing evenly over the cake and leave to set. Serve sliced, decorated with extra lavender, if liked.

VARIATIONS
◆ CLASSIC MADEIRA CAKE Omit the lavender from the cake and icing.
◆ ORANGE MADEIRA CAKE Omit the lavender. Flavour the sponge with the grated rind of 1 orange. Use orange rather than lemon juice in the icing.

3 Thoroughly drain the apples and pat dry on kitchen paper. Scatter half of the apples over the cake mixture, then sprinkle with the sultanas. Cover with the remaining apples, pushing them down gently into the cake mix.

4 Dust with the remaining sugar and bake at 190°C/fan oven 180°C (375°F) Mark 5 for about 45 minutes until pale golden and just firm. Sprinkle with a little more sugar and transfer to a wire rack to cool.

ICED ROSEMARY CAKE

A sweet orange glaze is the perfect contrast for this Madeira-type cake, which is delicately scented with fresh rosemary.

MAKES 12 SLICES ◆ PREPARATION 20 minutes ◆ COOKING TIME About 1 hour
◆ FREEZING Suitable (stage 4) ◆ 325 CALS PER SLICE ◆ COLOUR INDEX Page 40

3 tender fresh rosemary sprigs, each about 10cm (4 inches)
175g (6oz) unsalted butter, softened
175g (6oz) caster sugar
10ml (2 tsp) vanilla extract
3 eggs, beaten
225g (8oz) self-raising white flour
30ml (2 tbsp) milk

GLAZE
225g (8oz) icing sugar
finely grated rind of ½ orange
15ml (1 tbsp) orange juice

TO DECORATE
rosemary sprigs

1 Grease and line a 15cm (6 inch) round, deep cake tin. Strip the leaves from the rosemary stalks and chop finely. Set aside half for the glaze.

2 Cream the butter, sugar and remaining rosemary together in a bowl until pale and creamy. Stir in the vanilla extract.

3 Gradually beat in the eggs, a little at a time, adding a little of the flour to prevent curdling. Sift the remaining flour over the mixture. Add the milk and fold in.

4 Turn the mixture into the prepared tin and level the surface. Bake at 180°C/fan oven 170°C (350°F) Mark 4 for 50 minutes to 1 hour until firm and a skewer inserted into the centre comes out clean.

5 Meanwhile, put the remaining rosemary in a small pan with 30ml (2 tbsp) water. Heat gently for 2 minutes; set aside to infuse until cool.

6 To make the glaze, sift the icing sugar into a bowl and add the orange rind and juice. Strain the rosemary juice into the bowl and mix to the consistency of pouring cream, adding a little water if necessary.

7 Leave the cake to cool for 5 minutes, then run a knife between the cake and the lining paper. Pour the icing over the cake and leave to cool completely before removing the paper. Decorate with rosemary sprigs to serve.

NOTE It is essential to use young, tender rosemary leaves. Older, tougher ones would spoil the texture of the cake.

DANISH APPLE CAKE

This cake is so moist and delicious, it is difficult to resist. Serve warm with pouring cream for optimum appreciation.

MAKES 8 SLICES ◆ PREPARATION 20 minutes ◆ COOKING TIME 45 minutes
◆ FREEZING Not suitable ◆ 450 CALS PER SLICE

2 small cooking apples, about 450g (1lb) in total
15ml (1 tbsp) lemon juice
100g (3½oz) self-raising white flour
2.5ml (½ tsp) baking powder
2.5ml (½ tsp) ground cinnamon
125g (4oz) ground almonds

175g (6oz) caster sugar
150g (5oz) unsalted butter, softened
5ml (1 tsp) almond extract
2 eggs
125ml (4fl oz) milk
75g (3oz) sultanas
extra caster sugar, for sprinkling

1 Grease and line a 23cm (9 inch) spring-release cake tin. Peel, core and thinly slice the apples and put into a bowl of cold water with the lemon juice added to prevent discoloration.

2 Put the flour, baking powder, cinnamon, ground almonds and 150g (5oz) of the sugar in a food processor. Add the butter, almond extract, eggs and milk and process briefly until the ingredients are just evenly mixed to a smooth, thick paste. Turn into the prepared tin.

CARROT CAKE WITH MASCARPONE

Brazil nuts replace the more familiar walnuts in this carrot cake and crisp fried, sugared carrot shavings make an unusual topping. You could, of course, simply sprinkle with toasted chopped nuts instead.

MAKES 8-10 SLICES ◆ PREPARATION 20 minutes
◆ COOKING TIME 35-40 minutes ◆ FREEZING Suitable (stage 3)
◆ 735-570 CALS PER SLICE ◆ COLOUR INDEX Page 40

225g (8oz) unsalted
butter, softened
225g (8oz) caster sugar
175g (6oz) self-raising
white flour
5ml (1 tsp) baking powder
2.5ml (½ tsp) ground
allspice
4 eggs
grated rind of 1 orange
15ml (1 tbsp) orange juice
50g (2oz) ground almonds
350g (12oz) carrots,
peeled and finely grated
125g (4oz) brazil nuts,
coarsely chopped and
toasted

FROSTING
250g (9oz) mascarpone
5ml (1 tsp) finely grated
orange rind
30ml (2 tbsp) orange juice
30ml (2 tbsp) icing sugar

TO DECORATE
deep-fried carrot ribbons
(optional, see note)
icing sugar, for dusting

1 Grease and base-line two 18cm (7 inch) moule à manque tins or sandwich tins. Dust the sides of the tins with flour and shake out excess.

2 Cream the butter and sugar together in a bowl until pale and fluffy. Sift the flour, baking powder and allspice together over the mixture. Add the eggs, orange rind and juice, and the ground almonds; beat well. Stir in the carrots and brazil nuts.

3 Divide the mixture between the tins and level each surface. Bake at 180°F/fan oven 170°C (350°F) Mark 4 for 35-40 minutes until risen and firm to touch. Transfer to a wire rack to cool.

4 For the frosting, beat the mascarpone, orange rind, orange juice and icing sugar together in a bowl until smooth. Use half of the frosting to sandwich the cakes together. Spread the remainder over the top of the cake, swirling it attractively. Chill until required.

5 Scatter deep-fried carrot ribbons on top of the cake to decorate, if desired, and dust with icing sugar to serve.

NOTE To make the decoration, pare 1 large carrot into long thin ribbons, using a swivel vegetable peeler. Pat dry on kitchen paper, then deep-fry in hot oil, in two batches until golden and crisp. Drain on kitchen paper.

AMARETTI PLUM CAKE

MAKES 12-16 SLICES ◆ PREPARATION 25 minutes
◆ COOKING TIME 50 minutes ◆ FREEZING Suitable ◆ 445-335 CALS PER SLICE

100g (3½oz) amaretti
biscuits
50g (2oz) white sugar
cubes
250g (9oz) unsalted
butter, softened
225g (8oz) caster sugar
5 eggs, separated

finely grated rind of
1 lemon
60ml (4 tbsp) lemon juice
150g (5oz) self-raising
white flour
150g (5oz) ground
almonds
5 red plums, stoned and
thickly sliced

1 Grease and line a 23cm (9 inch) square cake tin. Break the amaretti biscuits into small chunks. Put the sugar cubes in a polythene bag and crush with a rolling pin to break into small pieces; set aside.

2 Cream the butter and caster sugar together in a bowl until light and fluffy. Beat in the egg yolks, lemon rind and juice.

3 Sift the flour into the bowl and add the ground almonds and 75g (3oz) of the broken biscuits. Carefully fold these ingredients into the mixture, using a large metal spoon.

4 Whisk the egg whites in a separate bowl until peaking. Fold a quarter into the almond mixture to lighten it, then fold in the remainder. (The egg whites will lose a lot of aeration, but the mixture should still be fairly light).

5 Turn into the prepared tin and scatter over the plum slices and remaining biscuits. Bake at 180°C/fan oven 170°C (350°F) Mark 4 for 50 minutes or until just firm in the centre and a skewer inserted into the centre comes out clean. Scatter with the crushed sugar and leave to cool in the tin.

6 Serve cut into slices or wedges. Store in an airtight tin in a cool place for up to 2 days.

CRUMBLE TOPPED FRUIT CAKE

An everyday fruit cake, dotted with dried fruits and topped with a sugary crumbly crust.

MAKES 12 SLICES ◆ PREPARATION 15 minutes ◆ COOKING TIME 1¼-1½ hours
◆ FREEZING Suitable ◆ 390 CALS PER SLICE

125g (4oz) margarine, softened
125g (4oz) caster sugar
2 eggs
225g (8oz) self-raising white flour
5ml (1 tsp) ground mixed spice
10ml (2 tsp) vanilla extract
250g (9oz) mixed dried fruit

100g (3½oz) dried apricots or peaches, chopped
15ml (1 tbsp) milk

TOPPING
150g (5oz) plain white flour
100g (3½oz) firm butter or margarine, cut into pieces
100g (3½oz) demerara sugar

1 Grease and line a deep 20cm (8 inch) round cake tin.
2 Put the margarine, sugar, eggs, flour, spice and vanilla extract in a bowl and beat until smooth and creamy. Stir in the dried fruit, apricots or peaches and milk until evenly combined. Turn into the prepared tin and level the surface.
3 To make the topping, put the flour in a bowl and rub in the butter or margarine until the mixture starts to bind together into large crumbs. (You can use a food processor for this). Stir in the sugar, then scatter the mixture into the tin.

4 Bake at 170°C/fan oven 160°C (325°F) Mark 3 for about 1¼-1½ hours until the cake is firm, and a skewer inserted into the centre comes out clean. Leave to cool in the tin. Wrap and store for up to 1 week.

GREEK YOGURT CAKE

This wonderfully simple cake is soaked in lemon syrup after baking to delicious effect. Served with fresh oranges, it makes a memorable pudding.

MAKES 10 SLICES ◆ PREPARATION 30 minutes, plus soaking
◆ COOKING TIME 1¼ hours ◆ FREEZING Suitable (stage 4)
◆ 340 CALS PER SERVING ◆ COLOUR INDEX Page 41

225g (8oz) plain white flour
10ml (2 tsp) baking powder
10ml (2 tsp) ground cinnamon
150g (5oz) caster sugar
150ml (¼ pint) sunflower oil
coarsely grated rind of 2 large lemons
150ml (¼ pint) Greek yogurt

4 large eggs, lightly beaten

SYRUP
225g (8oz) caster sugar
150ml (¼ pint) water
juice of 2 large lemons
15ml (1 tbsp) orange flower water (optional)

TO SERVE
6 large oranges (optional)
icing sugar, for dusting

1 Grease and base-line a deep 22cm (8½ inch) square or 24cm (9½ inch) round cake tin. Sift the flour, baking powder and cinnamon into a bowl and make a well in the centre.
2 In a separate bowl, whisk together the sugar, oil, lemon rind, yogurt and eggs. Mix into the flour until well combined.
3 Spoon mixture into the prepared tin. Bake at 170°C/fan oven 160°C (325°F) Mark 3 for 1¼ hours or until a skewer inserted into the centre comes out clean. Leave in the tin.
4 Meanwhile, for the syrup, put the sugar and water in a pan and dissolve over a low heat, then bring to the boil and bubble for 7-10 minutes until syrupy. Cool for 5 minutes, then add the lemon juice and orange flower water if using.
5 With the cake still in its tin, pierce the top with a fine skewer. Spoon over one third of the lemon syrup to moisten the crust, leave for 15 minutes, then spoon over the remainder. Leave to soak for 1 hour (see note).
6 With a peeler, thinly pare the rind from 2 oranges and cut into fine strips. Place in a bowl of boiling water for 2 minutes; drain and refresh with cold water. Set aside. Peel all of the oranges, discarding all white pith, then slice the flesh. Sprinkle the blanched rind over the oranges, cover and chill.
7 Remove the cake from the tin. Slice, dust with icing sugar and serve with the orange slices if appropriate.

NOTES
◆ The syrup must be thin enough to soak into the cake; add a little warm water if necessary.
◆ If using a loose-based tin, place on a tray to catch any syrup that seeps through.

2 Cream the butter and sugar together in a bowl until light and fluffy. Gradually add the eggs, beating well after each addition.

3 Sift the 125g (4oz) flour with the baking powder and allspice into the bowl, then fold in using a large metal spoon. Add the milk, polenta and chopped brazil nuts; fold in until evenly mixed.

4 Turn into the prepared tin and level the surface. Dip the halved nuts in flour and arrange around the edge of the mixture. Bake at 180°C/fan oven 170°C (350°F) Mark 4 for about 50 minutes until risen and just firm in the centre.

5 Leave the cake in the tin for 5 minutes, then transfer to a wire rack to cool. Drizzle with the honey to glaze. Store wrapped in greaseproof paper in an airtight tin for 4-5 days.

SUMMER BERRY CRUNCH CAKE

MAKES 8 SLICES ◆ PREPARATION 40 minutes ◆ COOKING TIME About 1 hour
◆ FREEZING Not suitable ◆ 435 CALS PER SLICE ◆ COLOUR INDEX Page 41

2 eggs
1 egg yolk
pinch of salt
150g (5oz) butter, softened
150g (5oz) caster sugar
150g (5oz) self-raising white flour, sifted
grated rind and juice of 1 lemon
125g (4oz) mixed raspberries and blueberries (see note)

TOPPING
25g (1oz) rough white sugar cubes
25ml (5 tsp) bottled lemon juice
225g (8oz) caster sugar

TO FINISH
icing sugar, for dusting
fresh berries and/or currants, to decorate

1 Grease and base-line a 900g (2lb) loaf tin. In a bowl, lightly beat the eggs and egg yolk with the salt.

2 Cream the butter and sugar together in a bowl until light and fluffy. Beat in the eggs, a little at a time.

3 Fold in the flour, together with the lemon rind and 30ml (2 tbsp) of the lemon juice. Fold in the berries.

4 Spoon into the prepared tin and bake at 170°C/fan oven 160°C (325°F) Mark 3 for 50 minutes - 1 hour. Leave in the tin for 5 minutes, then transfer to a wire rack to cool.

5 Lightly crush the sugar cubes. Mix together the reserved fresh lemon juice, bottled lemon juice and caster sugar. Spoon over the cake, then sprinkle with the crushed sugar. Set aside for 1 hour or until set.

6 Dust the cake with icing sugar. Serve sliced, topped with fresh berries and accompanied by crème fraîche or yogurt.

NOTES

◆ Don't worry if the berries sink towards the bottom of the cake during baking – this won't affect the flavour.

◆ Any combination of summer berries can be used in the cake – try blackberries, strawberries and black or white currants.

BRAZIL NUT AND POLENTA CAKE

Polenta gives an interesting grainy texture and accentuates the flavour of the brazil nuts in this delicious moist cake.

MAKES 10 SLICES ◆ PREPARATION 15 minutes
◆ COOKING TIME About 50 minutes ◆ FREEZING Suitable
◆ 380 CALS PER SLICE

150g (5oz) brazil nuts
150g (5oz) unsalted butter, softened
150g (5oz) light muscovado sugar
2 eggs, lightly beaten
125g (4oz) plain white flour, plus an extra 15ml (1 tbsp)

5ml (1 tsp) baking powder
5ml (1 tsp) ground allspice
75ml (3fl oz) milk
65g (2½oz) instant polenta
60ml (4 tbsp) clear honey or maple syrup

1 Grease and line an 18cm (7 inch) square, deep cake tin. Cut half of the brazil nuts in half and set aside for the topping; roughly chop the rest.

LEMON AND HAZELNUT CAKE

MAKES 8 SLICES ◆ PREPARATION 50 minutes ◆ COOKING TIME 25 minutes
◆ FREEZING Suitable (stage 4) ◆ 370 CALS PER SLICE ◆ COLOUR INDEX Page 40

I unwaxed ripe, juicy lemon
125g (4oz) ground hazelnuts
75g (3oz) plain white flour
5ml (I tsp) baking powder
150g (5oz) caster sugar
4 eggs

TO FINISH
90ml (6 tbsp) lemon curd (preferably homemade)
150ml (¼ pint) double cream, whipped
icing sugar, for dusting

I Grease and base-line two 20cm (8 inch) sandwich tins or moule à manque tins. Put the whole lemon in a small heavy-based pan and add sufficient hot water to just cover. Simmer gently for about 45 minutes until very tender. Drain, reserving 45ml (3 tbsp) of the juice. Quarter the lemon and remove the pips, then place in a food processor with the reserved juice and process until almost smooth.

2 Mix together the ground hazelnuts, flour, baking powder and 50g (2oz) of the sugar.

3 Put the remaining sugar in a heatproof bowl with the eggs. Whisk over a pan of simmering water until the mixture is thick enough to leave a trail when the whisk is lifted. Fold in the hazelnut mixture and lemon purée.

4 Divide the mixture between the prepared tins and level the surfaces. Bake at 170°C/fan oven 160°C (325°F) Mark 3 for about 25 minutes until risen and just firm. Transfer to a wire rack to cool.

5 Sandwich the cakes together with the lemon curd and whipped cream. Dust generously with icing sugar to serve.

CHERRY AND APPLE STREUSEL

MAKES IO SLICES ◆ PREPARATION 30 minutes
◆ COOKING TIME About 50 minutes ◆ FREEZING Suitable ◆ 405 CALS PER SLICE
◆ COLOUR INDEX Page 41

225g (8oz) self-raising white flour
finely grated rind of I lemon
175g (6oz) unsalted butter, diced
150g (5oz) light muscovado sugar
75g (3oz) ground almonds
I large egg

FILLING
5 tart juicy dessert apples, preferably Cox's
40g (I½oz) butter
425g (15oz) can pitted black cherries
5ml (I tsp) cornflour
5ml (I tsp) vanilla extract
juice of ½ lemon

TO FINISH
icing sugar, for dusting

I Lightly grease a 23cm (9 inch) spring-release cake tin. For the filling, peel, core and roughly dice the apples. Melt the butter in a frying pan, add the apples and fry gently for about 3 minutes until softened.

2 Drain the cherries, reserving 60ml (2fl oz) juice. Blend the reserved juice with the cornflour in a separate pan. Add the vanilla and lemon juice; bring to the boil. Add the cherries and cook for I minute until thickened. Leave to cool.

3 Put the flour and lemon rind in a food processor. Add the butter and process until the mixture starts to stick together. Add the sugar and ground almonds and blend until crumbly. (Alternatively, rub the butter into the flour by hand, then stir in the sugar and almonds.)

4 Set aside 175g (6oz) of the mixture for the crumble topping. Add the egg to the rest of the mixture and mix to a dough. Turn into the prepared tin and press firmly on to the base and 2.5cm (I inch) up the sides to make a case.

5 Stir the apples into the cherry mixture and spoon into the case. Scatter over the crumble topping. Bake at 180°C/fan oven 170°C (350°F) Mark 4 for about 50 minutes until slightly risen and pale golden.

6 Leave to cool in the tin. Serve dusted with icing sugar.

CAERPHILLY AND APPLE CAKE

MAKES IO SLICES ◆ PREPARATION 20 minutes
◆ COOKING TIME 50 minutes-I hour ◆ FREEZING Suitable ◆ 345 CALS PER SLICE
◆ COLOUR INDEX Page 41

575g (I¼lb) dessert apples
175g (6oz) self-raising white flour
5ml (I tsp) baking powder
75g (3oz) light muscovado sugar
50g (2oz) raisins
50g (2oz) sultanas

50g (2oz) brazil nuts, roughly chopped
2 eggs
90ml (3fl oz) sunflower oil
225g (8oz) Caerphilly or Wensleydale cheese

TO FINISH
icing sugar, for dusting

I Grease a 5cm (2 inch) deep, 23cm (9 inch) round loose-based flan tin. Peel, core and thinly slice the apples.

2 Sift the flour and baking powder into a bowl. Stir in the sugar, raisins, sultanas, nuts and apples, and mix until evenly combined. Beat the eggs with the oil and add to the dry ingredients. Stir until all the flour mixture is moistened and evenly incorporated.

3 Turn half the mixture into the prepared tin and level the surface. Crumble the cheese over the surface, to within Icm (½ inch) of the edge. Cover with the remaining cake mixture, spreading it roughly to give an interesting finish.

4 Bake at 180°C/fan oven 170°C (350°F) Mark 4 for 50 minutes to I hour until golden and just firm. Leave in the tin for 10 minutes, then transfer to a wire rack to cool. Serve warm, sprinkled with icing sugar.

FRUITED BUTTERMILK CAKE

MAKES 12 SLICES ◆ PREPARATION 10 minutes
◆ COOKING TIME About 1¼ hours ◆ FREEZING Suitable ◆ 330 CALS PER SLICE

350g (12oz) self-raising white flour

5ml (1 tsp) baking powder

15ml (1 tbsp) ground mixed spice

125g (4oz) firm unsalted butter or block margarine, in pieces

125g (4oz) dark muscovado sugar

350g (12oz) luxury mixed dried fruit

2 eggs

285ml (9½fl oz) buttermilk

30ml (2 tbsp) demerara sugar (optional)

1 Grease and line an 18cm (7inch) round, deep cake tin.

2 Sift the flour, baking powder and spice together into a bowl. Add the butter and rub in using fingertips until the mixture resembles fine breadcrumbs. Stir in the muscovado sugar and dried fruit.

3 In another bowl, beat the eggs with the buttermilk. Add to the fruit mixture and mix lightly until the ingredients are just combined. Turn into the prepared tin and level the surface.

4 Scatter with the demerara sugar if using. Bake at 180°C/fan oven 170°C (350°F) Mark 4 for about 1¼ hours until the cake feels firm in the centre, covering with foil after about 30 minutes to prevent overbrowning. To test whether the cake is cooked, insert a skewer into the centre: it should come out clean. Leave to cool in the tin. Store in an airtight container for up to 1 week.

FRUITED GINGERCAKE

A deliciously moist gingercake, packed with plenty of dried fruit, nuts and ginger pieces. This cake keeps well in an airtight container – for up to 10 days.

MAKES 16 SLICES ◆ PREPARATION 25 minutes ◆ COOKING TIME 1½-1¾ hours ◆ FREEZING Suitable (before decorating) ◆ 415 CALS PER SLICE

400g (14oz) plain white flour
5ml (1 tsp) baking powder
15ml (1 tbsp) ground ginger
225g (8oz) unsalted butter or block margarine
225g (8oz) golden syrup
150g (5oz) molasses sugar
150g (5oz) glacé cherries, halved
100g (3½oz) glacé or preserved stem ginger, chopped

100g (3½oz) glacé pineapple, roughly chopped
100g (3½oz) blanched almonds
150g (5oz) sultanas
100g (3½oz) dried pears, chopped
3 eggs, beaten

ICING
50g (2oz) icing sugar
10ml (2 tsp) water

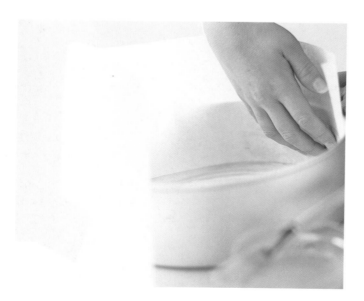

1 Grease and line a 23cm (9 inch) round cake tin. Sift the flour, baking powder and ground ginger into a large bowl. Melt the butter or margarine with the syrup and sugar in a saucepan over a low heat.

2 Set aside half of the cherries, ginger and pineapple with 25g (1oz) of the almonds for the topping; chop the rest of the nuts. Add the chopped almonds and remaining cherries, ginger and pineapple to the flour with the sultanas and pears; stir to mix.

3 Add the melted butter mixture to the bowl with the eggs and stir well until evenly combined. Turn into the prepared tin and level the surface.

4 Bake at 150°C/fan oven 140°C (300°F) Mark 2 for 1½-1¾ hours or until firm and a skewer inserted into the centre comes out clean. Leave to cool in the tin. Spread remaining almonds on a baking sheet and toast in the oven for 5-10 minutes until golden brown.

5 To make the icing, beat together the icing sugar and water until the consistency of thick pouring cream. Spread a little icing around the edges of the cake.

6 Scatter the reserved fruit and nuts on top of the icing and press gently to secure in position. Scribble the remaining icing over the fruit and nuts.

PISTACHIO ANGEL CAKE

MAKES 12 SLICES ◆ PREPARATION 25 minutes ◆ COOKING TIME 35-40 minutes
◆ FREEZING Not suitable ◆ 340 CALS PER SLICE ◆ COLOUR INDEX Page 42

75g (3oz) pistachio nuts
7 large egg whites
1.25ml (¼ tsp) salt
5ml (1 tsp) cream of tartar
5ml (1 tsp) almond extract
275g (10oz) caster sugar
175g (6oz) plain white flour

FROSTING
250g (9oz) mascarpone
10ml (2 tsp) lemon juice
120ml (4fl oz) coconut milk
125g (4oz) icing sugar

TO DECORATE
pistachio nuts

1 Oil a 1.7 litre (3 pint) ring mould, then dust with flour, shaking out excess. Soak the pistachio nuts in boiling water for 3 minutes. Drain, remove the skins by rubbing between layers of kitchen paper, then chop finely.
2 Whisk the egg whites in a large bowl until foamy. Add the salt and cream of tartar and whisk until stiff. Add the almond extract.
3 Gradually add the sugar, whisking well after each addition. Sift the flour over the mixture and fold in, using a metal spoon. Fold in the chopped pistachio nuts.
4 Turn the mixture into the ring mould and bake at 170°C/fan oven 160°C (325°F) Mark 3 for 35-40 minutes or until firm, and a skewer inserted into the centre comes out clean. Invert on to a wire rack but do not remove the tin. Leave to cool, then loosen and remove tin.
5 For the frosting, whisk together the mascarpone, lemon juice, coconut milk and icing sugar until smooth; chill until thickened. Transfer the cake to a serving plate and spread with the frosting. Scatter over pistachio nuts to decorate.

CHERRY AND ALMOND CAKE

MAKES 18 SLICES ◆ PREPARATION 20 minutes
◆ COOKING TIME About 50 minutes ◆ FREEZING Suitable ◆ 335 CALS PER SLICE
◆ COLOUR INDEX Page 42

300g (10oz) natural glacé cherries, rinsed and dried
150g (5oz) self-raising white flour, plus 15ml (1 tbsp)
250g (9oz) unsalted butter, softened
250g (9oz) caster sugar
finely grated rind of 2 lemons
5 eggs, separated

150g (5oz) ground almonds
45ml (3 tbsp) milk
25g (1oz) slivered or flaked almonds

GLAZE
100g (3½oz) caster sugar
100ml (3½fl oz) water
juice of 2 lemons
5ml (1 tsp) almond extract

1 Grease and line a 23cm (9 inch) square cake tin. Halve the cherries and toss in 15ml (1 tbsp) flour.
2 Cream the butter and sugar together in a bowl until light and fluffy. Stir in the lemon rind and egg yolks.
3 Sift the flour into the bowl. Add the ground almonds and milk and fold in, using a large metal spoon.
4 Whisk the egg whites in a clean bowl until peaking; fold a quarter into the creamed mixture to lighten it, then carefully fold in the remainder.
5 Turn the mixture into the prepared tin. Scatter over the cherries and almonds. Bake at 180°C/fan oven 170°C (350°F) Mark 4 for about 50 minutes until golden and just firm. Leave to cool in the tin.
6 For the glaze, put the sugar and water in a small heavy-based saucepan and heat gently until dissolved. Bring to the boil, add the lemon juice and almond extract and boil rapidly for 5 minutes until syrupy. Leave to cool, then spoon over the cake. Store in an airtight container for up to 5 days.

DARK, MOIST CHOCOLATE CAKE

MAKES 12 SLICES ◆ PREPARATION 30 minutes ◆ COOKING TIME 1¼-1½ hours
◆ FREEZING Suitable (stage 5) ◆ 460 CALS PER SLICE

250g (9oz) good quality plain chocolate (70% cocoa solids), in pieces
90ml (3 fl oz) milk
175g (6oz) unsalted butter, softened
175g (6oz) light muscovado sugar
4 eggs
150g (5oz) self-raising white flour

75g (3oz) ground almonds

TOPPING
100g (3½oz) plain chocolate, in pieces
25g (1oz) unsalted butter

TO DECORATE
25g (1oz) milk chocolate, melted

1 Grease and line a 20cm (8 inch) round, deep cake tin.
2 Melt the chocolate with the milk in a heatproof bowl over a pan of simmering water; stir until smooth. Let cool slightly.
3 Cream the butter and sugar together in a bowl until light and fluffy. Gradually beat in the eggs, adding a little of the flour to prevent curdling. Stir in the melted chocolate mixture.
4 Sift in the remaining flour and add the ground almonds. Fold in lightly until evenly combined.
5 Turn the mixture into the prepared tin and level the surface. Bake at 170°C/fan oven 160°C (325°F) Mark 3 for 1¼-1½ hours until a skewer inserted into the centre comes out clean. Leave in the tin for 5 minutes, then transfer to a wire rack to cool, placing the cake the right way up.
6 For the topping, melt the chocolate and butter in a heatproof bowl over a pan of simmering water; stir until smooth. Let cool for a few minutes until slightly thickened, then spread on top of the cake using a palette knife. Leave to set in a cool place. Drizzle with melted chocolate to decorate.

CREAM CAKES AND GÂTEAUX

Sophisticated cakes that are deceptively easy to create and taste as sensational as they look. Most are best eaten very fresh; many are ideal special occasion desserts

ITALIAN MERINGUES

Meringues which are crisp on the outside but give way to a soft centre are always a popular dessert.

SERVES 6 ◆ PREPARATION 20 minutes ◆ COOKING TIME 2-3 hours ◆ FREEZING Suitable ◆ 270 CALS PER SERVING

3 egg whites
175g (6oz) caster sugar

TO SERVE
200ml (7fl oz) double cream
strawberries, raspberries or sliced peaches

1 Line 2 baking sheets with non-stick baking parchment. Using an electric whisk on high speed, whisk the egg whites and sugar together in a large heatproof bowl set over a pan of gently simmering water until the mixture leaves a very thick 'trail' when the beaters are lifted. Immediately remove bowl from heat and continue whisking for 2 minutes until cooled.

2 Using 2 large spoons, shape the meringue into 12 ovals or rounds, spacing them well apart on the baking sheets.
3 Bake at 110°C/fan oven 100°C (225°F) Mark ¼ for 2-3 hours until the meringues are crisp and well-dried out, but still white; switch the baking sheets around halfway through baking to ensure even cooking. Carefully peel the meringues off the paper and transfer to a wire rack to cool.
4 Whip the cream until it just holds its shape. Sandwich the meringues together in pairs with cream and serve with fruit.

◆ CLASSIC MERINGUES These have a crisper, less melting texture than Italian meringues as the mixture is not heated during whisking. Whisk the egg whites in a large bowl until they are very stiff and hold a firm peak, but not dry. Gradually whisk in half of the sugar, a tablespoonful at a time, whisking well after each addition, until the meringue is very stiff. Lightly fold in the rest of the sugar, using a large metal spoon. Shape and bake as above.

PAVLOVA

SERVES 8 ◆ PREPARATION 30 minutes ◆ COOKING TIME 1¼-1½ hours
◆ FREEZING Not suitable ◆ 220 CALS PER SERVING ◆ COLOUR INDEX Page 43

3 egg whites
175g (6oz) caster sugar
5ml (1 tsp) cornflour, sifted
5ml (1 tsp) white wine vinegar
2.5ml (½ tsp) vanilla extract

FILLING
300ml (½ pint) double cream (or half Greek yogurt and half cream)
2 passion fruit, halved
2 kiwi fruit, peeled and sliced
225g (8oz) strawberries
225g (8oz) fresh pineapple, peeled, cored and chopped

1 Line a baking sheet with non-stick baking parchment and draw a 23cm (9 inch) circle on the paper; turn paper over.
2 For the meringue, whisk the egg whites in a bowl until stiff. Whisk in the sugar a third at a time, whisking well between each addition until stiff and very shiny. Fold in the cornflour, vinegar and vanilla extract.
3 Pile the meringue on to the marked circle, making a substantial hollow in the centre. Bake at 130°C/fan oven 120°C (250°F) Mark ½ for 1¼-1½ hours or until slightly browned and dry but a little soft in the centre; press lightly with a finger to test. Leave to cool slightly, then peel off paper. At this stage the meringue will probably crack and sink a little.
4 For the filling, whip cream until thick and, if using, mix with the yogurt; spoon on top of the Pavlova. Scoop out passion fruit pulp on to the cream and arrange the other fruit on top.

VARIATION For the fruit topping, use 450g (1lb) mixed soft fruits, such as strawberries, raspberries and redcurrants. Decorate with chocolate curls (see page 265).

CHOCOLATE AND HAZELNUT MERINGUES

SERVES 6 ◆ PREPARATION 25 minutes, plus chilling ◆ COOKING TIME 2 hours
◆ FREEZING Suitable ◆ 500 CALS PER SERVING ◆ COLOUR INDEX Page 43

125g (4oz) hazelnuts, toasted
125g (4oz) caster sugar
75g (3oz) good quality plain dark chocolate
2 egg whites

TO ASSEMBLE
300ml (½ pint) double cream
redcurrants, blackberries, and/or kumquats, caramel-dipped physalis fruit (see page 272)
chocolate shavings (optional)

1 Line 2 baking sheets with non-stick baking parchment. Put the toasted hazelnuts in a food processor with 45ml (3 tbsp) of the caster sugar and process to a fine powder. Add the chocolate and pulse until roughly chopped.

2 In a clean bowl, whisk the egg whites until stiff. Whisk in the remaining sugar, a spoonful at a time, until the mixture is stiff and shiny. Carefully fold in the chocolate and nut mixture.
3 Spoon the mixture into 12 small rough mounds on the baking sheets. Bake at 110°C/fan oven 100°C (225°F) Mark ¼ for about 45 minutes until the meringues will just peel off the paper. Gently push in the base of each meringue to form a deep hollow, then bake for a further 1¼ hours or until crisp and dry. Transfer to a wire rack to cool.
4 Whip the cream until it just holds its shape; use three quarters to sandwich the meringues together in pairs. Refrigerate for up to 2 hours to soften slightly.
5 Serve the meringues topped with the remaining cream, fruit and chocolate shavings.

CHOCOLATE AND CHESTNUT MACAROON

SERVES 6 ◆ PREPARATION 45 minutes, plus chilling
◆ COOKING TIME 1 hour 20 minutes ◆ FREEZING Suitable (stage 6)
◆ 750 CALS PER SERVING ◆ COLOUR INDEX Page 43

300g (10oz) icing sugar
2.5ml (½ tsp) bicarbonate of soda
4 egg whites
175g (6oz) hazelnuts, toasted and ground

FILLING
50g (2oz) plain chocolate, melted and cooled
125g (4oz) chestnut purée

15ml (1 tbsp) maple syrup
200ml (7fl oz) double cream
225g (8oz) mascarpone

TO DECORATE
chocolate curls (see page 265)
hazelnuts and/or gold-coated almonds (optional)
icing sugar, for dusting

1 Line 3 baking sheets with non-stick baking parchment and draw a 20cm (8 inch) circle on each; turn the paper over. Sift the icing sugar and bicarbonate of soda together.
2 Whisk the egg whites in a large bowl until very stiff, but not dry. Whisk in 50g (2oz) of the icing sugar. Carefully fold in the remaining icing sugar and ground hazelnuts.
3 Divide the mixture between the 3 circles and spread evenly into rounds. Bake at 130°C/fan oven 120°C (250°F) Mark ½ for 5 minutes. Lower oven setting to 110°C/fan oven 100°C (225°F) Mark ¼ and bake for a further 1¼ hours. Transpose the baking sheets during baking to ensure even cooking. Cool on a wire rack, then peel away the paper.
4 Beat the chestnut purée and maple syrup together.
5 Whip the cream until it just holds its shape, then fold into the mascarpone. Stir half into the cooled, melted chocolate; fold the remainder into the chestnut purée.
6 Place a meringue round on a serving plate. Spread with the chestnut mixture. Place a second meringue on top; press down lightly. Cover with the chocolate cream. Position the final meringue round on top. Refrigerate for at least 4 hours.
7 Decorate with chocolate curls, and the nuts if using. Dust with icing sugar to serve.

5 Drain the cherries, reserving 75ml (5 tbsp) of the juice. In a small pan, blend the cornflour with the reserved juice. Bring to the boil and cook, stirring, until thickened. Add the cherries and kirsch; cook for a further 30 seconds. Leave to cool.

6 Sprinkle a sheet of greaseproof paper with caster sugar and invert the roulade on to it. Lightly whip the cream until thickened, then spread on top of the sponge to within 1cm (½ inch) of the edges. Spoon the cherries and syrup over the cream. Starting from one of the short ends, carefully roll up. Transfer the roulade to a serving plate and chill until required. Serve sprinkled with sugar.

CHOCOLATE ROULADE

SERVES 10 ◆ PREPARATION 30 minutes, plus chilling
◆ COOKING TIME 20 minutes ◆ FREEZING Suitable (stage 7)
◆ 325 CALS PER SERVING ◆ COLOUR INDEX Page 44

175g (6oz) good quality plain dark chocolate (70% cocoa solids), in pieces
150ml (¼ pint) water
6 eggs, separated
175g (6oz) caster sugar

FILLING
300ml (10fl oz) whipping cream
5ml (1 tsp) caster sugar
2.5ml (½ tsp) vanilla extract

TO DECORATE
cocoa powder, for dusting
chocolate shavings

1 Grease and line a 38x28cm (15x11 inch) Swiss roll tin with non-stick baking parchment.

2 Melt the chocolate with the water in a small heatproof bowl over a pan of simmering water; stir until smooth.

3 Whisk the egg yolks and sugar together in a bowl, using an electric whisk, until pale and thick. Beat in the chocolate.

4 In a clean bowl, whisk the egg whites until they just hold a soft peak. Stir a quarter of the egg white into the chocolate mixture to loosen it, then carefully fold in the remainder, using a large metal spoon; do not overmix. Immediately pour into the prepared tin and spread into the corners.

5 Bake at 180°C/fan oven 170°C (350°F) Mark 4 for 20 minutes or until springy to the touch. Cover with a damp tea-towel and leave until cold. Once cold, cover the cloth with cling film, then refrigerate for at least 6 hours or overnight.

6 For the filling, whip cream until it starts to thicken. Add the sugar and vanilla and continue to whip until it holds its shape.

7 Lightly dust a large sheet of greaseproof paper with caster sugar. Uncover the roulade, then carefully turn out on to the greaseproof paper. Cut 5mm (¼ inch) off the two short sides to neaten. Spread the cream over the roulade and roll up tightly from a long side, using greaseproof paper to help. (Don't worry if the sponge cracks.)

8 Transfer to a plate, sprinkle with cocoa and serve decorated with chocolate shavings.

VARIATION At stage 7, scatter 175g (6oz) fresh raspberries over the cream before rolling up the roulade.

COCONUT ROULADE WITH CHERRIES

Unlike desiccated coconut, creamed coconut provides a rich flavour without the 'gritty' texture. For convenience, you can prepare this dessert up to the end of stage 4 a day in advance, assembling the roulade a few hours before serving.

SERVES 8 ◆ PREPARATION 30 minutes ◆ COOKING TIME 15-18 minutes
◆ FREEZING Not suitable ◆ 370 CALS PER SERVING

4 eggs, separated
140g (4½oz) caster sugar
45ml (3 tbsp) plain white flour
125g (4oz) chilled creamed coconut, finely grated

TO ASSEMBLE
420g (14½oz) can pitted black cherries
5ml (1 tsp) cornflour
60ml (4 tbsp) kirsch
caster sugar, for sprinkling
150ml (¼ pint) double cream

1 Grease a 33x23cm (13x9 inch) Swiss roll tin and line with greased non-stick baking parchment.

2 Whisk the egg yolks and 125g (4oz) of the sugar in a bowl until pale and fluffy. Sift the flour over the mixture. Add the grated coconut and fold the ingredients lightly together.

3 Whisk the egg whites in a clean bowl until stiff, then gradually whisk in the remaining sugar. Using a large metal spoon, fold a quarter of the egg white into the coconut mixture to lighten it, then carefully fold in the remainder.

4 Turn the mixture into the prepared tin and spread into the corners. Bake at 180°C/fan oven 170°C (350°F) Mark 4 for 15-18 minutes until risen and just firm to the touch. Cover with a dampened tea-towel and leave to cool.

CHOCOLATE AND CHERRY GÂTEAU

MAKES 10-12 SLICES ◆ PREPARATION 1 hour, plus soaking and chilling
◆ COOKING TIME 45 minutes ◆ FREEZING Suitable (stage 7)
◆ 625-520 CALS PER SLICE ◆ COLOUR INDEX Page 44

350g (12oz) fresh cherries, stoned, or 400g (14oz) pitted cherries, drained
45ml (3 tbsp) dark rum
50g (2oz) blanched almonds, toasted
50g (2oz) plain white flour
125g (4oz) good quality plain dark chocolate, in pieces
3 eggs, separated
125g (4oz) butter, softened
125g (4oz) caster sugar

GANACHE
225g (8oz) good quality plain dark chocolate, in pieces
450ml (¾ pint) double cream

TO DECORATE
chocolate curls (see below)
cocoa powder, for dusting

1 Put the cherries in a bowl with 30ml (2 tbsp) rum, cover and leave to soak for 6 hours or overnight.
2 Grease a 23cm (9 inch) deep round cake tin and line the base with non-stick baking parchment. Place the almonds in a food processor with the flour and process until finely ground.
3 Melt the chocolate with 45ml (3 tbsp) water in a bowl over a pan of simmering water. Remove from the heat, add the egg yolks and remaining rum and beat until smooth.
4 Beat the butter and sugar together in a bowl until light and fluffy. Stir in the chocolate mixture, then fold in the flour. Whisk the egg whites in a clean bowl until they form soft peaks, then fold into the chocolate mixture.
5 Pour the mixture into the prepared tin. Bake at 180°C/fan oven 170°C (350°F) Mark 4 for 30-35 minutes or until the cake is cooked. Leave in the tin for 10 minutes, then turn out on to a wire rack to cool completely.
6 To make the ganache, put the chocolate in a bowl. Slowly bring the cream to the boil in a small pan. Pour over the chocolate and leave to stand for 5 minutes, then stir until melted and smooth; cool. Using an electric whisk, beat the ganache until lighter in colour and thick.
7 Return the cake to the cleaned tin and scatter the cherries and any juice over the surface. Spoon the chocolate ganache on top, spread smoothly, then cover and refrigerate for at least 2 hours.
8 Decorate with chocolate curls and dust liberally with cocoa powder. Serve cut into thin slices, with cream, if wished.

◆ CHOCOLATE CURLS Use fine quality dark chocolate with at least 70% cocoa solids. Melt the chocolate in a bowl over a pan of barely simmering water, making sure it doesn't become too hot and that no moisture gets into the chocolate. Spread the melted chocolate in a thin layer over a marble slab or other clean, smooth surface. When it has just set, push a large knife across the chocolate at an angle of about 25° to scrape off curls. Store in an airtight container between sheets of greaseproof paper in a cool place for up to 1 week.

CITRUS MOUSSE CAKE WITH PLUMS

MAKES 12 SLICES ◆ PREPARATION 30 minutes ◆ COOKING TIME 35-40 minutes
◆ FREEZING Not suitable ◆ 305 CALS PER SLICE

6 eggs, separated
250g (9oz) caster sugar
finely grated rind of 2 lemons
45ml (3 tbsp) lemon juice
finely grated rind of 1 lime
30ml (2 tbsp) lime juice

150g (5oz) plain white flour
200ml (7fl oz) dessert wine
200ml (7fl oz) mild olive oil
900g (2lb) red or yellow plums
icing sugar, for dusting

1 Grease and line a 23cm (9 inch) spring-release cake tin.
2 Whisk the egg yolks and 175g (6oz) of the sugar together in a bowl until thickened and pale. Fold in the lemon and lime rind. Sift in the flour and fold in. Stir in 60ml (4 tbsp) of the wine, the lemon juice, then the olive oil.
3 Whisk the egg whites in a clean bowl until stiff. Using a large metal spoon, fold a quarter into the yolk mixture to lighten it, then carefully fold in the remainder. Turn into the prepared tin. Bake at 190°C/fan oven 180°C (375°F) Mark 5 for 35-40 minutes until well risen, golden and just firm to the touch. Cover with a damp tea-towel and leave to cool in the tin; the cake will sink slightly.
4 Quarter and stone the plums. Put the rest of the wine in a saucepan with the lime juice and remaining sugar and heat until the sugar is dissolved. Add the plums and simmer gently for about 3 minutes until slightly softened. Leave to cool.
5 Dust the cake with icing sugar. Serve cut into wedges, with the poached plums and lightly whipped cream.

CHOCOLATE AND RASPBERRY TORTE

This elegant gâteau makes an exquisite dessert to finish a special dinner party with a flourish.

MAKES 12 SLICES ◆ PREPARATION 45 minutes, plus chilling
◆ COOKING TIME 12-15 minutes ◆ FREEZING Not suitable ◆ 375 CALS PER SLICE

5 eggs
150g (5oz) caster sugar
125g (4oz) plain white flour
25g (1oz) cocoa powder

FILLING
4 egg yolks
50g (2oz) caster sugar
60ml (4 tbsp) cornflour
10ml (2 tsp) vanilla extract
450ml (¾ pint) milk
90ml (6 tbsp) Grand Marnier or other orange liqueur

300ml (½ pint) double cream
175g (6oz) raspberries
100g (3½oz) plain chocolate, grated or finely chopped
2 pieces preserved stem ginger in syrup, about 25g (1oz), finely chopped

TO FINISH
cocoa powder, for dusting

1 Grease and line a 23cm (9 inch) spring-release cake tin, and a 26x16cm (10½x6½ inch) shallow rectangular tin. Put the eggs and sugar in a large heatproof bowl set over a pan of hot water. Whisk until the mixture is pale and creamy and leaves a trail when the whisk is lifted from the bowl. Remove from the heat and whisk until cool.

2 Sift the flour and cocoa powder over the mixture, then carefully fold in, using a large metal spoon. Spoon a thin layer of the mixture into the rectangular tin, to give an 8mm (⅜ inch) depth. Turn the remainder into the spring-release tin. Bake both cakes at 200°C/fan oven 190°C (400°F) Mark 6 for 12-15 minutes until just firm. Leave to cool.

3 For the filling, beat the egg yolks, sugar, cornflour, vanilla extract and a little of the milk together in a bowl until smooth. Put the remaining milk in a heavy-based pan and bring to the boil, then pour on to the yolk mixture, stirring constantly. Return to the pan and heat gently, stirring until thickened; do not boil. Turn into a bowl, cover the surface closely with a disc of dampened greaseproof paper to prevent a skin forming and leave to cool.

4 Cut the round cake horizontally into two layers and fit one back into the cleaned tin, cut-side down. Trim off the edges of the rectangular cake, then cut into 4cm (1½ inch) wide strips. Fit these around the side of the tin to make a sponge case. Using a teaspoon, drizzle 45-60ml (3-4 tbsp) of the orange liqueur evenly over both round cake layers.

5 Whip the cream in a bowl until thickened, but not peaking. Fold in the cooled custard, raspberries, chocolate, ginger and remaining liqueur. Turn the mixture into the chocolate case and level the surface. Lay the reserved sponge round on top, cut-side up. Chill in the refrigerator overnight.

6 To serve, carefully release the side of the cake tin and invert the chocolate torte on to a large flat plate. Serve dusted with cocoa powder.

CHOCOLATE GÂTEAU WITH BRANDIED PRUNES

MAKES 16 SLICES ◆ PREPARATION 35 minutes ◆ COOKING TIME 25-30 minutes
◆ FREEZING Suitable (stage 4) ◆ 475 CALS PER SLICE ◆ COLOUR INDEX Page 44

75g (3oz) dark bitter
chocolate, in pieces
150ml (¼ pint) water
175g (6oz) unsalted
butter, softened
300g (10oz) light
muscovado sugar
3 eggs, beaten
300g (10oz) plain white
flour
5ml (1 tsp) bicarbonate of
soda
10ml (2 tsp) baking
powder
150ml (¼ pint) soured
cream

FILLING
175g (6oz) ready-to-eat
dried prunes
5ml (1 tsp) vanilla extract
2.5ml (½ tsp) cornflour
90ml (6 tbsp) brandy

TO DECORATE
450ml (¾ pint) double
cream
250ml (8fl oz) crème
fraîche
cocoa powder, for dusting

1 Grease and base-line three 20cm (8 inch) sandwich tins. Put the chocolate in a saucepan with the water and heat very gently until melted. Cool slightly.

2 Cream the butter and sugar together in a bowl until light and fluffy. Gradually beat in the eggs, a little at a time, adding a little of the flour to prevent curdling.

3 Sift together the remaining flour, bicarbonate of soda and baking powder. Stir the melted chocolate into the creamed mixture, then fold in the flour and soured cream.

4 Divide the mixture between the prepared tins and spread level. Bake at 190°C/fan oven 180°C (375°F) Mark 5 for 25-30 minutes until firm to the touch. Turn out and cool on a wire rack.

5 For the filling, roughly chop the prunes and place in a pan with the vanilla extract and 90ml (3fl oz) water. Bring to the boil, reduce the heat and simmer gently for 5 minutes. Blend the cornflour with 15ml (1 tbsp) water, add to the pan and cook, stirring, for 1 minute until thickened. Take off the heat, add the brandy and leave to cool. Once cool, the filling should still be juicy; if necessary moisten with a little water.

6 For the decoration, whip the cream in a bowl until just holding its shape. Fold in the crème fraîche.

7 Divide the prune filling between two of the sponge layers and spread evenly, then cover with a layer of cream. Sandwich these sponge layers together on a serving plate, then top with the final sponge round. Swirl the remaining cream on top and serve dusted with cocoa.

BUTTERSCOTCH AND BRAZIL NUT GÂTEAU

MAKES 12 SLICES ◆ PREPARATION 35 minutes, plus chilling
◆ COOKING TIME 15 minutes ◆ FREEZING Not suitable ◆ 580 CALS PER SLICE
◆ COLOUR INDEX Page 44

125g (4oz) brazil nuts
5 eggs
150g (5oz) caster sugar
150g (5oz) plain white
flour

FILLING
100g (3½oz) unsalted
butter
200g (7oz) dark
muscovado sugar
45ml (3 tbsp) cornflour
300ml (½ pint) milk
600ml (1 pint) double
cream
10ml (2 tsp) vanilla
extract

1 Set aside 12 nuts for decoration; finely chop the remainder. Line 3 baking sheets with non-stick baking parchment and draw a 25cm (10 inch) circle on each. Grease the circles.

2 Whisk the eggs and sugar together in a heatproof bowl over a pan of hot water until thick and pale, and the whisk leaves a trail when lifted. Remove from the heat and whisk until cool.

3 Sift the flour over the mixture. Add the chopped nuts and fold in, using a large metal spoon. Spread the mixture over the marked circles. Bake at 180°C/fan oven 170°C (350°F) Mark 4 for 15 minutes or until just firm. Leave to cool.

4 To make the filling, melt the butter in a pan, add the sugar and stir until dissolved, then boil for 1 minute. Add 50ml (2fl oz) boiling water; stir until smooth.

5 Blend the cornflour with a little of the milk. Put the remaining milk in a saucepan with 150ml (¼ pint) of the cream and bring to the boil. Pour over the cornflour mixture, stirring. Add to the butter mixture and cook, stirring, until thickened and smooth. Transfer to a bowl and leave to cool. Set aside 45ml (3 tbsp) for decoration.

6 Trim the sponges to neat 25cm (10 inch) rounds. Dampen and line the sides of a 25cm (10 inch) loose-based cake tin with greaseproof paper. Place one cake layer in the tin.

7 Whip the remaining cream in a bowl with the vanilla extract until holding its shape. Spread half of the cream over the sponge in the tin. Cover with a third of the butterscotch mixture. Repeat these layers, then top with the final sponge and the remaining butterscotch. Chill in the refrigerator for at least 2 hours to firm up.

8 Carefully unmould the gâteau and transfer to a serving plate. Arrange the reserved nuts around the edge. Using a piping bag fitted with a plain nozzle, drizzle the reserved butterscotch on top of the gâteau. Chill until ready to serve.

EXOTIC FRUIT GÂTEAU

A delicious layered fresh fruit gâteau, mildly spiced with star anise and cinnamon. For easier slicing, make a day in advance.

MAKES 12 SLICES ◆ PREPARATION 40 minutes, plus cooling
◆ COOKING TIME 30-35 minutes ◆ FREEZING Not suitable ◆ 370 CALS PER SLICE

50g (2oz) unsalted butter
6 eggs
175g (6oz) caster sugar
175g (6oz) plain white flour
45ml (3 tbsp) white rum

FILLING
1 medium mango
1 papaya
100g (3½oz) caster sugar

90ml (3fl oz) water
8 star anise
1 cinnamon stick, halved
300ml (½ pint) double cream
200g (7oz) Greek yogurt

TO DECORATE
mango slices
passion fruit wedges

1 Grease and line a 23cm (9 inch) spring-release or loose-based cake tin. Melt the butter and leave to cool slightly.

2 Put the eggs and sugar in a large heatproof bowl set over a pan of hot water. Whisk until pale and creamy, and the mixture leaves a trail when the whisk is lifted from the bowl. Remove from the heat and whisk until cool.

3 Sift half the flour over the bowl and fold, in using a large metal spoon. Pour the butter around the edge of the bowl. Sift the remaining flour over the mixture, then gently fold in, incorporating the butter.

4 Turn the mixture into the prepared tin. Bake at 180°C/fan oven 170°C (350°F) Mark 4 for about 30-35 minutes until just firm, covering with foil for the final 10 minutes if the cake appears to be overbrowning. Leave to cool.

5 For the filling, peel and thinly slice the mango, discarding the stone. Halve and deseed the papaya, then peel and slice.

6 Heat the sugar and water in a small, heavy-based pan until dissolved. Add the spices, mango and papaya and simmer gently for 2 minutes until the fruits have softened. Leave to cool, then drain the fruits, reserving the syrup; discard spices.

7 Split the cake horizontally into 3 layers and drizzle each with a little rum. Whip the cream until slightly thickened, then whisk in the yogurt. Gradually whisk in the reserved syrup.

8 Place one cake layer on a serving plate and spread with a quarter of the cream. Arrange half of the fruits on top. Repeat these layers, then top with the remaining cake layer.

9 Using a palette knife, spread the remaining cream over the top and sides of the gâteau. Chill until needed. Serve decorated with mango slices and passion fruit wedges, spooning some passion fruit pulp on top of the gâteau.

RICH CHOCOLATE LACE GÂTEAU

The lacy chocolate collar on this gâteau looks very impressive, but takes little time to create. It embraces a rich, liqueur-drizzled chocolate sponge concealed under a creamy ganache – a perfect choice for a special occasion. For optimum flavour, make sure you buy good quality chocolate, with a minimum of 70% cocoa solids.

MAKES 12 SLICES ◆ PREPARATION 40 minutes, plus chilling
◆ COOKING TIME 30 minutes ◆ FREEZING Not suitable ◆ 495 CALS PER SLICE

200g (7oz) plain dark chocolate, in pieces
175g (6oz) unsalted butter
5 eggs, separated
150g (5oz) light muscovado sugar
5ml (1 tsp) almond extract
75g (3oz) self-raising white flour, sifted
125g (4oz) ground almonds

60-75ml (4-5 tbsp) Grand Marnier or other orange liqueur

GANACHE
100ml (3½oz) double cream
150g (5oz) plain dark chocolate, in pieces

TO DECORATE
50g (2oz) plain dark chocolate

1 Grease and line a 25-26cm (10-10½ inch) round cake tin. Melt the chocolate and butter together in a heatproof bowl over a pan of simmering water; stir until smooth. Beat the egg yolks, sugar and almond extract together in a large bowl until pale and thick. Whisk in the melted chocolate mixture. Carefully fold in the flour and ground almonds, using a large metal spoon.

2 In a separate bowl, whisk the egg whites until stiff. Fold a quarter into the chocolate mixture to lighten it, then fold in the remainder. Turn into the prepared tin and bake at 180°C/fan oven 170°C (350°F) Mark 4 for about 30 minutes until risen and just firm. Leave to cool in the tin. Transfer the cake to a large, flat serving plate and drizzle with the liqueur.

3 To make the ganache, pour the cream into a small pan and bring almost to the boil. Remove from the heat and add the chocolate. Leave until melted, then stir until smooth. Transfer to a bowl and leave to cool until slightly thickened. Using a palette knife, spread the ganache over the top and sides of the cake to cover evenly.

4 Measure the circumference of the cake, using a piece of string. Cut a strip of greaseproof paper or non-stick baking parchment the length of the string and 6cm (2½ inches) deep. Melt the chocolate and put into a greaseproof paper piping bag. Snip off the merest tip, then scribble the chocolate randomly and quite heavily all over the paper strip.

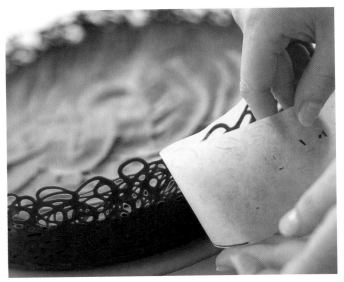

5 Carefully lift the strip and secure around the side of the gâteau, so the lower half of the strip touches the side of the cake while the top half stands proud. Carefully place the gâteau in the refrigerator and chill for about 30 minutes until the chocolate has set.

6 Carefully peel away the paper, leaving the chocolate lace collar in position around the side of the cake. Keep the gâteau in a cool place, or chill until required. Serve with softly whipped cream if desired.

NOTE Don't make the chocolate collar too delicate, otherwise it might break as you remove the paper.

PEAR AND GINGER WINE GÂTEAU

In this fresh-tasting gâteau, pears and mildly spiced sponge are encased in a delicious whipped, mousse-like mascarpone cream. Fresh pear slices, set in ginger wine jelly, make a simple integral decoration.

MAKES 12 SLICES ◆ PREPARATION 40 minutes, plus chilling
◆ COOKING TIME 25-30 minutes ◆ FREEZING Not suitable ◆ 370 CALS PER SLICE

3 pieces preserved stem ginger in syrup, about 50g/2oz

4 eggs

125g (4oz) caster sugar

125g (4oz) plain white flour

TO ASSEMBLE

10ml (2 tsp) powdered gelatine

60ml (4 tbsp) water

30ml (2 tbsp) lemon juice

4 firm pears

250ml (8fl oz) ginger wine, plus 90ml (6 tbsp)

250g (9oz) mascarpone

300ml (½ pint) double cream

50g (2oz) caster sugar

1 Grease and line a 23cm (9 inch) spring-release or loose-based cake tin. Rinse the ginger, pat dry on kitchen paper, then grate.

2 Put the eggs and sugar in a large heatproof bowl set over a pan of hot water. Whisk until thickened and pale, and the mixture leaves a trail when the whisk is lifted from the bowl. Remove from the heat and whisk until cool. Lightly whisk in the grated ginger.

3 Sift the flour over the bowl then carefully fold in, using a large metal spoon. Turn the mixture into the prepared tin and bake at 180°C/fan oven 170°C (350°F) Mark 4 for 25-30 minutes or until just firm to the touch. Leave to cool slightly in the tin, then transfer to a wire rack.

4 Sprinkle the gelatine over the 60ml (4 tbsp) water in a small bowl and leave to soften. Peel, core and thickly slice the pears lengthways, immediately immersing the pear slices in a bowl of cold water with the lemon juice added to prevent discoloration.

5 Drain the pears and put in a saucepan with the 250ml (8fl oz) ginger wine. Bring to a simmer and cook gently until slightly softened; 2-4 minutes, depending on the type of pear. Remove the pears with a slotted spoon. Add the softened gelatine to the syrup and stir until dissolved. Transfer the syrup to a jug; allow to cool.

6 Lightly grease the cleaned cake tin and line with non-stick baking parchment. Arrange a circle of pears decoratively over the base and refrigerate; chill the remaining pears, too. Cut the sponge horizontally into two layers and drizzle with the remaining ginger wine.

7 When the syrup is slightly thickened but not set, set aside 200ml (7fl oz), then carefully pour the remainder evenly over the pears in the tin. Position one sponge layer, cut-side down, on top.

8 Put the reserved syrup in a large bowl with the mascarpone, cream and sugar and whisk until smooth and slightly thickened. Spoon a little into the cake tin, making sure the mixture runs down the sides, between the edges of the cake and the tin. Scatter the remaining pear slices into the tin, making sure that some slices are pressed against the side of the tin.

9 Spoon the remaining cream mixture into the tin. Position the second sponge layer on top, cut-side down. Press the sponge down lightly into the cream until the sponge and cream around the edge are level. Chill for at least 4 hours until set, or overnight.

10 To serve, remove the side of the tin and peel away the paper. Invert the gâteau on to a flat plate and carefully lift away the base and lining paper.

NOTE Use a full-flavoured variety of pear, such as Comice or Williams Bon Crètien.

CHOCOLATE ORANGE TRUFFLE TORTE

MAKES 12 SLICES ◆ PREPARATION 30 minutes, plus chilling
◆ COOKING TIME 25-30 minutes ◆ FREEZING Suitable (stage 5)
◆ 560 CALS PER SERVING ◆ COLOUR INDEX Page 45

BASE
4 eggs
125g (4oz) caster sugar
40g (1½oz) plain flour
30ml (2 tbsp) cocoa powder
20g (¾oz) butter, melted and cooled
60ml (4 tbsp) Grand Marnier or brandy

TRUFFLE MIXTURE
450g (1lb) good quality plain dark chocolate (70% cocoa solids)

600ml (1 pint) double cream
4 egg yolks
50g (2oz) caster sugar
finely grated rind of 3 large oranges

TO DECORATE
cocoa powder, for dusting
12 caramel-dipped physalis fruit (optional)

1 Grease a 25cm (10 inch) loose-based cake tin and line the base with non-stick baking parchment. For the base, whisk the eggs and sugar together in a heatproof bowl over a pan of simmering water, using an electric whisk, until pale and thick, then remove from the heat and whisk until cool.
2 Sift the flour and cocoa together over the mixture, then fold in gently. Carefully fold in the melted butter.
3 Pour the mixture into the prepared tin and bake at 180°C/fan oven 170°C (350°F) Mark 4 for 25-30 minutes. Leave in the tin for 10 minutes, before turning out on to a wire rack. Drizzle with the Grand Marnier or brandy, then allow to cool. Return the cooled cake, upside down, to the clean tin. Press firmly on to the base.
4 For the truffle mixture, break the chocolate into a heatproof bowl and add half of the cream. Melt over a pan of simmering water; stir until smooth and leave to cool. Whip the remaining cream until it forms soft peaks.
5 Using an electric whisk, beat the egg yolks and sugar together in a bowl until pale and fluffy, then beat into the cooled chocolate. Fold into the whipped cream with the orange rind. Immediately pour the mixture over the cake in the tin and chill for at least 3 hours, preferably overnight, until the truffle mixture is set firm.
6 To serve, remove the torte from the tin and dust with cocoa. Decorate with caramel-dipped physalis fruit if wished.

◆ CARAMEL-DIPPED PHYSALIS FRUIT Fold back the dried 'petals' of 12 physalis to expose the orange berries; set aside. Dissolve 125g (4oz) caster sugar in 90ml (3fl oz) water in a small heavy-based pan over a low heat, then bring to the boil and bubble until the syrup is a rich caramel colour. Dip the base of the saucepan in cold water to stop the cooking process, then immediately dip the physalis berries into the caramel to coat. Leave to set on a lightly oiled baking sheet in a dry atmosphere for up to 3 hours.

PASSION FRUIT MERINGUE GÂTEAU

SERVES 10 ◆ PREPARATION 25 minutes ◆ COOKING TIME 1¼ hours
◆ FREEZING Not suitable ◆ 320 CALS PER SERVING

4 egg whites
225g (8oz) caster sugar
10ml (2 tsp) vanilla extract
50g (2oz) desiccated coconut

FILLING
12 passion fruit, halved
60ml (4 tbsp) white rum

250g (9oz) Greek yogurt
300ml (½ pint) double cream
30ml (2 tbsp) icing sugar

TO DECORATE
passion fruit quarters
lychees or mango slices
toasted coconut shavings

1 Line 3 baking sheets with non-stick baking parchment, then draw a 23cm (9 inch) circle on each; invert the paper.
2 Whisk the egg whites in a bowl until stiff. Gradually whisk in the sugar, a tablespoonful at a time, until the meringue is stiff and glossy. Fold in the vanilla and coconut.
3 Spoon on to the marked circles, peaking the meringue around the edges. Bake at 140°C/fan oven 130°C (275°F) Mark 1 for about 1¼ hours until crisp. Leave to cool.
4 Scoop the pulp from 8 passion fruit into a sieve over a bowl; press to extract the juice. Stir in the rum and yogurt. Whip the cream with the icing sugar, then fold in the yogurt.
5 Place one meringue round on a plate, spread with half the cream mixture and scoop the pulp from 2 passion fruit around the edge. Repeat these layers, then top with the final meringue round. Decorate with passion fruit, lychees or mango slices and coconut shavings.

DOUBLE CHOCOLATE RIBBON CAKE

This deliciously rich cake makes an irresistible treat. The chocolate ribbons add a stylish finishing touch.

MAKES 10 SLICES ◆ PREPARATION 30 minutes, plus chilling
◆ COOKING TIME 50 minutes ◆ FREEZING Suitable (stage 4)
◆ 855 CALS PER SERVING

BISCUIT BASE
40g (1½oz) butter
10ml (2 tsp) cocoa powder
125g (4oz) shortbread biscuits
75g (3oz) milk chocolate coated hazelnuts, or hazelnut chocolate

FILLING
125g (4oz) plain chocolate
125g (4oz) white chocolate
400g (14oz) full-fat cream cheese
125g (4oz) caster sugar
3 eggs, beaten
150ml (¼ pint) double cream

CUSTARD
1 vanilla pod, split
150ml (¼ pint) double cream
300ml (½ pint) milk
3 egg yolks
50g (2oz) caster sugar

CHOCOLATE RIBBONS
125g (4oz) plain chocolate, melted

TO FINISH
cocoa powder, to decorate
fresh orange segments, to serve (optional)

1 Line the base of a 23cm (9 inch) spring-release cake tin with non-stick baking parchment. For the biscuit base, melt the butter in a small pan, add the cocoa and cook for 30 seconds. Place the biscuits in a food processor with the chocolate hazelnuts and pulse until finely chopped. Stir in the butter mixture, then spoon into the prepared tin, pressing down well to make a smooth layer. Chill for 30 minutes.

2 For the filling, melt the plain and white chocolate separately in heatproof bowls over pans of simmering water; allow to cool. Beat the cream cheese and caster sugar together in a large bowl until smooth, then gradually beat in the eggs and cream. Divide the mixture equally between two bowls.

3 Stir the plain chocolate into one portion; stir the white chocolate into the other half. Spoon the plain chocolate mixture on to the chilled biscuit base and smooth with a palette knife.

4 Spread the white chocolate mixture in the tin and smooth again. Bake at 180°C/fan oven 170°C (350°F) Mark 4 for 50 minutes or until the filling is golden, just set around the outside and starting to shrink from the edge of the tin. Leave the cake to cool in the switched-off oven, then chill in the tin for at least 2-3 hours.

5 To make the custard, place the vanilla pod in a pan with the cream and milk and bring to the boil. Beat the egg yolks and sugar together in a bowl, then pour on the hot milk and stir well. Return to the clean pan and cook over a gentle heat, stirring continuously, until the custard thickens slightly. Do not allow the mixture to boil, or it will curdle. Pass through a sieve into a bowl and cover the surface closely with dampened greaseproof paper to prevent a skin forming. Allow to cool, then chill.

6 To make the chocolate ribbons, cut 12 strips of non-stick baking parchment, 30cm (12 inches) long and 3cm (1¼ inches) wide. Brush the melted chocolate thinly over the paper strips, then lay these across the handles of several wooden spoons to make waves. Leave to set for about 20 minutes. Remove the cake from the tin. Carefully peel away the paper from the chocolate ribbons, then use to decorate the cake. Dust with cocoa powder. Serve the cake with the vanilla custard, and fresh orange segments if wished.

BLUEBERRY AND VANILLA MALLOW

SERVES 8 ◆ PREPARATION 25 minutes ◆ COOKING TIME 45 minutes
◆ FREEZING Not suitable ◆ 320 CALS PER SERVING ◆ COLOUR INDEX Page 45

25g (1oz) flaked almonds, lightly toasted
1 vanilla pod, split
225g (8oz) caster sugar
4 egg whites
5ml (1 tsp) cornflour
5ml (1 tsp) lemon juice

FILLING
250g (9oz) blueberries
50g (2oz) caster sugar
250g (9oz) mascarpone
150ml (¼ pint) Greek yogurt
15ml (1 tbsp) lemon juice

TO FINISH
caster sugar, for sprinkling

1 Grease and line a 33 x 23cm (13 x 9 inch) Swiss roll tin and scatter with the toasted almonds. Scrape the vanilla seeds into a small bowl, add a little of the sugar and rub with the back of a spoon to distribute the seeds evenly. Stir in remaining sugar.
2 Whisk the egg whites in a large clean bowl until stiff. Gradually add the vanilla sugar, a spoonful at a time, whisking well after each addition until stiff and glossy. Fold in the cornflour and lemon juice.
3 Turn into the prepared tin and level the surface. Bake at 140°C/fan oven 130°C (275°F) Mark 1 for about 45 minutes until crisp. Leave to cool in the switched-off oven.
4 Put the blueberries in a small pan with 30ml (2 tbsp) sugar. Heat gently until the sugar is dissolved and the blueberries are just beginning to break up. Leave to cool.
5 Beat the mascarpone in a bowl to soften and stir in the remaining sugar, yogurt and lemon juice. Remove meringue from the tin and cut crosswise into 3 even rectangles.
6 Place one meringue rectangle on a plate and spoon on half the mascarpone mixture, then a third of the blueberries. Repeat these layers and top with the final meringue. Top with remaining blueberries and dust with sugar to serve.

ICED BERRY MERINGUE

SERVES 10 ◆ PREPARATION 30 minutes, plus freezing ◆ COOKING TIME 2½ hours
◆ FREEZING Suitable ◆ 155 CALS PER SERVING ◆ COLOUR INDEX Page 45

2 egg whites
125g (4oz) caster sugar

ICE CREAM
700g (1½lb) mixed soft fruits, such as strawberries, raspberries and redcurrants
175g (6oz) caster sugar

220ml (7fl oz) low-fat natural yogurt
200g (7oz) quark or other low-fat soft cheese

TO DECORATE
extra berries
icing sugar, for dusting

1 Line 2 baking sheets with non-stick baking parchment, draw a 21cm (8¼ inch) circle on each, then turn paper over.

2 To make the meringue, place the egg whites in a large, clean bowl and whisk until stiff. Gradually add the sugar, a spoonful at a time, whisking well after each addition until stiff and glossy.
3 Divide the meringue between the circles on the baking sheets, spreading evenly to make 2 thin rounds. Bake at 140°C/fan oven 130°C (275°F) Mark 1 for 2½ hours or until crisp and lightly coloured, transposing the baking sheets halfway through to ensure even cooking. Allow to cool.
4 To make the ice cream, put the fruit and sugar in a food processor and work to a purée, then pass through a sieve into a bowl to remove pips. Add the yogurt and quark; beat until smooth. Freeze in an ice-cream maker according to the manufacturer's instructions, or in a shallow container whisking twice during freezing to break down the ice crystals.
5 Line a 23cm (9 inch) spring-release cake tin with non-stick baking parchment. Place one of the cooled meringue rounds in the tin, flat-side down and cover with the ice cream, smoothing the surface. Place the second meringue round on top and press down lightly. Cover and freeze for at least 6 hours, or overnight.
6 About 1-1½ hours before serving, carefully remove the iced meringue gâteau from the cake tin and leave in the refrigerator to soften slightly. Serve decorated with extra berries and dusted with icing sugar.

CHOUX RING WITH PEACHES AND CARAMEL

SERVES 10-12 ◆ PREPARATION 40 minutes ◆ COOKING TIME 25 minutes
◆ FREEZING Not suitable ◆ 495-385 CALS PER SERVING

CHOUX PASTRY
65g (2½oz) plain white flour
50g (2oz) unsalted butter
150ml (¼ pint) water
2 eggs, lightly beaten
15g (½oz) flaked almonds

CARAMEL
175g (6oz) caster sugar
60ml (4 tbsp) water

TO FINISH
4 ripe peaches or nectarines
500g (1lb 2oz) mascarpone
150ml (¼ pint) double cream
60ml (4 tbsp) Cointreau or other orange liqueur

1 Draw a 23cm (9 inch) circle on a sheet of non-stick baking parchment. Draw a 14cm (5½ inch) circle inside the first to make a ring. Turn the paper over and grease the ring. Place on a baking sheet. Sift the flour on to a sheet of greaseproof paper.
2 Put the butter and water in a small pan. Heat gently until the butter has melted, then bring to the boil. Immediately shoot in the flour and beat well until the mixture comes away from the side of the pan. Leave to cool slightly, for 2 minutes.

3 Beat in the eggs, a little at a time, until the mixture is smooth and glossy. Put into a piping bag fitted with a large plain nozzle and pipe into the ring to fill evenly. Sprinkle with the almonds.

4 Bake at 220°C/fan oven 210°C (425°F) Mark 7 for about 20 minutes until well risen and golden. Remove from the oven and split in half horizontally. Place the top half, cut-side up, on another baking sheet and return both halves to the oven for 3 minutes to dry out the centres. Leave to cool.

5 To make the caramel, lightly oil a baking sheet. Heat the sugar and water in a small heavy-based pan until the sugar is dissolved, then boil rapidly until golden. Immediately dip the base of the pan in cold water to prevent further cooking. Using a teaspoon, drizzle a little of the syrup over the top half of the pastry. Pour the remaining caramel on to the oiled baking sheet and leave to set until brittle, about 30 minutes.

6 Halve and stone the peaches and cut into wedges. Place the brittle caramel between sheets of greaseproof paper and beat with a rolling pin to crush finely. Beat the mascarpone and cream together in a bowl, then mix in the crushed caramel and liqueur.

7 Place the pastry base on a flat plate and spread with half of the cream mixture. Pile the peaches on top and cover with the remaining cream. Position the pastry lid. Keep cool until ready to serve.

NOTES

◆ If you haven't got a large piping bag and nozzle, spoon the paste into the circle on the paper to make a more irregular shaped ring.

◆ If the remaining caramel sets before you have time to pour it on to the baking sheet, warm gently to dissolve.

CELEBRATION CAKES

Elegant cakes for birthdays, anniversaries, Christmas and other special occasions, plus a selection of easy novelty cakes for children's parties

CELEBRATION CAKES

Cakes for Christmas, birthdays, weddings and other special occasions are featured here. These generally require a richer, more substantial cake than a simple sponge, as they are usually covered with marzipan and ready-to-roll icing (sugar paste) or royal icing. The advantage of a rich fruit cake is its keeping qualities. A light fruit cake or Madeira cake may be used instead.

RICH FRUIT CAKE

This recipe makes a very moist rich cake suitable for any celebration cake. It can be made in stages, which is convenient if time is short or if you are making more than one cake. Most dried fruit is sold ready cleaned and dried so it does not need to be washed before use. The fruit can be weighed and mixed a day ahead, the tins prepared and lined in advance, and other ingredients weighed ready to mix. On the day of baking simply make the cake and bake.

The quantities have been carefully worked out so that the depth of each cake is the same. This is important when making several tiers for a wedding cake as they must all be the same depth to look aesthetically correct. For sizes and quantities, refer to the Rich Fruit Cake Chart (opposite). Use the same amount of brandy stated for the cake to 'feed' the cake after baking. Spoon half the amount over the surface after baking and the remainder about a week later.

METHOD

1 Grease and line the appropriate cake tin for the size of cake you wish to make, using a double thickness of greaseproof paper. Tie a double band of brown paper round the outside and stand the tin on a baking sheet, double lined with brown paper.
2 Prepare the ingredients for the appropriate size of cake according to the chart (opposite). Place the currants, sultanas, raisins, glacé cherries, mixed peel and flaked almonds in a large mixing bowl. Mix all the ingredients together until well blended, then cover the bowl with cling film. Leave for several hours or overnight in a cool place if required.
3 Sift the flour, mixed spice and cinnamon together into another mixing bowl.
4 Put the butter, sugar and grated lemon rind into a large bowl and cream together until pale and fluffy. Add the beaten eggs gradually, beating well after each addition.
5 Gradually fold the flour lightly into the mixture with a plastic-bladed spatula, then fold in the brandy. Finally fold in the fruit and nuts until evenly distributed throughout the mixture.
6 Spoon the mixture into the prepared tin and spread evenly. Give the tin a few sharp taps to level the mixture and to remove any air pockets. Smooth the surface with the back of a metal spoon, making a slight depression in the centre.
7 Bake in the centre of the oven at 150°C/fan oven 140°C (300°F) Mark 2, using the time suggested in the chart as an approximate guide. When baking large cakes, 25cm (10 inch) and upwards, it is advisable to reduce the oven setting to 130°C/fan oven 120°C (250°F) Mark 1 after two thirds of the baking time. Test the cake to see if it is cooked 15 minutes before the end of the baking time. If cooked, it will feel firm and a fine skewer inserted into the centre should come out cleanly. If the cake is not cooked, return to the oven, re-testing at 15-minute intervals. Remove the cake from the oven and allow it to cool in the tin.
8 Turn the cake out of the tin but do not remove the lining paper as it helps to keep the cake moist. Prick the top all over with a fine skewer and spoon over half the quantity of brandy, listed in the recipe. Wrap in a double thickness of foil.
9 Store the cake, the right way up, in a cool dry place for 1 week. Unwrap and spoon over the remaining brandy. Re-wrap and store the cake upside down, so the brandy moistens the top of the cake and helps to keep it flat. The cake should keep well for up to 2-3 months.

APRICOT GLAZE

MAKES 150ml (¼ pint) ◆ PREPARATION 5 minutes ◆ COOKING TIME 2 minutes ◆ FREEZING Suitable ◆ 55 CALS PER 25ml (1fl oz)

125g (4oz) apricot jam
30ml (2 tbsp) water

1 Place the jam and 30ml (2 tbsp) water in a small pan. Heat gently, stirring, until the jam begins to melt. Bring to the boil and simmer for 1 minute.
2 Strain the jam through a nylon sieve. Use while still warm.

ALMOND PASTE

MAKES 450g (1lb) ◆ PREPARATION 10 minutes ◆ FREEZING Suitable ◆ 135 CALS PER 25g (1oz)

225g (8oz) ground almonds
125g (4oz) caster sugar
125g (4oz) icing sugar
1 egg

5ml (1 tsp) lemon juice
5ml (1 tsp) sherry
1-2 drops of vanilla extract

1 Place the ground almonds, caster sugar and icing sugar in a bowl and mix together. In a separate bowl, whisk the egg with the remaining ingredients and add to the dry mixture.
2 Stir well to mix, pounding gently to release some of the oil from the almonds. Knead with your hands until smooth. Cover until ready to use.

NOTE If you wish to avoid using raw egg. Bind the almond paste with a little water instead.

IVORY CELEBRATION CAKE

Fresh flowers and delicate garlands of pearl beading make a simple, yet stylish decoration for this adaptable cake.

MAKES 36-40 SLICES ◆ PREPARATION 1½ hours, plus standing
◆ COOKING TIME 3½-4 hours ◆ FREEZING Not recommended
◆ 465-420 CALS PER SERVING ◆ COLOUR INDEX Page 46

25cm (10 inch) round rich fruit cake (see left)

TO DECORATE
60ml (4 tbsp) apricot glaze (see left)
900g (2lb) white almond paste
ivory food colouring

900g (2lb) ready-to-roll-icing
1.5 metres pearlised beading
pearl lustre dusting powder
selection of fresh flowers, such as gerberas, roses, etc

1 Place the cake on the cake board, brush with the apricot glaze, then cover with the almond paste (see page 70). Knead a little ivory colouring into the icing, then use to cover the cake (see page 71). From the trimmings, shape about 40 small balls, the same size as the beads. Leave to harden overnight.
2 Cut a strip of greaseproof paper, the circumference and depth of the cake. Fold into 8 equal portions. Make a deep semi-circle from two folded points, reaching almost to the base of the strip, and cut out through all thicknesses. Secure around the cake and transfer the curved outline on to the cake, using pin pricks.
3 Secure the beading around the cake over the pin pricks, brushing very lightly with water to secure. Cut a single bead and make 4-5 impressions below each garland in the icing. Moisten a little dusting powder with water. Roll the balls of icing in the powder, then press into the impressions.
4 Just before the gathering, arrange the flowers on the cake.

RICH FRUIT CAKE CHART

CAKE TIN	12cm (5in) square / 15cm (6in) round	15cm (6in) square / 18cm (7in) round	18cm (7in) square / 20cm (8in) round	20cm (8in) square / 23cm (9in) round	23cm (9in) square / 25cm (10in) round	25cm (10in) square / 28cm (11in) round
Currants	225g (8oz)	350g (12oz)	450g (1lb)	625g (1lb 6oz)	775g (1lb 12oz)	1.1kg (2lb 8oz)
Sultanas	100g (4oz)	125g (4½oz)	200g (7oz)	225g (8oz)	375g (13oz)	400g (14oz)
Raisins	100g (4oz)	125g (4½oz)	200g (7oz)	225g (8oz)	375g (13oz)	400g (14oz)
Glacé cherries	50g (2oz)	75g (3oz)	150g (5oz)	175g (6oz)	250g (9oz)	275g (10oz)
Mixed peel	25g (1oz)	50g (2oz)	75g (3oz)	100g (4oz)	150g (5oz)	200g (7oz)
Flaked almonds	5g (1oz)	50g (2oz)	75g (3oz)	100g (4oz)	150g (5oz)	200g (7oz)
Plain flour	175g (6oz)	215g (7½oz)	350g (12oz)	400g (14oz)	600g (1lb 5oz)	700g (1lb 8oz)
Mixed spice	1.25ml (¼ tsp)	2.5ml (½ tsp)	2.5ml (½ tsp)	5ml (1 tsp)	5ml (1 tsp)	10ml (2 tsp)
Cinnamon	1.25ml (¼ tsp)	2.5ml (½ tsp)	2.5ml (½ tsp)	5ml (1 tsp)	5ml (1 tsp)	10ml (2 tsp)
Butter	150g (5oz)	175g (6oz)	275g (10oz)	350g (12oz)	500g (1lb 2oz)	600g (1lb 5oz)
Soft brown sugar	150g (5oz)	175g (6oz)	275g (10oz)	350g (12oz)	500g (1lb 2oz)	600g (1lb 5oz)
Grated lemon rind	a little	a little	a little	¼ lemon	¼ lemon	½ lemon
Eggs, beaten	2½	3	5	6	9	11
Brandy	15ml (1 tbsp)	15ml (1 tbsp)	15-30ml (1-2 tbsp)	30ml (2 tbsp)	30-45ml (2-3 tbsp)	45ml (3 tbsp)
Baking time	2½-3 hours	3½ hours	3½ hours	4 hours	4½ hours	6 hours
Cooked weight	1.1kg (2½lb)	1.5kg (3¼lb)	2.1kg (4¾lb)	2.7kg (6lb)	3.8kg (8½lb)	4.8kg (10¾lb)

QUANTITIES FOR ALMOND PASTE, READY-TO-ROLL AND ROYAL ICING

CAKE TIN	12cm (5in) square / 15cm (6in) round	15cm (6in) square / 18cm (7in) round	18cm (7in) square / 20cm (8in) round	20cm (8in) square / 23cm (9in) round	23cm (9in) square / 25cm (10in) round	25cm (10in) square / 28cm (11in) round
Almond Paste	350g (12oz)	450g (1lb)	550g (1¼lb)	800g (1¾lb)	900g (2lb)	1kg (2¼lb)
Ready-to-roll Icing	350g (12oz)	450g (1lb)	700g (1½lb)	800g (1¾lb)	900g (2lb)	1kg (2¼lb)
Royal Icing	450g (1lb)	550g (1¼lb)	700g (1½lb)	900g (2lb)	1kg (2¼lb)	1.1kg (2½lb)

TIERED CELEBRATION CAKE

This versatile cake is an ideal choice for an anniversary, christening, special birthday or an informal wedding. A two-tier cake makes a stunning centrepiece for a large gathering, but the design works equally well using one or three tiers. Follow the rich fruit cake recipe and cake chart (on pages 280-281) and adjust the decoration accordingly. The royal icing is easy to apply as it needn't be completely smooth.

MAKES 80-100 SLICES ◆ PREPARATION 2-3 hours, plus standing
◆ COOKING TIME Large cake 4 hours; small cake 2½-3 hours
◆ FREEZING Not recommended ◆ 355-285 CALS PER SLICE

2 round rich fruit cakes:
23cm (9 inches) and 15cm
(6 inches) (see pages 280-1)
30cm (12 inch) round cake
board
100g (3½oz) apricot glaze
(see page 280)
1.5kg (3¼lb) homemade
(see page 280) or white
almond paste
icing sugar, for dusting

ROYAL ICING
4 egg whites
900g (2lb) icing sugar

TO DECORATE
30-40 small edible flowers,
such as primulas,
primroses, violets, apple
blossom or herb flowers
a little lightly beaten egg
white, for brushing
caster sugar, for dusting
450g (1lb) small fresh
strawberries
0.75 metre fine white
muslin
2 metres fine white ribbon
or paper cord

1 Place the large cake on the cake board and brush generously with apricot glaze. Lightly knead two thirds of the almond paste on a surface dusted with icing sugar and roll out to a 35cm (14 inch) round. Lift the almond paste over the cake and ease it to fit around the side; trim off any excess around the base. Position the small cake centrally on top and brush with more apricot glaze. Roll out the remaining almond paste to a 28cm (11 inch) round and use to cover the small cake in the same way.

2 To make the royal icing, whisk the egg whites in a bowl, gradually whisking in the icing sugar until peaking. Keep the surface of the icing closely covered with cling film until ready to use, to prevent it drying out. Set aside a little of the icing for securing the decorations. Using a palette knife, spread some royal icing over the small cake, covering in an even layer and spreading until fairly smooth. Cover the large cake in the same way, then cover the cake board with a thin layer of icing. Leave to dry.

3 To make the sugared flowers, brush both sides of the petals with a little beaten egg white, then sprinkle generously with caster sugar. Shake off excess sugar and place the flowers on a sheet of greaseproof paper. Leave for several hours or overnight to dry. Sugar the strawberries in the same way and leave to dry for 1-2 hours.

4 Cut the muslin into two long strips, one measuring 75x20cm (30x8 inches), the other 63x20cm (25x8 inches). Using short lengths of ribbon or cord, tie each strip tightly at regular intervals to form 5 or 6 even-sized swags.

5 Place the longer muslin strip around the top edge of the large cake, securing at the ties with a dot of icing. (If the muslin falls away from the cake, prop up with cocktail sticks until the icing has dried.) Secure the shorter strip around the top of the small cake.

6 Scatter caster sugar over the muslin and around the base of the cake board. Using more icing, secure the flowers and strawberries on top of the cake and around the edges. Store in a cool place until ready to serve.

NOTE Sugared flowers can be made up to 2 weeks in advance and stored in an airtight container. Don't arrange the strawberries until the day, just in case the juices run.

1 Place all the dried fruit in a bowl with the candied peel, glacé cherries and brandy. Stir well, cover and leave to macerate in a cool place for 1-2 days, stirring occasionally.

2 Grease a deep 20cm (8 inch) round cake tin and line with a double thickness of greaseproof paper. Sift the flour with the salt, cinnamon and a little nutmeg.

3 Beat the softened butter in a bowl until creamy, using a food mixer if available, or electric hand whisk. Add the sugar gradually, beating well between each addition until light and fluffy. Beat in the egg yolks one at a time, then fold in half of the flour mixture. Fold in the fruit with its soaking liquid, then incorporate the remaining flour.

4 In another bowl, whisk the egg whites until foamy. Add to the mixture with the cocoa and bicarbonate of soda; mix well.

5 Turn the mixture into the prepared tin, smooth the surface and bake at 150°C/fan oven 140°C (300°F) Mark 2 for about 2 hours until a skewer inserted into the centre comes out clean. Leave in the tin for 30 minutes, then transfer to a wire rack to cool completely.

6 Wrap the cake in greaseproof paper and foil, and store in a cool place for up to 6 weeks (or a minimum of 1 week). Every week for the first 4 weeks, prick the base of the cake and spoon over 15ml (1 tbsp) brandy. For the last 2 weeks leave to dry.

7 Place the cake on the cake board. Warm the honey and brush a thin layer over the cake. Roll out the almond paste on a surface dusted with cornflour to a 30cm (12 inch) round. Position over the cake and press lightly on to the top and sides; trim away the excess at the base. Leave in a cool place to dry for 1-2 days.

8 Thinly roll out 225g (8 oz) of the icing on a surface dusted with cornflour to a 30cm (12 inch) round. Position over the cake and press lightly on to the top and sides; trim away the excess at the base.

9 Cut a greaseproof paper triangle template, with 2 equal long sides measuring 20cm (8 inches), and a base measurement of 4cm (1½ inches). Roll out the remaining icing thinly and use the template to cut about 22 triangles; re-roll trimmings to cut more triangles as necessary.

10 Position the triangles on the cake with the narrow points to the centre, overlapping them and tucking in excess icing as you go. Secure silver braid around the base of the cake. Roll the icing trimmings into balls, covering some of them with silver leaf if using. Arrange on top of the cake, pressing gently, to secure. Position a few balls on the board to finish.

VARIATION At stage 8, roll out half of the icing and use to cover the cake as above. Buff the icing with the palm of your hand to give a smooth finish. Colour three quarters of the remaining icing green, then roll out and stamp out Christmas trees with a suitable cutter. Shape the remaining icing into snowballs. Stick the trees and snowballs on to the side of the cake, using a paste made from icing sugar and water.

THE ULTIMATE CHRISTMAS CAKE

A moist cake full of Christmas flavours. If you're short of time, leave the mixture in a cool place until the following day to bake; this will also ensure the cake has a flat top. Brush the surface very lightly with cold water before baking to prevent a hard crust forming.

MAKES 16-20 SLICES ◆ PREPARATION 1½ hours, plus maturing
◆ COOKING TIME 2 hours ◆ FREEZING Suitable (stage 5)
◆ 660-530 CALS PER SLICE

300g (10oz) raisins, preferably large ones
200g (7oz) sultanas
225g (8oz) currants
75g (3oz) candied peel
75g (3oz) glacé cherries
200ml (7fl oz) brandy
300g (11oz) plain white flour
pinch of salt
5ml (1 tsp) ground cinnamon
freshly grated nutmeg
150g (5oz) unsalted butter, softened
150g (5oz) soft dark brown (muscovado) sugar
4 eggs, separated

5ml (1 tsp) cocoa powder
pinch of bicarbonate of soda

TO FINISH
60ml (2fl oz) brandy
28cm (11 inch) round cake board
90ml (6 tbsp) thin honey or apricot jam
450g (1lb) white almond paste
cornflour, for dusting
about 900g (2lb) ready-to-roll icing
1 metre silver braid
silver leaf, to decorate (optional)

CANDLELIT CHRISTMAS CAKE

This unusual Christmas cake makes an impressive festive centrepiece and is lighter than a traditional rich fruit cake. Once cooled, the cake can be wrapped in greaseproof paper and foil and stored in a cool place to mature for up to 4 weeks – 'feed' with a little brandy if desired (as for the opposite recipe).

MAKES 24-30 SLICES ◆ PREPARATION 1 hour, plus standing
◆ COOKING TIME About 2½ hours ◆ FREEZING Suitable (stage 4)
◆ 715-575 CALS PER SLICE

225g (8oz) ready-to-eat dried apricots

225g (8oz) ready-to-eat dried pears

225g (8oz) sultanas

40g (1½oz) chopped glacé ginger

60ml (4 tbsp) brandy

400g (14oz) unsalted butter, softened

400g (14oz) caster sugar

4 eggs

350g (12oz) plain white flour

5ml (1 tsp) baking powder

15ml (1 tbsp) vanilla extract

110g (4oz) ground almonds

50g (2oz) blanched almonds, chopped

50g (2oz) hazelnuts, chopped

TO FINISH

30cm (12 inch) silver round cake board

60ml (4 tbsp) apricot glaze (see page 280)

1kg (2¼lb) ready-made white almond paste

icing sugar, for dusting

1kg (2¼lb) ready-to-roll icing

cornflour, for dusting

6 large sprigs of fresh bay leaves

1 egg white, lightly beaten

caster sugar, for sprinkling

6 nightlights

2 metres fine silver cord

1 metre thick silver cord

1 Roughly chop the dried apricots and pears in a food processor. Place in a bowl with the sultanas, glacé ginger and brandy, stir to mix well and leave to stand for about 30 minutes.

2 Grease and line a deep 23cm (9 inch) round cake tin. Tie a double thickness of brown paper band around the outside of the tin.

3 Cream the butter and sugar together in a large bowl. Gradually beat in the eggs, adding a little of the flour to prevent curdling. Sift the remaining flour and baking powder together over the mixture, then fold in. Add the soaked fruits, vanilla extract, ground almonds and chopped nuts; stir until evenly combined.

4 Turn the mixture into the prepared tin and bake at 150°C/fan oven 140°C (300°F) Mark 2 for about 2½ hours until a skewer inserted into the centre comes out clean. Leave to cool in the tin, then turn out on to a wire rack and leave until cold.

5 Place the cake on the cake board and brush with apricot glaze. Cover with the almond paste (see page 70). Leave in a cool dry place for 1-2 days before applying the icing.

6 Roll out the icing on a surface lightly dusted with cornflour and use to cover the cake (see page 71).

7 Wash the bay leaves and dry on kitchen paper. Brush with the egg white, then sprinkle generously with sugar. Leave on a wire rack to dry for several hours.

8 Arrange the nightlights in a circle on top of the cake, 1cm (½ inch) from the edge. Press the bay leaves into the icing around the candles, then trail the fine silver cord around the leaves. Secure the thick silver cord around the base of the cake. When ready to serve, light the nightlights.

NOTE Decorative silver cord is obtainable from haberdashery departments.

VARIATION Omit the nightlights. Arrange the frosted bay leaves in a garland on top of the cake and position a single candle in a suitable holder in the middle.

WHITE AND DARK CHOCOLATE GÂTEAU

This sensational gâteau is guaranteed to impress your guests, yet it is surprisingly straightforward to make.

MAKES 12-14 SLICES ◆ PREPARATION 45 minutes, plus chilling
◆ COOKING TIME 1¼-1½ hours ◆ FREEZING Suitable (stage 4)
◆ 600-515 CALS PER SERVING ◆ COLOUR INDEX Page 46

225g (8oz) good quality plain chocolate (70% cocoa solids), in pieces
125g (4oz) unsalted butter, cut into cubes
8 eggs, separated
225g (8oz) caster sugar

TO DECORATE
300g (10oz) white chocolate
450ml (¾ pint) double cream
15ml (1 tbsp) icing sugar, sifted, plus extra for dusting (optional)
350g (12oz) raspberries seasonal blossom or edible flowers

1 Grease a deep 20cm (8 inch) round cake tin and line the base with non-stick baking parchment. Melt the chocolate and butter together in a large heatproof bowl set over a pan of simmering water. Remove from the heat, stir until smooth and allow to cool slightly.

2 Using an electric whisk, whisk the egg yolks and sugar together in a bowl until pale and light in colour, then slowly whisk the mixture into the cooled, melted chocolate.

3 Whisk the egg whites in a clean bowl until they form soft peaks, then fold into the mixture until evenly combined.

4 Pour the mixture into the prepared tin. Bake at 190°C/fan oven 180°C (375°F) Mark 5 for 1¼-1½ hours, until well risen and just firm to the touch, covering with foil after 30 minutes if the cake appears to be overbrowning. Leave to cool in the switched-off oven for 30 minutes then take out, cover with a damp cloth and allow to cool completely before turning out on to a wire rack.

5 For the decoration, melt the white chocolate in a heatproof bowl over a pan of simmering water. Remove from the heat and wipe away any condensation from around the bowl. Stir the chocolate gently until smooth. Cut out a 38cm (15 inch) circle of greaseproof paper; place on a tray. Using a palette knife, spread the melted chocolate over the paper in a thin layer almost to the edges. Leave until the chocolate is just sufficiently set that it doesn't run as you pick up the paper.

6 Meanwhile, whip the cream in a bowl until it forms soft peaks, then fold in the icing sugar. Transfer the cooled cake to a serving plate and spoon the cream on top, spreading a little down the sides. Top with the raspberries.

7 Carefully lift the greaseproof paper by the edge and invert it on top of the cake, allowing the chocolate to drape softly around the sides to the base. Chill for 30 minutes, with the greaseproof paper on, or until the chocolate is set.

8 Starting at the base, gently peel off the paper in strips. Dust the cake with icing sugar and decorate with flowers to serve.

NOTE Do not allow the melted white chocolate to cool until firm, otherwise it will be too solid to drape over the cake to form soft folds.

CHOCOLATE CROWN

MAKES 12 SLICES ◆ PREPARATION About 1 hour ◆ COOKING TIME 50 minutes
◆ FREEZING Suitable (stage 2) ◆ 665 CALS PER SLICE

175g (6oz) self-raising white flour
5ml (1 tsp) baking powder
50g (2oz) cocoa powder
175g (6oz) soft margarine
175g (6oz) caster sugar
3 eggs

TO DECORATE
300ml (½ pint) double cream
300g (10oz) good quality plain chocolate, in pieces
8 Maltesers (optional)
450g (1lb) luxury bought chocolates in paper cases
8 gold wrapped sugared almonds
0.75 metre gold cord

1 Grease and line a deep 18cm (7 inch) round cake tin. Sift the flour, baking powder and cocoa powder together into a bowl. Add the margarine, sugar and eggs and beat well for about 2 minutes until smooth and creamy.

2 Turn the mixture into the prepared tin and level the surface. Bake at 170°C/fan oven 160°C (325°F) Mark 3 for about 50 minutes until firm. Leave in the tin for 5 minutes, then transfer to a wire rack to cool.

3 To make the chocolate ganache, pour the cream into a heavy-based pan and slowly bring almost to the boil. Remove from the heat and add 200g (7oz) of the chocolate. Leave until melted, then stir until smooth and transfer to a bowl. Leave until the mixture is cool and just holding its shape.

4 Cut the cake horizontally into 2 layers and sandwich together with some of the chocolate cream. Using a sharp knife, trim off the top edge to give a domed centre. Place the cake on a flat plate and spread the top and sides with the reserved chocolate cream, spreading as smoothly as possible.

5 To make the crown, melt the remaining chocolate in a heatproof bowl over a pan of simmering water; set aside. Measure the exact circumference of the cake with a piece of string. Cut 2 strips of greaseproof paper, the length of the string and 10cm (4 inches) wide. Fold one paper strip in half, then in half twice more to make a rectangle of eight thicknesses. Using a pencil, draw a curve between the two folded points, then cut along the curve through all thicknesses. Open out the paper to reveal the fluted edge and lay on top of the second paper strip. Draw the fluted outline on to the second paper strip; discard the cut strip.

6 Put the melted chocolate in a paper piping bag and snip off the tip. Pipe along the fluted edge and down the sides and base of the paper. Scribble diagonal lines all over the strip, within the chocolate border. Scribble more lines across in the

opposite direction to create a dense lattice design. (Reserve a little chocolate in piping bag). Leave until the chocolate is just sufficiently set that it doesn't run as you pick up the paper.

7 Carefully lift the paper strip, by the uncoated areas, and position around the cake so the chocolate rests against the side of the cake and the ends of the strip just meet. Chill or leave in a cool place until the chocolate has set.

8 Carefully peel away the greaseproof paper, leaving the chocolate collar in position. Pipe a dot of melted chocolate on each of the points of the crown and gently secure a Malteser if using. (If the chocolate has set in the piping bag, soften in the microwave). Pile the chocolates and sugared almonds on top of the cake. Secure the gold cord around the base. Store the cake in a cool place until ready to serve.

SPICED ALMOND CAKE

This has a layer of sticky almond paste running through the middle and a delicious fresh spicy flavour that improves with keeping. Home-made almond paste tastes wonderful and can be made in minutes, but if you're pressed for time, use 125g (4oz) ready-made almond paste.

MAKES 10 SLICES ◆ PREPARATION 45 minutes ◆ COOKING TIME 1¾ hours
◆ FREEZING Suitable (stage 5) ◆ 450 CALS PER SLICE ◆ COLOUR INDEX Page 47

ALMOND PASTE
50g (2oz) ground almonds
40g (1½oz) icing sugar
25g (1oz) caster sugar
grated rind of 1 lemon
15ml (1 tbsp) beaten egg (see cake)

CAKE
300g (11oz) plain white flour
10ml (2 tsp) baking powder
pinch of salt
2.5ml (½ tsp) ground coriander
2.5ml (½ tsp) ground cloves
5ml (1 tsp) ground ginger
5ml (1 tsp) ground cinnamon

175g (6oz) unsalted butter, softened
grated rind of 1 lemon
225g (8oz) light muscovado sugar
4 medium eggs, beaten (less 15ml (1 tbsp)

TO DECORATE
90-120ml (6-8 tbsp) apricot glaze or jam
15ml (1 tbsp) kirsch or Grand Marnier
8-10 kumquats
few ready-to-eat dried apricots or mango slices
4-5 physalis fruit
1 metre wide gold ribbon

1 Line a deep 23cm (9 inch) round cake tin with greaseproof paper. For the almond paste filling, in a small bowl, mix the ingredients together to a smooth paste, then cover and chill.
2 To make the cake, sift the flour, baking powder, salt and spices together. Beat the butter and lemon rind together in a bowl until creamy. Beat in the sugar, a spoonful at a time.
3 Beat in the eggs, a little at a time, until the mixture is light and fluffy, adding 15ml (1 tbsp) flour with the last addition. Using a large metal spoon, fold in the flour and spices.
4 Spoon half of the cake mixture into the prepared tin; smooth the surface. Roll out the almond paste on a sheet of greaseproof paper sprinkled with icing sugar to a 20cm (8 inch) round. Use the paper to help lift the almond paste on top of the mixture in the tin. Spoon the remaining cake mixture on top of the almond paste layer and smooth.
5 Bake at 150°C/fan oven 140°C (300°F) Mark 2 for about 1¾ hours, covering with greaseproof paper if the cake appears to be overbrowning. Leave in the tin for 30 minutes, then turn out on to a wire rack to cool completely.
6 To decorate the cake, warm the apricot glaze, add the kirsch, kumquats and apricots or mango slices and spoon on top of the cake. Leave for about 30 minutes until set. Open the physalis fruit and arrange around the edge of the cake. Tie the ribbon around the side to finish.

NOTE To add a special finishing touch, dip the physalis fruit in edible gold dust before positioning on the cake.

CARAMEL GARLAND CAKE

This elegant celebration cake is covered with a delicious crème au beurre. Delicately flavoured with orange liqueur, the cake itself has a moist, light texture as it is made with breadcrumbs and ground nuts instead of flour.

MAKES 12 SLICES ◆ PREPARATION 1 hour, plus cooling
◆ COOKING TIME 20-25 minutes ◆ FREEZING Suitable (cake only)
◆ 530 CALS PER SLICE

6 eggs, separated
5ml (1 tsp) almond extract
225g (8oz) caster sugar
225g (8oz) ground hazelnuts or almonds
50g (2oz) fresh white fine breadcrumbs
5ml (1 tsp) baking powder
45ml (3 tbsp) lemon juice
45ml (3 tbsp) Grand Marnier or other orange liqueur

CARAMEL
125g (4oz) granulated sugar
90ml (6 tbsp) water

CRÈME AU BEURRE
125g (4oz) granulated sugar
90ml (6 tbsp) water
3 egg yolks
250g (9oz) unsalted butter, softened

TO DECORATE
12 physalis fruit, opened
6-8 apricots, halved or quartered (optional)
150g (5oz) red grapes, in small bunches

1 Grease and line three 18cm (7 inch) round sandwich tins, preferably straight sided. Whisk the egg yolks in a large bowl with the almond extract and 200g (7oz) of the sugar until pale and thickened. Stir in the ground nuts, breadcrumbs, baking powder and lemon juice.
2 Whisk the egg whites in a clean bowl until stiff. Gradually whisk in the remaining sugar. Using a large metal spoon, fold a quarter of the egg whites into the cake mixture to lighten it, then carefully fold in the remainder.
3 Divide the mixture between the prepared tins and level the surface. Bake at 190°C/fan oven 180°C (350°F) Mark 5 for 20-25 minutes until risen and just firm. Transfer to a wire rack to cool.
4 Lightly oil 2 large baking sheets. To make the caramel, put the sugar and water in a small heavy-based pan and heat gently until the sugar is dissolved, then increase the heat. Bring to the boil and boil rapidly to a golden caramel. Dip the base of the pan in cold water to prevent further cooking, then immediately pour a little of the caramel on to one of the baking sheets, until it has spread to about 10cm (4 inches) in diameter.
5 Using a teaspoon, drizzle more syrup on to the baking sheet, to form 8 round lacy shapes about 7.5cm (3 inches) in diameter. Leave for about 30 minutes until brittle.
6 To make the crème au beurre, gently heat the sugar and water in a small heavy-based pan until the sugar is dissolved. Bring to the boil and boil steadily until the syrup registers 107°C (225°F) on a sugar thermometer.

7 Meanwhile, lightly beat the egg yolks in a bowl to break them up. Slowly pour the hot syrup on to the yolks, whisking well. Cream the butter in a separate bowl, then gradually beat in the syrup mixture until smooth.

8 Drizzle the cakes with the liqueur. Put the large piece of brittle caramel between sheets of greaseproof paper and crush quite finely, using a rolling pin. Mix the crushed caramel with a quarter of the crème au beurre. Use this to sandwich the cakes together on a large flat serving platter, at least 28cm (11 inches) in diameter. Using a palette knife, spread the remaining crème au beurre over the top and sides.

9 Arrange the fruits casually on the platter around the cake. Carefully lift the caramel shapes from the baking sheet, using a palette knife, and prop them between the fruits.

NOTES
◆ If the caramel hardens before you have shaped all of the decorations, reheat gently to melt.

◆ The caramel shapes can be made up to 2 days in advance and stored in an airtight container between sheets of oiled cling film. Assemble the other decorations a day in advance, tucking the caramel shapes in place shortly before serving.

SNOW COTTAGE

This delightful variation of a gingerbread house uses a spice-free biscuit mixture – making it ideal for a child's birthday party. For extra appeal, pile a selection of sweets or chocolate buttons into the centre of the cottage before fitting the roof.

To shape the cottage sections, you will need to cut out the following paper templates: two 17x9cm (6¾x3½ inch) rectangles for the roof; two 14x9cm (5½x3½ inch) rectangles for the long side walls; two 9cm (3½ inch) squares with a pointed gable on one side, extending 6cm (2½ inches) from the top edge of the square to the point, for the end walls.

SERVES 10 ◆ PREPARATION About 1½ hours, plus chilling
◆ COOKING TIME 12 minutes ◆ FREEZING Not suitable ◆ 375 CALS PER SERVING

75g (3oz) unsalted butter, softened

75g (3oz) dark muscovado sugar

1 medium egg, beaten

50g (2oz) golden syrup

300g (10oz) self-raising white flour

TO ASSEMBLE

28cm (11 inch) round cake board

250g (9oz) ready-to-roll icing

icing sugar, for dusting

1 egg white

225g (8oz) icing sugar

1 cereal biscuit bar

thin white chocolate squares, or 'After eight' mints

small sprigs of bay leaves and rosemary

1 Put the butter and sugar in a food processor and blend to a paste. Add the egg, golden syrup and flour and process until the mixture comes together into a ball. Wrap in cling film and chill for 30 minutes. Roll out the biscuit dough thinly on a lightly floured surface. Lay the paper templates (see above) on top of the dough and cut around them to shape the sections for the cottage. Transfer the cut-out shapes to 2 greased baking sheets.

2 Cut out an arched window from each of the side sections, and an arched door from one end section. Halve the cut out window shapes to make shutters and lay next to the larger pieces on the baking sheets. Bake at 180°C/fan oven 170°C (350°F) Mark 4 for about 12 minutes until beginning to colour around the edges. Leave on the baking sheets for 2 minutes, then transfer to a wire rack to cool.

3 Reserve 25g (1oz) ready-to-roll icing. Thinly roll out the rest on a surface dusted with icing sugar to a 30cm (12 inch) round and use to cover the lightly dampened cake board; trim off excess. Beat the egg white and icing sugar together in a bowl until smooth. Spread a little along the base of one end section, then press gently into the icing on the board; prop it against a jar for support. Spread a little icing along the base and sides of one side section and position at right angles to the end section. Secure the other two sides in the same way.

4 From the cereal bar, cut two strips for windowsills and two door steps; secure with icing. Secure the door and shutters at the sides of the windows. Spread more icing over the top edges of the cottage, then secure the roof sections; if necessary, prop up the overhanging edges on small containers until the icing has set slightly.

5 Using a palette knife, spread more icing over the roof. Let the icing overhang the edges of the roof, pulling it gently with a palette knife to resemble icicles. Put the remaining icing in a piping bag fitted with a writing nozzle and pipe further decorations on the door, shutters and cottage corners.

6 Shape reserved ready-to-roll icing into a chimney; secure to the roof. Cut little triangles from white chocolate squares and position on top of the roof as tiles. Cut paving stones from the white chocolate and position as a path leading to the steps. Arrange the herbs around the cottage, then dust with icing sugar to resemble snow.

VARIATION For a gingerbread house, add 10ml (2 tsp) ground ginger to the biscuit mixture.

BIRTHDAY BEAR CAKE

MAKES 24 SLICES ◆ PREPARATION 1½ hours ◆ COOKING TIME 1¼ - 1½ hours
◆ FREEZING Suitable (stage 2) ◆ 195 CALS PER SLICE ◆ COLOUR INDEX Page 47

275g (10oz) unsalted butter or margarine, softened

275g (10oz) caster sugar

4 eggs

175g (6oz) plain white flour

175g (6oz) self-raising white flour

FILLING

175g (6oz) strawberry jam

1 quantity Buttercream (see page 294)

TO ASSEMBLE

28cm (11 inch) round cake board

1.2kg (2¾lb) ready-to-roll icing

green, purple, orange, red and brown food colourings

icing sugar and cornflour, for dusting

coiled parcel ribbons or streamers

1 metre orange ribbon, 1cm (½ inch) wide

1 Grease and line a deep 23cm (9 inch) round cake tin. Cream the butter or margarine and sugar together in a bowl. Gradually beat in the eggs, adding a little of the flour to prevent curdling. Sift the remaining flour into the bowl and fold in until evenly combined.

2 Turn into the prepared tin, level the surface and bake at 170°C (325°F) Mark 3 for 1¼-1½ hours until just firm. Leave in tin for 10 minutes, then turn out; cool on a wire rack.

3 Cut the cake horizontally into 3 layers. Sandwich together with the jam, and all but 45ml (3 tbsp) buttercream. Place on the cake board. Spread thinly with reserved buttercream.

4 Colour 150g (5oz) of the ready-to-roll icing green, 150g (5oz) purple, 150g (5oz) orange, 100g (3½oz) red and 50g (2oz) brown, leaving the remainder white.

5 Roll out the white icing on a surface lightly dusted with icing sugar and use to cover the cake (see page 71). Smooth the icing around the sides of the cake, with cornflour-dusted hands. Trim off the excess icing around the base.

6 Shape 3 parcels, one from each of the green, purple and orange icings; position these towards the back of the cake, securing the bases with a lightly dampened paintbrush. Cut long thin strips of red icing and secure around the parcels to resemble ribbon.

7 Roll 15g (½oz) pieces of the coloured icings into balls, then elongate slightly into balloon shapes. Arrange in clusters around the parcels.

8 Shape a small teddy from the brown icing. Mould the body, head, ears, arms and legs separately, then assemble using a lightly dampened paintbrush to stick the pieces together. Prop teddy against one of the parcels. Shape a small snout in brown icing; press on to the face. Shape a party hat in coloured icing and press gently on top of teddy's head. Shape a coloured bow tie and press gently into position. Using a fine paintbrush and brown food colouring, paint features on teddy's face.

9 Lightly dampen the edge of the cake board. Thinly roll out a long strip of orange icing and use to cover the edge of the board; trim off excess icing at the edge.

10 Shape more balloons and arrange around the base of the cake. Press a small ball of icing on to the end of each balloon for the knot. Cut lengths of parcel ribbon and taper the ends to a point; press into each balloon. Secure the orange ribbon around the edge of the board.

NOTE Don't be restricted by the colourings listed. You can use any combination of bright colours to decorate this cake.

TRAIN CAKE

The simplicity of this design is wonderfully effective, making it a perfect choice for any small child. Once decorated, it will store well in a cool place for up to 5 days.

MAKES 16-20 SLICES ◆ PREPARATION 1½ hours ◆ COOKING TIME About 2 hours
◆ FREEZING Suitable (stage 2) ◆ 465-370 CALS PER SLICE

325g (11oz) self-raising white flour

5ml (1 tsp) baking powder

225g (8oz) unsalted butter or margarine, softened

225g (8oz) caster sugar

4 medium eggs

10ml (2 tsp) vanilla extract

FILLING

90ml (6 tbsp) raspberry or strawberry jam

1 quantity Buttercream (see page 294)

TO ASSEMBLE

20cm (8 inch) round cake board

750g (1lb 10oz) ready-to-roll icing

blue, green and red food colourings

icing sugar, for dusting

0.75 metre green ribbon

selection of liquorice sweets

birthday candles

1 Grease and line a deep 15cm (6 inch) round cake tin. Sift the flour and baking powder into a bowl. Add the butter or margarine, sugar, eggs and vanilla extract and beat with an electric whisk for about 2 minutes until creamy.

2 Turn half the mixture into the prepared tin and level the surface. Bake at 170°C (325°F) Mark 3 for about 1 hour until firm, then transfer to a wire rack to cool. Clean and re-line the tin, then bake the remaining mixture in the same way; turn out and cool.

3 Cut each cake horizontally into 2 layers. Sandwich all 4 layers together with the jam and all but 45ml (3 tbsp) of the buttercream. Place the cake on the board and spread thinly with the reserved buttercream.

4 Colour 450g (1lb) of the ready-to-roll icing pale blue. Colour 125g (4oz) green, and 125g (4oz) red, leaving the remainder white. Roll out a quarter of the pale blue icing on a surface dusted with icing sugar and cut out a 15cm (6 inch) circle. Fit on top of the cake.

5 Measure the circumference of the cake with a piece of string. Roll out the remaining blue icing to a strip, the length of the string and depth of the cake. Roll up lightly and position against the side of the cake, then unroll the icing around the side to cover it. Using hands dusted with icing sugar, smooth the icing around the join at the top edge.

6 Dampen the cake board and the icing at the base of the cake. Roll out the green icing to a long curved strip, about 46cm (18 inches) long and 5cm (2 inches) wide. Cut an uneven, wavy line along the inner edge. Fit the strip around the base of the cake so the wavy edge sits over the blue icing and the outer edge covers the base of the board. Trim off the icing around the edge of the board. Secure the ribbon around the side of the board.

7 To make the trains, thinly roll out the red icing. Cut out two inverted 'L' shapes for the engines, approximately 3cm (1¼ inches) high and 5cm (2 inches) long. Position on opposite sides of the cake, just above the green icing. To make the trucks, cut out four or six 4x2.5cm (1½x1 inch) rectangles. Secure these behind the engines.

8 Cut wheels, windows and funnels from the liquorice sweets. Finely chop some sweets for the cargo in the trucks. Dampen the sweets and press into position.

9 Thinly roll the white icing and cut out little cloud shapes in various sizes. Secure above the train and on top of the cake. Position the candles on top.

BASIC ICINGS AND FROSTINGS

Some icings are poured over the cake to give a smooth glossy finish; others need spreading or swirling to give a textured appearance. Fresh whipped cream and buttercream may be smoothed flat, textured with a palette knife or piped.

◆ Whether you are using cream or an icing to fill a cake, it must have the right consistency for spreading: if too firm it will pull the crumbs from the cake, making an untidy layer; if too soft it will cause the cake layers to slip and move around, and ooze out of the side of the cake. Use a palette knife dipped in hot water for spreading. Jam should be warmed gently to thin to a spreading consistency.

◆ To cover a cake with butter cream or crème au beurre icing, use a small palette knife dipped in hot water to spread the icing smoothly and evenly. For a textured effect, paddle the palette knife backwards and forwards, or swirl the icing decoratively.

◆ If you are covering a cake with frosting, make sure it is the correct consistency – thick enough to coat the back of a spoon. Frostings are often warm at this stage; if too thick, the bowl will need to be placed over hot water, or the frosting may be thinned with a little water. On the other hand, if the frosting is too slack, allow it to cool and thicken slightly. Pour all of the frosting over the top of the cake and allow it to fall over the sides, gently tapping the cake to encourage it to flow; don't be tempted to use a knife which would leave marks. Once the frosting has stopped falling, neaten the bottom edge and allow to dry.

◆ Once a cake has been covered with icing or frosting, the sides may be coated with crushed praline, grated chocolate or toasted chopped or flaked nuts; pistachio nuts, in particular, add colour as well as texture. Simple finishing touches are often the most effective – a drizzle of melted chocolate or caramel, fresh or frosted herbs and flowers, fresh fruit, toasted nuts and chocolate curls, for example.

GLACÉ ICING

MAKES 225g (8oz) ◆ PREPARATION 5 minutes ◆ FREEZING Suitable
◆ 100 CALS PER 25g (1oz)

225g (8oz) icing sugar
few drops of vanilla extract (optional)
30-45ml (2-3 tbsp) hot water

few drops of food colouring (optional)

1 Sift the icing sugar into a bowl. Add a few drops of vanilla extract if wished.

2 Using a wooden spoon, gradually stir in the hot water until the mixture is the consistency of thick cream. Beat until white and smooth and the icing is thick enough to coat the back of the spoon. Add colouring, if liked, and use at once.

NOTE This quantity is sufficient to cover the top of one large sandwich cake, or about 16 small cakes.

VARIATIONS

◆ ORANGE OR LEMON GLACÉ ICING Replace the water with strained orange or lemon juice.

◆ MOCHA GLACÉ ICING Dissolve 5ml (1 tsp) cocoa powder and 10ml (2 tsp) instant coffee granules in 15ml (1 tbsp) of the boiling water.

◆ CHOCOLATE GLACÉ ICING Sift 10ml (2 tsp) cocoa powder with the icing sugar.

◆ COFFEE GLACÉ ICING Flavour the icing with 5ml (1 tsp) coffee essence or dissolve 10ml (2 tsp) instant coffee granules in 15ml (1 tbsp) of the hot water.

BUTTERCREAM

MAKES 250g (9oz) ◆ PREPARATION 5 minutes ◆ FREEZING Suitable
◆ 130 CALS PER 25g (1oz)

75g (3oz) unsalted butter, softened
175g (6oz) icing sugar, sifted

few drops of vanilla extract
15-30ml (1-2 tbsp) milk or water

1 Put the butter in a bowl and beat with a wooden spoon until it is light and fluffy.

2 Gradually stir in the icing sugar, vanilla extract and milk. Beat well until light and smooth.

NOTE This quantity is sufficient to cover the top of a 20cm (8 inch) cake. To cover the top and sides use 110g (4oz) butter and 225g (8oz) icing sugar.

VARIATIONS

◆ ORANGE, LIME OR LEMON BUTTERCREAM Replace the vanilla extract with a little finely grated orange, lime or lemon rind to taste. Add 15-30ml (1-2 tbsp) juice from the orange, lemon or lime instead of the milk, beating well to avoid curdling the mixture. If the mixture is to be piped, omit the fruit rind.

◆ CHOCOLATE BUTTERCREAM Blend 15ml (1 tbsp) cocoa powder with 30ml (2 tbsp) boiling water and cool before adding to the mixture.

◆ COFFEE BUTTERCREAM Replace the vanilla extract with 10ml (2 tsp) instant coffee granules dissolved in 15ml (1 tbsp) boiling water; cool before adding to the mixture.

CRÈME AU BEURRE

MAKES 275g (10oz) ◆ PREPARATION 15 minutes ◆ COOKING TIME 5 minutes
◆ FREEZING Not suitable ◆ 155 CALS PER 25g (1oz)

75g (3oz) caster sugar
60ml (4 tbsp) water
2 egg yolks, beaten

175g (6oz) unsalted butter, softened

1 Put the sugar and water in a heavy-based pan and heat gently to dissolve the sugar, without boiling.
2 When the sugar is completely dissolved, bring to the boil and boil steadily for 2-3 minutes until the syrup registers 107°C (225°F) on a sugar thermometer (ie the thread stage – when a little syrup placed between two dry teaspoons and pulled apart forms a fine thread).
3 Put the egg yolks in a bowl and pour on the syrup in a thin stream, whisking all the time with an electric hand whisk. Continue to whisk until the mixture is thick and cold.
4 In another bowl, cream the butter until light and fluffy. Gradually add the egg yolk mixture, whisking well after each addition, until smooth and light.

VARIATIONS
◆ ORANGE OR LEMON CRÈME AU BEURRE Add the finely grated rind and a little juice to taste at stage 4.
◆ CHOCOLATE CRÈME AU BEURRE Melt 50g (2oz) plain chocolate cool slightly, then beat into the mixture at stage 4.
◆ COFFEE CRÈME AU BEURRE Dissolve 15-30ml (1-2 tbsp) coffee granules in 15ml (1 tbsp) boiling water. Cool, then beat into the crème au beurre mixture at stage 4.
◆ FRUIT CRÈME AU BEURRE Crush 225g (8oz) strawberries or raspberries and beat into the crème au beurre at stage 4.

ROYAL ICING

MAKES 450g (1lb) ◆ PREPARATION 20 minutes ◆ FREEZING Not suitable
◆ 100 CALS PER 25g (1oz)

2 egg whites or 15ml (1tbsp) albumen powder
10ml (2 tsp) liquid glycerine (optional, see note)

450g (1lb) icing sugar

1 If using the egg whites and the glycerine, place them in a bowl and stir just enough to break up the egg whites. If using albumen powder, mix according to the manufacturer's instructions.
2 Using a clean wooden spoon, add a little sieved icing sugar and start mixing gently, to incorporate as little air as possible.
3 Add a little more icing sugar as the mixture becomes lighter. Continue to add the sugar, stirring gently but thoroughly until the mixture is stiff and stands in soft peaks. If required for coating, it should form soft peaks; for piping it should be a little stiffer.
4 Transfer to an airtight container, cover the icing closely with cling film to exclude air and prevent the surface of the icing drying out, then seal. Stir the icing lightly before use.

NOTES
◆ Glycerine is added to royal icing to prevent it from becoming hard. Omit the glycerine from the recipe if the icing is required to cover a tiered cake, as a hard surface will be required to support the tiers.
◆ The chart on page 281 indicates the amount of royal icing needed to cover different sized cakes. It is better not to make up more than 900g (2lb) at a time.

COFFEE FUDGE FROSTING

MAKES 400g (14oz) ◆ PREPARATION 5 minutes ◆ COOKING TIME 5 minutes
◆ FREEZING Not suitable ◆ 105 CALS PER 25g (1oz)

50g (2oz) butter or margarine
125g (4oz) soft light brown sugar
30ml (2 tbsp) single cream or milk

15ml (1 tbsp) coffee granules
30ml (2 tbsp) boiling water
200g (7oz) icing sugar, sifted

1 Put the butter, sugar and cream in a saucepan. Dissolve the coffee in the boiling water and add to the saucepan. Heat gently until the sugar dissolves, then bring to the boil and boil briskly for 3 minutes.
2 Remove from the heat and gradually stir in the icing sugar. Beat with a wooden spoon for 1 minute until smooth.
3 Use immediately, spreading with a wet palette knife, or dilute with a little water to use as a smooth coating.

CHOCOLATE GANACHE

MAKES 200ml (7fl oz) ◆ PREPARATION 10 minutes, plus cooling
◆ FREEZING Suitable ◆ 165 CALS PER 25ml (1fl oz)

150ml (¼ pint) double cream

125g (4oz) plain or milk chocolate, in pieces

1 Pour the cream into a small pan and bring to the boil. Remove from the heat and add the chocolate; stir gently until the chocolate has melted and the mixture is smooth.
2 Return the mixture to the heat. Bring to the boil, remove from the heat and allow to cool. Use at room temperature: the mixture should be the consistency of softened butter.

GLOSSARY OF CULINARY TERMS

A brief guide to cooking methods, terms and ingredients used in the recipes featured in this book.

Acidulated water Water to which lemon juice or vinegar has been added in which fruit or vegetables, such as pears or Jerusalem artichokes, are immersed to prevent discoloration.

Al dente Italian term used to describe food, especially pasta and vegetables, which are cooked until tender but still firm to the bite.

Arrowroot Fine, white powder used as a thickening agent for sauces. Unlike cornflour, arrowroot gives a clear gloss.

Au gratin Describes a dish which has been coated with sauce, sprinkled with breadcrumbs or cheese and browned under the grill or in the oven. Low-sided gratin dishes are used.

Bain-marie Literally, a water bath, used to keep foods, such as delicate custards and sauces, at a constant low temperature during baking. The baking dish(es) is placed in a roasting tin containing enough hot water to come halfway up the sides.

Baking blind Pre-baking a pastry case before filling. The pastry case is lined with greaseproof paper and weighted down with dried beans or ceramic baking beans.

Baking powder A raising agent consisting of an acid, usually cream of tartar and an alkali, such as bicarbonate of soda, which react to produce carbon dioxide. This expands during baking and makes cakes and breads rise.

Balsamic vinegar Italian oak-aged vinegar, dark brown in colour with a superior sweet, mellow flavour.

Baste To spoon the juices and melted fat over meat, poultry, game or vegetables during roasting to keep them moist. The term is also used to describe spooning over a marinade.

Beat Method of incorporating air into an ingredient or mixture by agitating it vigorously with a spoon, fork, whisk or electric mixer. The technique is also used to soften ingredients.

Béchamel Classic French white sauce, used as the basis for other sauces and savoury dishes.

Beurre manié Equal parts of flour and butter kneaded together to form a paste. Used for thickening soups, stews and casseroles. It is whisked into the hot liquid a little at a time at the end of cooking.

Bind To mix beaten egg or other liquid into a dry mixture to hold it together.

Brûlée A French term, literally meaning 'burnt' used to refer to a dish with a crisp coating of caramelised sugar.

Calorie Strictly a kilocalorie, this is used in dietetics to measure the energy value of foods.

Candying Method of preserving fruit or peel by impregnating with sugar.

Caramelise To heat sugar or sugar syrup slowly until it is brown in colour; ie forms a caramel.

Chill To cool food in the refrigerator.

Clarify To remove sediment or impurities from a liquid. Stock is clarified by heating with egg white, while butter is clarified by melting and skimming. Butter which is clarified will withstand a higher frying temperature.

TO CLARIFY BUTTER heat until melted and all bubbling stops. Remove from the heat and let stand until the sediment has sunk to the bottom, then gently pour off the fat, straining it through muslin.

Coconut milk Used in curries and other ethnic dishes. Available in cans from larger supermarkets and ethnic stores. Alternatively creamed coconut sold compressed in blocks, can be reconstituted to make coconut milk.

Consistency Term used to describe the texture of a mixture, eg firm, dropping or soft.

Cream of tartar Also known as tartaric acid, this is a raising agent which is also an ingredient of baking powder and self-raising flour.

Cream To beat together fat and sugar until the mixture is pale and fluffy, and resembles whipped cream in texture and colour. Used in cakes and puddings which contain a high proportion of fat and require the incorporation of a lot of air.

Crimp To decorate the edge of a pie, tart or shortbread by pinching it at regular intervals to give a fluted effect.

Crystallise To preserve fruit in sugar syrup.

Curdle To cause sauces or creamed mixtures to separate once the egg is added, usually by overheating or over-beating.

Dariole mould Small, narrow mould with sloping sides used to make individual puddings.

Deglaze To heat stock, wine or other liquid with the cooking juices left in the pan after roasting or sautéing, scraping and stirring vigorously to dissolve the sediment on the base of the pan.

Dégorge To draw out moisture from a food, eg salting aubergines to remove bitter juices.

Dice To cut food into small cubes.

Dredge To sprinkle food generously with flour, sugar, icing sugar etc.

Dropping consistency Term used to describe the required texture of a cake or pudding mixture just before cooking. Test for it by taking a spoonful of the mixture and holding the spoon on its side above the bowl. The mixture should fall of its own accord within 5 seconds.

Dust To sprinkle lightly with flour, cornflour, icing sugar etc.

Emulsion A mixture of two liquids which do not dissolve into one another, eg oil and vinegar. Vigorous shaking or heating will emulsify them, as for a vinaigrette.

En croûte Term used to describe food which is wrapped in pastry before cooking.

En papillote Term used to describe food which is baked in a greaseproof paper or baking parchment parcel and served from the paper.

Enzyme Organic substance in food which causes chemical changes. Enzymes are a complex group. Their action is usually halted during cooking.

Extract Concentrated flavouring which is used in small quantities, eg yeast extract, vanilla extract.

Ferment Chemical change deliberately or accidentally brought about by fermenting agents, such as yeast or bacteria. Fermentation is utilised for making bread, yogurt and wine.

Filo Pastry A type of Greek pastry manufactured in wafer-thin sheets and sold in packets or boxes. It must be kept covered to prevent it drying out.

Folding in Method of combining a whisked or creamed mixture with other ingredients by cutting and folding so that it retains its lightness. A large metal spoon is used.

Frosting To coat leaves and flowers with a fine layer of sugar to use as a decoration. Also an American term for icing cakes.

Galette Cooked savoury or sweet mixture shaped into a round.

Garnish A decoration, usually edible, such as parsley or lemon, which is used to enhance the appearance of a savoury dish.

Gelatine An animal-derived gelling agent sold in powdered form, and as leaf gelatine.

Gelazone A vegetarian gelling agent sold in powdered form in sachets, and used as a substitute for gelatine.

Glaze A glossy coating applied to bread, pastry, teabeads and other items before or after baking to improve their appearance and sometimes flavour. Ingredients for glazes include beaten egg, egg white, milk and syrup.

Gluten A protein constituent of grains, such as wheat and rye, which develops when the flour is mixed with water to give the dough elasticity.

Grate To shred hard food, such as cheese and carrots, with a grater or food processor attachment.

Griddle A flat, heavy, metal plate used on the hob for cooking scones or for searing savoury ingredients.

Grind To reduce foods such as nuts and spices to small particles in a food mill, pestle and mortar, electric grinder or food processor.

Hull To remove the stalk and calyx from soft fruits, such as strawberries.

Infuse To immerse flavourings, such as aromatic vegetables, herbs, spices and vanilla, in a liquid to impart flavour. Usually the infused liquid is brought to the boil, then left to stand for a while.

Julienne Fine 'matchstick' strips of vegetables or citrus zest, sometimes used as a garnish.

Knead To work dough by pummelling with the heel of the hand.

Knock back To knead a yeast dough for a second time after rising, to ensure an even texture.

Kugelhopf mould Tube-shaped, deep container with fluted sides use for baking a traditional Austrian yeast cake of the same name.

Liaison A thickening or binding agent based on a combination of ingredients, such as flour and water, or oil and egg.

Macerate To soften and flavour raw or dried foods by soaking in a liquid, eg soaking fruit in alcohol.

Madeleine tray A baking tin with 12 shell-shaped indentations for baking traditional French Madeleines.

Mandolin(e) A flat wooden or metal frame with adjustable cutting blades for cutting vegetables.

Marinate To soak raw meat, poultry or game – usually in a mixture of oil, wine, vinegar and flavourings – to soften and impart flavour. The mixture, which is known as a marinade, may also be used to baste the food during cooking.

Mince To cut food into very fine pieces, using a mincer, food processor or knife.

Mocha Term which has come to mean a blend of chocolate and coffee.

Moule à manqué A French cake tin with sloping sides which creates a cake with a wider base than top, enabling the icing to run down and cover the sides.

Parboil To boil a vegetable or other food for part of its cooking time before finishing it by another method.

Pare To finely peel the skin or zest from vegetables or fruit.

Pâte The French word for pastry, familiar in pâte sucrée, a sweet flan pastry.

Patty tin Tray of cup-shaped moulds for cooking small cakes and deep tartlets. Also called a bun tin.

Pestle and mortar Heavy marble or porcelain bowl with a heavy grinding tool for grinding herbs, spices etc.

Pesto A paste-like sauce made from puréed herbs and oil, used to flavour pasta and vegetables. A classic pesto is made from basil, pine nuts, garlic and olive oil.

Pith The bitter white skin under the thin zest of citrus fruit.

Pizza stone A clay stone for pizza-baking which reproduces the intense heat of a professional pizza oven.

Poach To cook food gently in liquid at simmering point, so that the surface of the liquid is just trembling.

Prove To leave bread dough to rise after shaping.

Purée To pound, sieve or liquidise fruit, vegetables or fish to a smooth pulp. Purées often form the basis for soups and sauces.

Reduce To fast-boil stock or other liquid in an uncovered pan to evaporate water and concentrate the flavour.

Roulade Soufflé or sponge mixture rolled around a savoury or sweet filling.

Roux A mixture of equal quantities of butter (or other fat) and flour cooked together to form the basis of many sauces.

Rub-in Method of incorporating fat into flour when a short texture is required. Used for pastry, cakes, scones and biscuits.

Sauté To cook food in a small quantity of fat over a high heat, shaking the pan constantly – usually in a sauté pan (a frying pan with straight sides and a wide base).

Score To cut parallel lines in the surface of food to improve its appearance or help it cook more quickly.

Seasoned flour Flour mixed with a little salt and pepper, used for dusting meat, fish etc before frying.

Shred To grate cheese or slice vegetables into very fine pieces or strips.

Sieve To press food through a perforated sieve to obtain a smooth texture.

Sift To shake dry ingredients through a sieve to remove lumps.

Spring-release tin Also known as a springform pan, this is a round cake tin with a spring-release side and removable base which is clamped in. Used for cakes and desserts which are not to be inverted.

Simmer To keep a liquid just below boiling point.

Steam To cook food in the steam of rapidly boiling water.

Steep To immerse food in warm or cold liquid to soften it and draw out strong flavours.

Sterilise To destroy bacteria in foods by heating.

Suet Hard fat of animal origin used in pastry and steamed puddings. A vegetarian alternative is available.

Sweat To cook chopped or sliced vegetables in a little fat without liquid in a covered pan over a low heat.

Swiss roll tin Shallow, rectangular tin, available in several different sizes, used for baking sponges which are filled and rolled after baking – such as roulades.

Tepid The term used to describe temperature at approximately blood heat, ie 37°C (98.7°F).

Thermometer, Sugar/Fat Used for accurately checking the temperature of boiling sugar syrups, and fat for deep-frying respectively. Dual purpose thermometers are obtainable.

Whipping (whisking) Beating air rapidly into a mixture either with a manual or electric whisk.

Zest The thin coloured outer layer of citrus fruit which contains essential oil.

Zester Small bevelled tool with five holes drawn across citrus fruit to remove the zest in fine strips.

INDEX